Living and Working
in
Switzerland

A Survival Handbook

by
David Hampshire

SURVIVAL BOOKS • LONDON • ENGLAND

First published 1988
Second Edition 1989
Third Edition 1991
Fourth Edition 1993
Fifth Edition 1995
Sixth Edition 1997
Seventh Edition 1999
Eighth Edition 2002
Ninth Edition 2004
Tenth Edition 2005
Eleventh Edition 2007

Copyright © Survival Books 1988, 1989, 1991,
1993, 1995, 1997, 1999, 2002, 2004, 2005, 2007
Map and illustrations © Jim Watson
Cover photograph 🖥 www.shutterstock.com

Survival Books Limited
26 York Street, London W1U 6PZ, United Kingdom
☎ +44 (0)20-7788 7644, 🖨 +44 (0)870-762 3212
✉ info@survivalbooks.net
🖥 www.survivalbooks.net

British Library Cataloguing in Publication Data.
A CIP record for this book is available
from the British Library.
ISBN-10: 1-905303-15-7
ISBN-13: 978-1-905303-15-1

Printed and bound in Finland by WS Bookwell Ltd.

ACKNOWLEDGEMENTS

My sincere thanks to all those who contributed to the publication of this book and to the many people who took the trouble to read and comment on the draft versions. In particular I would like to thank Susan Vogel-Misicka for updating the book for its 11th Edition, Joanna Styles for editing, Joe Laredo for proofreading and Kerry Laredo for layout. Also special thanks to Erik Gottschalk and Adèle Kelham, without whom the book may never have seen the light of day, Gabrielle Grether (Grether Consulting) for updating previous editions, Nigel MacGeorge, Nicolas Vivion and Patric Eisele (all Grether Consulting), Dianne Kiefer-Dicks (Bergli Books), Christian Tromp (*Die Schweizerische Post*), Philipp Dubach (Bundesamt für Statistik) and Rolf Beeler (Strassenverkehrsamt Zurich). Also a special thank-you to Jim Watson for the superb illustrations, cartoons and cover design.

TITLES BY SURVIVAL BOOKS

The Best Places To Buy A Home
France; Spain

Buying a Home
Australia & New Zealand; Bulgaria,
Cyprus; France; Greece; Italy;
Portugal; South Africa; Spain;
Buying, Selling & Letting Property (UK)

Buying and Renting a Home
London; New York

**Foreigners Abroad: Triumphs
& Disasters**
France; Spain

Living and Working
America; Australia; Britain
Canada; France; Germany
The Gulf States & Saudi Arabia;
Ireland; Italy;

London; New Zealand;
Spain; Switzerland

Earning Money from Your Home
France; Spain

Making a Living
France; Spain

Retiring Abroad
France; Spain

Other Titles
Investing in Property Abroad;
Renovating & Maintaining
Your French Home;
Running Gîtes and B&Bs in France;
Rural Living in France;
Shooting Caterpillars in Spain;
Wild Thyme in Ibiza

WHAT READERS & REVIEWERS

When you buy a model plane for your child, a video recorder, or some new computer gizmo, you get with it a leaflet or booklet pleading 'Read Me First', or bearing large friendly letters or bold type saying 'IMPORTANT – follow the instructions carefully'. This book should be similarly supplied to all those entering France with anything more durable than a 5-day return ticket. It is worth reading even if you are just visiting briefly, or if you have lived here for years and feel totally knowledgeable and secure. But if you need to find out how France works then it is indispensable. Native French people probably have a less thorough understanding of how their country functions. – Where it is most essential, the book is most up to the minute.

LIVING FRANCE

Rarely has a 'survival guide' contained such useful advice. This book dispels doubts for first-time travellers, yet is also useful for seasoned globetrotters – In a word, if you're planning to move to the USA or go there for a long-term stay, then buy this book both for general reading and as a ready-reference.

AMERICAN CITIZENS ABROAD

It is everything you always wanted to ask but didn't for fear of the contemptuous put down – The best English-language guide – Its pages are stuffed with practical information on everyday subjects and are designed to complement the traditional guidebook.

SWISS NEWS

A complete revelation to me – I found it both enlightening and interesting, not to mention amusing.

CAROLE CLARK

Let's say it at once. David Hampshire's **Living and Working in France** is the best handbook ever produced for visitors and foreign residents in this country; indeed, my discussion with locals showed that it has much to teach even those born and bred in l'Hexagone. – It is Hampshire's meticulous detail which lifts his work way beyond the range of other books with similar titles. Often you think of a supplementary question and search for the answer in vain. With Hampshire this is rarely the case. – He writes with great clarity (and gives French equivalents of all key terms), a touch of humour and a ready eye for the odd (and often illuminating) fact. – This book is absolutely indispensable.

THE RIVIERA REPORTER

A mine of information – I may have avoided some embarrassments and frights if I had read it prior to my first Swiss encounters – Deserves an honoured place on any newcomer's bookshelf.

ENGLISH TEACHERS ASSOCIATION, SWITZERLAND

HAVE SAID ABOUT SURVIVAL BOOKS

What a great work, wealth of useful information, well-balanced wording and accuracy in details. My compliments!

THOMAS MÜLLER

This handbook has all the practical information one needs to set up home in the UK – The sheer volume of information is almost daunting – Highly recommended for anyone moving to the UK.

AMERICAN CITIZENS ABROAD

A very good book which has answered so many questions and even some I hadn't thought of – I would certainly recommend it.

BRIAN FAIRMAN

We would like to congratulate you on this work: it is really super! We hand it out to our expatriates and they read it with great interest and pleasure.

ICI (SWITZERLAND) AG

Covers just about all the things you want to know on the subject – In answer to the desert island question about the one how-to book on France, this book would be it – Almost 500 pages of solid accurate reading – This book is about enjoyment as much as survival.

THE RECORDER

It's so funny – I love it and definitely need a copy of my own – Thanks very much for having written such a humorous and helpful book.

HEIDI GUILIANI

A must for all foreigners coming to Switzerland.

ANTOINETTE O'DONOGHUE

A comprehensive guide to all things French, written in a highly readable and amusing style, for anyone planning to live, work or retire in France.

THE TIMES

A concise, thorough account of the DOs and DON'Ts for a foreigner in Switzerland – Crammed with useful information and lightened with humorous quips which make the facts more readable.

AMERICAN CITIZENS ABROAD

Covers every conceivable question that may be asked concerning everyday life – I know of no other book that could take the place of this one.

FRANCE IN PRINT

Hats off to *Living and Working in Switzerland*!

RONNIE ALMEIDA

THE AUTHOR

David Hampshire was born in England and after serving in the Royal Air Force was employed for many years in the computer industry. His work has taken him around the world and he has lived and worked in many countries, including Australia, France, Germany, Malaysia, the Netherlands, Panama, Singapore, Spain and Switzerland. It was while working in Switzerland in the '80s that David wrote his first book, *Living and Working in Switzerland*, which was published in 1988. He is now the author or co-author of over 15 titles, including *Living and Working* guides to America, Australia, Britain, France and Spain. David lives with his partner in England and Panama.

CONTENTS

14. FINANCE 279

15. LEISURE 299

IMPORTANT NOTE

Switzerland is a diverse country with many faces. It has four national languages, both federal and canton laws, a variety of religions and customs, and continuously changing rules and regulations, particularly with regard to foreigners.

Always check with an official and reliable source (not always the same) before making any major decisions or undertaking an irreversible course of action. However, don't believe everything you're told or read, even, dare it be said, herein. Comprehensive lists of useful addresses, publications and useful websites are included in **Appendices A, B and C** respectively, to help you obtain and verify information. Throughout this book certain points have been emphasised in bold print. **Ignore them at your peril or cost.**

Unless specifically stated, a reference to any company, organisation or product in this book doesn't constitute an endorsement or recommendation.

AUTHOR'S NOTES

- Times are shown using am for before noon and pm for after noon (see also **Time Difference** on page 382).

- His/he/him/man/men (etc.) also mean her/she/her/woman/women (no offence ladies!). This is done simply to make life easier for both the reader and, in particular, the author, and isn't intended to be sexist.

- Spelling is (or should be) British English and not American English. Names of Swiss towns and foreign words are generally shown in their English spelling, e.g. Basle (Basel), Berne (Bern), Geneva (Genf, Genève), Lucerne (Luzern) and Zurich (Zürich).

- Prices quoted usually include value added tax (VAT) and should be taken only as estimates, although they were mostly correct when going to print and fortunately don't usually change significantly overnight in Switzerland.

- Warnings and important points are shown in **bold** type.

- The following symbols are used in this book: ☎ (telephone), ▤ (fax), 💻 (internet) and ✉ (e-mail).

- Lists of useful addresses, further reading and useful websites are contained in **Appendices A**, **B** and **C** respectively.

- For those unfamiliar with the metric system of weights and measures, conversion tables are included in **Appendix D**.

- A map of Switzerland showing the 26 cantons is included in **Appendix E**.

INTRODUCTION

Whether you're already living or working in Switzerland or just thinking about it, this is **THE BOOK** you've been looking for. Forget about those glossy guide books, excellent though they are for tourists. This amazing book was written especially with you in mind and is worth its weight in Emmental.

In sharp contrast to the abundant information provided by Switzerland Tourism, information for foreigners living and working in Switzerland is often hard to come by – particularly in the English language. My aim in writing this book was to help redress the balance and try to fill the void (chasm?) that exists between the paucity of information available and the knowledge necessary for a relatively trouble-free life.

You may have visited Switzerland as a tourist, but living and working there is a different matter altogether. Moving to a new job and making a home in any foreign country can be a traumatic and stressful experience – and Switzerland is no exception. You need to discover the Swiss way of doing things – for example, finding an apartment, paying bills and obtaining insurance – and to adapt to your new surroundings.

For most foreigners in Switzerland, finding out how to overcome the everyday obstacles of Swiss life was previously a case of pot luck. However, with a copy of *Living and Working in Switzerland* to hand, you will have a wealth of information at your fingertips. Information derived from a variety of sources, both official and unofficial – not least the hard won personal experiences of the author, his friends, colleagues and acquaintances. This book isn't simply a monologue of dry facts and figures, but an entertaining, practical and occasionally humorous look at life in Switzerland. However, don't be mislead by the subtle and sophisticated witticisms – this is serious stuff!

Living and Working in Switzerland represents the most up-to-date source of information available to foreigners in Switzerland – in any language. It doesn't contain all the answers (most of us don't even know the questions), but it will help you make informed decisions instead of costly mistakes, calculated judgements rather than uneducated guesses, and, most importantly, it will help you save time, trouble and money.

A period spent in Switzerland is a wonderful way to enrich your life, broaden your horizons and hopefully please your bank manager. I trust that this book will help to smooth your way to a happy and rewarding life in your new home in Switzerland.

Viel Glück/Bon courage !

David Hampshire
August 2007

1.

FINDING A JOB

Finding a job in Switzerland isn't as difficult as official Swiss policy may lead you to believe, although obtaining a permit can prove a problem. Switzerland is known for its restrictive immigration policy and permit quota system, although the rules regarding executives and certain 'specialists' have been eased. By 2014 a bilateral agreement between the European Economic Area (EEA) countries and Switzerland will allow the free movement of people and remove the need for permits (there are currently no work permit quotas for EEA nationals). Switzerland's economic success is largely dependent upon the influx of foreign labour and foreigners are found in almost every walk of life. Many companies have a sizeable foreign labour force and foreigners fill almost half the top positions at the 25 largest Swiss companies. Foreign employees in Switzerland number around 1m or some 25 per cent of the workforce.

Labour relations in Switzerland are excellent and there are fewer strikes than in any other industrialised country. Increased global competition has meant that a large number of companies have streamlined their workforces over the last few years and many have moved their production and research facilities abroad (mainly to eastern Europe) to reduce costs. However, Switzerland has one of the lowest unemployment rates in Europe and a 'jobless Swiss' is almost a contradiction in terms – in mid-2007, national unemployment was 2.7 per cent. GDP growth was a healthy 4.1 per cent in 2000 but fell to 2.7 per cent in 2006 and forecasts for 2007 and 2008 are similar.

In 2007 there was a record resident population of over 1.54m foreigners or over 20 per cent of the population (Geneva has the highest concentration at 43 per cent). This figure doesn't include employees of international organisations, foreign embassies and consulates (and their families), or seasonal workers and asylum seekers, who together total a further 100,000. An additional 226,500 foreigners cross the borders each day to work in Switzerland. Some 67 per cent of foreigners are from EEA countries (nearly 20 per cent of these are Italians), 12.3 per cent from Serbia and Montenegro and almost 5 per cent from Turkey. Switzerland also exports workers and over 650,000 Swiss live and work abroad.

The employment of foreigners, albeit an economic necessity, is something of a political hot potato. The Swiss generally live and work harmoniously with their foreign 'guests', although there's a vociferous minority who would like to see the number of foreign workers drastically reduced. During the last 30 years they've gained sufficient support to stage a number of national referendums in an attempt to reduce the resident foreign population. All have been defeated but they've served to strain relations between the Swiss and resident foreigners.

Most positions held by foreigners fall into two main categories: seasonal jobs for a maximum of nine months a year and permanent staff positions. Seasonal workers include hotel and catering staff, building and construction workers, factory hands, farm workers, and most people in the tourist industry. Such jobs are available throughout Switzerland and aren't usually difficult to find. Permanent jobs are generally reserved for senior managers, professionals and specialists (e.g. computer experts and engineers), and require annual residence permits. Residence permits are also required by au pairs, students and trainees, for whom there are no quota restrictions (although permits are generally valid only for one year).

SWITZERLAND & THE EUROPEAN UNION

Despite being surrounded by EEA members and being a 'currency island' (all its neighbours use the euro), Switzerland is the only western European country that isn't a member of the European Union (EU) or EEA. The Swiss have twice voted in referenda against joining these entities – the first time in 1992, when they voted against joining the EEA, and in 2001, when they decided not to join the EU by a majority of 77 per cent. The referendum results highlighted a serious split between the Swiss Germans and Swiss French over Switzerland's future and created an acrimonious divide between them – French-speaking Swiss tend to be in favour of joining the EU, while German-speakers are generally against it. In 2006, the Swiss Parliament decided to keep open the country's invitation to join the EU, but another referendum isn't expected for several years. Surveys show that currently around a third of the Swiss population is in favour of EU membership, one third is against, and the remaining third undecided. Meanwhile, the EU remains open to Swiss membership and undoubtedly, the topic of European integration and EU membership will dominate Swiss politicians' thinking for the foreseeable future.

In spite of the referendum and survey results, there remains a mood for change in the country and the numerous bilateral agreements between Switzerland and the EU demonstrate a firm commitment to co-operation – one of the most important of these being the agreement on the free movement of EEA citizens in Switzerland and vice versa. Switzerland and the EU are dependent on each other – Switzerland is one of the EU's most important export markets and its second-largest supplier after the US, and almost 900,000 EU citizens work in Switzerland.

SEASONAL JOBS

The majority of seasonal jobs in Switzerland are available in the tourist industry. Most seasonal jobs last for the duration of the summer or winter tourist seasons, i.e. April to October and December to April respectively. To work in a seasonal job you need to obtain a (non-renewable) L permit for a maximum of 18 months or an annual B permit. Short-term permits (see **Chapter 3**) that allow foreigners to work in Switzerland for a maximum of three or four months a year are also available.

Although salaries are higher in Switzerland than in most other countries, you're expected to work **hard and long hours**, particularly in hotels and restaurants in winter resorts (summer is generally more relaxed). Many businesses must survive for a whole year primarily on their winter earnings and employers expect everyone to earn their keep. Language fluency is required for all but the most menial and worst paid jobs, and is at least as important as experience and qualifications (not that language proficiency alone will get you a well paid job). **The local language in Switzerland may be French, German or Italian, depending on the area** (see **Languages** on page 38). Fortunately, there's a great sense of camaraderie among seasonal workers, which goes a long way towards compensating for the often boring and hard work (the Swiss francs also help).

If accommodation isn't provided with a job, it can be expensive and difficult to find. Ensure that your salary is sufficient to pay for accommodation, food and other living expenses, and hopefully also allow you to save some money (see **Cost of Living** on page 295). Seasonal jobs include the following:

Year Round	Winter Only
Hotels & Restaurants	Chalet Staff
Bars & Clubs	Ski Technicians
Couriers or Resort Representatives	Ski Instructors or Guides
Sports Instructors	
Manual Worker	
Voluntary Workers	

Year Round Jobs

Bars & Clubs

Jobs in bars and clubs are available throughout Switzerland. English- and Irish-style pubs in many towns often hire native English-speaking bartenders and waiters to add a touch of authenticity. Winter resorts have many clubs and discotheques requiring disc jockeys, particularly those with a collection of up-to-date dance music. Jobs for disc jockeys are also advertised in British music newspapers. Casino staff, including croupiers, are also required in many areas of Switzerland.

Couriers & Resort Representatives

A courier's or resort representative's duties include ferrying tourist groups back and forth from airports, organising excursions and social events, arranging ski passes and equipment hire (rental), and generally playing the role of Jack (or Jill) of all trades. A job as a courier is demanding and requires resilience and resourcefulness to deal with the chaos associated with the package holiday business. The necessary requirements include the ability to answer many questions simultaneously (often in different languages), and to remain calm, charming and humorous under extreme pressure. Lost passengers, tickets, passports and tempers are everyday occurrences. It's an excellent training ground for managerial and leadership skills, pays well and often provides opportunities to supplement your earnings.

Couriers are required by many local and foreign tour companies in both winter and summer resorts. Competition for jobs is fierce and local language ability is always required, even for employment with British tour operators. Most companies have age requirements, the minimum usually being 21, although many companies prefer employees to be a few years older. The majority of courier jobs in Switzerland are available during the winter ski season with British ski-tour companies and school ski-party organisers.

A good source of information is ski magazines, which contain regular listings of tour companies showing which operates in which resorts. It's wise to find out the type of clients you're likely to be dealing with, particularly if you're allergic to children or yuppies (young urban professionals – similar to children but more immature). To survive a winter in a ski resort, it helps if you're a keen skier or a dedicated learner; otherwise you risk being bored to death by ski bums.

Some companies, such as Club Méditerranée (Club Med), operate both summer and winter hotels and camps throughout Switzerland. Employees are required to speak good French. For information write to Club Méditerranée, 11, Rue de Cambrai, F-75957 Paris Cedex 19, France (⌨ www.clubmed-jobs.com). Couriers or counsellors are also required for summer camps, which are organised for both adults and children. See also **Voluntary Workers** below.

Hotels & Restaurants

Hotels and restaurants are the largest employers of seasonal workers, and jobs are available at all levels, from managers to kitchen hands. Experience, qualifications and language fluency are required for all the best and highest paid positions, but a variety of jobs are available for the untrained and inexperienced. These include chambermaids, waiters and waitresses, cleaners, dishwashers, handymen, porters, messengers, drivers, kitchen assistants and MBOs (muscle-bound oafs).

The standards required by Swiss employers are high, and hard work and long hours are demanded, although the pay is usually good. The minimum monthly wage for employees in the hotel/restaurant industry is around SFr. 3,150 and a 13th month's salary (see page 46) is paid to full-time employees (but isn't usually paid to seasonal workers). Employees in hotels are usually provided with full board and you should avoid any job that doesn't include it, as the cost can be prohibitive. Reductions from gross salaries for board and lodging and compulsory insurance amount to some 50 per cent.

Official working hours vary between 44 and 48 hours per week depending on the job, or around nine to nine-and-a-half hours per day. Your contract will state maximum number of working hours per week (normal working hours should be a maximum of 45 per week), although in reality this may be the minimum. You're entitled to two free days each week and four weeks' paid holiday per year (around one-and-a-half days per month). Between Christmas and New Year you may be expected to work 12 hours a day, seven days a week, for which you will usually receive time off in January. Most jobs include a two-week trial period with a notice period of three days, after which the notice period is one month.

Waiters and waitresses are expected to provide their own 'uniform' and wallet and a cash float of around SFr. 200. The salary is often on a commission basis, where you're paid a percentage of your takings (plus tips – unless all your customers are Swiss). Aprons, hats and oven gloves are normally supplied for kitchen staff, and a free laundry service is usually provided for working clothes and uniforms. Other dress requirements vary according to the job; for example waiters require black trousers and shoes, white shirts and often jackets, and waitresses require black skirts, shoes and stockings, white blouses and possibly small aprons.

In addition to jobs in Swiss hotels and restaurants, jobs are available in hotels and chalets operated by British and other foreign tour operators, where local language ability may be unnecessary. Work is generally easier and the atmosphere more relaxed, but salaries are usually lower than those paid by Swiss-run hotels and may even be half the minimum wage.

Many agencies and a number of trade newspapers are available in Switzerland to help you find a job in a hotel or restaurant. Union Helvetia is the official Swiss union for hotel and restaurant staff, and anyone who has training or qualifications in the hotel and catering trades may become a member. Union Helvetia publishes an official rule book (*Obligationenrecht, droit des obligations*) for employers and employees and a list of official minimum salaries for all jobs. It also publishes a weekly newspaper, *Expresso*, listing job vacancies. It's available from news kiosks in Switzerland or on subscription from Hotel & Gastro Union, Zentralsekretariat, Adligenswilerstr. 22, PO Box 4870, CH-6002 Lucerne (☎ 041 418 22 22, ▣ www.gastroline.ch). Hotel & Gastro Union has its own employment agency at its head office in Lucerne and regional offices in Geneva, Lausanne and Zurich.

The Swiss Hotel Association (Schweizer Hotelier-Verein, Société Suisse des Hôteliers) publishes a newspaper, *Hotel + Tourismus Revue*, which usually contains more job vacancies than the *Expresso* newspaper. It's also available from news kiosks (on Thursdays) or on subscription from *Hotel + Tourismus Revue*, Monbijoustr. 130, PO Box 3001, CH-3007 Berne (☎ 031 370 41 11, ▣ www.htr.ch). Both *Expresso* and *Hotel + Tourismus Revue* contain articles in

French and German. Like Union Helvetia, the Swiss Hotel Association has its own employment agency and publishes a standard employment contract for hotel and restaurant staff, which is in use throughout the country.

Other weekly newspapers advertising job vacancies for hotel and restaurant staff include *Schweizer Gastronome* (🖥 www.gilde.ch). Besides answering advertisements and visiting agencies, you could try contacting Swiss hotel and restaurant chains directly.

Manual Workers

Jobs for manual workers are usually available throughout Switzerland, mostly in the construction and farming industries. The minimum salary in the construction industry is around SFr. 4,000 per month. Jobs are also available for cleaners and general labourers in hospitals, factories, warehouses and large hotels. Farmers often require extra labourers, particularly in the spring and autumn to help with the fruit, vegetable and grape harvests. Farming jobs entail hard physical work, usually for around 12 hours a day, six days a week, for a low salary.

One of the most popular jobs is grape picking, e.g. in the cantons of Valais and Vaud. Lasting for around eight to ten days in early October, the work is hard and the salary is around SFr. 65 per day, sometimes without accommodation or food. Even for this kind of work it may be important to have some knowledge of the local language.-

Unfortunately the worst abuses of seasonal workers' rights occur in the farming industry, particularly in the Geneva area, where complaints include low pay, long hours, inadequate living conditions and unpaid social benefits. If you're a seasonal worker from a country with a bilateral insurance agreement with Switzerland, the Swiss government doesn't repay federal social security payments (OASI/DI) when you leave Switzerland (see page 261). Therefore there's a temptation for dishonest employers to deduct the OASI/DI payment from your salary and not declare it, particularly as you're unlikely ever to claim a Swiss pension.

The Swiss are continually digging tunnels, building and repairing bridges and roads, and constructing office blocks and shopping centres – and it's mostly foreigners who do the manual work. Enquire at building sites in Switzerland – the bigger the site, the better your chance of success. In summer, jobs may be available in ski resorts installing new ski lifts, snow-making machinery and pipes, and building chalets and hotels. Ask local lift operating companies, estate agents and construction companies.

If you have experience or training in the building industry, e.g. as a bricklayer or carpenter, you should be able to command a higher salary, even without local language fluency. Outdoor jobs in the building and construction industries are usually restricted to the warmer months, as trying to find your shovel under two metres of snow can be a handicap in winter.

Sports Instructors

Instructors are required for a variety of sports, including badminton, canoeing, diving, golf, gymnastics, hang-gliding, horse riding, mountaineering, parachuting, rock-climbing, sailing, squash, subaquatic sports, swimming, tennis and windsurfing. Whatever the sport, it's probably played and taught somewhere in Switzerland. Most jobs for sports instructors are available in summer, as winter sports vacancies are generally filled by the Swiss (for information regarding **Ski Instructors & Guides** see page 28). However, if you're a qualified winter sports instructor, you can contact Swiss resorts or sports organisations for information about vacancies. You may require an officially recognised qualification to teach some sports, for example a life-saving certificate to teach swimming or a sailing instructor's certificate to teach sailing.

Voluntary Work

Voluntary work is primarily to enable students and young people to visit Switzerland for a few weeks or months to learn about the country and its people at first hand. Voluntary work is, of course, unpaid, although meals and accommodation are normally provided and a small amount of pocket money may be paid. This, however, may not be sufficient for expenses such as entertainment and drinks, so make sure that you bring enough money with you. The usual visa regulations apply to voluntary workers and your passport must be valid for at least a year. You will be informed whether you need a visa when you apply (a work or residence permit isn't required).

Various kinds of voluntary work are available, including the following.

Farm Work

Voluntary farm work is usually available from March to October (mainly in German-speaking areas) and is organised by the Swiss Farm Work Association. You must be aged between 17 and 30 with a basic knowledge of German or French (depending on the area) and be prepared to work for a minimum of three weeks and a maximum of eight. It certainly isn't a holiday, as the work is usually strenuous and the hours long, for six days a week (Sundays are free). Officially a maximum of 48 hours a week are worked, although more may be expected. Work may be in the fields, farmyard, farmhouse or farm garden. For this you're paid at least SFr. 20 a day (those aged over 18), plus board and lodging, and are insured against illness and accidents. You must pay for your own journey to and from the farm.

Many farms are in remote mountain areas, where living and working conditions may be primitive and there's little social life. If you like a hectic social life and companionship, this isn't the job for you. Friends applying together aren't usually placed with the same farmer, as only one worker is allocated per farmer due to a lack of applicants. Application forms are available from Landdienst - Zentralstelle, Archstr. 2, Postfach 2050, CH-8401 Winterthur ((052 264 00 30, 🖳 www.landdienst.ch). Registration should be made at least four weeks before you wish to start work (a deposit may be payable by overseas applicants and is forfeited if an application is cancelled or a position isn't taken up).

Farm jobs include work on an organically run farm, in return for which you receive free meals and accommodation (but no expenses). A year's membership and a list of participating farms costs SFr. 20 from WWOOF Switzerland, PO Box 59, CH-8124 Maur (🖳 www.welcome.to/wwoof). You should send an international reply coupon with your letter.

General

Many organisations requiring voluntary workers, mostly for holiday camps for children and the disabled, are listed in a brochure available from Pro Juventute, Seehofstr. 15, PO Box, CH-8032 Zurich (☎ 044 256 77 77, 🖳 www.pro juventute.ch). The *International Directory of Voluntary Work* (Vacation Work) also contains a wealth of information for prospective voluntary workers.

Winter Jobs

A seasonal job in a ski resort can be a lot of fun and very satisfying. You will get fit, learn or improve a language and make friends and may even save some money; all in addition to living in one of the most beautiful regions in the world. **However, although a winter job might be a working holiday to you (with lots of skiing and little work), to your employer it's exactly the opposite!** In general, hotel and restaurant staff work much harder in ski resorts during winter than in summer, when life is more relaxed. Some hotel and restaurant employers even forbid employees to ski (although this is rare), particularly key personnel (e.g. chefs) over the Christmas and New Year period.

Ski resorts require an army of temporary workers to cater for the annual invasion of winter sports enthusiasts. Besides jobs in the hotel and restaurant trades already described (on page 23), a variety of generally well paid winter jobs are available, some of which are described below. Usually the better paid the job, the longer the working hours and the less time off there is for skiing. Employment in a winter resort may entitle employees to reduced public transport fares and a discounted ski pass. An invaluable book for anyone looking for a job in a ski resort is *Working in Ski Resorts – Europe & North America* by Victoria Pybus (Vacation Work).

Note that seasonal workers in the tourist industry aren't covered by unemployment insurance, unlike, for example, workers in the construction industry. In a bad season, with little or no snow, you can therefore find yourself without work or money. Ski lift operators and others directly dependent on snow conditions for a living, should watch the weather forecast closely and pray for lots of snow. Even if you work in a hotel or restaurant, your contract could be cancelled or cut short when bookings are low or business is poor.

Chalet Staff

Hundreds of chalet workers (most are female, but males are also eligible) are required each winter to look after the everyday comforts of guests in holiday chalets and private hotels, many run by British and other foreign tour operators. The job of a chalet worker is hard work, generally offers low pay (as little as half the rate paid by Swiss hotels) and requires a variety of skills and experience. You must usually be able to cook to a high standard or have experience of catering for parties; do shopping, housekeeping and laundry; deal with obstreperous clients; and generally be a Jill of all trades. Nevertheless, once you get over the initial shock, you will probably find the job satisfying and challenging, and it allows plenty of time off for skiing. One thing for sure, you won't have time to be bored. You will also have to fight off the attentions of hordes of men and survive numerous late-night parties – it's a tough job but someone has to do it! A limited number of chalet workers are required in summer.

Ski Instructors & Guides

Jobs as ski instructors in Switzerland are almost impossible to obtain unless you've passed the Swiss ski instructors' examinations, although some resorts accept foreign qualifications, e.g. the advanced British Association of Ski Instructors (BASI) qualification or equivalent. Experience and local language fluency are also required. Jobs can more easily be found as ski companions, ski instructors for children and ski guides with foreign tour operators. Unfortunately in some resorts local ski instructors are hostile towards ski guides, particularly as there's often only a thin dividing line between guiding and instructing, and as a result guide jobs have been reduced.

The Ski Club of Great Britain (SCGB, 🖳 www.skiclub.co.uk) has representatives in many resorts, whose job is to take members on skiing excursions but not to teach them. Swiss resorts usually allow British and other foreign school parties to be taught by qualified foreign instructors. To teach children, the lowest BASI qualification or equivalent may be sufficient.

Working as an unofficial instructor without a permit or qualifications is strictly illegal. If you work as a ski guide or instructor and an accident occurs through your negligence (for example one of your customers falls down a precipice), you may be liable for damages.

Ski Technicians

A ski technician's job entails fitting and maintaining skis, bindings and boots. Although some employers require previous experience, many ski hire shops provide training, and courses are available in some countries. Besides doing the round of resort shops, contact tour companies and large luxury hotels, as they often have their own ski hire and service shops. Local language ability is usually required, although it may depend on the employer and his clientele.

PERMANENT POSITIONS

Permanent positions in Switzerland require an annual residence permit (see **B Permit** on page 67). Most permanent positions open to foreigners require special skills, qualifications and experience, which are usually more important than the ability to speak fluent French, German or Italian. In fact, you may not be expected to speak the local language at all if your mother tongue is English. This is often the case when you're employed by an American or British company, or work in a high-tech field where English is an important language spoken fluently by your colleagues. If you need to speak (or learn) the local language, you will be informed at your interview. When necessary, language tuition may be subsidised or paid for by your employer.

There's often a huge difference between working for a Swiss or foreign company employing many other English-speaking foreigners, and working for a company where you have few or no English-speaking colleagues. You will, of course, learn the local language much more quickly working with colleagues who don't speak English. However, you may find – as many other foreigners do – that the working environment and general lack of camaraderie, warmth and friendliness, isn't to your liking. The Swiss don't generally mix socially with their colleagues and this may even exclude the occasional drink after work at a local bar.

Foreign qualifications are recognised in many trades and professions, provided the length of training and syllabus was similar to those required for the equivalent Swiss qualification. Under bilateral treaties between Switzerland and the EU, Switzerland now recognises most EU-based diplomas and qualifications – even for formerly excluded professions such as teachers, barristers, lawyers, doctors, dentists, pharmacists and veterinarians. For non-EU citizens, restrictions remain but a non-EU foreigner entitled to live in Switzerland – for example as a result of long-term residence or marriage to a Swiss citizen – may be able to study or pass a Swiss examination entitling him to work in a restricted field. Regulations may also be relaxed by individual cantons when there's a shortage of qualified Swiss staff.

When applying for a job, always provide copies of all qualifications and references, as these tend to impress Swiss employers and may also influence the authorities when they're deciding whether to grant a permit.

JOB APPLICATIONS

How you apply for a job depends largely on whether it's a seasonal or permanent position.

Seasonal Jobs

Apply for jobs as early as possible, for example January for summer jobs and June or July for winter jobs. For summer jobs in mountain resorts, you should apply in March or April. If you apply too early, the worst that can happen is that you will be told to apply again later. The latest dates for applications are usually the end of September for winter jobs and the end of April for summer jobs. In some resorts, the season starts in spring (April), staff being recruited in January. Don't put all your eggs in one basket – the more job applications you make, the better your chance of success.

Many jobs require local language fluency (see **Languages** on page 38); therefore if you apply for a job in writing, it's best to write in the local language – but obtain help if you aren't fluent. You can brush up your language ability after you've secured a job, but it isn't advisable to exaggerate your language ability, experience or qualifications in a letter. If you're offered a job on the basis of non-existent qualifications, you will soon be found out and risk being fired. A good knowledge of the local language helps when dealing with local officials. For seasonal jobs, German is more advantageous than French, as the majority of jobs are in German-speaking resorts.

When applying for a job requiring experience, don't forget to provide your curriculum vitae and copies of qualifications and references. **Always** ask for a written job offer and a contract, and steer clear of employers who won't provide them (see **Illegal Working** on page 33). An official job entitles you to accident insurance, unemployment benefits, and in particular, official protection from exploitation.

Note that writing unsolicited letters for jobs is a hit-and-miss affair and is usually the least successful method of securing employment. An employer who doesn't know you from Adam or Eve may be unwilling to risk employing you because if you don't turn up he's left in the lurch. If you're really serious and can afford the journey, it may be worthwhile visiting prospective employers for an interview before the season starts.

Your best chance of obtaining a seasonal job may be to apply in person, particularly when looking for a winter job close to the start of the ski season. Success is often simply a matter of being in the right place at the right time, although you can give lady luck a helping hand by persistence and enterprise. Make an effort to look presentable, as Swiss employers expect a high standard of dress and cleanliness; hair must usually be short (except for women) and tidy, and beards aren't usually permitted. When looking for a job in person, try the following methods:

● Call on prospective employers, but avoid calling at hotels and restaurants during meal times.

● Ask prospective employers if they know of anyone looking for staff and leave your name and an address and a telephone number (if possible) where you can be contacted (an international mobile phone is handy).

● Check wanted boards or place an advertisement on local notice boards, for example in a Migros or Coop supermarket, or on the notice boards of expatriate clubs, churches and other organisations.

● Look in local newspapers or place an advertisement in the 'Wanted' section.

● Ask at tourist offices – many keep lists of job vacancies from September onwards for the coming winter season. Lists are regularly updated and the service is free.

● Ask other foreign workers.

If you're an English speaker, the best winter resorts to try are those with a large number of American and British skiers. These include Arosa, Champéry, Crans-Montana, Davos, Engelberg, Grindelwald, Gstaad, Klosters, Les Diablerets, Leysin, Saas Fee, St. Moritz, Verbier, Wengen and Zermatt. However, don't neglect the many smaller resorts; although jobs may be scarcer, there's less competition from other job hunters, who tend to focus on the major resorts.

Don't worry if you miss the start of the season, as jobs often become vacant at short notice to replace those who become sick or homesick, are injured or sacked, or who run off with a ski instructor. However, employers may have difficulty obtaining a permit during the season as allocated permits cannot be transferred to new employees. Don't forget to take enough money to see you through the job-hunting period. Allow at least two weeks and bear in mind that the cost of living (see page 295) is high in Switzerland.

Depending on your nationality, after you've found a job you may need to return to the nearest border point with your 'assurance of a residence permit' (see **Chapter 3**) for a health check. When leaving a job at the end of the season, it's advisable to ask for a reference if one isn't provided automatically, particularly if you intend to look for further seasonal work.

If you need a visa to enter Switzerland to take up employment (see Chapter 3), you will be unable to find a job on the spot, as the visa must be issued by an embassy abroad.

Permanent Positions

There are various ways to find a permanent position in Switzerland, including the following:

- Obtain copies of Swiss newspapers, most of which contain a positions vacant (*Stellenanzeiger/Stellenmarkt, offres d'emploi*) section on certain days. When the ability to speak English is paramount, a position may be advertised in English. Swiss companies sometimes advertise for C permit holders (see page 67) or Swiss nationals only. Outside Switzerland, Swiss newspapers may be available from international news agencies, Swiss embassies and consulates, Swiss trade and commercial centres, and Swiss social clubs. However, they don't always contain the positions vacant sections.

- Apply to American, British and other multinational companies which have offices or subsidiaries in Switzerland, and make written applications directly to Swiss companies. The 2,000 largest Swiss companies are listed in *Top 2006*, a book published by HandelsZeitung Fachverlag AG, Abo-Service, PO Box, CH-8027 Zurich (☎ 044 288 35 00, 🖳 www.handelszeitung.ch) – also available on CD. Many of the companies listed advertise jobs on their websites. When writing letters for jobs, you should address them to the personnel department manager (*Personalabteilungsleiter, Chef de Service du Personnel*). Include your curriculum vitae and copies of references and qualifications with your letter. If possible, offer to attend an interview in Switzerland and state when you're available.

- Apply to international recruiting agencies acting for Swiss companies. These companies chiefly recruit executives and key personnel, and many have offices worldwide, including Switzerland. A Swiss company may appoint a sole agent to handle recruitment in a particular country.

- Contact employment agencies in Switzerland. **Note that many Swiss agencies find positions for Swiss citizens only or for foreigners holding a B or C permit (see Chapter 3).** Some agencies specialise only in certain fields, for example the computer or catering industries. The Swiss labour exchange doesn't help foreigners find employment unless they're already resident in Switzerland. Swiss employment agencies are unable to apply for residence permits on your behalf and only a bona fide Swiss employer can do this.

- If you're a member of a recognised profession, you can place a 'position wanted' advertisement in a Swiss professional or trade newspaper or magazine. Publicitas SA, Département étranger, Rue Etraz 4, CH-1003 Lausanne (☎ 021 317 81 11, 🖳 www.publicitas.ch) can help you select the most appropriate publication.

- Apply in person to Swiss companies. This method is often successful but doesn't usually shorten the time required to process a job application and obtain a residence permit, which can take up to three months.

- Ask friends or acquaintances working in Switzerland if they know of an employer seeking someone with your experience and qualifications.

- Use the internet, an increasingly popular option among Swiss job hunters. There are numerous websites devoted to job-hunting in Switzerland, many of which are available in English, such as 💻 www.swiss-job.ch, 💻 www.stellen. ch and 💻 www.topjobs.ch, but note that some job descriptions are in French or German. Some sites specialise in English-speaking positions, such as 💻 www.jobsingeneva.com and 💻 www.jobsinzurich.com. Positions advertised in newspapers often invite candidates to apply online, but many Swiss companies (as well as the post office!) prefer traditional job applications sent by post.

WORKING ILLEGALLY

It isn't uncommon in Switzerland for foreigners to work without a residence permit, though the number of illegal workers in Switzerland has fallen considerably since measures were taken to address the problem. The illegal labour market (termed the black economy) thrives because employers are often unable to obtain permits for foreigners, and many foreigners are willing to risk the consequences for the high wages on offer. Some unscrupulous employers use illegal labour simply to pay low wages for long hours and poor working conditions (Geneva is the black economy's black spot). An employer may also be reluctant to pay for an employee's permit, particularly when he may need him for a few weeks only, e.g. to help with the grape harvest.

It's strictly illegal to work in Switzerland without a permit. If you're tempted to take a job without one you should be aware of the consequences, as the black economy is a risky business for both employers and employees. An employer faces a fine of up to SFr. 5,000 per employee and those who organise or help people enter Switzerland illegally can be imprisoned and fined up to SFr. 100,000. Anyone caught working without a permit is usually fined and deported, and may be refused a permit in future. You can even be black-listed (this also applies to those sacked for serious offences) or deported and your passport stamped so that you're unable to re-enter Switzerland. If you're caught working illegally, even for a few days while waiting for a permit to be issued, you can be fined and your permit application may be cancelled. **Employees without permits have no entitlement to federal or company pensions, unemployment pay, health or accident insurance (e.g. when skiing), and no legal job protection.**

SALARIES

It can be difficult to determine the salary you should receive in Switzerland, as salaries aren't quoted in job advertisements and are kept strictly confidential – the Swiss don't like to discuss money, which simply confirms that they've got heaps of it! Usually salaries are negotiable and it's up to you to ensure that you receive the level of salary and benefits commensurate with your qualifications and experience. Minimum salaries exist in all trades and professions. Age is usually a major consideration with many Swiss companies, and seniority and experience are favoured by most Swiss employers (unless you're over 50). Many employers, particularly larger companies, are reluctant to pay a young person (e.g. below 30) a top salary, irrespective of his qualifications and experience. If you have friends or acquaintances working in Switzerland or who have worked there, ask them what an average or good salary is for your particular trade or profession.

Surveys consistently show that Swiss salaries are among the highest in the world, particularly those of managers and executives, and the Swiss also have the highest net pay after the deduction of taxes and social security contributions. An executive or top manager earns over SFr. 100,000 and top executives around SFr. 250,000 or more, although management salaries have fallen in recent years. A top executive can earn at least 40 times that of the lowest paid worker, the highest differential in the world. Salaries of both skilled and unskilled workers are generally up to two or three times higher in Switzerland than in most other European countries.

Starting salaries with many large Swiss companies may, however, be lower than the national average. Small companies often pay higher salaries but have smaller permit allocations. Salaries paid by some foreign (e.g. American) companies tend to be, on average, higher than those paid by Swiss companies, partly because many staff are specialists, managers and executives imported from abroad. Your working hours (see page 50) may be longer than in other countries and should be taken into account when negotiating your salary (an extra two hours a week adds up to around two and a half weeks a year!). In recent years, salary increases have been low and often below the rate of inflation (salaries have largely stagnated in the last decade).

Some employers may underestimate the cost of living in Switzerland, particularly the cost of housing, which can be astronomical. On average, the cost of living (see page 295) is much higher than in other developed countries, although the gross earnings and purchasing power of the Swiss are among the highest in the world. Income tax and pension contributions are progressive; the higher your income, the higher your pension and income tax payments (see **Chapters 13 & 14** respectively). They are, however, lower than in most other countries.

Women make up 45.3 per cent of the Swiss workforce and around 57 per cent of Swiss women between 15 and 64 are employed, one of the highest proportions in Europe. However, over 56 per cent of women work part-time compared with just 12 per cent of men. Since 1981, employers in Switzerland have been legally required to pay equal wages to men and women doing the same job. Nevertheless, women's salary levels are (on average) around a third lower than men's, an inequality not entirely accounted for by their different occupations, and foreign women usually earn even less than Swiss women.

As in most countries, although there may be no official discrimination, in practice this isn't always so. Professional women are rarer in Switzerland than in many other developed countries and a woman often finds it difficult to reach the top ranks of her profession; only a small proportion are managers or executives – Switzerland has a concrete rather than a glass ceiling where career women are concerned! Swiss women have held a few one-day strikes to highlight salary inequalities, although they weren't well supported.

Married women usually face more discrimination in the workplace than single women, although it's no worse than in most other developed countries. Swiss employers must pay the salary of a female employee during pregnancy when she is absent from work, provided she intends to return to work after giving birth (see **Pregnancy & Confinement** on page 54). However, as no crèche service is provided by companies, this is often difficult; in Switzerland, a woman is usually either a mother or an employee – seldom both.

A useful guide to salaries and the cost of living is contained in a booklet entitled *Living and Working in Switzerland*, published in English by the Federal Office for Migration, Bundesgasse 8, CH-3003 Berne (☎ 031 322 21 11, 💻 www. swissemigration.ch). The United Bank of Switzerland publishes a free booklet (in English) entitled *Prices and Earnings Around the World*, which compares Swiss salaries with those of many other countries (it can be ordered from 💻 www. ubs.ch).

CONTRACT JOBS

Contract jobs, usually for a limited period, are available through many foreign and Swiss employment agencies specialising in freelance work. Most contract positions are for specialists in the computer, engineering and electronics fields. A number of agencies in Switzerland specialise in supplying contract staff to major companies and many post lists of day labourers required, in their windows. Foreign employees of a foreign company who are living in Switzerland and working temporarily for a Swiss employer require a work permit. This must be obtained by the Swiss employer, unless employment is for only a brief period.

SELF-EMPLOYMENT

Non-EU citizens require a C permit (*Niederlassungsbewilligung, permis d'établissement* – see page 67) to be self-employed. It's therefore virtually impossible to emigrate to Switzerland to become self-employed or to start a business (unless you have millions of francs and are going to create jobs and exports). There are sometimes exceptions in the fields of music and art, and in professions where Swiss nationals don't usually qualify, for example translating or writing in a non-Swiss language. Non-EU citizens married to Swiss nationals with a B permit may be allowed to be self-employed, although this is unusual.

EU citizens can start self-employment in Switzerland but must register with the authorities and obtain a work permit. This is usually granted if the self-employed person can prove that he has set up successfully and can make a living from his trade.

Non-resident foreigners who wish to establish a business in Switzerland may be able to negotiate a favourable tax deal with the canton authorities (e.g. in the canton of Vaud, where a ten-year tax exemption is possible) plus residence permits for the owner and his family.

TRAINEES

Switzerland is a participant in an international trainee (*Praktikant, stagiaire*) programme designed to give young people the opportunity for further education and occupational training, and to enlarge their professional experience and knowledge of languages. The programme has exchange agreements with Argentina, Australia, Austria, Belgium, Bulgaria, Canada, the Czech Republic, Denmark, Finland, France, Germany, Hungary, Ireland, Italy, Luxembourg, Monaco, the Netherlands, New Zealand, Norway, Poland, Portugal, Romania, Russia, Slovakia, South Africa, Spain, Sweden, the UK and the US. If you're between 18 and 30 (18 to 35 for Argentina, Bulgaria, the Czech Republic, Monaco, Romania, Slovakia, South Africa and the US) and have completed your vocational training (minimum of two years), you may be eligible for a position as a trainee in Switzerland. The trainee agreement covers all occupations except those normally barred to foreigners and employment must be in the occupation in which you were trained.

Permits are granted for one year and can, in exceptional circumstances, be extended for a further six months. Under the trainee agreement, the granting of a residence permit doesn't depend on quotas or the employment situation. After a training period in Switzerland, a non-EU trainee cannot be re-employed by the same or another employer in Switzerland for a period of 2 to 12 months. This is to prevent people using the trainee programme as a back door to securing a permanent job in Switzerland.

Information about the trainee programme can be obtained from the Bundesamt für Migration, Abteilung Arbeitsmarkt, Sektion Auswanderung und Stagiaires, Quellenweg 6, CH-3003 Berne (☎ 031 322 42 02, 🖳 www.bfm. admin.ch).

AU PAIRS

If you're between 17 and 30 (you don't have to be female) you're eligible for a job as an au pair in Switzerland. The au pair system provides you with an excellent opportunity to travel, learn a language and generally broaden your education by living and working abroad. The main aim of the au pair system is to give you the opportunity to learn a foreign language in a typical family environment. The au pair employment conditions state that you must attend language classes for a minimum number of hours a week (around four) and be given sufficient time off to study at home. Evidence of attendance at a language course may be required by the authorities.

Foreign au pairs are contracted to work for up to 18 months. Most au pairs in Switzerland come from Europe (particularly Scandinavian countries). British girls are popular, but you should make sure that a family isn't just looking for an unofficial English teacher. Young people from Australia, Canada, Europe, New Zealand and the US are permitted to work as au pairs in Switzerland.

You must be prepared to do most kinds of housework and various duties associated with children, including the preparation of their meals, washing and ironing their clothes, cleaning and baby-sitting. You aren't, however, a general servant or cook, although extra services are often taken for granted. You also shouldn't be expected to look after physically or mentally handicapped children. Working hours are officially limited to 30 a week (five hours per day, six days per week) plus a few evenings' baby-sitting, and include at least one full day and one half day free each week. You're paid between around SFr. 600 and 900 per month, depending on your age, experience and working hours and the canton in which you're employed; you may have fun as an au pair, but you're unlikely to get rich unless you marry a wealthy Swiss.

All meals and accommodation are provided and you have your own room with a lockable door. Your employer pays for your residence permit and may pay part of your language study costs and your journey to and from Switzerland, although this isn't usual. If you don't have the required insurance (see **Chapter 13**), he should deduct insurance contributions from your pay. **Check that this is the case, or you will be working illegally.** If you're under 20, you have five weeks' paid holiday per year, four weeks' if over 20. On days off, you're paid around SFr. 20 in lieu of board. You should obtain a statement of your precise duties, time off and salary in writing before your arrival in Switzerland.

You can find a position as an au pair through agencies both in Switzerland and abroad. The major au pair agencies in Switzerland include Pro Filia (🖥 www. profilia.ch) and Swissaupair (🖥 www.swissaupair.ch). These agencies charge registration and placement fees when a position is found. There are specialist au pair agencies in most European countries and in North America that can help you find a job as an au pair in Switzerland. It's possible to advertise for an au pair position in a local newspaper. Au pair jobs are also often advertised in tourist offices. The *Au Pair and Nanny's Guide to Working Abroad* by Susan Griffith & Sharon Legg (Vacation Work) may also be of interest.

The au pair system has been uncharitably referred to as a mine-field of guilt-ridden mothers, lecherous fathers and spoilt brats. Your experience as an au pair will depend on your family (and yourself). If you're fortunate enough to work for a warm and friendly host family, you will have a wonderful experience, lots of free time, and possibly holidays in both Switzerland and abroad. Many au pairs grow to love their children and families and form lifelong friendships. On the other hand, abuses of the au pair system are common in all countries and you may be treated as a servant or slave rather than a member of the family, and be expected to work long hours and spend most evenings baby-sitting. Many families employ an au pair simply because it costs only a fraction of the salary of a nanny. If you have any questions or complaints about your duties, you should refer them to the agency which found you your position (if applicable). **There are many families to choose from and you should never remain with a family if you're unhappy with the way you're treated.**

LANGUAGES

An important consideration for anyone seeking employment in Switzerland is the local language, which varies with the area. Switzerland has four official languages: German, spoken by around 65 per cent of the population (but note that the spoken and written languages differ – see **German** below), French (20 per cent), Italian (6 per cent) and Romansch (Rhaeto-Roman), which is spoken by around 35,000 people (0.5 per cent of the population) in the canton of Graubünden. The remainder are foreigners whose mother-tongue isn't one of the Swiss national languages. Although all official languages are equal in principle, this is often not the case in practice, and the German language and German speakers dominate many areas of public life, to the displeasure of the French-speaking Swiss. The cultural and linguistic division between the German and French-speaking Swiss cantons is referred to as the *Röstigraben* (the 'fried potato cake' divide). Italian is usually relegated to a distant third place (except in Ticino).

Although English could be called the *lingua franca* of Switzerland, most official publications, forms, warning signs, etc., are printed in French, German and Italian, and seldom in English. English is a mandatory subject in most state schools from the age of 13 or later and is widely spoken by the middle-aged and youths, although less so by the elderly and in rural areas. Nevertheless, it's an important business and commercial language, even within Switzerland. Some 15 per cent of all Switzerland's workforce uses English at work, with the German-speaking Swiss more likely to use it than French or Italian speakers. Wherever you work, you will be inundated with forms, documents, memos and other communications written in the local language. Don't ignore them, as some will be important. The same applies to private post – don't throw it away unless you're sure it's junk mail.

Berne, Fribourg and Valais are officially bi-lingual and have both French and German-speaking areas. Graubünden is tri-lingual, where (some) people speak German, Italian and Romansch. Some Swiss towns are totally bi-lingual and languages are even alternated during conversation (the Swiss are **very** democratic). In parliament, members are free to speak their mother tongue, which may explain why governmental decisions take so long in Switzerland (it's said that the Swiss get on so well because they don't understand each other). The problem of which language to use on stamps and currency is solved by using the Latin name for Switzerland, *Helvetia*.

Probably nothing will affect your lifestyle (and possibly your career prospects) in Switzerland more than your ability to speak the local language(s). **In an emergency, being able to make yourself understood in a foreign language could make the difference between life and death.** See also **Language** on page 156 and **Language Schools** on page 173.

German

The language spoken in German-speaking areas of Switzerland is Swiss German (*Schwyzertüütsch, suisse allemand*). It bears little resemblance to the High German (*Schriftdeutsch/Hochdeutsch, bon allemand*) of parts of Germany, which is a foreign language to the Swiss – although not half as foreign as Swiss German is to Germans, let alone the French- and Italian-speaking Swiss! There are over 100,000 recorded Swiss German words and although many have their origin in High German, the Swiss have successfully managed to make them unrecognisable to anyone but themselves. To the casual listener, Swiss German sounds like someone trying to speak while gargling and is often described as 'not so much a language as a throat disease'. There are many dialects of Swiss German and sometimes inhabitants of neighbouring villages, let alone cantons, have trouble understanding one another.

Most native High German speakers are initially just as confused as other foreigners. Most Swiss German speakers do, however, speak High German (fairly) fluently and, when talking to foreigners, many attempt to speak it, or at least will do so when asked. **Note, however, that the Swiss don't like speaking High German and most Germans don't like the way that the Swiss speak their language.**

Even if you don't understand what the locals are saying, the written language in Switzerland is High German, so if you understand High German you will at least be able to read the newspapers. Strictly speaking, Swiss German isn't a written language and it's never used in official communications (the most common usage is in advertising). Most people write Swiss German using completely arbitrary phonetic spelling and the Swiss cannot even decide how to spell *Schwyzertüütsch* (Swiss German). Nevertheless there are a few children's books in Swiss German dialects and some poets and authors use it. (It's all a fiendish plot to prevent foreigners from understanding what's going on.) All cantons except those listed under **French** and **Italian** below are Swiss German-speaking (some are bi-lingual with French or Italian).

There's a useful little book of Swiss German swear words entitled *Lappi, Lööli, Blööde Siech* (untranslatable in polite society) written by Andreas Lötscher. It might come in handy when motoring or repelling ski-lift queue-jumpers – that's if you can get your tongue around any of the words. See also **Swiss German** on page 39.

French

French is spoken in the cantons of Geneva, Jura, Neuchâtel and Vaud, in addition to the bi-lingual cantons of Berne, Fribourg and Valais. In French-speaking Switzerland (*Westschweiz, suisse romande*) the language is almost the same as in France, with few Swiss idiosyncrasies added. The accent is clear and good French is spoken, the purest in Neuchâtel, although the same claim is often made for the French of Geneva and Lausanne.

If you work in a French-speaking region, it's usually necessary to speak French at work. Social life in French-speaking areas of Switzerland can also be difficult without at least basic French, although in cities such as Geneva and Lausanne, English is widely spoken.

Italian

Standard Italian is spoken in the canton of Ticino and parts of Graubünden (as well as 'High Italian' and some local dialects). It would be almost impossible to work in Ticino without speaking Italian. Socially the language isn't such a problem, as Ticino is a popular tourist area where people are used to dealing with foreigners. German is widely spoken in Ticino, mainly due to the influx of German and Swiss German tourists and retirees.

2.

EMPLOYMENT CONDITIONS

Employment conditions (*Arbeitreglement, règlement de travail*) in Switzerland are largely dependent on canton laws, an employee's employment contract, and an employer's general terms. In general, foreigners are employed under the same working conditions as Swiss citizens. This usually means that salaries, fringe benefits and working conditions are among the best in the world. Employees hired to work in Switzerland by foreign (non-Swiss) companies and organisations may be offered even better terms and conditions (including higher salaries) than those provided by Swiss employers.

EMPLOYMENT CONTRACTS

Under Swiss law a contract exists as soon as you undertake a job for which you expect to be paid. For many Swiss, their word is their bond (in mountain areas, contracts are often oral and sealed by a handshake); however, even if you're employed only part-time, you should insist on a written contract. You and your employer are obliged to abide by the rules and regulations set out in the Swiss law of obligation (*Schweizerisches Obligationenrecht, Droit d'obligation suisse*), a copy of which can be purchased from most bookshops.

There are usually no hidden surprises or traps for the unwary in a Swiss employment contract (*Arbeitsvertrag, contrat de travail*). Nevertheless, as with any contract, you should know exactly what it contains before signing it. If you aren't fluent in the local language, you should try to obtain an English translation of your contract (your language ability would need to be excellent to understand the legal jargon that goes into some contracts). Swiss employers seldom provide foreigners with contracts in English, irrespective of the number of English-speaking staff employed. If you cannot obtain a written English translation of your contract, you should at least have it translated orally so that you don't receive any nasty surprises later – like discovering that you're required to give six months' notice.

In some trades or fields of employment (e.g. agriculture, domestic, and hotel and restaurant jobs) standard employment contracts are drafted by canton governments or a professional body, based on collective labour contracts or legislation (covering around half the workforce). These are usually applicable unless both employer and employee agree otherwise in writing. Employment contract disputes can be easily and inexpensively resolved by a court. For more information contact the Federal Aliens' Committee (Eidgenössische Ausländerkommission/EKA, Comission fédérale des étrangers/CFE), Quellenweg 9, CH-3003 Berne-Wabern (☎ 031 325 91 16, 💻 www.eka-cfe.ch). The EKA also publishes information (in French, German and Italian – unfortunately not yet in English) on a wide range of subjects.

Your employment contract may contain the following:

● the date from which it takes effect and to whom it applies;

- your job title;

- the name of your department and manager;

- your main duties;

- how your department relates to other departments;

- your place(s) of work;

- your salary details, including 13th month's salary and any agreed increases;

- confidentiality clauses and restrictions on private work;

- information about membership of a compulsory health fund (if applicable);

- requirement for a medical examination (if applicable);

- a clause stating that the contract is subject to a residence permit or permission to change jobs being granted by the canton authorities;

- details of probationary and notice periods;

When you sign your contract, you're also confirming your agreement with your prospective employer's general employment terms. Before signing the contract you should therefore obtain a copy of these and ensure that you understand them.

Checklist

- Do you have a written list of your job responsibilities?

- Have your employment conditions been confirmed in writing?

- If a dispute arises over your salary or working conditions, under the law of which country will your employment contract be interpreted?

SALARY & BENEFITS

Your salary (*Salär/Gehalt*, *salaire*) is stated in your contract, where salary reviews, planned increases and cost of living rises may also be covered. Only general points, such as the payment of your salary into a bank or post office account and the date of salary payments, are usually included in an employer's general terms. If the salary payment day varies each month, your employer may provide you with a list of payment dates. Salaries are usually paid earlier in December.

Salaries in Switzerland are generally reviewed once a year around November/December, pay rises taking effect from 1st January of the following year. Annual increases include a percentage to cover a rise in the cost of living, although if there's a decrease in the cost of living (which **has** happened in Switzerland!), your salary may be **reduced**.

13th Month's Salary & Bonuses

Most employers in Switzerland pay their employees' annual salary in 13 instalments and not 12: in December you receive, in effect, two months' salary (which helps pay your end-of-year bills, Christmas and New Year party expenses, etc.), although sometimes you receive half in July and half in December.

Note, however, that a 13th month's salary isn't a bonus but, in effect, a delay in payment. When a 13th month's salary (*13. Salär, 13ème salaire*) is paid it's stated in your employment contract. Some companies don't pay a 13th month's salary but compensate by paying a higher monthly salary. When negotiating your salary with a prospective employer, ask whether a 13th month's salary is paid, i.e. whether you should divide your annual salary by 12 or 13. In your first and last year of employment, your 13th month's salary is paid pro rata if you don't work a full calendar year.

Some employers operate an additional annual voluntary bonus (*Gratifikation, gratification*) scheme, based on each employee's performance or the employer's profits. If you're employed on a contract basis for a fixed period, you may also be paid an end-of-contract bonus. **If you pay direct income tax, then you will pay a higher overall rate of tax if your 13th month's salary and bonus are paid in the same month.**

Allowances

In addition to your salary, you may be paid various allowances, including the following.

Area Allowance

If you're a civil servant employed by the federal government or a canton or community, you may receive an area allowance or weighting (*Ortzuschlag, allocation locale*), depending on the region where you work. The allowance, which may total a few thousand francs a year, is paid in monthly instalments with your salary.

Child Allowance

In Switzerland, parents receive a monthly child allowance (*Kinderzulage, allocations familiales*) of between around SFr. 150 and 450 per child per month. Child allowance is paid by your employer and varies from canton to canton. The majority of cantons pay a fixed allowance for each child, while some cantons pay an increased allowance for the third and subsequent children (to encourage the Swiss to have more children). The cantons with the smallest population or lowest birth rates usually pay the highest child allowances. The allowance is usually paid up to a child's 16th birthday (15 in Fribourg and Geneva) or until the age of between 18 and 25 when he remains in full-time education or occupational training. Registration is made by your employer and the allowance is usually paid to the family's main breadwinner (you can choose) in his or her monthly salary payment. Around ten cantons pay a birth allowance of SFr. 600 to 1,500.

Expenses

Expenses (*Spesen, frais*) paid by your employer are usually listed in his general terms. These may include travel costs from your home to your place of work, usually consisting of a second-class rail season ticket or the equivalent cost, paid monthly with your salary. Companies without a staff restaurant or canteen may pay a lunch allowance or provide luncheon vouchers. Expenses paid for travel on company business or for approved training and education may be detailed in a separate document.

Travel & Relocation Expenses

Travel (*Reisespesen, frais de voyage*) and relocation expenses to Switzerland depend on your agreement with your employer and are usually included in your employment contract or the employer's general terms. If you're hired from outside Switzerland, your air ticket (or other travel costs) are usually booked and paid for by your employer or his agent abroad. In addition, you can usually claim any extra travel costs, for example the cost of transport to and from airports. If you travel by car to Switzerland, you can usually claim a mileage rate or the equivalent air fare cost. Most Swiss employers pay your relocation expenses up to a specified amount, although you may be required to sign a special contract which stipulates that if you leave the employer before a certain period elapses (e.g. five years), you must repay a percentage of your removal costs, depending on your length of service.

An employer may pay a fixed relocation allowance based on your salary, position and size of family, or may pay the total cost of removal. The allowance should be sufficient to move the contents of an average house (castles aren't usually catered for) and you must normally pay any excess costs yourself. If you don't want to bring your furniture to Switzerland or have only a few belongings to ship, it may be possible to purchase furniture locally up to the limit of your allowance. Check with your employer. A company may ask you to obtain two or three removal estimates when it's liable for the total cost of removal.

Generally you're required to organise and pay for the removal yourself. Your employer usually reimburses the equivalent amount in Swiss francs **after** you've paid the bill, although it may be possible to get him to pay the bill directly or provide a cash advance. If you change jobs within Switzerland, your new employer may pay your relocation expenses when it's necessary for you to move house. Don't forget to ask, as he may not offer to pay (it may depend on how desperate he is to employ you).

Checklist

General Positions

- Is the total salary (including expenses) paid in Swiss francs or will it be paid in another country (in a another currency) with expenses for living in Switzerland?

- Is the total adequate, taking into consideration the high cost of living in Switzerland (see page 295)? Is the salary index-linked?

- When and how often is the salary reviewed?

- Does the salary include a 13th month's salary and annual or end-of-contract bonuses?

- Are removal expenses or a relocation allowance paid?

- Does the allowance include travelling expenses for all family members?

- Is there a limit and is it adequate?

- Is free air travel to your home country or elsewhere provided for you and your family, and if so, how often?

- Are you required to repay relocation expenses (or a percentage) if you resign before a certain period has elapsed?

- Are you required to pay for your relocation in advance? This can run into many thousands of francs for normal house contents.

- If employment is for a limited period, will your relocation costs be paid by the employer when you leave Switzerland?

- If you aren't shipping household goods and furniture to Switzerland, is there an allowance for buying furnishings locally?

- Do relocation expenses include the legal and estate agent's fees incurred when moving home?

- Does the employer use the services of a relocation consultant?

- Will the employer pay for a hotel (or pay a lodging allowance) until you find permanent accommodation?

- Is subsidised or free (temporary or permanent) accommodation provided? If so, is it furnished or unfurnished?

- Must you pay for utilities such as electricity, gas and water?

- If accommodation isn't provided by the employer, is assistance provided to find accommodation? What does it consist of?

- What will accommodation cost?

- Are your expenses paid while looking for accommodation?

- Are free or subsidised language lessons provided for you and your spouse?

- Is a travelling allowance paid from your Swiss residence to your place of work?

- Is free or subsidised parking provided at your place of work?

- Is a free or subsidised company restaurant provided? If not, is a lunch allowance paid? Some Swiss companies provide excellent staff restaurants, which save you both money and time.

- Are free work clothes or overalls provided? Does the employer pay for the cleaning of work clothes (both workshop and office)?

- Does the employer provide any fringe benefits, such as subsidised in-house banking services, low-interest loans, inexpensive petrol, staff shop or product discounts, sports and social facilities, and subsidised tickets, e.g. for local theatres or sports events?

- Will the employer provide or pay for any professional training or education required, if necessary abroad? Will he pay for a part or the total cost of non-essential education, e.g. a computer or language course?

Executive Positions

- Is private schooling for your children paid for or subsidised? Will the employer pay for a boarding school in Switzerland or abroad?

- Is the salary index-linked or protected against devaluation and cost of living increases? This is particularly important if you're paid in a foreign currency that fluctuates wildly or could be devalued (many currencies have lost ground against the Swiss franc in recent years). Are you paid an overseas allowance for working in Switzerland?

- Is there a non-contributory pension fund besides the compulsory company scheme? Is it transferable, and if so, what are the conditions?

- Are the costs incurred by a move to Switzerland reimbursed? For example, the cost of selling your home, employing an agent to let it for you or storing household effects.

- Will the employer pay for domestic help or a contribution towards the cost of a servant or cook?

- Is a car provided? With a chauffeur?

- Are you entitled to any miscellaneous benefits, such as membership of a club or free credit cards?

- Is there an entertainment allowance?

- Is a clothing allowance available? For example, if you arrive in the middle of winter from the tropics, you will probably need to buy some winter clothes.

- Is compensation paid if you're made redundant or fired? Redundancy or severance pay (or a golden handshake) is unusual in Switzerland (see **Unemployment Insurance** on page 267) and when applicable it should be noted in your employment contract.

WORKING HOURS

Working hours (*Arbeitsstunden, heures de travail*) in Switzerland vary with the employer, your position and the industry in which you're employed, the average being around 41. Under Swiss employment law, normal working hours should be a maximum of 45 per week. Employees in industry work around 40 hours per week, while workers in the service sector, such as banking, generally work slightly longer hours (around 42 per week). Employees in hospitals, catering and hotels, however, may work up to 60 hours per week, although the average is between 45 and 48. Whatever your working hours are in Switzerland, they may be longer than you're used to working. Of the leading industrial nations, only the Japanese and Americans work longer hours than the Swiss.

The Swiss have voted against shorter working hours on a number of occasions. In 2002, an initiative to reduce the normal working week to 36 hours was rejected by almost 75 per cent of voters. Many Swiss believe their long working hours are partly responsible for their economic success, but most analysts reckon that, although the Swiss work longer hours than many other Europeans, they don't actually do more work. Some people (especially wives and mothers) choose to work reduced hours, e.g. four days a week (usually Friday is the free day).

If a company closes between Christmas and New Year or on other unofficial holidays, employees must usually compensate by working around one hour extra each week. If applicable, this will be stated in your terms of employment. Your working hours cannot be increased above the hours stated in your contract or terms without compensation or overtime being paid.

It may come as a nasty surprise to some foreigners to discover that many Swiss employers (including most large companies) require all employees to clock in and out of work. Anyone caught cheating is liable to instant dismissal.

Flexi-time

Most Swiss companies operate a flexi-time (*Gleitzeit, horaire flexible*) system, which requires all employees to be present between certain hours, known as the core or block time (*Blockzeit, temps bloqué/heures de présence obligatoire*). For example, from 8.30 to 11.30am and from 1.30 to 4pm. Block time can start as early as 7.30 or 8am (which isn't early by Swiss standards). Employees may make up their required working hours by starting earlier than the start of block time, reducing their lunch break (a minimum 30-minute lunch break is a legal requirement) or working later. Most business premises are open between around 6.30am and 7pm. Smaller companies may allow employees to work as late as they wish, provided they don't exceed the maximum permitted daily working hours stipulated by canton or federal governments.

Working hours for employees who work a flexi-time system (see above) are usually calculated on a monthly basis, during which time they may run up a credit or deficit, e.g. 15 or 25 hours. Hours can be compensated or increased in the following month(s) by working fewer or extra hours. **Note that some companies automatically cancel hours worked in excess of 15 or 25 hours if an employee doesn't take time off in lieu of hours worked (*Kompensation, compensation*) within a certain time limit (they never, however, forget about the hours you owe the company!).** Employees who work a flexi-time system may usually take a day or a half-day off work each month, provided the hours are made up either beforehand or afterwards, without needing to request 'permission'. Because flexi-time rules are often complicated, they may be contained in a separate set of regulations.

Overtime

Overtime (*Überstunden, heures supplémentaires*) payments may be made for extra hours worked, depending on company policy or your employment conditions. Most companies pay overtime only for work that's urgent and officially approved. Overtime is generally paid at the normal rate plus 25 per cent on weekdays and Saturdays, and plus 50 per cent on Sundays and public holidays. Companies must generally obtain permission from the canton authorities for employees to work on Sundays and official holidays (see below).

Sunday Working

In Switzerland there's a law against working on Sundays and official holidays unless absolutely necessary (some people would like it extended to the other six days of the week!). When necessary, an official form must be completed by your employer and approved by the canton authorities. Fines can be imposed for ignoring the Sunday working law, although as a foreigner you may just be given a warning (usually by your upstanding Swiss neighbours). Sunday working laws may be less strict or less strictly observed in country areas, where farmers are permitted to work on most Sundays. See also **Social Customs** on page 382.

Checklist

- What are the weekly working hours?

- Does the employer operate a flexi-time system? If so, what are the block working hours? How early may you start and finish? Can you carry forward extra hours worked and take time off at a later date or carry forward a deficit and make it up later?

- Are you required to clock in and out of work?

- Can you choose to take time off in lieu of overtime or be paid for it?

- Are you required to work additional hours each week to compensate for extra official company holidays?

HOLIDAYS & LEAVE

Annual Holidays

Your annual holiday (*Ferien, congé/vacances*) entitlement depends on your profession, position and employer. Most Swiss companies allow four weeks' annual holiday up to the age of 50 and five weeks' over 50. Some companies may allow a fifth week's holiday at an earlier age, e.g. 45. Top managerial positions may offer additional annual holiday (but no time to take them!). The average number of paid holidays a year is around 23 days.

Before starting a job, check that your new employer will approve any planned holidays. This is particularly important if they fall within your probationary period (usually three months), when holidays aren't usually permitted.

Public Holidays

Public holidays (*Feiertage, jours fériés*) vary from canton to canton, depending on whether the predominant local religion is Catholic or Protestant. The following dates or days are public holidays in most Swiss cantons; those marked with an asterisk are Swiss national holidays.

Date	Holiday
*1st January	New Year's Day (*Neujahr, Jour de l'An*)
2nd January	St. Berchtold's Day (*Berchtoldstag, le 2 janvier*)
*March or April	Good Friday (*Karfreitag, Vendredi Saint*)
	Easter Monday (*Ostermontag, Lundi de Pâques*)
1st May	May Day (*Tag der Arbeit, Fête du Travail*)
May	Ascension Day (*Auffahrt, Ascension*) – Thursday 40 days after Easter
*June	Whitsuntide (*Pfingsten, Pentecôte*) – ten days after Ascension
*1st August	Swiss National Day (*Bundesfeiertag, Fête nationale*)
*25th December	Christmas Day (*Weihnachtstag, Noël*)
*26th December	Boxing Day (*Stefanstag, le 26 décembre*)

There are also half-day public holidays in some cantons, e.g. Zurich.

If a public holiday falls on a weekend, there's no substitute weekday holiday unless the number of public holidays in a particular year falls below a minimum number. When a holiday falls on a Thursday or a Tuesday, many employees take the Friday or Monday (respectively) off to make a long weekend, although the extra day must come out of their annual holiday entitlement.

Many Swiss companies close down during Christmas and New Year, e.g. from midday or 4pm on 24th December until 2nd or 3rd January. To compensate for this shutdown (and perhaps other company holidays), employees are required to work around one hour per week extra, throughout the year.

Pregnancy & Confinement

Time off for sickness in connection with a pregnancy (*Schwangerschaft*, *grossesse*) is usually given without question but may not be paid without a doctor's letter.

Some companies pay a monthly allowance to pregnant women (pregnant men receive the Nobel Prize for medicine!). Around ten cantons pay a birth allowance of SFr. 600 to 1,500. In 2005, the Swiss introduced state maternity insurance which pays working mothers 80 per cent of their average salary for 14 weeks after giving birth. The benefits are paid by the *Erwerbsersatzordnung* – the fund that pays the salary of Swiss men when on military service. The maximum amount paid is SFr. 172 per day.

Pregnant and nursing mothers cannot be required to work overtime and cannot be given notice during the pregnancy or the 16 weeks after a birth. You cannot (by law) return to work during the eight weeks after delivery and you can choose to stay at home for another eight weeks.

Sick Leave

You're usually required to notify your employer as soon as possible by phone of sickness or an accident that prevents you from working. If you're away from work for longer than two or three days, you may be required to produce a doctor's certificate. (The period is stated in your general terms of employment.) Your salary insurance policy will determine how much money you receive while unable to work (see **Salary Insurance** on page 267).

Compassionate Leave

Most Swiss companies provide additional days off for moving house, your own or a family marriage, the birth of a child, the death of a family member or close relative, and other milestones in life. Grounds for compassionate leave (*Sonderurlaub*, *congé spécial*) should be listed in your general employment terms.

Checklist

● What is the annual leave entitlement? Does it increase with age?

● What are the paid public holidays?

INSURANCE

Accident Insurance

Accident insurance (*Unfallversicherung, assurance accidents*) is mandatory for all employees in Switzerland. Occupational accident insurance is paid by your employer and covers accidents or illness at work, and accidents that occur when travelling to and from work, or when travelling on company business.

Private accident insurance contributions vary according to your employer from nothing (in a non-contributory scheme) to around 1.5 per cent of your gross monthly salary. For information see page 266.

Federal Social Security

Swiss federal social security offers old age and survivors' insurance/OASI (*Eidgenössische Alters- und Hinterlassenenversicherung/AHV, assurance-vieillesse et survivants/AVS*) and disability insurance/DI (*Invalidenversicherung/IV, assurance d'invalidité/AI*), and contributions are obligatory for most residents of Switzerland. A flat rate of 5.05 per cent of your gross salary is deducted at source by your employer. For details see **Social Security System** on page 260.

Salary Insurance

Many companies provide salary insurance (*Salärausfallversicherung/ Salärlosenversicherung, assurance perte de gain*) to cover periods of sickness or injury. The cost to employees varies from nothing to around 1 per cent of gross monthly salary. For further information see page 267.

Unemployment Insurance

Unemployment insurance (*Arbeitslosenversicherung, assurance chômage*) is compulsory for all employees of Swiss companies. You pay 1 per cent of your gross monthly salary, which is deducted by your employer. Payment may be included with your OASI/DI payments on your pay slip (total 6.05 per cent). For details see page 267.

Miscellaneous Insurance

Other insurance provided by your employer is listed in his general terms. It may include free life and health insurance when travelling outside Switzerland on company business. Some companies have compulsory health insurance schemes.

Checklist

- Is insurance cover provided other than obligatory insurance (see above)?
- Is free life insurance provided?
- Is health insurance provided for you **and** your family? What does it include?
- For how long will your salary be paid if you're ill or have an accident?

RETIREMENT & PENSIONS

Your employment conditions may be valid only until the official Swiss retirement age (*Ruhestand, retraite*), which is currently 64 for women and 65 for men. If you wish to continue working after you've reached retirement age, you may be required to negotiate a new employment contract (you should also seek psychiatric help).

Company Pension Fund

Membership of a company pension fund (*Berufliche Vorsorge/BVG, prévoyance professionelle/LPP*) is compulsory for all employees earning over SFr. 19,890 a year. The amount you pay varies from around 6 to 15 per cent of your gross monthly salary, depending on your age and your employer's pension fund. See page 263 for further information.

Checklist

- What percentage of your salary must you pay towards a pension fund and what does it entitle you to?
- Are you able to pay a lump sum into the pension fund in order to receive a full or higher pension?

OTHER CONDITIONS

Education & Training

Education and training (*Schulung und Ausbildung, enseignement et formation*) provided by your employer should be stated in his general terms. This may include training abroad, provided it's essential to your job (although you may need to convince your employer). In addition to relevant education and training, employers must provide the essential tools and equipment for a job, which is, however, open to interpretation.

If you need to learn a language or improve your language knowledge to perform your job, the cost of language study is usually paid by your employer. If it isn't essential, some employers will pay only a part of the cost or nothing at all (one of the penalties of being an English speaker). Employees who aren't of English mother-tongue may be paid to learn or improve their English if it's necessary for their job. An allowance may be paid for personal education or hobbies such as flower arranging, kite flying or break dancing, which aren't work related or of any direct benefit to your employer.

Acceptance of Gifts

Employees are normally forbidden to accept gifts (*Geschenkannahme, accepter des dons*) of more than a certain value (e.g. SFr. 50) from customers or suppliers. Many suppliers give bottles of wine or small gifts at Christmas that don't breach this rule. (If you accept a bribe, make sure it's a big one and that your bank account is covered by the Swiss secrecy laws.)

Changing Jobs & Confidentiality

Companies in a high-tech or highly confidential business may have 'competition restrictions' (*Konkurrenzklausel/Konkurrenzverbot, clause de non-concurrence*) regarding employees working for a competitor in Switzerland or elsewhere. You should be aware of these restrictions as they're enforceable by Swiss law, although it's a complicated subject and disputes must often be resolved by a court of law.

Swiss laws regarding industrial secrets and employer confidentiality are **very** strict. If you breach this confidentiality it may not be simply a matter of dismissal and perhaps subsequently having to leave Switzerland. You may also find yourself subject to criminal proceedings, resulting in a fine or even imprisonment. Keep our secrets **secret** is the byword of **all** Swiss companies – not just Swiss banks.

If you wish to change jobs, you may be affected by permit restrictions (see page 72). Note also that the Swiss don't generally change jobs often and some employers may think that you're unreliable if you change jobs more often than a few times during your lifetime (although this has changed in recent years, during which redundancies have become commonplace).

Other matters to take into account when changing jobs are:

- If you're a member of a company health fund (*Krankenkasse, caisse de maladie*), you may wish to transfer your family's health insurance to another health fund or health insurance company, as you will no longer benefit from the (usually substantial) company discount.

- If you're moving to another Swiss company, your accrued company pension fund benefits will be transferred to a private pension fund account in your name. If you're leaving Switzerland the accrued benefits will be paid to you in full.

If changing jobs entails moving house within Switzerland, see **Chapter 20.**

Dismissal

Dismissal is usually legal in exceptional circumstances only, depending on your contract (although an employer can make you redundant for any number of reasons). For example, refusing to work, cheating or stealing from your employer, competing with your employer, insulting your employer or colleagues, assaulting your employer or a colleague, and drunkenness during working hours on your employer's premises (office parties excepted). Under normal circumstances, you cannot be fired in the first four weeks of an illness, during pregnancy or the 16 weeks after giving birth, or during compulsory military service.

Military Service

Salary payment during Swiss military service (*Militärdienst, service militaire*) and time off for military and civil defence duties are included in your employment terms. These are of no interest to foreigners, as they aren't liable for Swiss military service unless they become Swiss citizens or have dual nationality, haven't already served in a foreign army, and are young enough to be eligible (see **Military Service** on page 373).

Part-time Job Restrictions

Restrictions on part-time employment (*Nebenarbeit, travail accessoire*) are usually detailed in your employment conditions. Most Swiss companies don't allow full-time employees to work part-time (i.e. moonlight) for another employer, particularly one in the same line of business. You may, however, be permitted to take a part-time teaching job or similar part-time employment (or you can write a book!).

Probationary & Notice Periods

For most jobs there's a probationary period (*Probezeit, période d'essai*), ranging from two weeks for seasonal workers to three months or longer for permanent employees. Seasonal workers or their employer can usually terminate their contract with a notice period (*Kündigungsfrist, délai de résiliation*) of three days during the probationary period. For permanent employees, notice can be given at the end of any week, with a notice period of one or two weeks. After the probationary period, an employment contract may be terminated by either party at the end of any month, when the contract notice period applies.

Your contract notice period depends on your employer, profession and length of service and is usually noted in your employment contract and general terms. If it isn't stated, the notice period is usually one month during the first year, two months during the second to ninth years, and three months from the tenth year of service. The notice period for many professions is three months and may be longer for executive or key employees, e.g. six months. Your notice period may be extended after a number of years' service. If an employer goes bankrupt and cannot pay you, you can terminate your employment without notice. Other valid reasons for an employee not giving notice are assault or abuse of you or a colleague by your employer, and failure to pay (or persistent delay in paying) your salary.

Trade Unions

Switzerland has an almost impeccable record of industrial peace, and strikes are virtually unheard of. Although strike action isn't illegal, the Federal Council prohibits industrial action that affect the security of the state, external relations or the supply of vital goods to the country, which helps to explain the reliability of Swiss public transport.

There isn't a strong trade union movement, but some 40 per cent of private-sector employees work under collective agreements negotiated between employers and the trade unions. Travail.Suisse (Hopfenweg 21, PO Box 5775, CH-3001 Berne, ☎ 031 370 21 11, 💻 www.travailsuisse.ch) is the umbrella organisation for several Swiss workers' unions.

3.

PERMITS & VISAS

Before making any plans to live or work in Switzerland, you must ensure that you have a valid passport (with a visa if necessary) and the appropriate documentation to obtain a residence permit.

With the bilateral treaty between Switzerland and the European Economic Area (EEA) that came into force in 2002, the laws on work and residence permits changed considerably. There are now two distinct categories of foreigner living and working in Switzerland: EEA citizens, who in many ways have similar rights to Swiss citizens, and non-EEA citizens, for whom it has become even more difficult to obtain work and/or residence permits (see page 66).

Most Swiss companies and many foreigners in Switzerland, sooner or later become entangled in the complex and bureaucratic nightmare of the Swiss permit system (do Swiss officials **really** understand it?). You may hear a variety of stories about how foreigners can obtain residence permits, many of which appear contradictory. Although a prospective employer may tell you in good faith that he can obtain a permit, he cannot guarantee that approval will be granted. It's impossible to state absolute rules as the criteria for the granting of permits are many and varied, and include qualifications, experience, profession, quotas, canton and federal government approval, the nationality of the applicant (priority is given to nationals from EEA countries) and his spouse, and the area of Switzerland. Ultimately permit approval may simply be decided on the whim of a government official. If a permit application is denied, your prospective employer may be able to appeal.

Any infringements concerning residence permits or registration of foreigners are taken very seriously by the Swiss authorities. There are penalties for breaches of regulations, including fines and even deportation for flagrant abuses. Note in particular the following:

- It can take up to three months to obtain a residence permit to live in Switzerland – from the initial job application, interview and written job offer, until receipt of your permit approval.

- You must enter Switzerland within three months of the date of issue of your residence permit approval. If you're unable to take up employment within this period, you should inform your prospective employer so that he can apply for an extension.

- If the alien's registration office rejects an application for a permit, the reason will be given to the prospective employer in writing, who will inform you of any right of appeal, the relevant appeal authority and any time restrictions that apply.

- Older children without residence permits should carry passports or identity cards to verify their age, for example to purchase reduced price public transport tickets and cinema tickets for age-restricted performances. Secondary school children are often issued with a school identity or student card (*Schülerausweis/Studentenausweis, carte d'identité scolaire/carte d'étudiant*).

- Although it isn't mandatory, it's advisable to carry your Swiss residence permit, passport or other official form of identification with you at all times within Switzerland (except when swimming).

- It's advisable to keep a copy (not the originals) of all your family's official papers, permits, passports, birth certificates and other important documents in a safe place, e.g. a safety deposit box.

Foreigners entitled to live or work (or both) in Switzerland are issued with a residence permit (*Aufenthaltsbewilligung, autorisation de séjour*) in a plastic cover entitled 'foreigners' permit' (*Ausländerausweis, livret pour étrangers*). Foreigners working for international organisations located in Switzerland are issued with an identity card (*Identitätskarte, carte de légitimation*) and not a residence permit, and aren't subject to quotas or the same regulations as people working for Swiss employers.

VISAS

Some foreigners require a visa to enter Switzerland, whether as a visitor or for any other purpose. This includes most people who aren't citizens of a western European country (if in doubt, check with a Swiss embassy or consulate). Visas are usually valid for one to three months only and are often expensive. There may also be restrictions on the number of entries permitted on a single visa.

If you need a visa for employment (*Einreisevisum zum Stellenantritt, visa d'entrée pour prise d'emploi*) the procedure is as follows:

1 An offer of employment is sent to you by your prospective Swiss employer, stating your anticipated start date.

2 Take this with your passport to the Swiss embassy or consulate in your country of residence. You will be asked to complete a number of forms and provide passport photographs, which are sent to Switzerland for processing. The Swiss embassy or consulate will tell you exactly what to provide.

3 On receipt of your acceptance of the job offer, your prospective Swiss employer will apply to the canton alien's police for a residence permit.

4 When the application is approved, authorisation to issue the visa is sent to the Swiss embassy or consulate in your country of residence. They will contact you and ask you to visit them with your passport, in which a visa is stamped permitting you to enter Switzerland to take up employment.

Note that if you require a visa to enter Switzerland, you may also need visas to visit other European countries. Check with your country's embassy or consulate in Switzerland.

When you're resident in Switzerland, you may need to obtain a character reference (*Leumundszeugnis, certificat de bonne vie et moeurs*) from your community (fee around SFr. 20) in order to obtain a visa for some countries.

VISITORS

Foreigners who visit Switzerland for under three months without taking up employment, don't require a permit, although some foreigners need a visa (see above) to enter Switzerland. Nationals of EU countries including Austria, Belgium, France, Germany, Liechtenstein, Luxembourg, Monaco, the Netherlands, Portugal, San Marino and Spain, can enter Switzerland using an identity card or passport that expired no more than five years previously. All other foreigners require a full and current passport to enter Switzerland.

Visitors without permits may not exceed a total of six months' residence a year. According to federal regulations, foreign visitors must be registered by their landlord with their local community if their stay exceeds three months (this period can be reduced by some cantons). To extend a stay beyond three months without leaving Switzerland, you should apply to the local canton's 'alien's police'. If you wish to establish temporary residence for longer than six months, you must apply at a Swiss embassy or consulate **before** coming to Switzerland.

A leaflet issued by Swiss embassies states: 'Anyone entering Switzerland as a tourist will not be able to obtain a residence permit. An application will be considered only after his departure from Switzerland.' In practice, however, this isn't always true. Non-EEA citizens entering Switzerland as tourists are generally unable to obtain an annual residence (B) permit (although an L permit may be issued within a few weeks under certain conditions) – see **Residence Permits** on page 66. An application for a B permit is officially considered only after the departure of the applicant from Switzerland. On the other hand, many employers of seasonal workers rely on hiring workers on the spot. If you apply in person for a seasonal job, an employer may be able to get a permit issued within a few weeks. Before applying for an annual permit for a foreign worker from outside the EEA, however, a Swiss employer must have previously advertised the job vacancy in Switzerland. There are strict annual permit quotas in each canton, plus a federal government quota that can be used in exceptional circumstances. Each canton's quota is based on economic factors and manpower requirements in the canton. In deciding whether to grant a permit, the authorities consider the provision of essential services and supplies, economic necessity due to lack of personnel, and the promotion of commercial development. The authorities can usually exercise their discretion within the bounds of the law.

EU citizens are allowed to come to Switzerland for up to three months to look for employment. Non-EEA citizens must obtain an 'assurance of a residence permit' (*Zusicherung der Aufenthaltsbewilligung, assurance d'autorisation de séjour*) before entering Switzerland. This is an official document issued by the Swiss federal government stating that you've been offered a position with a Swiss employer or have been given permission to live in Switzerland, and that you will be granted a residence permit after arrival. The assurance must be obtained **before** arrival in Switzerland to take up residence. Some foreigners also require a visa to enter Switzerland, even when coming to take up employment or residence (see **Visas** above).

WORK PERMITS

EEA Citizens

The following information applies to all EEA nationals except those from Bulgaria, the Czech Republic, Estonia, Hungary, Latvia, Lithuania, Poland, Romania, Slovakia and Slovenia, who are excluded from the bilateral agreement for the time being, and considered to be non-EEA citizens with regard to work permits in Switzerland.

On 1st June 2002, a new permit system was introduced for EEA citizens under a bilateral agreement between Switzerland and the EEA. This will eventually (expected in 2014) culminate in EEA citizens having freedom of movement within Switzerland and Swiss citizens within EU countries. Under the bilateral agreement, Swiss employers are no longer required to prove that they cannot find a Swiss person to do a job before employing an EEA citizen and employers don't have to disclose the salary to the authorities. In 2007, quotas for EEA work permits were suspended, although the Swiss authorities can reintroduce the quotas in 2009 if the flood of non-Swiss workers is overwhelming.

Companies registered in an EEA country can send their employees to work in Switzerland for a maximum of 90 days per calendar year without obtaining a work permit. They must, however, register the employee with the Federal Office for Migration (🖳 www.bfm.admin.ch) and provide the same conditions with regard to working time, salary and holidays as are mandatory in Switzerland.

For stays of up to 18 months, an L-EG/EFTA permit is issued, which can be transferred between employers and can be renewed if the employment continues or a new job is found after that time. L-EG permit holders can bring their families to Switzerland.

EEA citizens with an employment contract for an unlimited term receive a B-EG/EFTA permit that's valid for five years, which allows employees to move jobs or cantons without any restrictions. If a B-EG permit holder loses his job he can stay in Switzerland for the duration of the permit provided he has sufficient funds to live and doesn't become dependent on social welfare. He can also claim unemployment benefits under the same conditions as a Swiss citizen, look for a new job or become self-employed. After five years the B-EG permit is automatically converted to a C permit (*Niederlassungsbewilligung/permis d'établissement* – see **Settlement (C) Permits** on page 67).

EU citizens wishing to work but not to become resident in Switzerland can obtain a G-EG cross-border permit.

Non-EEA Citizens

Since the introduction of the Swiss-EEA agreement it has become more difficult for non-EEA nationals to obtain a work permit. Employers must prove they cannot find a Swiss or an EEA citizen for the job (this restriction doesn't apply to highly qualified specialists, who usually require a university degree, and top executives) and work permit approval is given by the federal authorities in Berne, rather than by canton authorities.

Nevertheless, your success in applying for a work permit varies hugely according to the canton and often depends on the number of unemployed people in a particular canton. Other factors include the level of demand in certain fields; for example in 2002 and 2003 some international banks and other companies had vast IT projects requiring large numbers of specialists, which made it difficult for other employers to obtain work permits, particularly in Geneva.

Employees of International Organisations

Foreigners employed in Switzerland by international organisations, e.g. the United Nations in Geneva, have a special status. They don't require a normal residence permit, but are issued with an identity card (*Identitätskarte, carte de légitimation*) obtained by their employer. Customs, immigration and housing regulations for employees of international organisations differ considerably from those of 'normal' permit holders (if it had had to put up with the usual Swiss red tape, the UN would have gone elsewhere!).

RESIDENCE PERMITS

Swiss residence permits fall into a number of categories, as follows.

Limited Validity (L) Permits

An 'L' permit (*Aufenthaltsbewilligung L, permis de séjour L*), issued (in a purple cover), is for a limited period (*begrenzte Gültigkeit/limitierte Gültigkeit, durée limitée*) of up to 18 months. It's generally granted to students, trainees, au pairs and specialists employed by foreign companies and sent as consultants to a Swiss-based company. It's closely linked to the job for which it has been granted and, should this be terminated early, is revoked, whereupon the employee must leave Switzerland. The authorities may allow a change of employment where the employee can prove, for example, that he was made redundant through no fault of his own. The permit automatically ends after 18 months and a new permit can be obtained only after a period of one year spent outside Switzerland (in most cases). At the end of 2006 there were some 114,000 L permit holders (both EU and non-EU) in Switzerland.

Annual (B) Permits

A 'B' permit (*Aufenthaltsbewilligung, permis de séjour B/permis B*) is usually valid for one year and is renewable. It's generally issued only to qualified and experienced people in professions where there's a shortage of skilled labour, and to spouses of Swiss citizens. However, there are also B permits for those who establish companies in Switzerland and invest at least SFr. 60,000. and so called 'fiscal deal' permits for those wishing to live but not work in Switzerland (who usually require a certified net wealth of at least SFr. 2m and need to spend at least 180 days a year in the country).

B permits (enclosed in a grey cover) are normally renewed annually on application, although this isn't an automatic entitlement. If you aren't an EEA citizen, an application for the renewal of a B permit must be made by your employer, although it's your responsibility to ensure that your permit is renewed. EEA citizens can obtain the relevant renewal forms from their local authority. There are fees for the renewal of annual permits, usually paid by the permit holder.

Each canton has an annual quota for new B permits (i.e. excluding renewals of existing B permits). Holders of B permits are usually discouraged from changing employment or profession in their first few years in Switzerland (see **Changing Jobs** on page 72). At the end of 2006 there were nearly 403,000 B permit holders in Switzerland.

Settlement (C) Permits

A 'C' permit (*Niederlassungsbewilligung, permis d'etablissement/permis C*) entitles you to permanent residence and, although it may be reviewed from time to time, it can be renewed indefinitely provided the holder resides in Switzerland. C permits are issued (in a green cover) automatically to B permit holders after five or ten consecutive years as a resident in Switzerland. EEA citizens (with the exception of those from Bulgaria, the Czech Republic, Estonia, Hungary, Latvia, Lithuania, Poland, Romania, Slovakia and Slovenia) and US nationals generally qualify for a C permit after five years.

The qualification period for citizens of all other countries is ten years, although a C permit can be granted after five years if the foreigner claims to be well integrated in Switzerland – the 'test' for this usually being that he masters the relevant language. The ten-year qualification period is also reduced to five years for a non-EEA foreigner married to a Swiss.

C permits are also issued to stateless people and official refugees after five years and to the families of C permit holders. Holders of C permits don't require permission to change jobs, to change their cantons of residence or work, or to become self-employed. At the end of 2006 there were over 1m C permit holders in Switzerland.

Border Crossing (G) Permits

A 'G' permit (*Grenzgängerbewilligung, permis frontalier*) gives a person living in a neighbouring country the right to work in Switzerland (many people choose to live in a neighbouring country, where the cost of living is significantly lower, and commute to their jobs in Switzerland). Unlike L, B and C permits, a G permit doesn't include residential rights in Switzerland. G permit holders are required to leave Switzerland at least once a week, meaning it's possible to stay in Switzerland, for example, from Monday to Friday but still keep a main residence outside the country, although only spending the weekends there.

To qualify you must usually have been resident near a Swiss border for at least six months. A G permit is renewed annually and cannot be converted into a B permit. There's no quota for G permits but positions must be advertised in Switzerland and companies must still satisfy the authorities that no equally qualified unemployed Swiss resident is available to fill a vacancy. Permits are usually initially valid for one year. When changing employers or even jobs within the same company, a new permit application is necessary. The total number of G permit holders in 2006 was around 226,500, virtually all (99 per cent) held by EEA nationals.

Dependants

The following entitlements and restrictions apply to dependants of residence permit holders:

- **L permit holders** – The families of L permit holders (including students and trainees) can be granted residence permits, although they don't have an automatic entitlement. If a permit isn't granted, visits are limited to six months per year and shouldn't exceed three months at any time, with a month between visits. The 'visit only' rule isn't, however, always strictly enforced.

- **B permit holders** – Recent legislation has improved the situation for the families of 'B' permit holders: within five years of a permit holder starting work in Switzerland, the spouse and children up to 18 years of age can also move to Switzerland and the spouse and children aged 14 or older are automatically entitled to a work permit. This also applies to spouses of international civil servants and members of diplomatic missions.

- **C permit holders** – There are no restrictions on the residence or employment of the families of a C permit holder.

- **Common-law & same-sex partners** – If you have a common-law partner or partner of the same sex, it may be possible for him to accompany you if you can prove that you've been living together for at least five years and you will be living at the same address in Switzerland. It's usually easier if you have children and/or can provide good reasons for not getting married.

- **Dependants of Swiss nationals** – The foreign spouse of a Swiss citizen must have lived in Switzerland for five years and been married for three years before he can apply for Swiss citizenship, or have been married for six years and show 'a close relationship with Switzerland'.

  Non-Swiss children with one Swiss parent must follow the normal immigration procedures for foreigners. They aren't, however, subject to quota restrictions and there are no limitations on their freedom to live and work in Switzerland.

Part-time Workers

Permits are required for all part-time occupations with the exception of voluntary work, which comes under special regulations. This applies to all members of a foreigner's family living in Switzerland. A permit is required even when a part-time job is for a few weeks only, for example temporary work in the farming industry.

Students

Foreign students in Switzerland require a B permit (see above) and the application procedure is as follows: the student must find accommodation and obtain a certificate from the educational establishment stating that he's a full-time student. He must then take proof of accommodation and the certificate to the local community office of the local town or area and apply for a residence permit in the normal way (see **Registration** on page 78). Foreign students must prove they can support themselves financially and the authorities may check that students are attending classes. With a student B permit you're permitted to get a job and work a maximum of 15 hours a week. There are special regulations for students or trainees studying with international organisations. Student permits don't count towards obtaining a C permit.

Non-employed Foreign Residents

Foreigners wishing to live but not work in Switzerland (euphemistically called 'leisured foreigners' by the Swiss authorities) must apply for a residence permit from a Swiss embassy or consulate before arriving in Switzerland. Permits are normally issued only to those aged over 55 (i.e. pensioners) or people of independent means, particularly the **very** rich and famous. You're required to furnish proof that you have sufficient assets or income to live in Switzerland, usually in the form of a statement from your bank.

Other information required may be a curriculum vitae, a statement of why you want to live in Switzerland, and the name of someone in Switzerland who will guarantee to look after you in an emergency. If you're a pensioner, you must have retired from all gainful employment. Regulations vary from canton to canton (contact the canton authorities in Switzerland for local residence qualifications).

PERMIT APPLICATIONS

EEA citizens can travel to Switzerland and remain there for up to three months while looking for a job before they must apply for a work permit or leave the country. For non-EEA citizens, the normal procedure for obtaining an annual residence permit in Switzerland is as follows:

1. An offer of employment is sent to you by your prospective Swiss employer, stating your anticipated starting date.

2. When you accept the offer of employment, your prospective employer applies to the canton alien's police for an 'assurance of a residence permit'. (Only bona fide Swiss companies or employers can apply for a residence permit for a foreigner.)

3. On receipt of the assurance document, your prospective employer sends it to you with an employment contract, stating your employment starting date.

4. On arrival in Switzerland, you must present your 'assurance of a residence permit' document to the border or airport immigration officials.

5. Within the next eight days, you must register – at your local community office (*Gemeindehaus, maison communale*) in country areas or an area office (*Kreisbüro, bureau d'arrondissement*) in cities – where you will be

asked to present a number of documents and fill in a form (see **Registration** on page 78).

Your permit will then be sent to you. Annual B permits are issued within a few weeks via your employer or community office. The fee for your permit depends on your family size and the period covered by the permit, and may be paid by your employer.

RENEWAL & CANCELLATION

If you're moving to a new community or leaving Switzerland permanently, you must complete a 'de-registration' (*Abmeldeung, déclaration de départ*) in your present community up to eight days before your departure, and register in your new community within eight days of taking up residence (if applicable).

B Permits

B permits are cancelled when **any** of the following occurs:

- the permit expires and isn't renewed;

- the permit holder leaves Switzerland;

- the permit holder has lived outside Switzerland for an uninterrupted period of six months, without applying for leave of absence (see below);

- it can be assumed that the permit holder has left Switzerland, for example he has given notice of termination of employment or taken up employment abroad, even if he hasn't notified the Swiss authorities.

If you're a B permit holder and live and work in different cantons, your residence permit won't be renewed by your canton of residence until your permission to work has been approved by the canton where you're employed.

C Permits

C permits are cancelled when **any** of the following occurs:

- the permit holder notifies the local authority of his permanent departure;

- the permit holder has lived outside Switzerland for an uninterrupted period of six months, without applying for leave of absence (see below).

Under certain circumstances the B or C permit of the spouse of a permit holder can be cancelled when he or she is widowed or divorced.

LEAVE OF ABSENCE

If you plan to be absent from Switzerland for longer than six months and want to be sure of retaining your permit on your return, you can obtain an 'assurance of residence permit' (*Zusicherung der Aufenthaltsbewilligung/assurance de l'autorisation de séjour*) if you're a B permit holder, or an 'authorisation of absence' (*Aufrechterhaltung der Niederlassungsbewilligung/maintien de l'autorisation d'établissement*) if you're a C permit holder. The 'assurance of residence permit' for a B permit holder must be requested by your employer. It's granted for an absence of up to four years, provided your employer states that you will return to his employment within this period.

If you're a C permit holder, your employer or you must request an 'authorisation of absence' from your canton authorities. It's granted for a maximum of three years, provided you can justify the necessity of your absence – for example study abroad, special education or training, or a special assignment for your employer.

CHANGING JOBS

The rules regarding changing jobs vary according to whether you're an EEA national, whether you're married to a Swiss citizen, and your type of residence permit. EEA nationals can change professions and jobs with no permit restrictions. Non-EEA L permit holders cannot change jobs without permission, and non-EEA B permit holders aren't generally permitted to change jobs without permission until they've worked five years in Switzerland. It's easier to change jobs within the same canton, provided your employment contract was terminated through no fault of your own and the unemployment rate is low.

When you change jobs, you may have to resign from your present position before your prospective employer can apply for a new residence permit. Your new employer will need a copy of the letter from your current employer confirming your resignation. The authorities may also ask for an official letter (*Freigabe, libération*) from your present employer, stating that you've resigned voluntarily and that they don't object to your leaving. Your former employer must provide (by law) a reference (*Zeugnis, attestation*) in the local language and a salary statement (*Lohnausweis, certificat de salaire*) for tax purposes. Some companies will provide a reference in English on request.

A job offer doesn't guarantee that a residence permit application will be approved. This means, at least in theory, that changing jobs in Switzerland before you have a C permit (a permanent residence permit) can be a risky business. In reality, companies usually know when they can obtain a residence permit for a foreigner and wouldn't expect you to resign unless they were confident of receiving the permit approval, **but take care**. Check the notice period in your employment contract or conditions before resigning (see **Probationary & Notice Periods** on page 59) and whether there are any employment restrictions, e.g. with regard to working for a competitor.

Your resignation letter should be sent by registered post to reach your employer by the last working day of the month at the latest, or it can be presented personally to your employer, when a signed and dated receipt should be provided.

The Swiss don't generally change jobs often and some employers may think that you're unreliable if you change jobs more often than a few times during your lifetime (although this has changed in recent years, during which redundancies have become commonplace). On the other hand, experienced and qualified foreigners with a C permit may find they can job-hop every few years when there are labour shortages.

4.

ARRIVAL

On arrival in Switzerland to take up employment or residence, there are a number of formalities that must be completed. These are described in this chapter, where you will also find suggestions for finding local help and information and useful checklists.

BORDER CONTROL

On arrival in Switzerland present your passport and 'assurance of a residence permit' (*Zusicherung der Aufenthaltsbewilligung, assurance d'autorisation de séjour et de travail*) document, if applicable (see **Visitors** on page 64), to the immigration authorities at the frontier or airport. If you have an entry visa (see page 63) it will be cancelled by the immigration official. Officially you also require an employment contract, although it's unlikely that anyone will ask to see it.

Ask the immigration official to stamp your 'assurance of a residence permit' document to verify your date of entry. This isn't obligatory but, in the words of the Federal Office of Public Health, 'strongly recommended'.

Foreigners from certain countries planning to work in Switzerland may be required to have a health check (usually consisting of an X-ray only) within 72 hours (three days) in order to detect contagious diseases. The health check is no longer required for people from EEA countries, Australia, Canada, New Zealand and the US. When applicable, the health check is carried out by a Swiss doctor of your choice and you receive a stamp in your passport confirming that it has been carried out.

CUSTOMS

When you enter Switzerland to take up residence, household or personal effects that you've used for at least six months can be imported without incurring duty or VAT. A complete list of the items being imported must be provided at the time of entry, together with a request for duty-free import (a form is provided). VAT (7.6 per cent) must be paid on any articles you've used for less than six months; itemised invoices should be provided. Certain items are exempt from customs duty, e.g. wedding gifts and inheritances.

You will also require the following:

● an inventory of all goods to be imported. Articles which don't fulfil the conditions for duty-free importation (see above) should be itemised at the end of the list as 'goods for normal customs clearance'.

● your Swiss residence permit or assurance of a residence permit (see **Chapter 3**);

- the official foreign registration certificate for cars, motorcycles, motorboats and aeroplanes;

- a contract for the lease or purchase of a property or other proof of accommodation;

- a photocopy of the passports of everyone taking up residence in Switzerland;

- a completed form 18.44 (declaration/application for clearance of household effects), available from the Federal Administration (Bundesverwaltung) website (💻 www.ezv.admin.ch (follow links to *Dienstleistungen*, *Publikationen und Formulare bestellen*, and *Übersiedlungs- und Erbschaftsgut*; the form includes instructions in English).

If you import a car duty-free and sell it in Switzerland within one year of your arrival, you're required to inform the customs authorities at the location where it was imported and pay import taxes, which are calculated on the age, value and sale price of a vehicle.

If you plan to enter Switzerland with a foreign-registered car and household effects (for example on a trailer), it's advisable to enter via a major frontier post, as smaller posts may not be equipped to deal with you unless they're informed of your arrival in advance. Note also the following:

- Switzerland has no currency restrictions – the Swiss love all currency.

- A licence is required to import any guns and ammunition.

- There are restrictions on the type and quantity of plants and bulbs that may be imported.

Information regarding the importation of cars can be found on page 204 and of pets on page 375, and details of duty-free allowances (e.g. alcohol and tobacco) on page 359. Information concerning Swiss customs regulations is contained in a leaflet entitled *Customs Regulations for Travellers Domiciled Abroad*, available from customs offices, Switzerland Tourism offices or the Head Customs Office, (*Eidgenössische Zollverwaltung/EZV, Administration fédérale des douanes/ AFD*) Monbijoustr. 40, CH-3003 Berne (☎ 031 322 65 11, 💻 www.zoll.admin.ch).

MOTORWAY TAX

On entering Switzerland you may be asked whether you intend to use Swiss motorways, particularly if you enter via Basle, and if you answer yes you're expected to pay an annual motorway tax of SFr. 40 on the spot. This tax is payable in addition to Swiss road tax (see page 217) and is applicable to all motor vehicles (including motorcycles) under 3.5 tonnes using Swiss motorways, whether Swiss or foreign-registered.

On payment of the tax, you're given a sticker (*vignette*) which must be affixed to your windscreen on the left hand side (top or bottom) or centre top. The *vignette* isn't transferable between vehicles and tears to pieces if you attempt to remove it (unless you know how!). If you have a trailer or caravan, it requires an additional *vignette*. Vehicles weighing over 3.5 tonnes are subject to a 'heavy vehicles' tax which is payable daily, monthly or annually (a 10-day pass is also available for those who visit Switzerland frequently for periods of one or two days).

If you don't buy a *vignette* and are subsequently stopped by the police on a motorway, you're fined SFr. 100 and must also pay the road tax on the spot. It is, of course, possible to drive around Switzerland without using motorways, but (very) time consuming. In fact, the motorway tax is a small price to pay for the convenience of using some of the finest roads in Europe, particularly when you consider that there are no road tolls in Switzerland. To put it into perspective, the annual Swiss motorway tax is about the same price as a **single day's** motoring on French, Italian or Spanish motorways!

The *vignette* is valid for a calendar year, with a month's overlap at each end, e.g. 1st December 2007 to 31st January 2009. It can be purchased in advance (although it's unnecessary) at Switzerland Tourism offices or from automobile associations throughout Europe. In Switzerland it's sold at border crossings, customs offices, post offices, garages, service stations and canton motor registries.

REGISTRATION

Within eight days of arrival in Switzerland and before starting work, you (and your family) must register (*anmelden, s'annoncer*) in the local community (*Gemeinde, commune*) where you're living, **even if you're in temporary accommodation, e.g. a hotel.** This is done at your local community office (*Gemeindehaus, maison communale*) in country areas or an area office (*Kreisbüro, bureau d'arrondissement*) in cities. Cities and large towns often have an ominous-sounding 'residents' control' department (*Einwohnerkontrolle, contrôle des habitants*).

Switzerland has strict regulations regarding registration for a number of excellent reasons, the most important of which is that most residents pay taxes levied by their local community from their date of registration. Another reason is that each new resident foreign worker is deducted from his canton's annual permit quota. In any case, you must register in order to obtain your annual residence permit (see **Permit Applications** on page 70). If applicable, you must have a health check (see **Border Control** above) **before** you can register. Registration is obligatory for all residents, both foreigners and Swiss nationals.

At your community registration office you will be asked to produce the following (as applicable):

● your passport (containing the border health check stamp, if applicable) and your spouse's and children's passports (if separate);

● your 'assurance of a residence permit' document, which will be retained by your community registration office;

● your marriage certificate;

● birth certificates for each member of your family;

● two passport-size photographs (black and white or colour) for each member of your family up to 18 years of age (family members over 18 must present their own documents).

It's useful to have a supply of passport-size photos for all members of your family, for example for school ID cards, train and bus season tickets, ski passes and Swiss driving licences. Photographs are available from machines at most railway stations and in town centres.

You must complete a form that includes (vital) information such as your mother's and father's Christian names, and (for men) your mother's and wife's maiden names or (for women) you husband's mother's maiden name (make sure he knows this!). If you're divorced, separated or widowed, you should state this on the registration form, as you may be entitled to a small tax concession. You're also asked to state your religion (see **Church Tax** below).

Annual B permit applicants receive their permits within a few weeks via their employer or community.

If you're moving to a new community or leaving Switzerland permanently, you must complete a 'de-registration' (*Abmeldeung, déclaration de départ*) in your present community up to eight days before your departure, and register in your new community within eight days of taking up residence (if applicable). Note also that, if you're a B permit holder and live and work in different cantons, your residence permit won't be renewed by your canton of residence until your permission to work has been approved by the canton where you're employed.

CHURCH TAX

When you arrive in Switzerland and register in your local community (see **Registration** above) you must complete a form asking you to state your religion. All communities in Switzerland levy a church tax (*Kirchensteuer, impôt ecclésiastique*) on members of the three main Swiss churches: Catholic, Old Catholic (Protestant) and Reformed. (Now you know why Swiss churches are in such excellent repair.) If you enter 'Protestant', for example, you're registered as a member of the relevant church and must pay church tax. Members of other religions such as the Church of England, Methodists and Baptists, can indicate their religion on the application, although they aren't required to pay tax. If you aren't a member of any church, enter 'NONE' as your religion. In both cases, you will be entitled to reclaim any church tax deducted from your salary (see below).

Almost all foreigners pay direct income tax (*Quellensteuer, impôt à la source*) and in most cantons church tax is deducted at source from your gross salary, **often without your knowledge or permission**. It doesn't appear on your pay slip or your annual salary statement (*Lohnausweis, certificat de salaire*) and many foreigners are unaware that they pay it. **Nevertheless, if you pay direct income tax, in some cantons you automatically pay church tax, even, for example if you're registered as an atheist.** However, if you aren't registered as a member of an official Swiss church, you can reclaim your church tax every one to three years, via a form available from your community or by writing a letter to the relevant tax office. Enter your personal particulars and bank account information and attach a copy of your salary statement (*Lohnausweis, certificat de salaire*) for the period in question. Send the form to your canton's tax office (Steueramt, Service des contributions), the address of which is printed on the form. You will be advised by letter when your money (excluding interest!) has been credited to your account, usually after six to eight weeks.

If you're wrongly registered as a member of a taxable religion, you can have your records officially changed and reclaim any tax paid, although you can reclaim church tax for a limited period only, for example the last three years. The procedure depends on the canton where you live and the religion under which you're registered. If you do this you cannot get married or buried by this church (without paying a huge fee) and it may affect your children's religious status, for example they may no longer receive religious instruction at school. Nevertheless, there are plenty of other churches only too happy to have you as a tax-free member, e.g. Anglicans, Baptists, Methodists, Pentecostals, the Salvation Army and many others, not to mention any number of religious sects.

If you don't reclaim wrongly paid church tax, the three churches divide the spoils among themselves – the interest alone must be worth a Pope's ransom.

The amount of tax payable depends on your salary (church tax is calculated as a percentage of your basic tax value – see **Income Tax** on page 287), your community (parish), your canton tax rates and your religion, and can amount to several thousand francs a year if you earn a high salary.

EMBASSY REGISTRATION

Nationals of some countries are required to register with their local embassy or consulate, as soon as possible after arrival in Switzerland. Even if registration isn't mandatory, it's wise to do so in case of emergency.

FINDING HELP

One of the biggest difficulties facing new arrivals in Switzerland is how and where to obtain help with day-to-day problems. This book was written in response to this need. However, in addition to the comprehensive information provided herein, you will require detailed local information. How successful you are in finding help depends on your employer, the town or area where you live (e.g. Geneva's residents are better served than Zurich's), and your nationality, language proficiency and sex (women are better served than men through numerous women's clubs). There's an abundance of general local information available in the Swiss national languages (French, German and Italian), although it usually isn't intended for foreigners and their particular needs, but little in English and other foreign languages. You may find that friends and colleagues can help, as they're often able to proffer advice based on their own experiences and mistakes, but this is often irrelevant to your circumstances and needs. More reliable sources of local information include the following.

Local Community

Your community is usually an excellent source of reliable information, but you will probably need to speak the local language to benefit from it. Some companies may have a department or staff whose job is to help newcomers or they may contract this task out to a relocation company. Unfortunately many employers in Switzerland seem totally unaware of (or uninterested in) the problems and difficulties faced by their foreign employees. In some cities, e.g. Geneva and Zurich, there are free advice centres for foreigners.

Women's Clubs

If a woman lives in or near a major town, she is able to turn to many English-speaking women's clubs and organisations for help. The single foreign male (who of course cannot possibly have any problems) must usually fend for himself, although there are men's expatriate clubs in some areas and mixed social clubs throughout the country (see **Appendix A**).

FAWCO

One of the best sources of information and help for women are the Swiss branches of the Federation of American Women's Clubs Overseas (FAWCO, 💻 www.fawco.org) located in Berne, Basle, Geneva, Lausanne and Zurich. FAWCO clubs provide comprehensive information in English about both local matters and topics of more general interest. They can provide detailed information about all aspects of living in Switzerland including accommodation costs, school profiles, names of English-speaking doctors and dentists, shopping information and much more.

FAWCO clubs produce data sheets and booklets containing a wealth of valuable local information, and they also run libraries open to non-members. FAWCO publications can be purchased directly from FAWCO clubs or from local bookshops. Clubs organise a variety of social events, plus many day and evening classes, ranging from local cooking to language classes.

The main disadvantage for many foreigners is that FAWCO clubs have quotas for non-American members (i.e. anyone who isn't an American citizen, married to an American or the daughter or mother of a member). The rules vary slightly from club to club, although in general members must speak fluent English and have strong links with the US, e.g. through study, work or a husband who works for a US company or the US government. Anyone can, however, subscribe to their newsletters.

FAWCO run excellent orientation programmes for newcomers to Switzerland, open to both men and women, including non-members. Courses are usually held once a year and consist of a series of meetings over a period of weeks, normally during the day (which can be a problem if you're working). Places are limited, so apply early. Course participants receive a comprehensive resource book, which may be available to non-participants for a fee. FAWCO clubs are non-profit, charitable organisations and are staffed by volunteers.

AngloPhone Information Service

A good source of information for both newcomers and long-term residents is the AngloPhone Information Service (PO Box 2024, CH-1227 Carouge, ☎ 0900 576 444 (SFr. 3.12 a minute), 🖥 www.anglophone.ch). AngloPhone provides information on finding help in emergencies, classes (in English), activities, professionals and their services (such as tax planners, accountants and lawyers), leisure and entertainment, sports activities and facilities, shopping, clubs and associations, and myriad other subjects. In fact AngloPhone staff will attempt to answer question on almost any subject, whether it's related to Switzerland or not. They will also try to find English-speaking tradesmen and professionals for those who don't speak the local language, and provide a message service, e.g. for family, friends, business associates and club members. AngloPhone also publishes a free newspaper, *Swiss Style*, containing information for both residents and tourists (also available on subscription).

Other Sources

In addition to the above, there are numerous social clubs and other organisations for foreigners in Switzerland, whose members can help you find your way around. Many embassies and consulates provide information, particularly regarding clubs for their nationals, and many businesses (e.g. Swiss banks) produce booklets and leaflets containing useful information (see **Appendix A**). Bookshops may stock useful publications (see **Appendix B**), and Swiss English-language periodicals (see page 352) provide useful information and contacts. Local tourist and information offices can also be of assistance.

CHECKLISTS

Before Arrival

The following checklist contains a summary of the tasks that should (if possible) be completed before your arrival in Switzerland:

● Obtain a visa, if necessary, for you and all your family members (see **Chapter 3**). Obviously this **must** be done before your arrival in Switzerland.

● If possible visit Switzerland to compare communities and schools, and arrange schooling for your children (see **Chapter 9**).

● Find temporary or permanent accommodation and arrange for shipment of your personal effects to Switzerland (see **Chapter 5**).

● Arrange health insurance for yourself and your family (see **Chapter 13**). This is essential if you aren't already covered by a private insurance policy and won't be covered automatically by your Swiss employer.

● Open a bank account in Switzerland and transfer funds (you can open an account with some Swiss banks from abroad). It's best to obtain some Swiss francs before your arrival in Switzerland as this will save you having to spend time changing money on arrival.

● Collect and update personal records including medical, dental, schools, insurance (e.g. car insurance), professional and employment (including job references).

● Obtain an international driving permit, if necessary.

● Obtain an international credit or charge card, which will prove invaluable during your first few months in Switzerland.

Don't forget to bring all your family's official documents including birth certificates, driving licences, marriage certificate, divorce papers or death certificate (if a widow or widower), educational diplomas, professional certificates and job references, school records and student ID cards, employment references, medical and dental records, bank account and credit card details, insurance policies, and receipts for any valuables. You also need the documents necessary to obtain a residence permit (see **Chapter 3**) plus certified copies, official translations and numerous passport-size photographs (students should take at least a dozen).

After Arrival

The following checklist contains a summary of tasks to be completed after arrival in Switzerland (if not done before arrival):

● On arrival at the Swiss border or airport, give your permit approval document and passport to the official for date stamping.

● If you're importing a car, complete a form for temporary importation. If you don't own a car, you may wish to hire (rent) one for a week or two until you buy one locally. See **Chapter 11**.

● Visit a health clinic within 72 hours (three days) for a health check if necessary.

● Open a post office or bank account and give the details to your employer in order to receive your salary.

● Register at your community registration office within eight days of arrival.

● Register with your local embassy or consulate.

● Arrange schooling for your children (see **Chapter 9**).

● Arrange whatever insurance is necessary for you and your family (see **Chapter 13**) and **Car Insurance** on page 214.

5.

ACCOMMODATION

In many areas of Switzerland, finding reasonably priced accommodation is becoming increasingly difficult (if not impossible) and finding accommodation at almost any price isn't easy in the major cities. In the cantons of Basle-City, Geneva, Zug and Zurich there's an acute shortage of accommodation due to the lack of building land and high demand. House prices are high and rental prices can be astronomical. For those on low incomes, and for most foreigners, homes are unaffordable, and they have no option but to rent; even then, they often struggle.

Housing accounts for around 25 to 30 per cent of the average family's budget, although it can easily amount to a third or more in high cost areas. Although the federal government subsidises the construction of low-cost housing for low-income families, invalids and pensioners, the growing lack of inexpensive rental accommodation has led to demonstrations in some cities and is one of Switzerland's most urgent needs.

This chapter contains information on buying property, renting accommodation, moving house, utilities and obtaining home help.

LOCATION

Employees of Swiss companies must usually live in the canton where they work and which issued their residence permit. However, there are numerous beautiful areas to choose from in every canton, all within easy travelling distance of a town or city. When looking for an apartment, bear in mind the travelling time (particularly in winter when it can increase significantly) and travel costs, for example to your place of work, shops and schools.

It may be possible for some foreign workers to live in one of Switzerland's neighbouring countries. In general, however, if you don't live in Switzerland you aren't entitled to a Swiss residence permit and your employer must apply for a frontier crossing (*Grenzgänger, frontalier*) G permit (see page 68). Permission may depend on your nationality and whether you work for an international organisation. If you decide to live outside Switzerland, you will be subject to the laws of the country where you're resident, including for example registration with the local police, payment of taxes and car registration. Your rent and general living costs may be lower outside Switzerland, but the advantages may not be as clear-cut as they first appear, e.g. higher taxes.

Employees of international organisations aren't subject to the same regulations as employees of Swiss companies and there are generally no restrictions on where they may live in Switzerland.

BUYING PROPERTY

Although currently growing, home occupier-ownership in Switzerland is about 35 per cent and the lowest in Europe (compared with around 45 per cent in

Germany, 55 per cent in France, 65 per cent in the UK, 70 per cent in Italy and 80 per cent in Spain and Ireland). And among the 'lucky' 35 per cent, most never actually own their homes, as the capital on part of the mortgage is never paid off during their lifetime, just the interest.

Restrictions

The Swiss authorities have traditionally placed many restrictions on foreigners buying property in Switzerland, although these restrictions have been relaxed in recent years, particularly for European Economic Area (EEA) nationals. In any case, the Swiss' fear that foreigners would buy up all their property is largely unfounded, as high property prices mean that most foreigners (and the average Swiss family) can only dream of owning their own home. (In fact many thousands of Swiss live (often illegally) outside Switzerland in what are ostensibly 'second' homes and commute to their jobs in Swiss cities such as Basle and Geneva.) Working foreign residents and their families comprise around 20 per cent of the Swiss population and own less then 1 per cent of property (although some 5 per cent of Switzerland's total housing is foreign-owned). It's also possible to buy a self-contained apartment in a hotel (aparthotel) in some areas, purchased purely for investment purposes, or a purpose-built retirement home (a growth industry in Switzerland).

EEA Nationals

Residents: EEA nationals living in Switzerland can buy and own property (whether a primary residence, second or holiday home, business premises or land) with no restrictions. You can continue to own property when you leave Switzerland and use it as a second home or rent it to a third party.

Non-residents: If you're an EEA national but not resident in Switzerland, you're subject to quota and canton restrictions on the purchase of a second or holiday home (see **Other Property** below).

Non-EEA Nationals

Primary residence: Non-EEA nationals living and working in Switzerland are permitted to buy a primary residence with no restrictions.

Other property: The purchase of other property, including second homes and buy-to-let properties, by non-EEA nationals (and non-resident EEA nationals) is subject to restrictions. These include:

● a national quota set annually by the federal authorities and divided between the cantons (in 2007 the annual quota was 1,440 properties) – once this quota is filled no further purchases are permitted, although quotas aren't always filled and cantons that don't fill their quotas can pass their availability to other cantons;

● restrictions on the size of the property that may be purchased (e.g. no more than 100m² in living area and 1,000m² of land);

● a limit of one property purchase per family or buyer (i.e. you cannot buy one property in your name and another in your spouse's or child's);

● restrictions on the use of the property, for example many cantons specify that you can use the property only for up to three months at a time and for a maximum of six months a year;

● and resale restrictions in some cantons, for example the property cannot be resold for five years after purchase.

Property Prices

Buying a house or apartment in Switzerland is a good investment if you intend to live there permanently or for many (many) years, although you shouldn't expect to make a quick profit. Due to the high prices and relatively low profit margins – Swiss property generally just keeps pace with inflation – **buying property in Switzerland should be viewed as a lifetime commitment rather than a quick way to turn a profit.**

Homes cost **a lot of** money due to the phenomenally high land prices, particularly in the cities; for example, property in Zurich's Bahnhofstrasse has been sold for over SFr. 250,000 per square metre and is therefore among the most expensive in the world. Prices vary considerably with the location and age of a property. On average a two-bedroom apartment costs around SFr. 350,000 and a four-bedroom semi-detached or detached house costs at least SFr. 800,000. These are average prices for new properties around 25 to 50km (15 to 30mi) from a major city; property in and close to major cities and other high-priced areas is **much** more expensive. A parking space or garage isn't usually included in the cost of an apartment and costs from around SFr. 25,000. Not surprisingly, Switzerland has the world's highest per-capita indebtedness in the mortgage sector.

The holiday-home market also has high prices, which usually start at over SFr. 100,000 for a studio apartment and increase to SFr. 1m or more for a self-contained chalet. A two-bedroom chalet apartment costs from SFr. 250,000 to 400,000 and three-bedroom apartments start at around SFr. 400,000. Three-bedroom apartments in exclusive developments cost from SFr. 500,000 to SFr. 800,000. The approximate average price per square metre of new buildings in Switzerland is around SFr. 6,500 (the highest in the world).

If you wish to buy a house it may be cheaper, depending on where you work, to move somewhere more remote where houses are cheaper and commute to work by car, train or air.

Despite the high prices, in most areas there isn't a lot of property for sale, as people seldom move house (it's too expensive) and buyers spend many months or even years looking.

A number of foreign agents deal in property in the most expensive areas of Switzerland, where property is often built especially for sale to foreigners. Agents arrange inspection flights to Switzerland and often refund the cost of flights (up to a certain limit) on completion of a sale. Most agents offer rental and management services and will arrange to let your property. **Note, however, that a property cannot be let for long periods, e.g. more than 250 days a year.**

Property Taxes

Annual property taxes are payable to the community, the canton and the federal government, and generally total around 1 to 1.5 per cent of the value of a property.

Quality

If you can afford to buy a home in Switzerland, the good news is that buildings are built to last at least a thousand years and the quality of workmanship and materials (triple glazing, etc.) are of the highest standard. Houses, unless new, are usually sold without a guarantee. New houses are guaranteed by the builder or architect, e.g. five years for construction defects and ten years for other defects.

If you have any alterations made to a new home before taking possession, you should negotiate directly with the company involved, e.g. a kitchen or bathroom manufacturer or installer, rather than the architect or builder, who will add a hefty percentage as their fee. Always carefully scrutinise any bills before paying them, as it isn't unusual for them to be incorrect.

Mortgages

Residents

Swiss banks, other financial institutions and some companies are only too willing to provide a mortgage (or two) to qualifying residents. You must put down a deposit of around 15 to 20 per cent, the actual amount depending on your lender. The larger the deposit, the lower your monthly mortgage payments, although repayments mustn't usually be more than a third of your gross salary. The balance is financed through a first (60 to 65 per cent) and a second mortgage (15 to 20 per cent) at different interest rates. The first mortgage is usually never paid off as you just pay the interest, while the second mortgage is repaid over 10 to 20 years.

Given that Swiss mortgages are 'life-long', you will be pleased to hear that Swiss interest rates are the lowest in Europe and among the lowest in the world. The mortgage rate is usually variable, although fixed rate mortgages, which must be re-negotiated every three to five years, are also available. The variable mortgage rate usually ranges from 3 to 5 per cent; in June 2007 it was just over 3 per cent, and the fixed rate for two years was 4.1 per cent and for five years 4.19 per cent (from the Zürcher Kantonalbank). Note that a 1 per cent increase in the mortgage rate translates into a 15 to 20 per cent increase in monthly mortgage payments! There's a fee of around 0.5 per cent of the value of a property to establish a mortgage.

Non-residents

Swiss mortgages of between 50 and 75 per cent of the sale price are available to non-residents over a period of 15 to 50 years. If you have additional security, other than the property that you're buying, you may qualify for a larger mortgage. Mortgage rates for non-residents are usually around 1 per cent higher than those for residents (see above).

The Purchase Process

Property conveyancing must be done by a notary (*Notar, notaire*), whose primary role is to protect the interests of the buyer. In any case, due to the complexities of Swiss property ownership laws, it would be almost impossible to find your way through the paper jungle without a notary. On completion of the purchase and registration of ownership, legal fees, land registry fees and a transfer tax (*Handänderungssteuer, droits de mutation*) totalling from 2.5 to 5 per cent of the purchase price, are payable to the notary. VAT at 7.6 per cent may also be levied on the purchase of new property in Switzerland and is included in the sale price. **Take care before signing any legal papers in connection with buying property and have your lawyer and lender check all contracts.**

RENTED ACCOMMODATION

Rented accommodation (*Mietwohnung, appartement à louer*) in Switzerland usually consists of an unfurnished apartment. Furnished accommodation isn't easy to find (except in holiday areas) and is generally expensive. Unfurnished apartments, both old and new, are generally available in all areas, the latter usually being easier to find but more expensive. In some areas there's a glut of apartments to rent, although in major cities such as Geneva and Zurich rented accommodation is in short supply and **very** expensive. Houses to let (furnished or unfurnished) are usually rare and always expensive, and rents range from SFr. 2,000 to SFr. 10,000 or more per month in the best areas. Contracts for house rentals tend to be longer than those for apartments and some landlords rent only to Swiss or C permit holders.

Furnished rooms can be rented in private houses and apartments in most towns for around SFr. 400 to 800 per month, depending on the size, amenities and location. Sharing accommodation can be a solution to high rents, particularly for seasonal workers, for whom rental costs are prohibitively high.

In the farming, restaurant and hotel trades, an employee's salary or benefits may include a furnished room or apartment. Seasonal workers in the building trade may be accommodated in barrack-type buildings near building sites.

Finding Accommodation

The chief sources of rental accommodation are local newspapers, the best days for advertisements usually being Wednesdays, Fridays and Saturdays. Apartments and houses for rent are also advertised (*Wohnungen zu vermieten, appartements à louer*) in free local newspapers, delivered in most areas along with copious 'junk' post (Switzerland is a world leader in the production of junk post, a major industry). Some cities have free newspapers devoted solely to accommodation, e.g. *WIM* in eastern Switzerland (🖳 www.wim.ch). There are also numerous websites (e.g. 🖳 www.homegate.ch, 🖳 www.immosky.ch, 🖳 www.immostreet.ch), where you can also subscribe to an email newsletter that informs you daily about new property that's available in your chosen area. There are also free classified advertisements pages such as 🖳 www.basel expats.com or 🖳 www.xpatxchange.ch.

Advertisers may be private owners, property managers or rental agencies. Most advertisements include a telephone number, although some, particularly those for exclusive properties, provide a box number (*Chiffre Nr., chiffre No./sous chiffres*) and you must apply in writing. If you're interested in a property, apply as soon as possible and be prepared to inspect the property at short notice – in major cities, an advertisement for a desirable apartment for rent may attract over 100 replies.

Most towns have rental and estate agencies (*Immobilien, agences immobilières*), listed in local telephone directories. These usually charge a registration fee of around SFr. 50 that's valid for three months. After signing a contract, you must pay an additional fee. Fees vary from agency to agency but are usually equivalent to a month's rent. **Find out what you're expected to pay before signing a contract.**

Apartments and houses for rent are also advertised on company bulletin boards, in company magazines and newspapers, and in official canton newspapers. Some communities publish a list of vacant accommodation. You can insert a 'rental wanted' (*Mietgesuche, recherche appartement/maison*) advertisement in most newspapers and on bulletin boards in supermarkets, churches, consulates and clubs (many have newsletters where you can place a wanted ad). Finally don't forget to ask friends, relatives and acquaintances to spread the word, particularly if you're looking in the area where you already live.

Fixtures & Fittings

Apartments normally include an oven (usually without a grill), a refrigerator, fitted kitchen units and sometimes a dishwasher or freezer. Note that kitchens are often tiny, even in many large houses. Apartments may be partly or fully carpeted; parquet (wooden) flooring is also fairly common. Larger apartments (from three bedrooms) usually have a second toilet and may have an ensuite shower off the main bedroom in addition to a separate bathroom.

Unfurnished apartments usually have light fittings only in bathrooms, kitchens and occasionally hallways (most rooms just have bare wires). Fitted wardrobes in bedrooms are rare and curtain rails aren't provided unless they're built-in. A number of built-in linen cupboards and a cloakroom unit may be provided. The hot water supply is often shared and can run out during times of heavy use, although modern apartments usually have their own boilers(s).

A storage room is usually provided in an apartment, and a lockable storage room in the cellar of the building, which doubles as the mandatory nuclear shelter (no joke). Many apartment blocks also have a bicycle storage room. Luxury apartment blocks may have a communal sauna or heated swimming pool.

Most apartment blocks have a communal laundry room with a washing machine and tumble dryer and a separate drying room. Some apartment blocks have outside clothes lines, where tenants may hang their clothes to dry. The sharing of washing machines can be most unsatisfactory for families, particularly in large apartment blocks; tenants may be allocated the use of the communal washing machine for a few hours a week only and at an inconvenient time. In larger, more expensive apartments, a personal washing machine and drier may be provided, which may be located in a private laundry/drying room. If you wish to buy your own washing machine and wash at your convenience, ensure that you have room to install it in your apartment and an appropriate power point (see **Electricity** on page 104) – and don't forget to ask your landlord for permission!

Rental Costs

The cost of renting an apartment varies considerably according to its size, age, facilities and location. Rents (*Miete, location/loyer*) are high (especially in cities) and have risen rapidly in the last decade. In response to an increase in property speculation, a law was passed giving prospective tenants the right to know the rental charge paid by the previous tenant (so don't forget to ask). If your rent is increased sharply, you can usually have it reviewed independently; ask your community for information. Subsidised housing is available in some areas for low-income families, invalids and pensioners. Owing to a shortage of low-income tenants, however, it's often possible to obtain subsidised accommodation irrespective of your salary.

Rental prices are linked to mortgage rates in Switzerland and when the mortgage rate increases, landlords have the right to increase rents. When mortgage rates go down tenants may ask for a reduction, although landlords aren't obliged to agree. In practice, however, good tenants usually obtain a reduction because most landlords are keen to keep good tenants.

The number of rooms advertised excludes the kitchen (except in Geneva), bathroom and toilet, although the total area (given in square metres) includes all rooms. Average rental costs for unfurnished apartments are shown in the table below:

No. of Bedrooms	Average Monthly Rent		
	Basle	Zurich	Geneva
0 (studio)	SFr. 650	SFr. 800	SFr. 700
1	SFr. 900	SFr. 1,100	SFr. 950
2	SFr. 1,100	SFr. 1,300	SFr. 1,250
3	SFr. 1,500	SFr. 1,600	SFr. 1,550
4	SFr. 2,000	SFr. 2,100	SFr. 2,000
5 or more	SFr. 2,700	SFr. 2,700	SFr. 3,000

The rents shown are for good quality new or recently renovated apartments in most rural and suburban areas, inclusive of extra costs (see page 96), but excluding a garage (see page 96). **They don't include apartments located in the central area of towns or in major cities, exclusive residential areas, houses or furnished accommodation – for which the sky's the limit.**

An apartment with a patio (*Gartensitzplatz, terrasse*) is usually cheaper than a top floor apartment, which may have a small balcony only. Generally the higher the floor, the higher the cost (you pay for the rarefied air). Top floor or attic apartments (*Dachwohnung, un attique*) are the most expensive and are often fitted with an open fireplace (*Cheminée/avec cheminée*), considered a luxury in Switzerland – though lugging wood up several flights of stairs is anything but luxurious.

Rents are highest in cantons Zug and Zurich, and lowest in Jura, Neuchâtel and Valais. In some areas you can pay over SFr. 10,000 per month for a furnished three- or four-bedroom house. It's possible to find cheaper, older apartments, but they're rare, generally smaller and don't usually contain the standard 'fixtures and fittings' of modern apartments, e.g. no central heating or double-glazing. **Heating in old houses can be highly eccentric.**

Extra Costs

Extra costs (*Nebenkosten/NK, charges/frais immobiliers*), totalling roughly 10 to 15 per cent of the rent, are payable in addition to the monthly rent of an apartment. When a property is advertised for rent, it's usually stated whether extra costs are included in the rent. Extra costs cover central heating, communal electricity, waste collection, the services of a caretaker (*Hauswart, concièrge*) and cable television. They vary from community to community (*Gemeinde, commune*) and are usually divided between all tenants in a building according to their apartment size. You receive an itemised account, usually in the autumn, detailing the amount to be paid. In some (rare) cases, you receive a refund of overpaid charges. If you pay your rent via a standing order, refunds are normally paid directly into your bank or post office account.

Garage or Parking Space

A garage or parking space (*Parkplatz, parking/place de parque*) isn't usually included in the rent of an apartment. A single lock-up garage or a parking space in an underground garage is common in modern apartment blocks and costs from SFr. 100 to 200 per month. A covered parking space costs around SFr. 80 to 120 per month and an outside parking space from SFr. 75 to 100. Most developments have adequate parking for both tenants and visitors (which is a legal requirement).

If a block has no parking spaces, it may be possible to rent one, for example in the underground garage of a hotel or in a private car park. You must sign a separate contract for a garage if it isn't rented with your apartment. It's possible to rent a garage for the winter months only, although the contract must usually start and end on fixed dates, for example from 1st October to 1st April (see **Termination** on page 98). A garage is useful, particularly in winter – unless of course you enjoy trying to find your car among the snow drifts. A garage also keeps your car cool in summer.

Free street parking is difficult or impossible to find in most cities and large towns. In many towns, tenants must obtain a resident's parking permit for on-street parking or face a fine.

Contracts

When you find a suitable apartment, you must sign a contract (*Vertrag, contrat*) with the landlord or owner. Apartment contracts are usually for a minimum of a year but otherwise an unlimited period, with a notice period of three or six months. House contracts are usually for between two and five years with a notice period of three or six months. A standard contract form is provided in most cantons, although you should take special note of any added or deleted clauses or passages. Your contract should include details of when your rent and extra costs will be increased, if applicable. An unscheduled rent rise, e.g. due to a mortgage interest rate increase, must be notified by registered post at least three months in advance.

A landlord may ask to see your residence permit (and in some cases may let an apartment only to a Swiss national or a foreigner with a C permit). Students and others with low or no regular income may need a Swiss guarantor to co-sign their contract. Among the most important considerations are the minimum tenancy period before you can move (e.g. one year) and the official moving dates, which are usually fixed for each canton (see **Termination** on page 98). **Before** signing a contract, you should find out the following:

- whether there's a minimum or maximum limit on your tenancy period;
- on which dates the contract can be terminated;
- whether a deposit is required (maximum three months' rent);
- how many people may live in the apartment;
- what laundry facilities are provided and when they're available;
- if cable television is available and what channels;
- if satellite television is available or whether it's possible to install an aerial;
- whether any telephone sockets are installed (otherwise, you must pay for them);
- if pets are allowed (you can be evicted if you keep a pet against your landlord's wishes);
- when the rent and extra costs are to be reviewed or increased;
- what the parking facilities are (particularly covered parking in winter) and the cost;
- when the tenant or landlord is required to redecorate the apartment;
- what the house rules are (see page 100);

- whether there are any churches or shooting ranges in the neighbourhood (if there's a church within 'donging' distance, you will be woken early on Sundays);

- any unusual rules or restrictions;

- whether there's a lift or a goods lift for furniture (some cantons rule that lifts must be provided in all buildings with four or more floors).

If you rent a house, it's **even more** important to check the rules and regulations for tenants because you will probably be responsible for the following:

- the gardens and grounds;

- the heating system maintenance, insulation, ordering fuel, etc.;

- maintenance of the water supply;

- chimney-sweeping twice a year, which is compulsory for oil- and wood-burning systems (your landlord may pay for this);

- fire precautions (regular inspections may be required by your insurance company, including checking the chimneys).

A deposit (*Kaution, caution*) equal to one to three months' rent must be paid and is deposited in an interest-bearing account. It's repaid with interest when you leave, provided there are no outstanding claims, e.g. for damages or cleaning (see **Termination** below).

Don't sign the contract (both husband and wife must sign) until you're sure that you fully understand all the small print. Ask one of your Swiss colleagues or friends for help, obtain legal advice or join an association such as ASLOCA (🖳 www.mieterverband.ch), which defends the rights of tenants and has offices in most towns.

Termination

You must generally give a minimum of three months' notice **by registered letter** (*Einschreiben Brief, lettre recommandée*) when you wish to terminate the lease on your apartment. This applies to most contracts in Switzerland. Notice letters must be signed by both the husband and wife, where applicable. The contract may usually be terminated only on the dates listed in your contract, normally the end of any month except December or, in older contracts, 31st March, 30th June or 30th September. If it isn't terminated by either party, a lease is normally automatically extended for a further period, as stated in your contract.

If you wish to terminate your contract outside the official dates or at short notice, you must find a replacement tenant who is acceptable to your landlord.

For example, a prospective tenant must be able to pay the rent, and there shouldn't be a good reason not to accept him, e.g. a registered drug addict or someone with a police record. If you don't find a replacement tenant before you move, you're liable for the rent due until the next official moving date or until a new tenant is found, if earlier.

You're expected to leave your apartment **spotlessly clean**, as it was when you took it over, and the return of your deposit depends on this. In Switzerland 'godliness is next to cleanliness' and the Swiss have a lot of spotlessly clean churches to prove it. Your landlord may even don white gloves to check that the oven is clean. One method of avoiding any problems is to employ professional cleaners, which many people consider well worth the money. Look in your local newspapers or telephone directory under 'Removal cleaning' (*Umzugsreinigung*, *nettoyage pour remise d'appartement*). Professional cleaning can be expensive, for example SFr. 1,000 or more, depending on the size of your apartment. Charges vary from company to company, so shop around and don't pay the bill until the apartment has been cleaned to your landlord's satisfaction (it pays not to move too often in Switzerland, as it can be an expensive business). The following checklist may convince you to use a cleaning company:

● The cleaning of your apartment should include **everything**, including carpets (professional cleaning), floors, walls, paintwork, windows (if double glazed, also **between** the glass), oven, cupboards, bath/WC, lampshades, refrigerator, dishwasher, blinds, pipes and radiators in all rooms, garage, patio, balcony, storeroom, attic and basement and the decalcification of your boiler. A cleaning company contract should include all the above.

● Any stains or scratches on floors (e.g. parquet floors, which must also be polished), paintwork and walls must be repaired. This may require painting, papering or sanding.

● Any holes made in walls for pictures, mirrors and other fittings must be filled.

● The garden and house surrounds must be in good order, e.g. no weeds on your patio or balcony.

● Any alterations or improvements made to the property must be sold to the next tenant or 'given' to the landlord. (The landlord may insist on professional alterations or restoration, usually stated in your contract, and not do-it-yourself.)

● Fixtures or fittings that are easily removed and which weren't part of the original inventory, e.g. light fittings, must be removed.

You must pay for any damage to fixtures and fittings and you may also be required to redecorate the apartment, depending on its condition when you moved in, how long you've lived there and the terms of your contract. Necessary repairs or replacements may depend on the length of your tenancy and if you're a long-term tenant certain things may be overlooked, e.g. 'normal' wear and tear. If you have public liability insurance (see page 274), it may pay for accidental damage caused to a rented apartment, although glass may be excluded.

You can obtain a written statement from your landlord to the effect that the apartment is in acceptable condition and that no further claims will be made, although this is usually unnecessary. You may wish to make a note of your electricity, water and gas meter readings and ensure that the telephone is disconnected. Finally, if applicable, ensure that your deposit is repaid with interest. Any deductions from your deposit should be accompanied by an itemised list of repairs and a copy of bills. See also **Chapter 20**.

House Rules

All apartment blocks have house rules (*Hausordnung, règlement d'immeuble*), some of which may be dictated by your local community and enforceable by law (particularly those regarding noise and siesta periods). You should receive a copy on moving into your apartment; if you don't understand them, have them translated. They may include the following:

- a noise curfew between 8pm and 6am (this may start at 9 or 10pm depending on the time of year). The Swiss generally take this seriously, as most go to bed early and rise at the crack of dawn. They may hammer on your door, walls, floor or ceiling, or even call the police if you play music or hold a noisy party after 10pm. Even inviting your Swiss neighbours to a party doesn't always do the trick, as they've been known to call the police and complain about the noise as soon as they're back in their own apartment! Some apartment blocks have a party room for the use of tenants. You can be fined or evicted for persistently making too much noise.

- absolutely no loud noise (e.g. drilling, banging in nails or playing loud music) on Sundays and public holidays. Sunday is a day of rest, when working is forbidden by law (see **Sunday Working** on page 52).

- a siesta (*Mittagsruhe, sieste*), e.g. from noon to 1 or 2pm, during which you mustn't make any loud noise. This is to allow young children and pensioners an undisturbed afternoon nap.

- no bathing or showering between 10pm and 7am;

- no pets without written permission (dogs aren't always permitted, but cats usually are);

- restrictions regarding children, e.g. no ball games or cycling on grass areas;

- no leaving footwear outside the door;

- hanging net curtains at your windows – compulsory in some apartments;

- airing bedding, i.e. hanging it from windows, only at certain times, which may be dictated by canton law;

- restricted use of the laundry room and cleaning after use;

- sorting of rubbish (special bags must be used – see **Waste Disposal** on page 107);

- no toilet flushing between 10pm and 6am and even a request to **'gentlemen to please sit down when using the toilet between these hours'** (seen in an expensive apartment block in Zurich – presumably with **very** thin walls).

Your Swiss neighbours will usually be happy to point out any transgression of house rules on your part. In apartment blocks, problems regarding the use of communal areas are dealt with by the caretaker, whereas problems with other apartments should be reported to your landlord.

Inventory

One of the most important tasks on moving into a new apartment is to complete an inventory and report on its condition (*Hauszustand/Mängelliste, état des lieux*). This includes the condition of fixtures and fittings, the cleanliness and state of the decoration, and anything missing or in need of repair. The inventory form is provided by your landlord and must be completed, signed and returned, within 14 days of occupying your apartment. If you're taking over an apartment from the previous tenant, the landlord may arrange for the hand-over to be done when you're both present, so that any problems can be sorted out on the spot.

Note the reading on your meters (electricity, gas and water) and check that you aren't overcharged on your first bill. **Your apartment should be spotless when you move in, as this is certainly what your landlord will expect when you move out** (the meaning of life in Switzerland is a spotless, highly polished stove) – see **Termination** on page 98. Most landlords in Switzerland are honest and won't try to deceive you; nevertheless, it's better to be safe than sorry.

Keys

You usually receive two or three keys to an apartment or house and two keys for the post box. If you require extra keys you must pay for them. Your house key may also fit your garage door, if applicable. The locks fitted to most apartments and houses are usually of a high security type. Keys have individual numbers, and copies cannot be cut at a local hardware store; if you require additional keys, you must ask your landlord, who will arrange for copies to be made and sent to you (along with the bill).

If you lock yourself out of your apartment (or car), there's usually a local locksmith on call day and night to help. Ask the telephone operator for the number on ☎ 111. This service is, however, **very** expensive and it may be much cheaper to break a window to gain entry to your apartment (unless you live on the 14th floor!). Whatever you do, don't call the locksmith out at night or at weekends – it could bankrupt you (stay in a hotel). If you're a habitual key loser, there are a number of companies that provide a key-return service. For around SFr. 20 they provide you with a coded key-ring tag which you attach to your key-ring. A note on the key-ring tag asks anyone finding the keys to drop them in the nearest post box. Return rates of over 90 per cent are claimed, including keys lost outside Switzerland.

If you vacate your apartment for an extended period, it may be obligatory to notify your caretaker and leave a key with him or with a neighbour in case of emergencies. If you don't have all the copies of your keys when you move out of an apartment, the barrel of a lock for which you've lost a key may need to be changed at your expense.

REMOVALS

After finding an apartment, it normally takes just a few weeks to have your belongings shipped from within Europe – from anywhere else it varies considerably. If you're flexible about the date, it's cheaper to have your move done as a part load, rather than a special delivery. If large items of furniture need to be taken in through an upstairs window or balcony, you may need to pay extra. Obtain a number of estimates in writing before committing yourself, as costs vary considerably. However, you should be wary of a company whose estimate is much lower than others'. Some removal companies promise anything to obtain a contract and increase the cost later, and many don't deliver on the planned date. Always use an established removal company with a good reputation. Check that a company uses its own vans and staff, as some companies use sub-contractors, known in the trade as 'cowboys'. For international house moves it's best to use a company specialising in international removals.

Try to use a removal company that's a member of an organisation such as the Federation of International Furniture Removers (FIDI, 💻 www.fidi.com) or the Overseas Moving Network International (OMNI, 💻 www.omnimoving.com). These, and some national removal companies, are usually members of an advance payment scheme that provides a guarantee: if a member company fails to fulfil its commitments to a customer, the removal will be completed at the agreed cost by another company or your money will be refunded.

Make a list of everything to be moved and give a copy to the removal company. Don't include anything illegal (e.g. guns, bombs or drugs) with your belongings, as customs checks can be rigorous and penalties severe. Give your removal company a telephone number and address in Switzerland where you can be contacted, and ask a relative or friend to handle any problems in the country from where your belongings are being shipped.

Be sure to fully insure your household contents during removal with a reputable insurance company. Don't insure with a shipping company that carries its own insurance as it will usually fight every cent of a claim. In some countries almost all removal companies' insurance policies restrict their liability to a pittance, which also applies to goods held in storage. **Make sure that insurance covers your belongings for their true value and have the policy small print checked by an independent expert.** It's advisable to make a photographic or video record of valuables for insurance purposes.

If you need to make a claim, be sure to read the small print, as some companies require you to make claims within three or seven days. **Any claims outside this period aren't considered!** Send your claim by registered post. If you need to put your household effects into storage, it's imperative to have them fully insured against fire, as warehouses occasionally burn down (often as a result of arson). **Note also that many warehouses have no fire alarms, sprinklers or fire-fighting equipment.** It's better to be safe than sorry!

If you plan to transport your belongings to Switzerland personally, check the customs requirements in the countries you must pass through. To expedite customs formalities, it's advisable to inform Swiss customs of the date and approximate time of your arrival in Switzerland. If your household and personal effects are sent unaccompanied, the receiving freight company sends you a customs form (18.44) to be completed and signed. In addition, they require a photocopy of your residence permit, a copy of the personal details pages of your passport and proof of accommodation, e.g. a copy of a rental contract.

For removals within Switzerland, vans and trucks can be rented by the hour, half-day, or day (local rental companies are the cheapest). Some companies allow employees the use of company vehicles free of charge. Many removal companies sell packing boxes in numerous sizes and rent or sell removal equipment (e.g. trolleys and straps) for those who feel up to doing their own house moving.

Bear in mind when moving home that everything that can go wrong often does, so allow plenty of time and try not to arrange your move to your new home on the same day as the previous owner is moving out. That's just asking for fate to intervene! **Last but not least, if your Swiss home has poor or impossible access for a large truck you must inform the shipping company (the ground must also be firm enough to support a heavy vehicle).** You can ask the local police to reserve a parking space for a removal truck when moving house (at a cost of around SFr. 50).

The cost of moving your house contents from your previous country of residence to Switzerland may be paid by your Swiss employer (see **Chapter 2**). You're officially allowed a day off work when moving house, provided you don't move every month! See also **Customs** on page 76 and **Chapter 20**.

UTILITIES

Registration & Billing

You don't always need to apply to your local electricity, gas and water companies (*Städtische Werke-Elektrizität, Gas und Wasser, centrale des services techniques: électricité, gaz, eau/services industriels*) to have your supply connected and/or transferred to your name. This may be done automatically by your landlord or community, although a deposit (e.g. SFr. 250) is required in some areas.

You're billed quarterly and may pay your bills automatically via a bank or post office account. You may receive a single bill for your electricity, gas, water and sewerage or separate bills. Meters are usually read every six months, so that the first bill received in a six-month period (i.e. after three months) is an estimate and the second bill contains an itemised list of your actual consumption and costs. If you think the estimate is wildly inaccurate, you can ask for an adjustment. (See also **Paying Bills** on page 123.)

Electricity

Some 56 per cent of electricity in Switzerland is generated by hydroelectric power, around 38 per cent by nuclear power and less than 6 per cent by oil and waste product combustion and solar power.

Power Supply

The electricity supply in Switzerland is 220 volts AC, 10 amps maximum, with a frequency of 50 hertz (Hz). This is suitable for all electrical equipment with a power consumption of up to 2,200 watts. For equipment with a higher power consumption (oven, washing machine, dishwasher), a single or three-phase 380 volts AC, 20-amp supply is necessary.

Power cuts, while not unknown, are rare and usually happen on average once a year in most areas. When your electricity supply is to be switched off, e.g. for repairs, you will be notified by your community. The electricity supply to washing machines and dryers (communal and private machines) and to dishwashers may be cut for around two hours during the lunch period (for example noon to 2pm) each day, to conserve electricity for cooking. This may occur only during the 'winter' months (October to March) in some areas.

A low electricity rate is in operation from around 8pm to 6 or 7am, Mondays to Fridays, Saturday afternoons and all day on Sundays, depending on the area and the time of the year. These are good times to run your washing machine or dishwasher.

Converters & Transformers

Some electrical appliances (e.g. electric razors and hair dryers) are fitted with a 110/220 volt switch. Check for the switch, which may be inside the casing, and make sure it's switched to 220 volts **before** connecting it to the power supply. Electrical equipment rated at 110 volts AC (for example from the US) without a voltage switch requires a transformer to convert it to 220 volts AC. Transformers are available from most electrical retailers and they can be purchased second-hand from Americans returning home. Add the wattage of the devices you intend to connect to the transformer and make sure that its power rating exceeds this sum. Generally all small high-wattage electrical appliances, such as kettles, toasters, heaters and irons need large transformers. Motors in large appliances such as cookers, refrigerators, washing machines, dryers and dishwashers, will need replacing or fitting with a large transformer. In most cases it's less trouble and expense to buy new appliances in Switzerland.

Note that the dimensions of Swiss cookers, microwave ovens, refrigerators, washing machines, dryers and dishwashers differ from those in most other countries, and equipment purchased abroad won't necessarily fit into a standard Swiss kitchen.

Another problem with some electrical equipment is the frequency rating, which in some countries, e.g. the US, is designed to run at 60Hz and not Switzerland's 50Hz. Electrical equipment **without** a motor is generally unaffected by the drop in frequency to 50Hz. Equipment with a motor may run with a 20 per cent drop in speed, but automatic washing machines, cookers, electric clocks, clock radios and record players must usually be converted from the US 60Hz cycle to Switzerland's 50Hz cycle. To find out if a machine needs converting, look at the label on the back of the equipment. If it says 50/60Hz, it should be okay. If it says 60Hz, you can try it, **but first ensure that the voltage is correct as outlined above.** If the equipment runs too slowly, seek advice from the manufacturer or the retailer. Bear in mind that the transformers and motors of electrical devices designed to run at 60Hz will run hotter at 50Hz, so equipment must have sufficient space around it for cooling.

Fuses, Plugs & Bulbs

Most apartments and all houses have their own fuse boxes. Fuses may be of two types. Older houses often have screw fuses with a coloured disk, which **when not displayed** indicates that the fuse has blown. These fuses, which have different amp ratings, can be purchased in most electrical stores and supermarkets. The other type of fuse, found in newer houses and apartments, consists of a simple switch, which when a circuit is overloaded, trips to the OFF position. After locating and remedying the cause, simply switch it back to the ON position.

Switzerland has three different plug configurations with two, three or five contact points (including the earth) and a 16-amp rating. Modern Swiss plugs are of the two- or three-pin or two-pin/earth socket type. Pins are round with a 4mm diameter, with live and neutral pins 2cm apart. **When wiring a Swiss plug, it's advisable to put a drop of glue on the screw threads as screws often work loose after a time.** Electric light bulbs are of the Edison screw type. Bayonet-fitting bulbs for British-type lamp fittings aren't available in Switzerland but can be purchased in France.

In many cantons, only a qualified electrician is allowed to install electrical wiring and fittings, particularly in connection with fuse boxes.

Gas

Gas is piped from Germany, the Netherlands and France to the major Swiss cities but isn't but isn't used in many homes, although the use of gas is steadily rising and it now accounts for around 12 per cent of total energy consumption (mainly industrial). If you want to cook by gas, you may be able to find a house or apartment that has it. In areas without mains gas and particularly in remote areas, homes may have a cooker that uses bottled gas.

Water

In Switzerland the left tap is always the hot water tap. In times of drought, you're forbidden by your community to water your lawn or wash your car.

Quality

Water in Switzerland is usually hard, which means you will need a copious supply of decalcification liquid to keep your kettle, iron and other equipment and utensils clean. Stainless steel pots and pans stain quickly when used to boil water unless they're cleaned soon after use. Tap and shower filters must be decalcified regularly. You can have decalcification equipment installed in your water system, which is rarely fitted as standard equipment in apartments. There are various systems available, most of which are expensive and not all very effective. Distilled water or water melted from ice from your refrigerator or freezer, should be used in steam irons (mineral water is also okay).

Tariffs

Water rates are calculated by one of two methods. If your apartment has a water meter, you're billed for the amount of water you use. Otherwise you pay a fixed rate according to the size of your house or apartment and possibly the number of taps. Water costs are generally low, e.g. SFr. 1.25 per cubic metre, although there have been large increases in some areas in recent years.

Central Heating

Most apartments in Switzerland have central heating (*Zentralheizung, chauffage central*), the cost of which is included in your extra costs (see page 96). Heating is usually switched on in autumn and off in spring by the caretaker or landlord, or it may be thermostat controlled all year. In most apartment blocks, the cost of heating for the whole building is divided among tenants according to their apartment size. In others, radiators may be individually metered, so you pay only for the heating you use. Some modern apartments have under-floor heating.

Central heating dries the air and can cause your family to develop coughs. Those who find dry air unpleasant can buy a humidifier (costing from around SFr. 50 to 200) to add moisture to the air. Humidifiers which don't generate steam should be disinfected occasionally (to prevent nasty diseases).

WASTE DISPOSAL

Switzerland produces around 675kg of waste per head of population annually, around half of which is recycled. The country has one of the highest rates of waste recycling in the world and most Swiss religiously sort their rubbish (where there's muck there's money!), which in many cases is obligatory. Recycling is a way of life in Switzerland, where there's a successful national campaign to reduce household waste under the slogan 'reduce, reuse and recycle' (see **Recycling** below).

For non-recyclable waste, most apartments have large rubbish disposal bins in which rubbish must be deposited in plastic bags (*Kehrichtsäcke, sacs à ordures*). In most communities you must deposit rubbish in 'official' bags, usually coloured and printed with the community name, sold in local stores and supermarkets. These bags, which come in various sizes, carry a tax and usually cost from SFr. 2 (35 litre) to SFr. 6 (110 litre) each, depending on their size and the community. Waste deposited in these bags is usually restricted to materials that can be incinerated. If you use unofficial rubbish bags, they won't be collected and the local waste 'detective' may track you down and fine you, e.g. SFr. 100 (you have been warned!). In some cantons you must purchase a stamp to put on each rubbish bag. The aim is to encourage recycling and avoid the unnecessary use of wrapping and packaging, which has already prompted many people to deposit unwanted packaging in supermarket dustbins. It must be working, because since the tax was introduced waste has been reduced by as much as 50 per cent in some areas. Some communities, however, charge residents an annual waste tax, e.g. SFr. 30 irrespective of the amount of waste they generate.

In some communities you may need to buy a dustbin (garbage can), which are usually emptied once or twice a week.

Recycling

Many kinds of waste are recycled or reused in Switzerland including the following:

● **paper and cardboard**, which should be tied in bundles with string and shouldn't include any plastic or metal, e.g. covers or bindings. Collection is organised by the canton authorities. However, in some communities there are no collections and paper must be deposited in a special container or storage area.

● **large objects** (e.g. old furniture, carpets, skis and appliances), which are collected periodically (e.g. once a month) in some areas, usually just after the official house moving dates (dates are announced in local newspapers). Second-hand junk and furniture stores, often operated in aid of a charity such as the Salvation Army, may collect old furniture free of charge.

● **bottles**, which should be deposited in bottle banks provided in all towns and villages. Bottle banks are divided into sections for green, brown and white bottles. Their use may be restricted, for example no deposits between 8pm and 7 or 8am and on Sundays and public holidays (or as listed). Some bottle banks are reserved for large bottles (0.5l or larger) of all colours, which are washed and reused. Switzerland is the world leader in glass recycling with a 94 per cent recovery rate. However, there's a returnable deposit of SFr. 0.30 to 0.50 on most one-litre glass bottles, so don't throw them away!

● **tin cans**, which may be taken to collection areas or deposited in can-crunching machines. They should be washed and squashed flat after the label, lid and base have been removed, and should be deposited only in the specified container.

● **household cooking oils**, which shouldn't be flushed down sinks as they clog the pipes. Not all collection bins have containers for oil.

● **batteries**, which should be returned to retailers, who must provide containers, or taken to a designated dump (some are recycled). Car batteries should be returned to a garage.

● **vegetable or organic waste**, including garden rubbish, which may be collected and used as compost (designated bins may be provided) – or you can make your own compost heap;

- **oil and old tyres**, which can be deposited at a designated dump or returned to the suppliers;

- **hazardous and toxic waste** such as paints and thinners, which should be taken to designated dumps;

- **aluminium** (e.g. cans, tops and frozen food containers), which is collected or can be dumped once or twice a year. A magnet is built into containers for aluminium waste: if it's magnetic it **isn't** aluminium (see **Tin Cans** above). There are crushing machines in some areas.

- **old clothes**, which are collected by charitable organisations, usually once or twice a year. Note, however, that some commercial collectors masquerade as charitable organisations and, if you don't want anyone to make money from your old clobber, you can deliver it directly to a bona fide charity such as the Red Cross or Salvation Army. A women's group in your local community may organise a clothes exchange once or twice a year and will collect and sell nearly-new clothing for a 10 to 20 per cent commission. Old shoes are collected by local shoe stores in some towns and sent to third-world countries (opticians may also collect old prescription spectacles).

- **unused medicines and poisons**, which should be returned for disposal to a chemist's (pharmacy) or the shop where they were purchased;

- **old electronics products**, which must be returned to the seller, who must take them back free of charge;

- **plastic bottles**, which must be returned to shops.

In some communities there are also collection bins for other types of plastic, e.g. soft PVC, metal (other than that specified above), electrical apparatus, mineral items and various other waste.

All communities publish instructions on what to do with different waste and a list of waste collection times and depots. Many large stores, e.g. Migros, Coop and Manor, have collection bins for aluminium, batteries, tins and certain types of bottle. **The indiscriminate dumping of rubbish is strictly forbidden in Switzerland.**

HOME HELP

The following pages contain information regarding the various types of home help available in Switzerland, which may be of particular interest to working parents. All the organisations mentioned below are listed in local telephone directories or registered with your local community. See also **Home Care Services** on page 252.

Part-time

There are various ways to find part-time domestic help (*Putzfrau, femme de ménage*):

- Place an advertisement (*Inserat, annonce*) in your local newspaper. This is usually the cheapest way of finding help. Your community may have a notice board (*Notizbrett, tableau d'affichage*) where you can place a free advertisement and many stores and supermarkets, e.g. Migros and the Coop, have a free or inexpensive notice board.

- Look under 'positions wanted' (*Stellengesuche, marché du travail*) in your local newspapers.

- Contact employment agencies (*Stellenvermittlungsbüro, bureau de placement*) listed in your local telephone directory.

Expect to pay a minimum of around SFr. 25 per hour – twice as much if you use an agency. **You must pay old age and survivor's insurance (see page 261) and accident insurance (see page 266) for part-time domestic helpers.**

Many communities provide families with a cleaning and general household service (including cooking) when the housewife (or househusband) is ill. The service is cheaper if you're a member of a housekeeping and nursing service association (see **Home Care Services** on page 252).

Full-time

There are regulations concerning the employment of full-time domestic helpers (*Diener/Dienerin, domestique*) in Switzerland. These include minimum salaries, maximum working hours, meal allowances, time off and paid holiday. Regulations are usually detailed in a booklet available from canton authorities. Salaries may vary considerably according to the nationality, age and experience of a domestic helper. If your servant isn't Swiss and doesn't have a C permit, you must apply for work and residence permits and pay his pension and accident insurance. Tax must be deducted at source from the salary, and all associated paperwork must be completed. Bringing a foreign servant with you to Switzerland is usually difficult and may be permitted only in exceptional circumstances upon proof of a special need.

Au Pairs

Regulations regarding the employment of au pairs vary from canton to canton. In some cantons priority is given to working mothers, while in others a mother must spend a minimum number of hours a week with the au pair, thus restricting her ability to work full-time. A permit for an au pair is issued for up to 18 months. Although families may hire a succession of au pairs, parents should take care that young children aren't unsettled by the frequent change of 'minder'. It may be better from your child's point of view to find a local person who will work for you for several years.

English-speaking families in Switzerland are unable to employ a Swiss or foreign au pair who wants to learn English. However, if one parent is a native German, French or Italian speaker, and the family speaks that language at home, they may be given permission to employ an au pair wishing to learn that language. For more information see **Au Pairs** on page 37.

Baby-sitters

Some women's organisations, for example American Women's Clubs, have baby-sitting lists or circles (see **Appendix A**). The Red Cross (💻 www.srk.ch) runs a training and referral service in some areas. (It may even be worthwhile starting your own baby-sitting circle with other local couples.)

Alternatively you can use a baby-sitting agency (*Babysitter-Vermittlungsbüro, agence de babysitting*), which can be found in major towns and cities. The hourly rate charged by baby-sitting agencies depends on the number of children to be cared for. You must pay for public transport for your baby-sitter to and from your home. If this is unavailable, you must take him home yourself or pay for a taxi. In rural areas, some communities keep a list of baby-sitters. You can also advertise for a baby-sitter in your local newspaper or on a supermarket notice board.

The cost of a baby-sitter varies from around SFr. 15 an hour for a person found through word of mouth to more than double for someone from an agency.

Many villages and towns run a child minding service (*Kinderhütedienst, garderie d'enfants*) that provides baby-sitting facilities during the day for working mothers. Child minding services are also provided by 'day mothers' (*Tagesmütter, Mamans de jour/gardiennes d'enfants*), whose fees are from around SFr. 20 for a half-day and SFr. 30 for a full day. Children aged from three to five are usually accepted. Many village women's groups take care of pre-school-age children one afternoon a week. Many holiday resorts have nurseries where you can leave your children while you ski or hike. Child-minding centres (*Kinderparadies, paradis des enfants*) are also provided by many shopping centres and large stores.

Playgroups & Day Care Centres

There are playgroups (*Spielgruppe, groupe de jeux/classe enfantine*) for children in all cities, but few in rural areas. Children are usually required to be over three years old, or at least toilet trained. Groups usually meet for two to three hours, several times a week.

Day care centres (*Kinderhort, crèche*) are also quite common and accept children of any age. Children are usually accepted on a part-time basis as often as required, although some centres provide full-time care only. They provide hot lunches, daytime sleeping facilities and outdoor activities. Fees are usually fixed but are sometimes reduced for low-income families.

6.

POSTAL SERVICES

There's a post office in most towns in Switzerland, although many smaller post offices have been closed in recent years. In addition to the usual post office services to be found in most countries, the Swiss post office provides a number of unique services, most of which are described in this chapter. In surveys the Swiss postal service is consistently rated one of the world's best (if not **the** best) and delivers some 2.8bn letters, 1.2bn newspapers and magazines, and 104m parcels a year. Information in English about post office services is available on the internet (💻 www.post.ch).

BUSINESS HOURS

Post office business hours in Switzerland are usually from 7.30am to noon and 1.30 or 1.45pm to 6pm, Mondays to Fridays, and from 7.30 to 11.30am or 12 noon on Saturdays. Small post offices in major towns may open later, e.g. 8 or 8.30am, and close for lunch from 11.30am until 2pm. In small towns and villages, opening hours are often restricted, e.g. 7 to 10.30am, 1.45 to 3.30pm and 4.30 to 6pm from Mondays to Fridays, and 7 to 11am on Saturdays. Main post offices in major towns don't close for lunch and provide limited services for urgent business outside normal business hours. In major towns and cities, some post offices may have extended opening hours, e.g. at railway stations. The opening hours for all post offices can be found on the internet (💻 www.post.ch – go to 'Services' and then 'Post offices search').

LETTER POST

Switzerland has a two-tier domestic letter postal service: 'A' and 'B' class . 'A' class domestic post is usually (around 99 per cent) delivered the day after posting and costs SFr. 1. for items up to size B5 (250 x 176mm) and 100g; SFr. 1.30 for items up to B5 and 101 to 250g; and SFr. 2.20-2.40 for items from size B5 to B4 (353 x 250mm) up to 500g. Delivery of A class post takes two to five days in Europe and four to ten days to other countries.

Delivery of B class domestic post takes two to three working days and costs SFr. 0.85 for items up to B5 and 100g; SFr. 1.10 up to B5 and 101to 250g; and SFr. 1.80-2.00 for items from B5 to B4 up to 500g. Delivery of B class post (surface mail) takes four to ten days in Europe and four to eight weeks to other countries.

'A' class stamps have a screen printed on them to allow for automatic sorting and an *A Prioritaire* sticker is required for post to European and overseas addresses (A class is sent by airmail, while B class post goes by surface mail). The cost of posting a letter or postcard in Switzerland is shown in the table below:

| Size | Weight | Thickness | Price (SFr.) | | | | | |
| | | | Switz. | | Zone 1* | | Zone 2** | |
			A	B	A	B	A	B
B6/B5	Up to 20g#	20mm	1.00	0.85	1.30	1.20	1.80	1.40
B6/B5	21 to 50g	20mm	1.00	0.85	2.40	2.00	3.50	2.60
B6/B5	51 to 100g	20mm	1.00	0.85	3.50	2.70	4.70	3.30
B6/B5	101 to 250g	20mm	1.30	1.10				
B4	Up to 100g	20mm	2.20	1.80	3.80	3.40	5.50	3.80
B4	101 to 250g	20mm	2.40	2.00	6.50	4.50	8.80	5.80
B4	251 to 500g	20mm	2.40	2.00	12.00	7.50	15.50	9.00
B4	501g to 1kg	20mm	5.00	4.00	16.00	9.50	25.00	14.00
B6/5	Up to 100g	20 to 50mm	3.30	3.15	13.00	8.00	19.00	10.00
B6/5	Up to 250g	20 to 50mm	3.90	3.40	13.00	8.00	19.00	10.00
B4/5/6	Up to 500g	20 to 50mm	8.00	6.00	13.00	8.00	19.00	10.00
B4/5/6	501g to 1kg	20 to 50mm	8.00	6.00	21.00	12.00	33.00	18.00
B4/5/6	1kg to 2kg	20 to 50mm	8.00	6.00	32.00	21.00	45.00	32.00

* Zone 1 – Europe

** Zone 2 – Rest of the world

Includes postcards

Note the following when posting letters in Switzerland:

- Letters up to 50mm thick and up to 250g can be sent within Switzerland for a surcharge of up to SFr. 2.30. Larger letters are classed as parcels (see page 119).

- It's necessary to use an *A Prioritaire* or airmail (*Luftpost, par avion, via aerea*) label for A class international post, although all letters to Western European countries are transported by air, including B class post.

- Post for the blind weighing up to 7kg is delivered free.

- Letters sent with insufficient postage are usually delivered, but not by A-Post. If known, the sender is sent a card showing the postage due plus a surcharge of SFr. 0.50, to which you must affix stamps equal to the amount due and re-post. If you **receive** a letter with insufficient postage, you're required to pay the postage due, either to the postman or at your local post office (a collection form will be left – see **Post Collection** on page 120).

- Post boxes are yellow and are usually set into (or attached to) a wall.

- There's one post delivery a day, in the morning, including Saturdays (which is restricted to A class post only).

- It's possible to send international letters and parcels by express (*Urgent*) to most western European countries. The fee depends on the size and the weight of the letter or parcel (minimum SFr. 39). There are also a number of domestic express post services offering guaranteed delivery taking a maximum of two hours (City-Express) or five hours (Intercity-Express) or next day (Swiss-Express). If you receive an express letter, a sticker reading *Achtung!* or *Attention!* is affixed to your letter box or door, advising you of this. **Note that express post has replaced the telegram service, which has been discontinued.**

- Aerogrammes (*Aerogramm, aérogramme*) are available from stationery stores (not post offices) and don't include postage.

- Christmas surface mail should be sent by around 1st November for North America and by 25th November for Europe. For other destinations enquire at a post office.

- All letters to Swiss addresses sent from outside Switzerland should have 'CH' (Confederatio Helvetica) before the town's postal or zip code (*Postleitzahl/PLZ, numéro postal/NPA*), which is the European postal designation for Switzerland. A typical Swiss address is shown below; in German, street (*strasse*) may be abbreviated as *str.* and the house number is listed after the street name:

> Heidi Schweizer
> Hauptstr. 10
> CH-3000 BERNE
> Switzerland

All Swiss postal codes are listed in the pink section of Swiss telephone directories (see page 132). Postal codes are also available via the internet (🖳 www.post.ch).

- A brochure showing how post should be addressed is available from post offices. A green sticker may be attached to incorrectly addressed letters, asking you to inform your correspondent of your correct address (*Bitte richtige Adresse dem Absender melden, veuillez communiquer votre adresse exacte à l'expéditeur*).

- Parcels must not be tied with string (otherwise you will be given scissors and sticky tape to re-seal it) and the address must be in the upper right corner.

- A surcharge of SFr. 5-6 is made for registered letters (*Eingeschriebener Brief/lettre recommandée*) within Switzerland and SFr. 6 for destinations outside Switzerland, plus the standard postage cost. The sender's address must be written on the back of registered letters. You receive a receipt for a registered letter or parcel. Proof of receipt (delivery) costs SFr. 3 (a card is returned to the sender). Registered letters and packages can be insured. Insured registered letters and packages over 1kg in weight and with a value of over SFr. 5,000 must be security sealed with wax/lead or special tape. The highest insured value for unsealed packages is SFr. 5,000.

- Stamps (*Briefmarke, timbre*) can be purchased from stamp machines outside most post offices. A change machine for one and two franc coins is provided at larger post offices, plus a machine that dispenses books of stamps. Stamps are also sold by shops and kiosks selling postcards (*Postkarte, carte postale*). Books of five plain stamped postcards can be bought from post offices.

- Special stamps are sold to celebrate Swiss National Day on 1st August (*Bundesfeiermarke, timbre de la fête nationale*) which have a surcharge, proceeds from which support Swiss social and cultural organisations. Other special charitable stamps are also sold occasionally. A magazine and brochures describing special stamps and first day covers are published for philatelists and are available from main post offices. For information about services for philatelists visit 🖳 www.post.ch and then click on 'stamps'. This website enables you to view and order stamps online. In addition the website gives addresses of the regional philatelist centres (there is one centre for each of the six postal regions).

PARCEL POST

For standard parcels (*Paket, paquet/colis*) of any size the postage depends on their weight, as shown by the examples in the table below.

| Weight | Price | |
	Economy Class	Priority Class
Up to 2kg	SFr. 6	SFr. 8
2 to 5kg	SFr. 8	SFr. 10
5 to 10kg	SFr. 11	SFr. 13
10 to 20kg	SFr. 16	SFr. 19
20 to 30kg	SFr. 23	SFr. 26

Priority parcels are delivered on the next working day if posted before 12 noon. Economy parcels are delivered within two working days. International parcels may be sent by economy (delivery by rail in Europe and air elsewhere), priority (airmail, e.g. two to three days in Europe) and EMS world-wide (courier). Airmail parcels, regardless of destination, take the same time to be delivered as airmail letters. A form must be completed when sending an international parcel weighing over 2kg.

The post office is strict regarding how parcels must be wrapped (see above) and how the address is written (ask your local post office for labels). For any parcel (too small, too big, too thick, too thin) that isn't considered 'standard' a charge of SFr. 3 for manual handling is levied. It's often worthwhile to enquire at the post office before sealing a parcel. A brochure is available from post offices describing how to pack goods for sending by post.

The Express Mail Service (EMS) to over 160 countries is available from all Swiss post offices for urgent parcels, usually weighing a maximum of 10 or 20kg, depending on the destination. Parcels sent via EMS take one to two days to be delivered within Europe and from two to four days overseas, depending on the destination. The post office also provides an Expresspost courier service and many international airfreight and courier companies (e.g. DHL, TNT and UPS) also operate in Switzerland.

Parcels sent to addresses outside Switzerland must be accompanied by a customs declaration form. Parcels weighing up to 1kg and not more than 90cm in circumference require an international green customs form CN22 and are sent at a small parcel postage rate. The value of such a parcel should generally not exceed SFr. 50. When sending an international parcel weighing over 1kg, special customs forms must be completed. Parcels can be insured when they're sent by registered post. Parcels sent within Switzerland can be registered for SFr. 1.50. Most post offices have scales and special post boxes for parcels – **don't put letters in them** and bear in mind that you don't receive a receipt when using a post box.

Cardboard boxes, called POST PACs, and padded 'jiffy' bags (*Luftpolster Couvert, enveloppe capitonée*) are available from post offices and most department and stationery stores. POST PACs are available in six sizes (costing from SFr. 2 to 4.70) and include sealing tape.

All domestic parcels have had a barcode sticker affixed by the post office to enable them to track stray parcels and check delivery times. The sender receives a receipt with a matching barcode sticker (keep it in case of late delivery, loss or damage).

POST COLLECTION

If the postman calls with post requiring a signature, payment of duty or excess postage when you aren't at home, he leaves a collection form (*Abholungseinladung, avis de retrait*). Present this form with some identification (for example your Swiss residence permit, passport or driving licence) at your local post office, the address of which is printed on the form. The collection form includes the date when the item can be collected and when it will be returned to the sender if it isn't collected (usually after seven days). This is a good reason to inform the post office if you're going to be away from home for some time (see **Change of Address** below), as they will hold your post for a small fee.

You can receive post via the main post office of any town in Switzerland through the international *poste restante* (*Postlagernd*) service. Post sent to a *poste restante* address is returned to the sender if it's unclaimed after 30 days. Identification is necessary for collection (see above).

You may be able to obtain a post office box number at your local post office **free of charge**. If you do, all your post will be stored there and the postman will no longer deliver to your home (it may be quicker to pick it up than wait for the postman). You can arrange to be informed when registered or express post arrives.

CHANGE OF ADDRESS

If you're going to be away from your home for up to two months, you can ask the post office (five days in advance) to hold your post for the sum of SFr. 10. You can either collect it at the end of the period or the postman will deliver it on the date you specify. Your post can be redirected to a new or temporary address in Switzerland or abroad for a nominal fee. All post sent within Switzerland, including parcels, is redirected (excluding circulars, which are returned with your new address to the sender). Only cards and letters are redirected abroad. A temporary forwarding order must be completed at your local post office. The post office provides free (no stamp required) change of address cards in local languages for a move within Switzerland.

Printed matter sent from abroad, e.g. magazines, newspapers and newsletters, won't usually be forwarded and will be returned to the sender, possibly without your new address. You may be able to request that all post is redirected, including post from abroad, provided you're willing to pay for the extra service. If a letter is unable to be delivered due to the wrong address, the addressee no longer being at the address, or the redirection period having expired, it will be returned with a note stating this, i.e. 'moved; redirection period expired' (*Weggezogen; Nachsendefrist abgelaufen, A déménagé; Délai de réexpedition expiré*).

POST ACCOUNTS

Anyone over the age of 16 can open a postcheque account (*Postcheckkonto, compte de cheque postal*) at any post office or by contacting Schweizerische Post, Postfinance, Nordring 8, CH-3030 Berne (☎ 0848 888 710, 💻 www.post

finance.ch). Postcheque accounts are popular in Switzerland and many people have postcheque and bank accounts. Postcheque accounts provide the following services:

- the facility to pay bills direct from your account;

- longer opening hours than banks (the post office is also open on Saturday mornings);

- two or more people can share the same account (a joint account);

- standing orders can be paid via the account;

- a PostFinance Visa or Mastercard is available for SFr. 50 a year.

For the basic post account, two accounts (known as 'sets') are available with different access and charges: The Private-Set includes two payment orders for all debits and deposits per month for an annual fee of SFr. 48 (the fee is waived if you have a balance above SFr. 7,500). If you prefer internet banking, you can use the Online-Set where you complete all payment advices via the internet. The annual fee for the Online-Set is SFr. 24 (waived if your balance is above SFr. 7,500). For further information see 🖥 www.yellownet.ch.

Additional accounts such as a savings account (Deposito-Konto) and foreign currency accounts are also available and offer the following advantages:

- cash can be sent via the post office to other European countries);

- interest is paid on deposits (a higher rate is paid on youth accounts for 14 to 26 year-olds);

- overdrafts of SFr. 1,000 are allowed for a 28-day period (interest is payable on overdrafts).

Postcards

A free cash card, called a 'Postcard', is available to account holders. It allows cash withdrawals of up to SFr. 1,000 a day to be made from post office ATMs, called 'Postomats', located at over 400 major post offices and from ATMs (indicated as Eufiserv) in several countries. When combined with a debit card, the Postcard also allows holders to pay bills in selected stores up to a total value of SFr. 3,000 per month and to obtain up to SFr. 300 per day in cash from selected stores. Purchases are automatically deducted from your postcheque account. Postcards can also be used to buy petrol, make telephone calls from payphones and obtain cash from ATMs abroad (fee SFr. 4). The debit Postcard is issued to foreigners only if they have their salary transferred to a post account by their employer or make regular deposits of around SFr. 2,000.

A Postcard can be combined with a Swiss Federal Railway (SBB) half-fare travel card (see page 189), when a photo is added to the card (the charge is automatically deducted from your account). It can also be combined with an annual rail season ticket (with a photo) and paid in monthly instalments.

When you open a postcheque account, you receive transfer forms and a supply of post-paid envelopes with which to pay bills via the post office. **Note that all postcheques must be written in the local language and not in English.**

PAYING BILLS

In contrast with many other countries, cheques drawn on bank accounts aren't the most important everyday means of payment in Switzerland (in fact cheques are hardly ever used in Switzerland due to the high fees imposed by banks). Many people pay their bills (except when paying in cash) via the post office giro service. A blue or red giro payment form (*Einzahlungsschein, bulletin de versement*) is usually included with every bill you receive by post, with which you can pay the bill at any post office or through your bank. You don't need a giro account to pay bills at a post office or to have money paid into a bank account via a post office, **but note that there's a fee for these services.**

Payment forms produced by a computer include all the necessary details including your name and address, the payee's name and account number, and the amount. If it's a non-computerised form you need to enter these details. Post office payment forms must be completed in blue or black ink and in BLOCK CAPITALS. If you make a mistake you must complete a new form as, unlike personal bank cheques, you **aren't** permitted to make corrections. The left hand stub of the payment form is your receipt and is stamped by the post office clerk and returned to you. Payments may be made at any post office, either in cash or through a girocheque account, as follows:

Payment at a Post Office

The procedure for paying bills at a post office is as follows:

1 Take the payment form(s) to the payments and withdrawals (*Ein- und Auszahlungen, versements et paiements*) window.

2 If you're making a number of payments, the clerk totals the amount due. Add up the total in advance so that you can confirm it (write it down if you don't speak the local language).

3 Payment must be in cash or by cheque from a postcheque account. Cash means **CASH** (the folding stuff) and bank cheques and credit cards aren't accepted.

4   The stamped receipt portion of the payment form will be returned to you (check that it's stamped!).

When you want to make a payment at the post office, it is best to go early in the morning, e.g. on your way to work, to avoid queues.

Payment Through a Girocheque Account

If you have a girocheque account, you can make all your giro payments simply by completing a single form and sending it to the post office with the payment slips that came with your invoices. The procedure is as follows:

1   Complete the form with the name, account number and the amount to be paid for each bill.

2   Sign and date the cover form that shows the total amount of all payment slips and the number.

3   Enclose the form with the blue/red giro payment slips in a pre-addressed envelope and post.

Payment of bills can be made in the same way through a bank account (see page 284). This is a more secure way of paying large bills than using cash.

Giro payment forms are provided by most companies in Switzerland for regular payments, such as rent, health insurance and credit (time) payments (e.g. one giro form per month, up to the total number of monthly payments due). If you prefer you can have them paid by standing order (*Dauerauftrag, ordre permanent*) from your bank or girocheque account. Just take them to your bank or a post office and they will complete the formalities.

Books of receipts (*Empfangsscheinbuch, livret de récépissés*) are available for SFr. 2 or 4 from any post office. Complete a receipt for each giro payment you make. All receipts are date stamped, thus providing you with a permanent record of all your giro payments in a single book. (All stubs and receipts should be kept for a period of five years, which is the statute of limitations period in Switzerland.) There's a space provided on giro payment forms for notes (*Mitteilungen, communications*), for example to draw attention to a new address. There are different giro payment forms (*Postanweisung, mandat de Poste*) for transferring money to giro account and non-account holders in Switzerland, account and non-account holders in continental Europe, and internationally.

When sending money abroad, just fill in the name and address of the creditor and the amount in local currency; the post office calculates the amount due in Swiss francs. You receive the payment advice stub as a receipt and payment is made directly to the payee by the post office.

The Swiss don't appear as anxious to be paid as creditors in most other countries. Don't be surprised if you aren't billed for weeks, or even months after you've purchased something – they haven't forgotten you. You aren't normally required to pay in advance when you order goods and are rarely asked to pay a deposit. You are, however, expected to pay all bills when due. The payment date (*Fällig am . . ./Zahlbar bis . . ., payable le . . ./échéance . . .*) is usually stated on the bill accompanying the giro payment form, or the number of days within which you must pay the bill. Payment is usually due immediately or within 10, 30 or 60 days. Some creditors offer a discount for prompt payment of bills or payment in cash. If you don't pay a bill on time, you're sent a reminder (*Mahnung, rappel/sommation*) and you may be charged interest. Usually only two reminders are sent, after which your creditor may take legal action if you don't pay within the specified period.

Post offices keep a directory of all Swiss postal account holders, which can be used to check account numbers. Cash can be sent to any Swiss bank account holder via a giro transfer. Just enter the bank name and giro number, the account holder's name and account number, and the reason for the payment.

You may receive a giro cheque (*Auszahlungsschein, bulletin de paiement*) as a payment, for example for an income tax or road tax refund. This can be cashed at any post office on production of proof of identification (Swiss residence permit, passport or driving licence). A **giro cheque must usually be cashed within four to six weeks (the validity period is printed on the cheque).** Foreign national girobank postcheques can be cashed at any Swiss post office, provided you have a guarantee card (Postcard).

When writing figures in Switzerland (or anywhere in continental Europe) the number seven should be crossed to avoid confusion with the number one, written with a tail and looking like an uncrossed seven to many foreigners. The date is written in the standard European style, for example 10th September 2006 is written 10.9.06 (not as in the US, 9/10/06).

7.

TELEPHONE

Among the various reasons for Switzerland's economic success are the many unfair advantages that it has over other countries, one of which is that its telephones always work. In Switzerland you rarely get a bad or crossed line and the quality and range of services are second to none. Switzerland has one of the highest numbers of telephones per head of population in the world (some 700 per 1,000 inhabitants, not including mobile phones) and nearly every household has a telephone.

The Swiss telecommunications market has been open to competition since 1st January 1998, when Telecom PTT became Swisscom (an independent company). You can now choose your phone operator from a number of companies including Abalon (☎ 041 747 17 00, 💻 www.abalonag.com), EconoPhone (☎ 0800 188 188, 💻 www.econophone.ch), Sunrise (☎ 0800 707 707, 💻 www.sunrise.ch), Orange (☎ 0800 700 700, 💻 www.orange.ch), Tele2 (☎ 0800 242 424, 💻 www.tele2.ch), Vtx Datacomm (☎ 0800 883 883, 💻 www. vtxnet.ch) and, of course, Swisscom (☎ 0800 800 800, 💻 www.swisscom.com). There are also smaller companies operating in certain cantons or cities and direct call (previously call-back) companies offering low-cost international calls.

Swisscom retains part of its monopoly because irrespective of which phone company you use you must still pay a fee of SFr. 25.25 per month to Swisscom for the line rental. The only way to avoid paying this fee is to choose Cablecom (☎ 0800 660 800, 💻 www.cablecom.ch), which has its own cable network, although it isn't generally available in rural areas.

Switzerland's mobile phone system, previously operated by Swisscom, has also been opened to competition with the entry of Orange and Sunrise into the market. There are also 'dozens' of internet providers in the country. As a consequence of deregulation, telephone rates have tumbled in recent years and are set to fall even further.

A list of emergency numbers is provided on page 135.

INSTALLATION & REGISTRATION

If you move into an old apartment, i.e. any apartment where you aren't the first occupant, a telephone line will usually have been installed but there will be no telephone. A new apartment, however, may just have a few holes in the wall in preparation for the installation of telephone sockets. Foreigners without a B, C, G or diplomat's permit (see **Chapter 3**) must pay a deposit of SFr. 300 before they can have a telephone line connected or installed. This deposit is returned with interest when you leave the country or obtain a qualifying permit, or may be repaid after one to two years if you pay your bills regularly (although you must sometimes request it).

To have a telephone line installed or connected, contact your nearest Swisscom office or telephone freephone ☎ 0800 800 800. Line installation is usually quick and takes an average of around seven days (where a line is already installed connection takes one or two days) and costs SFr. 43. When you've paid your deposit, Swisscom will arrange for the connection or installation to be completed at a convenient time. If your apartment doesn't already have a telephone socket(s), then you need to pay additional installation costs. You can rent a telephone from Swisscom (from around SFr. 5 a month) or buy one from Swisscom (from SFr. 30 for the cheapest pushbutton phone) or an independent supplier, which may be cheaper.

USING THE TELEPHONE

Using a telephone in Switzerland is much the same as in any other country. Telephone numbers consist of a three-digit area code, e.g. 044 for Zurich and 022 for Geneva, and a seven-digit subscriber number. Numbers are usually written as 044 123 45 67 (as in this book) or 044 123.45.67. An area code may cover a city or a much wider area. **When dialling a number in Switzerland, even a number with the same area code, you must always dial the area code.** When dialling Switzerland from overseas, you dial the local international code (e.g. 00 from the UK), followed by Switzerland's international code (41), the Swiss area code **without** the first 0, e.g. 44 for Zurich, and the subscriber's number. See also **International Calls** on page 131.

Service numbers (such as six-digit 0800 numbers) are toll-free numbers provided by companies and organisations. Numbers beginning with 156, 157 and 0900/0901/0906 are service numbers (or information lines) where calls cost a flat fee, e.g. SFr. 80, are charged per minute (e.g. SFr. 5) or have a basic charge of e.g. SFr. 10 in addition to an extra charge per minute charge (e.g. SFr. 5). **These include 'sex lines' and there is no upper limit for charges! There are also many new service numbers and it's difficult to know which are service numbers and how much calls cost.**

Standard telephone tones, i.e. the strange noises you hear when you aren't connected to a subscriber, are provided to indicate the progress of calls. The following standard tones are used in Switzerland and are different from those used in some other countries:

● **Dialling tone** – A steady note is heard after you lift the receiver, indicating that the telephone is working and that you can start dialling.

● **Ringing tone** – A single note repeated at long intervals means that the call has been connected and the number is ringing.

● **Engaged tone** – A short single note repeated at short intervals means that the number or all lines are busy.

● **Information tone** – A repeated sequence of three notes in rising pitch means that the party called cannot be reached on the dialled number. If you don't understand the recorded announcement following the tone, call the operator on 1811. If you dial a non-existent number, you receive a message informing you of this and telling you to check your telephone directory (see page 132). If you dial a number that has changed, you hear a message stating the new number or that the number no longer exists. Call 1811 and ask for the subscriber's new number.

MOBILE PHONES

There are three mobile phone providers in Switzerland: Orange (🖳 www.orange.ch), Sunrise (🖳 www.sunrise.ch) and Swisscom (🖳 www.swisscom.com). Rates vary greatly between providers, although Swisscom charges are the highest. However, Swisscom also has the widest network; with both Sunrise and Orange you may find yourself without a signal in remote areas, which is particularly annoying if you rely on your mobile when hiking or skiing (see **Chapter 16**). A useful website for comparing mobile phone rates is 🖳 www.comparis.ch.

Mobile phones – which the Swiss call a 'Natel' (*natel/portable*) or a 'Handy' – can be bought in department stores or specialised shops. Mobile phones linked to a provider are cheaper, but there's usually is a contract of 12 to 24 months which can make the telephone quite expensive, particularly if you don't use it very often. 'Prepaid' cards are a more flexible option; you can either buy new cards as needed or top-up your account online with a credit card.

CHARGES

Since deregulation of the Swiss telecoms market and the influx of new companies, it has been difficult to compare rates, although you can do so on Allo (🖳 www.allo.ch) and Comparis (🖳 www.comparis.ch). All companies have at least two tariff periods per day. Sunrise has a graduated system of discounts where the more you spend the more you save. It's important to compare rates, particularly when making international calls, when huge savings can be made by choosing the cheapest carrier.

Swisscom (☎ freephone 0800 800 800) has two basic tariff periods: peak (from 8am to 5pm Mondays to Fridays), and off-peak (from 5pm to 8am, Mondays to Fridays, and on Saturdays, Sundays and public holidays). Swisscom also offers several discount schemes such as 'frequently called numbers' (☎ 0800 86 87 88 for information); *Half price national* (SFr. 9.80 per month) providing national calls at a 50 per cent discount from 7am to 7pm Mondays to Fridays. Evening and weekend calls are free; *Half price international* (SFr. 9.80 per month) offering a 50 per cent discount on international calls; and *Half price combined* (SFr. 17.80 per month) allowing free evening and weekend national calls. National calls made during the day plus international calls made at any time are half price. The fees of most companies are now similar, although all have different special offers and 'discount days' which they announce in the media.

When using a company other than Swisscom, the company obtains your authorisation to inform Swisscom and have you connected to their network directly (a prefix isn't required). However, Swisscom may continue to charge you so you need to check your bills to confirm that you're connected to the correct company. Despite offering lower rates than Swisscom, new companies are held back by the high interconnection fees they must pay Swisscom to access their network.

Swisscom bills you for your monthly line rental, calls and telephone rental, as applicable. Your telephone bill doesn't contain an itemised list of calls, which is available for an extra charge if you have a tone phone. It does, however, separate domestic and international calls (subdivided into Europe and overseas), and calls made during different tariff periods. VAT at 7.6 per cent is levied on all telephone charges. Bills must be paid by the date shown.

INTERNATIONAL CALLS

The Swiss make more international calls per capita than any other nation and all private telephones in Switzerland are on International Direct Dialling (IDD). Dial 1811 for the international operator to make non-IDD calls, person-to-person calls and international enquiries. Information regarding international calls, including a world time-zone map, can be found in your local telephone directory. For operator connected calls made via Swisscom you pay a flat fee of SFr. 1.60 (national) or SFr. 2.50 (international) plus a per-minute rate for the time spent talking to the operator, in addition to the cost of your call.

To make an international call, dial 00 followed by the country code, then the area code **without** the first zero and finally the subscriber's number. The area codes for major towns in most countries are listed in telephone directories, along with the tariff per minute. International calls can be timed by the operator or you can buy a telephone with a meter to monitor the cost. International call information is provided in English in telephone directories.

If you make a lot of international calls, it's important to shop around and compare rates, as huge savings can be made by choosing the cheapest carrier (see **Charges** above). You can buy or rent a device (from electronics shops such as Media Markt and Interdiscount) that automatically selects the lowest cost routing for each call.

For example, in spring 2007, MyTel Swiss Select (☎ 0848 848 890, 💻 www.mytel.ch) were charging SFr. 0.07 per minute (inclusive of VAT) at all times to Austria, Germany, France, Italy, and the US and SFr. 0.08 per minute to the UK, Belgium, Denmark, the Netherlands, and Spain. In comparison Swisscom were charging SFr. 0.12 per minute (weekdays) and SFr. 0.10 (weekends) for calls to Australia, Austria, Canada, Denmark, Finland, France, Germany, Israel, Italy, Liechtenstein, Luxembourg, New Zealand, Norway, Sweden, the UK, the US and Vatican City. In addition, Swisscom has a special night and weekend rate of only SFr. 3 for 60 minutes on landlines in those countries. **Note that if you terminate**

the call before the 61st minute and dial the same number again, the low-tariff period starts again. Swisscom charges between SFr. 0.20-0.65 per minute for calls to most other countries. No matter where you're calling, extra charges apply to calls to foreign mobile networks.

One of the best ways to save money on international calls is to buy prepaid-cards, which you can use from any touch-pad telephone. After dialing a free access number (indicated on the card) a multi-lingual operator asks you to enter the card number followed by the subscriber's phone number. Prior to the call the operator tells you how many minutes credit you've left and whether it's sufficient for your call. This 'pedestrian' method is particularly useful when making calls from public telephones or to exotic destinations. There are a number of companies offering telephone cards including Econophone, Telecom FL and Teleline which cost SFr. 10, 20 or 30 from post offices, kiosks, petrol stations, newsagents and shops. **Note that there may be an extra charge of around SFr. 0.50 for calls made from public telephones and cards have an expiry date!**

DIRECTORIES

Swiss telephone subscribers are listed in directories (*Telefonbuch, annuaire téléphonique*) divided into cantons (the smaller cantons share directories). If you don't have the latest local directory when you move into an apartment, you can obtain one free of charge from your local post office. Directories for cantons other than your canton of residence cost around SFr. 10 each.

Information in telephone directories is separated into sections, as follows:

1   advertisting and information about entries;

2   international connections;

3   short numbers;

4   pink pages – a list of all Swiss postcodes, including the codes by street for large towns and cities;

5   white pages – private subscriber listings by town in alphabetical order (businesses and services may be listed under their type of business or service and/or their name).

Private subscribers are usually listed under the husband's name (if applicable) in telephone directories and also include the wife's maiden name (in brackets) and may include the subscriber's profession. If you want to have more than one entry in your local telephone directory, e.g. when a husband and a wife both retain their family names or when two or more people share a telephone, there's a charge each time a new directory is published. Subscribers are listed under their town or village and not alphabetically for the whole of a canton or city. Businesses aren't always listed under their name but under a group heading, for example a restaurant may be listed under restaurants and not under its name.

Calls to directory enquiries (valid for two queries) cost SFr. 1.60 plus SFr. 0.25 per minute for the first 60 seconds plus SFr. 0.08/0.04 from the 61st second. Alternatively, you can access all 4m Swiss subscribers on the internet phone directory (🖳 http://tel.search.ch) or on CD. New hardcopy directories are published every two years, although not all at the same time, while new CD directories (Twixtel) are published twice a year. The latter also usually includes a train timetable, the most important Swiss laws and other information about Switzerland. Yellow pages are also available via the internet (🖳 www.gelbe seiten.ch).

Yellow pages are available for most areas and for the major areas are produced by Swisscom Directories AG, Die Gelben Seiten, Morgenstrasse 131b, CH-3050 Berne (☎ 0848 868 086, 🖳 www.directories.ch). While your local yellow pages are free, directories for other regions are relatively expensive. Note that unlike Swisscom directories, subscribers in yellow pages are listed under a business or service heading for the whole area covered by the directory. Yellow pages in Switzerland aren't as widely used as those produced in North America or the UK, where they're indispensable (and free!). Free local telephone directories containing only business numbers are produced by council boroughs (*Bezirk, district*).

Swisscom has pioneered a new electronic telephone directory (Teleguide) that enables users of payphones to obtain Swiss telephone numbers and addresses at the touch of a button. Teleguides are gradually replacing paper telephone directories in public call boxes, where you can look up several addresses and numbers for a charge of SFr. 0.50 and also send emails, faxes or sms (short message service).

PUBLIC TELEPHONES

Most public telephones (*öffentliche Sprechstelle, téléphone public*) or payphones have International Direct Dialling (IDD). International calls can also be made via the operator. Payphones in Switzerland are owned and operated by Swisscom and most accept pre-paid cards, called **Taxcards**, rather than coins. You can buy a Taxcard for SFr. 5, 10 or 20 from post offices, Swisscom shops, railway station booking offices, petrol stations, campsites, newsagents, kiosks, hotels, government buildings and hospitals. You need to insert the Taxcard into a special slot in the payphone and the cost of calls and the remaining credit on the card will be indicated on a digital display. A card can be changed during a call without interrupting it simply by inserting a new card within 30 seconds. All cards have an expiry date printed on them. Taxcards are produced in a variety of designs and (as in many other countries) have become collectors' items. Some payphones also accept Postcards (see page 122), credit cards and coins.

Coin Payphones

While most payphones now accept Taxcards (see above), some accept coins. The coins required for payphones vary; some accept 10 and 20 cent coins and SFr. 1 and 5 coins, while others don't accept SFr. 5 coins, but do accept 50 cent coins. Some also accept euro coins. Call charges are the same as for private telephones, plus a 'user charge' of SFr. 0.20 a call. Calls to service numbers cost a minimum of SFr. 0.70 from payphones. **Emergency calls are free.** Where applicable your money is returned at the end of the call. Instructions for using payphones are listed in English, French, German and Italian and are as follows:

1   Lift the handset and wait for the dialling tone (a continuous beep).

2   Insert the minimum call charge of SFr. 0.60 (not required for emergency numbers). For a long distance call insert more money, depending on the cost per minute and the time required. The credit display, which shows how much money you have in credit, stops flashing.

3   Dial the number required.

4   When your credit is exhausted, the credit display starts flashing again and a warning tone is given on the line. **You have ten seconds to insert more coins before the call is disconnected**.

5   If you wish to make another call **don't replace the handset**, but press the **red button** located below the handset rest and, if necessary, insert additional coins. This prevents the loss of partly used coins.

6   To retrieve a partly used coin that is still in credit, **don't replace the handset** but press the **red button** and insert some coins until the credit display shows the value of a coin that can be retrieved, rather than an intermediate value.

7   Replace the handset and any unused coins will be returned.

There are special Swisscom telephone offices that can be found at main post offices, airports and main railway stations for international calls. Opening times are usually from 6.30 or 7am until between 8.30 and 10.30pm, Mondays to Saturdays. There are usually reduced opening hours on Sundays.

MOVING OR LEAVING SWITZERLAND

When moving house or leaving Switzerland, you must notify Swisscom and other telephone companies (as applicable), preferably 30 days in advance. **It's particularly important to notify Swisscom early if you're leaving Switzerland and need to get a deposit refunded.**

If you move within the same code area you can retain your number.

EMERGENCY NUMBERS

The following national emergency numbers (*Notfallnummern, numéros d'appel en cas d'urgence*) are listed on page one of all telephone directories.

Number	Service
☎ 117	**Police** (*Polizeinotruf, police secours*)
☎ 118	**Fire** (*Feuermeldestelle, feu centrale d'alarme*)
☎ 144	**Ambulance** (*Sanitätsnotruf, appel sanitaire d'urgence*)
☎ 1414	**Helicopter Rescue** (REGA – *Rettung mit Helikopter, sauvetage par hélicoptère*) – see below (SFr. 0.20 per call)
☎ 145	**Poison Emergency Service** (*Vergiftungsnotfall, intoxication en cas d'urgence*) (SFr. 0.08/0.04 per minute)
☎ 143	**Samaritans** (*Die dargebotene Hand, La main tendue*) – see below (SFr. 0.20 per call)
☎ 140	**Vehicle Breakdown** (*Strassenhilfe, secours routier*)

The above telephone numbers are staffed or provide recorded information 24 hours a day and can be dialled from anywhere within Switzerland. Recorded information is given in the local language (French, German or Italian); SFr. 0.50 is required to dial an emergency number from a coin payphone (but is returned).

Fire Service

The fire service, besides extinguishing fires, attending traffic accidents and natural disasters, also deals with the victims of accidents such as drowning, asphyxiation (lack of oxygen), choking, electrocution, serious burns and hanging. They're certainly the best people to call when faced with a life or death situation.

Swiss Air Rescue Service

The Swiss air rescue service (known as REGA) has 13 bases from which a helicopter or an air ambulance jet can be dispatched. Everywhere in Switzerland (except the Valais) is within 15 minutes flying time. The service also covers the whole world using jet aircraft.

The cost of the REGA service is covered by Swiss third party car insurance. **If you happen to fall down a mountain and are rescued by REGA, it will cost you around SFr. 2,000 if you aren't insured.** You can become a member of REGA for SFr. 30 a year for a single person over 16, or SFr. 60 a year for a couple. The annual fee for families, including all children under 18, is SFr. 40 (one parent) or SFr. 70 (two parents). Contact REGA, PO Box 1414, CH-8058 Zurich Airport (☎ 044-654 33 11, 🖳 www.rega.ch). Some towns (e.g. Sion, Zermatt) also have local helicopter rescue services.

Samaritans

The Samaritans (*Die dargebotene Hand*, *la main tendue* – ☎ 143, 🖳 www.143. ch; SFr. 0.20 per call) provide a confidential and anonymous counselling service for times of personal crisis and receive over 200,000 calls a year. If the duty counsellor doesn't speak English, he'll ask you to call at a time when an English-speaking counsellor will be present (if necessary).

TeleAlarm

Swisscom provides an emergency TeleAlarm call service (*Telefon-Notruf*, *téléphone-alarme*) for elderly or disabled people for SFr. 34.50 a month (including the base station and transmitter bracelet). In the event of an accident, subscribers can transmit an emergency pre-recorded call for help by simply pressing a button on the bracelet.

Service Numbers

The following service numbers (*Dienstnummern*, *numéros de service*) are described in the blue section at the front of telephone directories and can be called from anywhere in Switzerland. Unless specified, recorded information is given in the local canton language or languages (French, German or Italian). If you dial a service number where no information is available, you're informed of this via a recorded message.

Number	Service
☎ 1811 or ☎ 1818	National enquiries (SFr. 1.60 basic fee plus 0.25 for the first minute and standard rates after 60 seconds) and international enquiries (SFr. 2.50 basic fee plus 0.59 for the first 90 seconds and 0.25 per minute after 90 seconds).

☎ 1812	Automated enquiries (SFr. 0.80 basic fee plus 0.10 per minute).
☎ 140	Roadside assistance (SFr. 0.20 per call).
☎ 1600	*Regional News and information about exhibitions and fairs (SFr. 0.50 basic fee plus 0.50 per minute).
☎ 161	*Speaking clock (SFr. 0.50 per call).
☎ 162	*Weather forecasts (SFr. 0.50 basic fee plus 0.50 per minute).
☎ 163	*Traffic reports (SFr. 0.50 basic fee plus 0.50 per minute).
☎ 164	*Sports news and lottery results (SFr. 0.50 basic fee plus 0.50 per minute).
☎ 175	Fault repair service (*Störungsdienst*, *Service des dérangements*).
☎ 187	*Avalanche bulletins (winter) and lake wind conditions (summer, SFr. 0.50 per call).
☎ 0900 77	Automatic wake-up service (SFr. 0.50 per call).
☎ 0800 80 1141	Reverse charge calls.

* Recorded information.

INTERNET

The Swiss are among the world's most avid internet users. According to the OECD, nearly 75 per cent of Swiss households had internet access in 2005, a figure that grows annually. Broadband (via ASDL and cable) has become increasingly popular in recent years, with nearly 30 subscribers per 100 inhabitants. For the occasional user, a dial-up service is a good option. For example, Swisscom's Bluewin (🖥 www.bluewin.ch) offers connection at between SFr. 0.70 and 2.80 per hour, depending on the time and day. You get one free email account with this service, and there's no monthly fee. However, if you feel the need for speed, or if you use the internet frequently, you will want a faster connection. With some 150 internet service providers (ISPs) to choose from, getting online is fairly easy.

It's possible to access the internet via mobile phone. This technology is still being developed and connection packages change rapidly. Check with your mobile service provider for the latest information (see **Mobile Phones** on page 130).

Broadband

In Switzerland, most home broadband connections are via ADSL. Fees vary with the provider and the usage, but you can expect to pay around SFr. 50 per month for unlimited connection time and download speeds of up to 3,500 Kbits per second. Such a subscription typically includes five email addresses. Consumers with simpler needs can pay about SFr. 10 per month for a slower connection of 300 Kbits per second. There may be initial charges such as connection fees or modem costs, so it pays to shop around. The minimum contract length is usually one year. Comparis offers an overview of ADSL offers (🖳 www.comparis.ch). Popular providers include Bluewin (☎ 0844 844 884, 🖳 www.bluewin.ch), Econophone (☎ 0800 188 188, 🖳 www.econophone.ch), Orange (☎ 0800 700 700, 🖳 www.orange.ch), Sunrise (☎ 0800 707 707, 🖳 www.sunrise.ch) and Tele2 (☎ 0800 24 24 24, 🖳 www.tele2.ch). The last three have English web pages.

Cable internet access accounts for around a third of broadband subscriptions. Prices vary, for example SFr. 0.33 per MB or SFr. 45 per month. Major providers include Cablecom (☎ 0800 66 08 00, 🖳 www.cablecom.ch), Datazug (☎ 041 748 49 59, 🖳 www.datazug.ch) and Quickline (☎ 0800 84 10 20, 🖳 www.quickline.com). For a map showing providers by canton, visit 🖳 www.ablemodem.ch and click on *Anbieter- /Providerliste*. Cable tends to be unavailable in rural areas.

See also **TV via Broadband** on page 144.

8.

TELEVISION & RADIO

Television (TV) and radio services in Switzerland are operated by the Swiss Broadcasting Corporation (Schweizerische Radio und Fernsehgesellschaft, Société Suisse de Radiodiffusion et Télévision – SRG/SSR), which is a private, non-profit company and a public service financed by advertising and licence fees.

TELEVISION

The quality of Swiss TV leaves much to be desired, although it's no worse than the fare served up in most other European countries. The German-speaking Swiss reportedly watch less TV than almost anyone in Europe and other Swiss also watch much less TV than the European average. The choice of Swiss TV stations has increased in the last few years with the introduction of a number of local cable TV companies. Cable TV is available throughout the country and some 90 per cent of homes in Switzerland receive their TV programmes via a communal aerial or cable. Due to the wide availability of cable TV, satellite TV (see page 144) isn't common in Switzerland, although it's popular with expatriates. TV programmes are listed in daily and weekly newspapers (see page 352), and published in weekly TV magazines.

Television Standards

The standard for TV reception in Switzerland **isn't the same as in some other countries**. Due to differences in transmission standards, TVs and video recorders from the UK, France and the US won't function in Switzerland or the rest of Europe unless they're dual standard. Most continental countries use the PAL B/G standard except for France, which has its own standard which is called SECAM-L that's different from the SECAM B/G employed in the Middle East and North African countries, and SECAM D/K in eastern European and many African countries. The British use a modified PAL (PAL-I) system and the US use the North American NTSC standard. If you bring a TV to Switzerland from the UK or the US, you will receive either just a picture or just sound – **but not both**. Most modern TVs that are sold in France are multi-standard (e.g. SECAM and PAL B/G) and they can therefore be used in Switzerland. TVs can be converted to work in Switzerland, but it isn't usually worth the expense.

Video cassettes/DVDs can only be played on a video cassette recorder (VCR)/DVD player and a TV operating on the same system (e.g. PAL or NTSC, or Region 1 or 2) as that on which they were recorded. So if you bring DVDs or videos from the US, you must also have a compatible TV and DVD player or VCR. Videos recorded in the UK can be shown on Swiss VCRs and TVs (and British VCRs can be used to show video tapes that were recorded in the UK on a Swiss TV). You cannot, however, make video recordings from a TV designed for use in Switzerland with an incompatible video machine, for example one designed for use in the UK or the US. If you bring a TV and VCR to Switzerland from the US designed for use on 110 volts, you will need a transformer (see **Electricity** on page 104).

It's possible to buy a multi-standard TV or VCR that can handle PAL, SECAM-L and NTSC standards (or two of these three standards). You can also buy a PAL TV with an NTSC-in jack plug connection, allowing you to play American videos. Some DVD players can handle all regional codes. Many people buy a stereo TV in order to take advantage of dual-language broadcasts, where films and some sports events are broadcast in French, German or Italian plus the original language, which is often English. If you decide to buy a TV in Switzerland, it's worth buying one with teletext, which apart from allowing you to display programme schedules also provides a wealth of useful information.

Television Stations

In most cities and many rural areas, the majority of buildings are wired for cable TV (see below), which enables households to receive up to 70 TV stations (average around 40) and some 30 radio stations. The TV stations available include the six Swiss stations (two French, two German, two Italian), plus Austrian, French, German and Italian stations, and a variety of cable and satellite TV (see page 144) stations. Without cable TV, only five or six stations (including the Swiss stations) can be received, depending on the area.

The SRG/SSR is responsible for producing and relaying programmes in the four Swiss national languages (Swiss TV programmes are listed on teletext). Other stations broadcast in English, French, German or Italian. Foreign programmes, including films, are usually dubbed in the language of the broadcasting channel, the main exception being the occasional old black and white film. Note, however, that many recent films have dual soundtracks (see above).

The amount of advertising permitted on Swiss TV is strictly controlled and is 8 per cent of air time. Information regarding the SRG/SSR is available from Belpstrasse 48, 3000 Berne 14 (☎ 031 350 91 11, 🖳 www.srg.ch).

Cable Television

Cable TV (*Gemeinschaftsantenne, antenne collective*) is available in most areas of Switzerland, but is restricted to towns and buildings wired for cable TV. All you need to do to receive cable TV is to connect your TV aerial to a special wall socket. Around 90 per cent of Swiss households are connected to a communal antenna or to a cable network, making Switzerland third in the world in cable TV availability after Belgium and the Netherlands. Cable TV consists of cable relays of Swiss and foreign national TV stations, dedicated cable-only stations and satellite stations. The average Swiss household can receive around 40 TV channels, although some areas receive many more (e.g. 70 in Geneva). English-language cable TV stations are widely available and include CNN International,

Eurosport, MTV Europe and NBC Superchannel. Digital TV is available in most areas through a cable provider and, apart from a huge range of Eastern Europe TV stations, also includes BBC 1 and BBC 2.

Cable TV isn't always available in remote areas of Switzerland, in older buildings, and in small towns and villages. If you want to receive English-language cable TV, check that it's available (and which stations) before signing a lease. Cable TV usually costs between SFr. 20 (analogue) and SFr. 25 (digital) per month, depending on the channels provided, and is included in your apartment's monthly extra costs or billed annually. If you don't own a TV, you may be able to get the cable TV company to seal the aerial outlet and thus avoid paying the monthly rental charge. This is easy enough if you live in a house, but may be impossible if you live in an apartment, where cable TV costs are shared and are included in your apartment's extra costs.

In addition to unscrambled cable TV channels, scrambled TV channels are available in many areas. Like some satellite TV stations (see below), you require a decoder (which can be installed by most TV shops) to receive them and must pay a monthly subscription.

TV via Broadband

In common with many countries, Switzerland offers a television service delivered via your phone line. The service, called Bluewin TV, requires a Swisscom telephone line and a Bluewin ADSL connection. Bluewin TV features more than 120 channels, 21 of which are in English, and BBC radio is also available. The cost is SFr. 95 for installation plus SFr. 29 per month. Further information is available from ☎ 0800 081 081 and 🖥 www.tv.bluewin.ch.

Satellite TV

There are a number of satellites positioned over Europe carrying over 200 stations broadcasting in a variety of languages. Satellite TV has been growing apace in Europe in recent years, although most homes in Switzerland with satellite TV are owned by foreigners.

Astra

The Astra satellites offer a huge choice of English and foreign-language channels, at least 100 (or over 500 with digital TV) of which can be received throughout Switzerland with a 60 or 85cm dish. Among the many English-language channels available on Astra are Channel 5, The Discovery Channels, The Disney Channel, Eurosport, Film Four, Plus, Sky Cinema 1 & 2, Sky Movies 1–9, Sky News, Sky One, Sky Sports (three channels), TCM, UK Gold and UKTV

Gold. Other channels are broadcast in Dutch, German, Japanese, Swedish and various Indian languages. The signal for many channels is scrambled (the decoder is usually built into the receiver) and viewers must pay a monthly subscription to receive programmes. The best served by unscrambled (clear) channels are German-speakers. Further information can be found on Astra's website (🖳 www.astra.lu).

A bonus of Astra is the availability of radio stations, including all the national BBC stations (see **Radio** on page 148).

Sky Television

In order to receive Sky television you need a Sky digital receiver (digibox) and a dish. There are two ways to obtain the equipment and the necessary Sky 'smart' card. You can subscribe in the UK or Ireland (personally, if you have an address there, or via a friend) and then take the Sky receiver and card to Switzerland, although for the first year of your contract the digibox must be connected to a telephone line (so that Sky can sell you interactive services); if you export it during this period and connect it to a foreign telephone line, Sky will terminate your contract (Sky's call centre can tell what country a call/connection is being made from). After the first year, the digibox no longer needs to be connected to a telephone line and so can (although strictly should not) be exported. Similarly, a Sky card shouldn't be used outside the UK.

Alternatively, you can buy a digibox and obtain a Sky card 'privately' in Switzerland (a number of satellite companies supply Sky cards); however, you're subject to the same restrictions as noted above. To receive Sky TV in Switzerland, a dish must be at least 60 or 85cm in diameter.

You must subscribe to Sky to receive most English-language channels (other than Sky News, which isn't scrambled). If you subscribe to the basic package, costing around GB£15, you will have access to around 100 channels, including BBC1, BBC2, ITV1, CH4 and CH5. Various other packages are available costing up to around GB£42.50, for which you have access to the Movie and Sports channels, along with many interactive services such as Sky News Active.

Further information about Sky installation (in the UK) and programme packages can be found on Sky's website (🖳 www.sky.com).

Eutelsat

Eutelsat was the first company to introduce satellite TV to Europe and it now runs a fleet of communications satellites carrying TV stations to over 50m homes. The English-language stations on Eutelsat include Eurosport, BBC World and CNBC Superchannel. Other stations are broadcast in Arabic, French, German, Hungarian, Italian, Polish, Portuguese, Spanish and Turkish. Further information can be found on Eutelsat's website (🖳 www.eutelsat.org).

BBC

The BBC's commercial subsidiary, BBC Worldwide Television, broadcasts two 24-hour channels: BBC Prime (general entertainment) and BBC World (24-hour news and information). BBC World is free-to-air, while BBC Prime is encrypted and requires a D2-MAC decoder and a smartcard, available on subscription from BBC Prime, PO Box 5054, London W12 0ZY, UK (☎ 020-8433 2221, 🖳 www. bbcprime.com). For more information and a programming guide contact BBC Worldwide Television, Woodlands, 80 Wood Lane W12 0TT, UK (☎ 020-8433 2000, 🖳 www.bbcworldwide.com). A programme guide is also available on the internet (🖳 www.bbc. co.uk/schedules) and both BBC World and BBC Prime have websites (🖳 www.bbcworld.com and 🖳 www.bbcprime.com). When accessing them, you need to enter the name of the country (e.g. Switzerland) so that schedules appear in local time.

Equipment

A satellite receiver should have a built-in Videocrypt decoder (and others such as Eurocrypt, Syster or SECAM if required) and be capable of receiving satellite stereo radio. A 60cm dish may be adequate in some areas of Switzerland, although an 85cm dish or a signal booster is better and necessary in some regions. A basic fixed satellite system (which will receive programmes from one satellite only) costs around SFr. 500 and a motorised dish (which will automatically adjust its orientation so that you can receive programmes from other satellites) will set you back three or four times as much.

If you wish to receive satellite stations on two or more TVs, you can buy a satellite system with two or more receptors. To receive stations from two (or more) satellites simultaneously, you need a motorised dish or a dish with a double feed antenna (dual LNBs). There are many satellite sales and installation companies in Switzerland. Shop around and compare prices. Alternatively you can import your own satellite dish and receiver and install it yourself. Before buying a system, ensure that it can receive programmes from all existing and planned satellites.

Location & Installation

To be able to receive programmes from any satellite, there must be no obstacles between the satellite and your dish, i.e. no large obstacles such as trees, buildings or mountains must obstruct the signal, so check before renting an apartment or buying a home.

Before buying or erecting a satellite dish – or even before buying or renting a home – check whether it's possible to install it and whether you require permission from your landlord or a permit from the local authorities.

Dishes can usually be mounted in a variety of unobtrusive positions and can be painted or patterned to blend in with the background. New apartment blocks may be fitted with at least one communal satellite dish.

Programme Guides

Many satellite stations provide teletext information and most broadcast in stereo. Sky satellite programme listings are provided in a number of British publications such as *What Satellite, Satellite Times* and *Satellite TV Europe*, which are available on subscription and from newsagents in Switzerland. Satellite TV programmes are also listed in expatriate newspapers and magazines in Switzerland. The annual *The Directory of Global Broadcasting* (available from World Radio TV Handbook/WRTH – ☎ UK 01865-514 405, 🖳 www.wrth.com) contains over 600 pages of information and the frequencies of all radio and TV stations worldwide.

Television Licence

A TV licence (*Fernsehempfangskonzession, concession de réception de télévisuelle*) which costs SFr. 293 per year is required by all TV owners. The registration of a TV licence and a radio licence can be done together by contacting Billag (☎ 0844 83 48 34, 🖳 www.billag.ch). The TV licence fee is payable quarterly with your radio licence fee (if applicable) and can be paid by direct debit. The licence fee covers any number of TVs owned or rented by you, irrespective of where they are located, e.g. holiday homes, motor vehicles or boats. Registration must be made within 14 days of buying or importing a TV. **You're fined if you have a TV and don't have a licence when an inspector calls**. However, if your TV is used only for video/DVD playback or as a computer monitor, no licence fee is payable – but you mustn't be able to receive any TV broadcasts.

Videos & DVDs

English-language videos and DVDs can be rented from around SFr. 6 to 10 per day from video shops and postal video clubs throughout Switzerland. Rental costs can often be reduced by paying a monthly membership fee or a lump sum in advance. **Check the conditions before hiring, as some companies levy exorbitant 'fines' if you forget to return films on time (possibly more than the value of the video)**. Most public libraries also offer a variety of videos and DVDs available for rent for a nominal fee, e.g. SFr. 2 per week.

Since 2003, video shops in Switzerland have been forbidden by law to import original UK or US videos and DVDs, but can sell only German, French or Italian versions that are expressly licensed for Switzerland. However, there's no restriction on individuals buying videos from the UK or USA (e.g. via the internet).

RADIO

The good news for radio fans is that radios have the same standards the world over, although bandwidths vary. FM (VHF) stereo stations flourish in Switzerland and Medium Wave (MW or AM) and Long Wave (LW) bands are also in wide use throughout Europe. A Short Wave (SW) radio is useful for receiving international stations such as the BBC World Service, Voice of America, Radio Canada and Radio Sweden. The BBC World Service and the Voice of America are also available via cable radio in many areas (see below). Portable digital radio receivers are available that provide good reception, particularly on short wave, and expensive 'professional' receivers are capable of receiving stations from almost anywhere. If you're interested in receiving radio stations from further afield, obtain a copy of the *World Radio TV Handbook* (see **Programme Guides** on page 147).

Swiss Radio

There are over 40 private local radio stations in Switzerland, some broadcasting in English, e.g. Radio 74 (88.8 MHz FM) and World Radio (88.4 MHz FM) in Geneva. Advertising is forbidden on radio stations run by the SRG/SSR, but is permitted on local radio stations. Swiss Radio International (SRI) transmits programmes via short wave, cable and satellite in Arabic, English, French, German, Italian, Portuguese and Spanish. The English language programme (24-hours a day) can be heard via the Astra satellite. For more information contact SRI, Giacomettistr. 1, CH-3000 Berne 15 (☎ 031 350 92 22, 💻 www. swissinfo.org). Swiss Radio publishes a *Radio Magazin* available on subscription from Radio Magazin, Aboverwaltung, PO Box 75, CH-8024 Zurich (☎ 044 253 90 65, 💻 www.radiomagazin.ch).

BBC & Other Foreign Stations

The BBC World Service is broadcast on short wave on several frequencies (e.g. 12095, 9760, 9410, 7325, 6195, 5975 and 3955 Khz) simultaneously and you can usually receive a good signal on one of them. The signal strength varies depending on where you live in Switzerland, the time of day and year, the power and positioning of your receiver, and atmospheric conditions. All BBC radio stations, including the World Service, are also available via the Astra satellite (see below) and BBC World Service is available via cable radio (see below). You can view detailed programme information online at (🖥 www.bbc.co.uk/radio). Many other foreign stations publish programme listings and frequency charts for expatriates seeking news from home, including Radio Australia, Radio Canada, Denmark Radio, Radio Nederland, Radio Sweden International and the Voice of America.

Satellite Radio

If you have satellite TV you can also receive many radio stations via your satellite link. For example, BBC Radio 1, 2, 3, 4 and 5, BBC World Service, Sky Radio, Virgin 1215 and many foreign (i.e. non-English) stations are broadcast via the Astra satellites. Satellite radio stations are listed in British satellite TV magazines such as *Satellite TV*. If you're interested in receiving radio stations from further afield you can obtain a copy of *The Directory of Global Broadcasting* (available from WRTH – ☎ UK 01865-514 405, 🖥 www.wrth.com).

Cable Radio

If your apartment is wired for cable TV (see page 143), it will also be wired for cable radio, providing reception of around 30 stereo stations. Many cable networks provide the BBC World Service, BBC Foreign Language Service, Voice of America, Swiss Radio International (English service) and Sky Radio, in addition to a wide selection of FM stereo stations from Switzerland (national and local), France, Germany and Austria. All you need do is connect your radio or hi-fi tuner aerial to a special wall socket (cables are available from TV stores).

Radio Licence

A radio licence (*Radioempfangskonzession, concession de réception radio*), which costs SFr. 169 per year (SFr. 14.10 per month), is required by all owners of radios (including car radios). Both radio and TV licence (see page 147) registration can be done together by contacting Billag (☎ 0844 83 48 34, 🖥 www.billag.ch). The radio licence fee is payable quarterly with your TV licence fee (if applicable). It covers any number of radios irrespective of where they're located, e.g. holiday homes, motor vehicles or boats (but not radios in the workplace which should be covered by an employer's radio licence). Registration must be made within 14 days of buying or importing a radio and failure to register can result in a fine.

9.

EDUCATION

Switzerland is renowned for the excellence and diversity of its private schools. Although it isn't so well known abroad, Swiss state (i.e. publicly funded) schools also have a good reputation in academic circles. The Swiss have always been in the forefront of educational progress and have produced a number of world-renowned philosophers (e.g. Froebal, Pestalozzi, Piaget and Steiner) whose pedagogical theories and research remain a strong influence throughout the world. Even today, Swiss teaching methods are in advance of those of most other countries, many of which send delegations to Swiss schools.

Compulsory schooling begins at seven (some children start just before they're seven), after an optional period at nursery school for four to six-year-olds (there are no state nursery schools in Switzerland), and continues for eight or, more often, nine years (an optional tenth year exists in most cantons) until the age of 15 or 16. On average, the Swiss attend school until the age of 17, one of the highest average school-leaving ages in the world.

There are many things to take into account when choosing an appropriate school for your children in Switzerland, among the most important of which is the language of study. The only schools using English as the teaching language are international private schools. If your children attend any other school, they must study in a foreign language. For most children, studying in a foreign language isn't such a handicap as it may at first appear. The majority adapt quickly and soon become fluent in the local language, assisted by the extra language tuition usually provided for foreign children. Naturally all children don't adapt equally well to a change of language and culture, particularly teenage children. Before making any major decisions about your children's future education, it's important to consider their individual ability, character and requirements.

For many children, the experience of going to school and living in a foreign country is a stimulating change and a challenge that they relish, providing invaluable cultural and educational experiences. Your children will become 'world' citizens, less likely to be prejudiced against foreigners and foreign ideas, particularly if they attend an international school with pupils from many countries. Swiss state schools also have pupils from a number of countries, with an average of around 20 per cent being non-Swiss.

In addition to a detailed look at the Swiss state school system and private schools, this chapter also contains information about children's holiday camps, apprenticeships, universities, further education and language schools.

STATE OR PRIVATE SCHOOL?

If you're fortunate enough to be among those who can afford to send your children to a private school, you may be surprised to learn that the vast majority of Swiss parents choose to send their children to a state school, even when the cost of private education isn't an important consideration. If you're able to choose between state and private education, the following checklist of questions to ask yourself (or schools) will help you decide:

- How long are you planning to stay in Switzerland? If you're uncertain, it's probably best to assume a long stay. Due to language and other integration problems, enrolling a child in a Swiss state school is advisable only if you're planning to stay for at least a year, particularly for teenage children.

- What are the state schools like in the area you plan to live in? Bear in mind that the area where you choose to live may affect your choice of school(s). For example, if you choose state education, it may be compulsory to send your children to the state school nearest your home.

- Do you know where you're going after Switzerland? This may be an important consideration with regard to your children's language of tuition and system of education in Switzerland. How old are your children and what age will they be when you plan to leave Switzerland? What plans do you have for their education and in which country?

- What educational level are your children at now and how will they fit into a private school or the Swiss state school system? The younger they are, the easier it will be to place them in a suitable school.

- How do your children view the thought of studying in a foreign language? What language(s) is best from a long-term point of view? Is schooling available in Switzerland in your children's mother tongue?

- Will your children require your help with their studies and, more importantly, will you be able to help them, particularly with the language(s)?

- Is special or extra tutoring available in the local language or particular subjects, if required?

- What are the school hours? What are the school holiday periods? Some state schools in Switzerland have compulsory Saturday morning classes. How will the school holidays and hours affect your family's work and leisure activities?

- Is religion an important aspect in your choice of school? In Swiss state schools religion is usually taught as a compulsory subject. Parents may, however, request permission for their children not to attend.

- Do you want your children to attend a single-sex school? Swiss state schools are usually coeducational (mixed).

- Should you send your children to a boarding school? If so, where?

- What are the secondary and further education prospects in Switzerland or another country? Are Swiss examinations or the examinations set by prospective Swiss schools recognised in your home country or the country where you plan to live after leaving Switzerland?

- Does the school have a good academic record? Most schools provide exam pass rate statistics.

- How large are the classes? What is the pupil-teacher ratio?

Obtain the opinions and advice of others who have been faced with the same decisions and problems as you're facing, and collect as much information from as many different sources as possible before making a decision. Speak to teachers and the parents of children attending schools on your shortlist.

Many cantons have schools with facilities for physically and mentally disabled children. Switzerland doesn't, however, provide special teaching facilities for gifted children with exceptionally high IQs, although in some cases bright children are allowed to skip a grade.

STATE SCHOOLS

The term 'state' schools is a misnomer, as there are no state (federal) schools in Switzerland, education being the jealously guarded responsibility of the cantons. Nevertheless, state is used here in preference to 'public' (to prevent confusion with the British term 'public school', which refers to a private, fee-paying school) to refer to non-fee-paying schools funded by the cantons from local taxes.

The state school (*öffentliche Schulen*, *écoles publiques*) system in Switzerland is complicated compared with many other developed countries and differs considerably from the school systems in, for example, the UK and the US, particularly regarding secondary and university education. The Swiss canton education system results in 26 school systems, with many minor and some major differences between them. The school timetables and curricula and even the categories of schools may vary from canton to canton, and even from community to community. However, although the lack of a standardised national state school system may appear strange, it usually affects children (and their parents) only when they move to another canton. Even then, provided the teaching language remains the same, the differences are usually insignificant.

It's usually necessary to send your children to a school in your canton of residence where you pay your taxes. Some cantons, however, have agreements allowing children resident in neighbouring cantons to attend their schools. Pupils usually go to a nearby primary school, although attending secondary school often entails travelling quite long distances.

State schooling is free for all foreign children of parents with Swiss annual or permanent residence permits (B or C) and who work in Switzerland, although some school books must be purchased by parents.

Most foreign parents (plus the vast majority of Swiss parents) send their children to a Swiss state school for reasons that aren't entirely financial. Swiss state schools have an excellent academic record, aided by the small average class size (around 20 pupils), and are rated among the best in the world. In international tests, Swiss pupils regularly outperform children in most other countries (particularly in maths and science, as Swiss pupils don't usually use calculators until secondary school) and Swiss schools have far fewer low-achieving pupils. Attending a state school helps children integrate into the local community and learn the local language.

Swiss state schools usually impose more discipline than many foreign children are used to, for example regular homework, which may initially cause some stress and increases with the age of the child. Generally, the younger children are when they arrive in Switzerland, the easier they will cope. Conversely the older they are, the more problems they will have adjusting, particularly as the school curriculum is more demanding. Parents should try to empathise with their children's problems. If you aren't fluent in the local language, you will already be aware of how frustrating it is being unable to express yourself adequately. Lack of language ability can easily lead to feelings of inferiority or inadequacy in children (and adults!). State schools may provide supervised homework or extra classes for children who require them.

In general, the Swiss state school system is more disciplined and less flexible than schooling in many countries, but the results are generally good, every child being given the opportunity to study for a trade, diploma or a degree.

Having made the decision to send your child to a state school, you should persevere for at least a year to give it a fair trial. It may take your child this long to adapt to a new language, the change of environment and the different curriculum. A book may be available from your community explaining the intricacies of your canton's secondary school system. For example, excellent guides are published by the cantons of Zurich, *Volksschule wohin?* (*What Next? Primary School*) and Vaud, *Présent et Avenir des Ecoliers* (*Present and Future of School Children*).

Language

In the French- and Italian-speaking regions of Switzerland, the teaching language is the same as the spoken language and therefore foreign children are able to improve their language ability through their constant exposure to it. In German-speaking Switzerland the position isn't so straightforward. In kindergarten and early primary school classes, teachers speak the local Swiss German dialect. In primary school they officially begin to teach academic subjects in High German (*Schriftdeutsch/Hochdeutsch, bon allemand*), although this isn't always the case. In later years, generally all non-academic study is in Swiss German, while all academic subjects are taught in High German, particularly when text books are required. One of the problems for both Swiss and foreign children, is that because most lessons are conducted in Swiss German, there's little opportunity to practise High German. This has led to all subjects being (officially) taught in High German in secondary schools in some cantons.

The Swiss German dialect isn't formally taught in any schools (nobody would know where to start!). This makes school life more difficult for foreign children, particularly teenagers, although young children (e.g. 5 to 12 years) generally have few problems learning Swiss German. If you prefer your children to be educated in the French language and you live in a German-speaking canton, it may be possible to send your children to a school in a neighbouring French-speaking canton. You may, however, be required to live in the canton where your children go to school and may not be permitted to move cantons if you're a new arrival (Catch 22!).

Children who don't speak the local language, particularly children of secondary school age, are usually placed in a 'reception' or special class, depending on the degree of language assistance necessary. This allows them more time to concentrate on learning the language (with extra language tuition), as they will usually have already covered the syllabus. They integrate into the normal stream only when they've learnt the language and can follow the lessons. When the next promotion stage is reached, they must have reached a satisfactory standard in the local language or the year must be repeated.

All children must learn a second national language from their seventh school year at the latest. The compulsory second language in secondary schools in German-speaking Switzerland is French and in French-speaking Switzerland it's High German. However, many Swiss German parents would prefer English to be taught as a second language in place of French and this has already been adopted in some cantons, e.g. Zurich (much to the ire of the French Swiss).

Children don't usually start learning English in Swiss state schools until the age of 12 to 14 and even then it may be voluntary (although some cantons, such as Zurich, teach English in primary school). English becomes compulsory only when a child is studying modern languages, for example in a high school (*Gymnasium/Kantonsschule, gymnase/école cantonale*), or when a specialist subject requiring English language proficiency is being studied. English Fun Language Clubs for children aged three to ten are becoming increasingly popular (they also offer French, German and Spanish, but English is the most popular).

For more information about Swiss languages and learning them, see **Languages** on page 38 and **Language Schools** on page 173.

Enrolment

When you arrive in Switzerland and register in your local community (*Gemeinde, commune*), you're informed about schooling and told when and where to apply for school entrance for your children. In city areas you must apply to your area school commission (*Kreisschulpflege, commission scolaire du district*). School registration dates are announced in local newspapers. The start of the school year throughout Switzerland is between mid-August and mid-September. A detailed list showing school start (and holiday) dates for all cantons is available at 🖥 www.edk.ch.

School Hours

Swiss school hours differ considerably from those in most other countries and often vary from school to school, as it's generally left to individual teachers to schedule their own classes. Children rarely spend all day at school and if you have children of different ages attending school (even the same school), they may be coming and going at different times. This is particularly true for the youngest children, where classes may be divided into sections with varied hours. This is a difficult system for working parents, so many cantons have now introduced 'block times' (*Blockzeiten*). At a school with block times, classes typically start at 8am and end at noon with a second session from 2 to 4pm in the afternoon. A two-hour lunch break is normal, during which schools are closed (state schools in Switzerland don't usually provide school lunches). Older children who have a long journey to school may take a packed lunch to eat on the school premises, for which a room is provided. Some high schools have canteens.

In secondary schools, hours are generally anywhere between 7 to 11am or noon and 1.30 or 2pm to 6pm. In a higher grade secondary school, e.g. a high school (*Gymnasium/Kantonsschule*, *gymnase/école cantonale*), the school day can last from 7.30am to 5pm (around 40 hours a week), which is a long day, particularly when travelling time is added.

The average travelling time to and from school in German-speaking Switzerland is around 40 minutes, which together with the demanding school schedule is blamed for the high stress levels of some children. It isn't usual for parents to take their children to school in Switzerland; depending on the distance, children walk, ride a bike or use public transport. Going to school on their own is considered an important part of children becoming independent, and parents taking their children to school and picking them up by car is frowned upon in some areas. School buses are generally provided only for the disabled in the public sector; some private schools operate buses. See also **Health Insurance** below.

One or two afternoons or one day a week (usually Wednesday or Thursday) are free and Saturday morning school is normal in some areas of Switzerland.

Provisions & Equipment

At kindergarten, children usually take a snack for both morning and afternoon breaks (hungry work being a kid). Teachers recommend fruit, vegetable or bread, rather than biscuits or cakes. On their birthdays, children are allowed a treat and it's customary to take a cake for the whole class. (This custom is continued throughout adult life in most of the country and you will notice that many adult Swiss provide cakes on their birthdays.)

Primary school children require a school bag or satchel (usually different for boys and girls, for reasons best known to the Swiss); a pencil case and pencils, etc.; slippers, gym shoes (plimsolls), shorts and a towel for games and exercise periods; and a sports bag for the above if the satchel is too small. (The school bag and pencil case are usually provided by a child's godparents, who play an important role in a Swiss child's life.)

Parents are required to supply all sorts of odds and ends for handicraft lessons, from toilet roll tubes to empty boxes. Keep a junk supply handy if you don't want to be caught short.

Children require hiking boots for their annual school hike (*Schulreise, course d'école*). This entails children getting up in the middle of the night for a 10 to 30km hike (the distance depends on their age) around Switzerland to admire the cows and flowers.

Curriculum & Grading

Most state schools have little extracurricular activity; for example, there are no school clubs or sports teams. If your children want to do team sports, they must join a local club, which means that parents are required to ferry them back and forth for games and social events. In state schools, subsidised music lessons are given, although parents must usually provide the instruments. In some cases, instruments are loaned by the school for a period.

Two or three times a year children receive a school report. Satisfactory progress is graded as 'definitive' and at the end of the school year the child goes up into the next class. If progress is unsatisfactory, a child's report is graded as 'provisional' – two 'provisional' reports means the child must automatically repeat the year. Foreign children who fail to reach a satisfactory standard in the local language must also repeat a year (see **Language** above). Children often repeat a year or even two (the maximum) and there's usually a fairly wide age range in the higher school classes. There's generally no stigma attached to this repetition of classes, though some children resent it. Children, like adults, learn at different speeds and the Swiss school system simply recognises this fact. If a child fails to maintain the required standard in a higher grade secondary school, e.g. a high school, he may be required to join another school with a less demanding curriculum.

Health Insurance

All children are required to belong to a health insurance scheme, which must be specified on the school application form. Some aspects of children's health are supervised or carried out by the school authorities. All Swiss state schools have an extensive programme of vaccinations (inoculations) against polio, diphtheria, tuberculosis, whooping cough, measles, German measles and mumps. If your child has already undergone a course of vaccinations before arrival in Switzerland, you should show the certificates to the school health authorities.

In all primary and some secondary schools, children receive a free annual dental inspection by a school-appointed dentist or your family dentist. An estimate is provided for any dental treatment required and some communities pay a percentage of bills for low-income families. Your health insurance company may also pay a percentage, but only if your child is insured for dental treatment (see page 274).

Schools provide insurance against accidents at school and on the journey to and from school. For this reason, children are required to go by a direct or approved route to school, and if cycling, must use cycle paths to avoid invalidating their insurance policy. Outside these times children should be covered against accidents by your family health insurance policy.

Holidays

The typical state school holiday (*Schulferien, vacances scolaires*) periods are shown below, although the dates and length of holidays vary with the canton:

Month	Length of Holiday
January to March	1 to 2 weeks
April	2 to 3 weeks
July/August	5 to 7 weeks
September/October	1 to 3 weeks
December/January	1 to 2 weeks

Schools are also closed on public holidays (see page 53), if these don't fall within school holiday periods. School holiday dates are published by schools and local communities well in advance, thus allowing you plenty of time to schedule family holidays during official school holidays. For a list of school holidays in all cantons, see 💻 www.edk.ch.

Normally you aren't permitted to withdraw your children from classes at any time during the school term, except for visits to a doctor or dentist, when the teacher should be informed in advance (if possible). In primary school, a note to the teacher is sufficient. In secondary school you must complete an official absence form, which must be signed by the teacher concerned and delivered to the school office. For reasons other than sickness, children are generally allowed only one half day off school each year. Anything longer isn't allowed without written permission, which is difficult to obtain in some areas. If you're refused permission and insist on withdrawing your child from school, **you can be prosecuted and fined or even imprisoned on your return!** Unfortunately some school authorities don't make allowances for families who want to make, for example, a 'once in a lifetime' trip to visit relatives overseas and who are unable to go during official school holidays.

Kindergarten

Attendance at a kindergarten (*Kindergarten, école enfantine/jardin d'enfant*) is voluntary in all cantons except Geneva, where one year is compulsory. Each

© Kevan O'Meara (www.shutterstock.com)

The Matterhorn, Valais
© Susan Vogel-Misicka

© WizData, inc. (www.shutterstock.com)

Lucerne © D. H. Snover (www.shutterstock.com)

Bernese Mountain Dog
© Peter Weber (www.shutterstock.com)

▲ Saanen, Berner Oberland
© Vera Bogaerts (www.shutterstock.com)

◀ © Karen Hadley (www.shutterstock.com)

▲ Swiss Alps, Glarus © Beat Glauser (www.shutterstock.com)

◀ (www.bigstockphoto.com)

▼ Lake ferry © Vladislav Bukin (www.shutterstock.com)

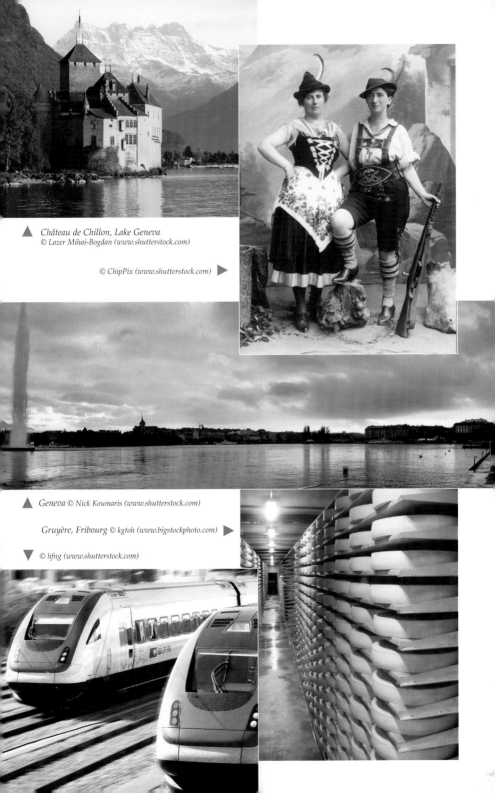

Château de Chillon, Lake Geneva
© Lazer Mihai-Bogdan (www.shutterstock.com)

© ChipPix (www.shutterstock.com) ▶

Geneva © Nick Koumaris (www.shutterstock.com)

Gruyère, Fribourg © kgtoh (www.bigstockphoto.com) ▶

© hfng (www.shutterstock.com)

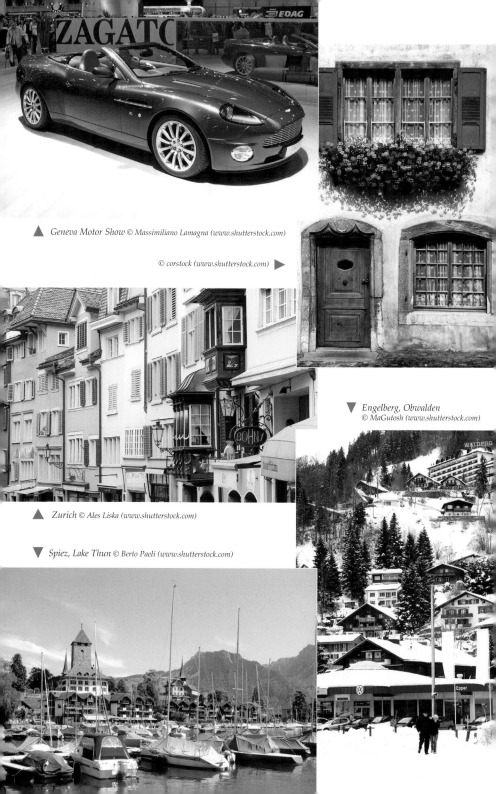

Geneva Motor Show © Massimiliano Lamagna (www.shutterstock.com)

© corstock (www.shutterstock.com) ▶

Engelberg, Obwalden
© MaGutosh (www.shutterstock.com)

Zurich © Ales Liska (www.shutterstock.com)

Spiez, Lake Thun © Berto Paeli (www.shutterstock.com)

community is required to provide a kindergarten for six-year-olds and often takes four- and five-year-olds also, although places may be limited. Kindergarten lasts for two-and-a-half to three hours in the mornings, or two hours both mornings and afternoons. Classes are generally held five days a week, with some afternoons free, or a few mornings only, possibly including Saturdays.

Kindergarten is highly recommended, particularly if your children are going to continue with a state education. After one or two years in kindergarten they're integrated into the local community and have learnt the local language in preparation for primary school. Children are given road safety training by policemen and are provided with reflective clothing to wear to and from kindergarten. Pre-primary school children aren't allowed to ride their bicycles on public roads.

In major cities, private playgroups are available which accept children as young as three (see page 111).

Primary School

In most cantons, children must be six years old before 1st January (or 30th June in some cantons) to start primary school (*Primarschule, école primaire*) the following year. To register your children for primary school, contact your local community in rural areas or your local school commission in cities. This may be unnecessary if your children have attended a local kindergarten. Coeducation (mixed classes) is normal, and primary classes have an average of around 20 pupils and pupils are generally taught all subjects by one teacher.

Primary education lasts from four to six years, depending on the canton, until children are 11 to 13 (in most it's six). When primary school is for six years, classes are split into three grades or steps (*Stufe, degré*). The first two years are termed lower grade (*Unterstufe, premier degré*), the next two years middle grade (*Mittelstufe, deuxième degré*) and the final two years upper grade (*Oberstufe, troisième degré*).

In their first or second year of primary school, children receive bicycle road safety training from local policemen, who may also warn them about the risks of talking to strangers. Children must be seven years old **and** attending primary school before they're allowed on public roads (kindergarten doesn't count, even when a child is already seven). For many young children (and some adults!), a scooter is the vehicle of choice. These are permitted on pavements, which makes them a bit safer traffic-wise (though not for pedestrians), but scooters are hard to steer and pick up speed quickly, so caution is advised.

In the Swiss state school system, a child's marks in his last primary school year usually determine what sort of secondary school he goes to (see below). Children are normally assessed on the average results of tests set by their teacher throughout the year. The most important primary school subjects are the local language, mathematics, local history and geography (*Heimatkunde, histoire et géographie régionales*). While it's important for children to do well in their last primary school year, a child's future education isn't, however, fixed on leaving primary school.

Secondary School

Secondary school (*Sekundarschule, école secondaire*) education in Switzerland lasts for three to seven years, depending on the type of school and the canton. The Swiss secondary school system allows for promotion and demotion, both within a school and from school to school, up to the age of 15 or even later. If your children receive good marks in their last primary school year, they have a better chance of going to an advanced secondary school or high school (*Gymnasium/Kantonalschule, lycée/école cantonale*), possibly leading to a university or technical institute. If you think your child has been incorrectly graded, you can apply for him to take an entrance examination to a higher or lower school.

In some cantons, a so-called *Orientierungsstufe/cycle d'orientation* has been introduced, where pupils of varying ability share the same class, rather than being streamed into different classes. Some main subjects are, however, divided into courses of different grades. The types of secondary school vary from canton to canton; those listed below, based on the structure in Canton Zurich, serve as an example.

- **Secondary modern school** (*Oberschule, école supérieure*) – This type of school provides three years' general education in a practical curriculum that includes woodwork, metalwork and home economics, as a preparation for an apprenticeship in the manual trades. Secondary modern schools are for less academically gifted children, usually around 5 per cent of the total.

- **Technical school** (*Realschule, école technique*) – Technical schools provide three years of more demanding academic education than secondary modern schools but also directed towards training in the manual trades. The second-largest number of children (around 35 per cent) attend a technical school.

- **Secondary school** (*Sekundarschule, école secondaire*) – Secondary schools provide three or more years' education in languages, sciences, geography and history as a preparation for entrance to a higher school. Most children (around 50 per cent) go to a secondary school, many going on to apprenticeships. Some parents prefer to send their children to secondary school, at least for a few years, rather than to a more demanding high school. Many will have an opportunity to attend a high school or vocational school later, when they may be better equipped to handle the curriculum.

- **Pre-high school** (*Progymnasium/Untergymnasium/Bezirks-schule, prégymnasium/lycée inferieur*) – Pre-high school, as the name implies, prepares children for high school in some cantons.

- **High school** (*Gymnasium/Kantonsschule*, *lycée/école cantonale*) – High school education prepares students for a university or technical college education and lasts for six to seven years, when the 'maturity examination' is taken (see below). A written entrance examination in French, German and mathematics is necessary, and only the top students (around 10 per cent of the total) are admitted. Children are on probation for the first three to six months to see how they progress. A Swiss high school provides roughly the same standard of education as an English grammar or high school, but higher than that provided by an American high school or two-year college.

Vocational Schools

The following schools are attended after two or three years in secondary school (with the exception of High School) from the age of 15 or 16. All require students to pass an entrance examination.

- **Commercial or business school** (*Handelsmittelschule*, *école de commerce*) – provide three years' training (federally recognised) for a commercial diploma and a good basic grounding for a business career, but also useful for a career in social work, nursing or as an interpreter;

- **Teacher training school** (*Lehramtschule/Unterseminar*, *école normale*) – The course lasts four to five years and qualifies only primary school teachers. Entrance qualifications vary and training may include a two- to three-year practical period. Training for secondary school teaching (two to three years) and higher school teaching (four to five years) is undertaken at university.

- **Diploma middle school** (*Diplommittelschule*, *école professionelle*) – a three-year preparatory school for kindergarten teachers, nurses and medical technicians.

Maturity Examination

Students at a high school study for the maturity (*Matura*, *maturité*) examination, usually consisting one of six syllabuses. If they pass the maturity examination, they obtain the maturity diploma (*Maturitätsdiplom*, *diplôme de maturité*). All students generally study French, German, mathematics, geography, history, biology, physics, chemistry and music or art. Other subjects depend on the syllabus chosen and are typically as follows:

- **Syllabus A** – Classical languages (Latin and Greek compulsory);

- **Syllabus B** – Latin plus English or Italian;

Understand more about living in Switzerland

Understand the language:

Get to grips with Swiss German in a fun way! Hoi contains over 200 cartoons and a handy phrase book & dictionary.

Hoi – your Swiss German survival guide
by Sergio J. Lievano & Nicole Egger
200 colour illustrations, 168 pages, paperback, CHF 29.80

Understand the culture:

This book will help you make sense of Swiss culture and avoid tricky situations at home and in the workplace.

Beyond Chocolate – understanding Swiss Culture
by Margaret Oertig-Davidson
Illustrated, 240 pages, paperback CHF 38.00

Understand Switzerland for children:

Your whole family can discover what Switzerland is all about. Chock full of cartoons and facts to help kids of all ages quickly feel at home.

Ticking Along with Swiss Kids
by Dianne Dicks & Katalin Fekete
Illustrated, 128 pages, hardback, CHF 34.00

Contact us for a free catalog and information about events at the Bergli Bookshop in Basel:

books

Bergli Books & Bookshop
Rümelinsplatz 19, 4001 Basel, Switzerland
Tel.: +41 61 373 27 77, Fax: +41 373 27 78
e-mail: info@bergli.ch   www.bergli.ch

- **Syllabus C** – mathematics, sciences and descriptive geometry; English or Italian are compulsory;

- **Syllabus D** – modern languages; German, French and English are compulsory, plus Italian, Spanish or Russian;

- **Syllabus E** – economics, including science of industrial management and political economy and social sciences; English or Italian are compulsory.

- **Syllabus M** – music and art as a preparation for academies of music and the other arts.

Some cantons have given up the traditional syllabi and now allow students to choose their own subjects within a certain range. However, in most cases German, French, mathematics and sciences are still compulsory.

All European universities and most American colleges recognise the Swiss maturity diploma as an entrance qualification, although foreign students must provide proof of their English language ability to study in the UK or the US.

PRIVATE SCHOOLS

Switzerland is famous for the quality and variety of its some 600 private day and boarding schools (*Privatschulen, écoles privées*). Schools cater for as few as 20 to as many as 2,000 pupils – a total of around 100,000, two-thirds of whom are Swiss. Fees vary considerably according to (among other things) the quality, reputation and location of the school. Day school fees vary from around SFr. 5,000 to 25,000 per year (e.g. the International School of Basle charges the latter fee), while annual boarding school fees are anywhere between SFr. 25,000 and 65,000.

Fees aren't all-inclusive and extra obligatory charges are made – e.g. for clothing, health and accident insurance, text books and stationary. Some schools charge parents for every little thing. There may be additional optional charges, e.g. for outings, and you may have to provide items such as art supplies and sports equipment. (Some schools will even arrange to have your child met at Geneva or Zurich airport and conducted by private plane and chauffeured limousine to school – for a price.) Most private schools have an entrance examination, e.g. in English and mathematics, plus an IQ test.

Private schools have a more relaxed, less rigid regime and curriculum than Swiss state schools. They provide a more varied and international approach to sport, culture and art, and a wider choice of academic subjects. Their aim is the development of the child as an individual and the encouragement of his unique talents, rather than teaching on a 'production line' system. This is made possible by small classes that allow teachers to provide pupils with individually tailored lessons and tuition.

The results speak for themselves and many private secondary schools have a near 100 per cent postgraduate university placement rate. Private school pupils are more likely to question rules and regulations (no wonder most Swiss prefer to send their children to state schools!), be open-minded, express themselves more spontaneously, and be more aware of world problems and politics.

You should make applications to private schools as far in advance as possible. You're usually asked to send previous school reports, exam results and records. Before enrolling your child in a private school, make sure that you understand the withdrawal conditions in the school contract. **Not all Swiss private schools live up to the reputed high standards and there are a number of schools that simply cash in on the good reputation of the best schools.** Always use the utmost caution when selecting a school and don't accept what's stated in the school brochure or prospectus at face value. The checklist below will help you choose an appropriate private school and avoid the charlatans.

A booklet entitled *Private Schools in Switzerland*, containing a complete list of private day and boarding schools in Switzerland, is available for free from the Swiss Federation of Private Schools (SFPS) Hotelgasse 1, PO Box 245, 3000 Bern 7 (☎ 031 328 40 50, 🖳 www.swiss-schools.ch), which represents some 260 schools. For detailed research on private schools (in German only) including a copy of the Federation's annual booklet, *Privatschulen*, see also 🖳 www.privatschulverzeichnis.com.

You may prefer to send your children to an international school (see below) or private day school across the border, for example in France. Alternatively you can send them to a boarding school in Switzerland or abroad, e.g. in the UK or the US.

International Schools

There are international primary and secondary day schools in or close to all major cities in Switzerland, where demand exceeds supply. One of the main advantages of an international school is that lessons are generally conducted in English, though there are also French-speaking international schools in Geneva and in recent years, private bilingual primary schools teaching in English/French or English/German have become more widespread and popular. There are also private schools in Switzerland for children with special language requirements other than English, for example the Japanese School in Zurich.

International schools offer curricula designed for a wide variety of examinations including the Swiss maturity examination (see page 163), British A-Levels, the French *baccalauréat*, the German Abitur and the Italian Maturita. Many international schools offer curricula tailored to the American college entrance CEEB and British GCSE examinations, and may also offer the International Bacclaureate (*Bakkalaureat*, *baccalauréat*) school leaving certificate, an internationally recognised university entrance qualification. **Note that some Swiss international schools have examinations that are**

recognised everywhere except in Switzerland, where they aren't accepted for entry to Swiss universities.

Another negative aspect of international schools, apart from the high fees, it's usually the high pupil turnover. This can have an adverse effect on some children, particularly when close friendships are severed. Some international schools have pupils from as many as 80 countries.

Choosing a Private School

The following checklist is designed to help you choose an appropriate and reputable private school in Switzerland:

● Does the school have a good reputation? How long has it been established? Does it belong to one of the Swiss private school associations?

● Does the school have a good academic record? For example, what percentage of pupils obtain good examination passes or go on to good universities? All the best schools provide exam pass rate statistics.

● How large are the classes and what is the student/teacher ratio? Does the class size tally with the number of desks in the classrooms?

● What are the qualification requirements for teachers? What nationality are the majority of teachers? Ask for a list of the teaching staff and their qualifications.

● What are the classrooms like? For example, their size, space, cleanliness, lighting, furniture and furnishings. Are there signs of creative teaching, e.g. wall charts, maps, posters and students' work on display?

● What is the teacher turnover? A high turnover is a bad sign and may suggest underpaid and poorly motivated teachers and poor working conditions.

● What extras must you pay?

● Which countries do most students come from?

● Is religion an important consideration in your choice of school?

● Are special English classes provided for children whose English (or other language) doesn't meet the required standard?

● What standard and type of accommodation is provided?

● What is the quality and variety of food provided? What is the dining room like? Does the school have a dietician?

● What languages does the school teach as obligatory or optional subjects?

● What is the student turnover?

- What are the school terms and holiday periods? Private school holidays are usually much longer than state schools, e.g. four weeks at Easter and Christmas and ten weeks in the summer, and often don't coincide with state school holiday periods.

- If you're considering a day school, what are the school hours?

- What are the withdrawal conditions, should you need or wish to remove your child? A term's notice is usual.

- What does the curriculum include? What examinations are set? Are examinations recognised both in Switzerland and internationally? Do they fit in with your long-term education plans? Ask to see a typical pupil timetable to check the ratio of academic/non-academic subjects. Check the number of free study periods and whether they're supervised.

- What sports instruction and facilities are provided? Where are the sports facilities located?

- What are the facilities for art and science subjects, for example arts and crafts, music, computer studies, biology, science, hobbies, drama, cookery and photography? Ask to see the classrooms, facilities, equipment and some of the students' projects.

- What sort of outings and holidays does the school organise and are they included in the fees?

- What medical facilities does the school provide, e.g. infirmary, resident doctor or nurse? Is medical and accident insurance included in the fees?

- What sort of punishments are applied and for what offences?

- What reports are provided for parents and how often?

- Last but not least (unless someone else is paying), what are the fees?

Before making a final choice, it's important to visit the schools on your shortlist during term time and talk to teachers and students, and if possible, former students and their parents. **Where possible, check the answers to the above questions in person and don't rely on the school's prospectus to provide the information.** If you're unhappy with the answers, look elsewhere. Finally, having made your choice, keep a check on your child's progress and listen to his complaints. Compare notes with other parents. If something doesn't seem right, try to establish whether the complaint is founded or not and, if it is, take action to have the problem resolved. Don't forget that you or your employer is paying a lot of money for your child's education and you should demand value for money. See also **State or Private School?** on page 152.

HOLIDAY CAMPS

Holiday camps (*Ferienlager, camps de vacances*) for children are organised during school holidays throughout the year. These include both day and residential camps run by private and state schools, clubs and organisations (e.g. youth organisations, scouts and brownies), churches and private organisations. Activities include skiing, swimming and various other sports; excursions; arts and crafts; and academic subjects. Most camps are reasonably priced. 'Club Migros' (*Klubschule Migros, école club Migros*) has a summer and autumn holiday centre: Milandia, Migros Sport- und Erlebnispark Grossried, CH-8606 Greifensee (☎ 044 905 66 66, 💻 www.milandia.ch).

Most cantons organise a variety of sports courses during summer holidays. Village Camps (14, Rue de la Morâche, CH-1260 Nyon, ☎ 022 990 94 00, 💻 www.villagecamps.com) is one of the largest Swiss operators of summer and winter camps (both in Switzerland and in other European countries) for boys and girls aged 8 to 18. Eurocamp Travel AG (Diessenhoferstr. 14, CH-8252 Schlatt, ☎ 052 646 01 01, 💻 www.eurocamp.ch) operates family holiday camps throughout Europe.

Ask your school or community office for information about holiday camps. A list of children's camps is available from offices of Pro Juventute (see your telephone directory), which also runs holiday camps for the disabled.

APPRENTICESHIPS

Around 70 per cent of young people in Switzerland undertake an apprenticeship or vocational training. A Swiss apprenticeship (*Lehre, apprentissage*) is a combination of on-the-job training and further education, where one or two days a week are spent at a training college and the remainder in the workplace. The syllabus for both schoolwork and practical training is co-ordinated by the Federal Office for Education and Technology. There are plans to introduce a new scheme where apprentices do a year of theoretical education in school followed by two years of practical work.

An apprenticeship lasts from two to four years and can be in almost any vocation, for example waitressing, secretarial work, cooking, plumbing and chimney sweeping. The employer pays a small salary that increases with age and experience, and he may pay for apprenticeship schooling and the cost of travel to and from school. An apprentice has five weeks' holiday a year. School careers officers are available to advise parents and students on a choice of career.

The Swiss apprenticeship system is one of the best in the world. It isn't for failures or students who aren't sufficiently academically gifted to go to high school or university (many successful businessmen and politicians in Switzerland were apprentices). If desired, it's possible to go on to higher education later, for example at a college of technology or a university, after completion of, or even during an apprenticeship. Around 12 cantons pay a vocational training allowance of between SFr. 150 and 450 for children who are in full-time education or training.

You may also be interested in the activities of Intermundo, the Swiss umbrella association for many international youth exchange organisations. There are 14 member organisations, all of which are non-profit with no political or religious ties. Exchanges are organised worldwide to further cultural understanding, provide work and practical experience, and learn languages. Participants vary in age from 15 to over 30, depending on the particular exchange programme. Exchanges can last from one week to one year. For further information contact Intermundo (Gerechtigkeitsgasse 12, PO Box, CH-3000 Berne 8, ☎ 031 326 29 20, 🖳 www.intermundo.ch).

Many books are published in Switzerland detailing career possibilities for school leavers. One such book is *Studieren und dann?*, *Carrefour Uni* (*Study and then?/University Crossroads*) published in both French and German by AGAB (Bleichemattstr. 15, CH-5000 Aarau, ☎ 062 823 57 30, 🖳 www.agab.ch).

HIGHER EDUCATION

Around 30 per cent of Swiss attend one of Switzerland's higher educational establishments, which is slightly below average for OECD countries. The country has ten universities (*Universität, université*), in Basle, Berne, Fribourg, Geneva, Lausanne, Lucerne, Neuchâtel, St. Gallen, Ticino and Zurich, plus two Federal

Institutes of Technology, in Lausanne (EPFL) and Zurich (ETHZ). In addition, there are a number of schools for applied sciences (business and technical) under the name of *Fachhochschule/haute école spécialiséé*. These are open to students who may not have a maturity or similar qualification but have completed a three- or four-year apprenticeship and obtained a federal diploma.

The minimum age for enrolment is 18 and university education lasts for at least four years, but there's no fixed study period for a degree and students may take as long as they like – up to nine years to complete a degree is common.

All Swiss higher education facilities, including several technical colleges, are open to foreign students, who comprise around 20 per cent of the total intake. There are usually quotas for foreign students and the number of places available is strictly limited at some universities and for particular courses, e.g. medicine. Foreigners with a B permit (see page 67) are always subject to foreign student quotas and those with a C permit (see page 67) are accepted only they've attended a Swiss state school for a number of years.

The maturity examination (see page 163) is the usual entrance requirement for Swiss nationals and foreigners who have studied in Switzerland. A Swiss university may accept three British A-Level passes but an American high school diploma isn't usually accepted; American students usually require a minimum of a BA, BBA or BSc degree. All foreign students require a thorough knowledge of the language of study (French or German), which is usually examined unless a certificate is provided. A Swiss university degree (*Lizenziat, licence*) is, on an academic scale, somewhere between a British BA or MA (or an American MA) and a doctorate (PhD). Swiss universities are currently adapting their curricula to the Bologna system and switching to the BA and MA system.

Fees, which are between SFr. 500 to 2,000 per year, are payable each term or semester and there's usually a higher fee rate for foreign students, although students (or their parents) who have been residents and taxpayers for at least two years in the canton where the university is located pay the Swiss rate. Scholarships and student low-interest loans may be available to foreigners after completion of four terms (semesters) and fees may be reduced after the tenth term. Cantons without their own universities must pay fees for students studying in another canton, but fees for foreign students are usually partly subsidised by the federal government.

Although fees have increased in recent years, it's mainly the high cost of living that makes studying in Switzerland expensive. For example, in Geneva the authorities recommend a minimum of around SFr. 1,500 to 2,000 per month for accommodation and food, plus university and local taxes, and health insurance (compulsory for university students). **Parents are legally obliged to support their children during their full-time education in Switzerland** and not surprisingly, many students go on living with their parents until they've finished their degree courses. For those who don't live at home, student accommodation is available in university cities.

FURTHER EDUCATION

Switzerland has over 50 private colleges and university-level institutions, many affiliated to foreign (often American) universities. These include business and commercial colleges, hotel and tourism schools, and the world-famous Swiss finishing schools for young ladies. Fees at finishing schools are around SFr. 50,000 per year and students are usually aged from 16 to around 24. The traditional training in French cooking, domestic science, floral art, etiquette and savoir vivre is nowadays supplemented by courses in commerce, languages and catering.

Study in all further education establishments is in small groups and may be full or part time, including summer courses. Many schools offer an American Master of Business Administration (MBA) course and subjects may include banking, communications, economics, European languages, information systems, management, marketing, public relations, and social and political studies.

Switzerland is also renowned for its hotel and restaurant training schools (where classes are often taught in English), widely recognised as the best in the world. These include the world-famous Swiss Hotel School in Lausanne, where parents enrol their children 'at birth' to ensure a place.

Tuition costs are high and study periods strictly organised. Most establishments have a good reputation, particularly in the business world.

The Federation of Swiss Private Schools (Verband Schweizerischer Privatschulen, Fédération Suisse des Écoles Privées) publishes a booklet entitled *Private Schools in Switzerland* containing the names of many further education establishments in Switzerland. It's available from Switzerland Tourism (ST, 🖳 www.myswitzerland.com), Swiss embassies and consulates, and from the Verband Schweizerischer Privatschulen (see **Private Schools** on page 165). A list of institutes of higher education and hotel and tourism schools is available from ST. See also **Day & Evening Classes** on page 312 and Intermundo under **Apprenticeships** on page 171.

LANGUAGE SCHOOLS

If you don't speak the local language fluently, you may wish to take a language course. It's possible, even for the most non-linguistic person, to acquire a working knowledge of French, German or Italian. All that's required is a little help and some perseverance – or a lot of perseverance if you're surrounded by English-speaking colleagues and only have English-speaking friends! A big handicap for English-speakers in Switzerland is that there's often someone around who speaks English (even on top of a mountain), particularly when you want to practise the local language. Don't get caught in the trap of seeking

refuge in the English language or allowing others to practise their English at your expense. You must persist in speaking the local language; give in too easily and you will never learn. **Most foreigners in Switzerland find that their business and social enjoyment and success is directly related to the degree to which they master the local language(s).**

There are language schools (*Sprachschule, école de langues*) in all cities and large towns. Most schools offer various classes depending on your language ability, how many hours you wish to study a week, how much money you want to invest, and how quickly you wish (or reasonably expect) to learn. Some Swiss employers provide free in-house language classes or pay their employees' course fees (corporate courses for executives and managers are big business).

Courses generally fall into three categories. 'Extensive' courses involve between 4 and 15 hours' training a week and 'intensive' courses from 15 to 30 hours'. For those for whom money is no object (hopefully your employer), there are 'total immersion' (i.e. sink-or-swim) courses for two to six weeks, where you study from 8am to 5pm, five days a week. The cost for a Berlitz two-week total immersion course is around SFr. 13,000. At the other end of the scale, free language courses are available in some cities, e.g. at the Worker's and Popular universities in Geneva.

Don't expect to become fluent in a short period unless you have a particular flair for languages or already have a good command of a language. Unless you need to learn a language quickly, it's better to arrange your lessons over a long period. However, don't commit yourself to a long course of study (particularly an expensive one) before ensuring that it's the right course. Most schools offer free tests to help you find your level and a free introductory lesson, and a choice between small groups or individual tuition.

Among the cheapest language schools is Migros Club School (🖳 www.klubschule.ch), a subsidiary of the Migros supermarket chain. Migros offers inexpensive evening courses at all levels, usually consisting of two two-hour sessions per week. The People's High School (*Volkshochschule, université populaire* – 🖳 www.up-vhs.ch), Coop leisure centres (*Coop Freizeit Center, centre de loisirs Coop*) and various voluntary organisations (e.g. FAWCO – 🖳 www.fawco.org – see page 81) also run inexpensive classes. Many language schools run inexpensive classes designed for au pairs. **However, the quality of language teaching is extremely variable and many schools hire 'teachers' without formal training.**

You may prefer to have private lessons, which are a quicker but more expensive way of learning a language. The main advantage of private lessons is that you learn at your own speed and aren't held back by slow learners or left floundering in the wake of the class genius. You can advertise for a teacher in your local newspapers, on shopping centre bulletin boards or university notice boards, and through your or your spouse's employer. Your friends or colleagues may also be able to help you find a suitable private teacher or choose a language school.

Swiss universities hold summer language courses and many holiday language courses are organised (summer and winter) throughout Switzerland for children and young adults aged up to 25. Switzerland Tourism (ST) publish a brochure entitled *Holidays and Language Courses* listing summer language courses in English, French, German, Italian, Romansch and Spanish. Eurocentres (Seestrasse 247, CH-8038 Zurich, ☎ 044 485 50 40, 💻 www.eurocenters.com), operated by a Swiss charitable foundation, offer reasonably priced intensive language courses both in Switzerland and other countries, inclusive of accommodation with a local family. If you already speak the local language(s) but need conversational practice, you may wish to enrol in a course at an institute or local club, for example pottery, painting or photography (see **Day & Evening Classes** on page 312). For further information about languages in Switzerland, see **Languages** on page 38 and on page 156.

Swiss German

It's rarely necessary for foreigners to master Swiss German (*Schwyzertüütsch, suisse allemand* – see page 39), although you may find yourself excluded from everyday life in German-speaking Switzerland if you don't understand it. You will find that speaking Swiss German opens doors, both in business and socially, and is particularly important if you plan to settle permanently in a German-speaking area of Switzerland or are thinking of applying for Swiss citizenship.

Opinion is divided over whether it's an advantage to speak High German before attempting to learn Swiss German. If your High German is poor, learning Swiss German won't help you speak, read or write High German and may even be a hindrance. There are a significant number of foreigners in Switzerland who can speak Swiss German reasonably fluently but are unable to speak, read or write High German properly.

The Federation for Swiss German (Verein Schweizerdeutsch) organises Swiss German classes (in local dialects!) in Basle, Winterthur, Zurich and occasionally Zug and insists that all students have a good command of High German before enrolling in courses. For information contact Dr. Alfred Egli, Unt. Heslibachstr. 1, CH-8700 Küsnacht (☎ 044 910 73 78). The Migros Club School (*Klubschule Migros, école club Migros*) and People's High School (*Volkshochschule, université populaire*) also run Swiss German classes in many areas (see above and **Day & Evening Classes** on page 312).

Various books are available for students of Swiss German including *Schwyzertüütsch* by Arthur Baur (Gemsberg Verlag, Winterthur), *Dialect and High German in German Speaking Switzerland* by Alfred Wyler (Pro Helvetia) and *Hoi, your Swiss German survival guide* by Sergio J. Lievano and Nicole Egger (Bergli Books).

10.

PUBLIC TRANSPORT

Public transport services (*öffentlicher Verkehr, transport public*) in Switzerland are excellent and provide a frequent, convenient and inexpensive service to every corner of the country. The government firmly believes that the benefits of a first class public transport system far outweigh the cost, even if it means increased public subsidies (although costs are causing concern). All modes of public transport are highly efficient, completely integrated, clean and usually punctual to the minute (among the most reliable clocks in Switzerland are those at railway stations).

With some 24,500km (around 15,300mi) of fixed transport lines (trains, trams, trolley-buses and cableways), Switzerland has the densest public transport network in the world. It isn't essential to own a car in Switzerland, particularly if you live in or near a large town or city. For example, Zurich has one of the world's best public transport systems, which even includes the loan of bicycles. This is verified by the frequency of use by its citizens, which is double the average in other major European cities. However, if you live in a remote village or a town off the main train and bus routes, you will find it more convenient or even essential to have your own transport.

On first acquaintance, Swiss public transport may seem expensive to some foreigners. However, if you take advantage of the often bewildering range of discounts and season tickets available, public transport provides excellent value and is often a bargain (particularly in relation to Swiss salaries).

If you find all the different tickets for buses and trains bewildering, it's hardly surprising. With such an abundance of season and discounted tickets, the only thing you can be sure of is that unless you're travelling free, you're probably paying too much! The solution is simply to tell the ticket office clerk where you want to go, when and how often you want to travel, and (for train journeys) whether first or second class. You can generally rely on him to provide you with the cheapest ticket available – unless it's his first day on the job, in which case he will be just as confused as you are!

Even greater savings can be made with tickets combining travel on different public transport systems, e.g. railways, buses and trams. For example, there's a 'junior' card (*Junior-Karte, carte junior*), which is valid for one year and entitles children aged up to 16 to travel free when accompanied by a parent. The parent may have a full-fare or half-fare ticket, but not a commuter ticket. The junior card can be used on all SBB trains, private railways, PostBuses and lake steamers. It can also be used in around 35 towns to purchase city bus and tram day-cards under the same conditions as for trains. Junior cards are available from railway stations (and PostBus depots) for SFr. 20 for the first and second children, free for subsequent children. A junior card must be signed and dated by the holder. Other discounted tickets and passes are detailed below.

Any journey by rail, boat or PostBus (see page 192) may be broken without cost or formality, provided your ticket remains valid. It's advisable to notify the conductor when planning to break your journey, however, or he may retain or cancel your ticket.

HOLIDAY & VISITORS' TICKETS

Visitors to Switzerland and Swiss residents travelling within Europe can buy a range of discounted holiday and visitors' tickets and passes. One of the most interesting journeys for visitors is the 'Golden Pass' taking in Lucerne, Interlaken, Zweisimmen and Montreux, while another is the Lake Geneva region pass which includes railways, funiculars and boats of the Lake Geneva Shipping Company. **Note that some tickets are valid only if your permanent residence is outside Switzerland.** A useful brochure for visitors entitled *Discover Switzerland by Train, Bus and Boat*, is published by the SBB.

Swiss Pass

Visitors to Switzerland can buy a Swiss Pass (🖥 www.swisstravelsystem.ch), which provides unlimited travel by rail, PostBuses and ferries throughout the country, plus buses and trams in 38 towns and cities. There are also reductions on many mountain railways and aerial cableways. It's available outside Switzerland at Switzerland Tourism (ST) offices and travel agents', and in Switzerland at international airports and at a few main railway stations, on production of your passport or identity card. A Swiss Pass is available only to those with their permanent residence outside Switzerland and Liechtenstein.

The prices of a Swiss Pass are as follows:

Age	Validity	Cost	
		1st Class	2nd Class
Over 26	4 days	SFr. 383	SFr. 255
	8 days	SFr. 552	SFr. 368
	15 days	SFr. 669	SFr. 446
	22 days	SFr. 771	SFr. 514
	1 month	SFr. 849	SFr. 566
16 to 26	4 days	SFr. 288	SFr. 192
	8 days	SFr. 414	SFr. 276
	15 days	SFr. 502	SFr. 335
	22 days	SFr. 579	SFr. 386
	1 month	SFr. 637	SFr. 425

As a Swiss Pass holder you can obtain a free junior card, which allows children aged from 6 to 16 to travel free when accompanied by a parent with a Swiss Card (see below) or a Swiss Pass/Swiss Flexi Pass. There's a 15 per cent discount for two or more people travelling together.

When you arrive in Switzerland with a Swiss Pass, for example at an international airport, you must have it validated (stamped and dated) at the SBB desk.

Swiss Flexi Pass

A Swiss Flexi Pass allows between three and eight days' unlimited travel within one month. It also offers a 15 per cent discount for two or more people travelling together. The costs for adults are shown below; children pay half these rates.

Validity	Cost	
	1st Class	2nd Class
3 days	SFr. 366	SFr. 244
4 days	SFr. 444	SFr. 296
5 days	SFr. 513	SFr. 342
6 days	SFr. 584	SFr. 389
8 days	SFr. 683	SFr. 455

Swiss Transfer Ticket

The Swiss Transfer Ticket provides you with return travel from the Swiss border or a Swiss airport to any railway station in Switzerland. It's valid for up to one month and costs SFr. 124 second class and SFr. 188 first class. It's available only abroad. Be sure to check the regular fares before buying a Transfer Ticket, especially if your journey is short; a single second-class ticket from Zurich Airport to Lucerne, for example, costs just SFr. 26.

Swiss Card

The Swiss Card provides return travel from the Swiss border to any hotel in Switzerland, plus unlimited half-fare travel on Swiss federal railways (SBB), PostBuses and ferries for a period of one month. It can be purchased at the same locations abroad as the Swiss Pass (see above), but not in Switzerland. The cost for an adult is SFr. 178 (second class) and SFr. 250 (first class).

Rail Passes

A range of rail passes is available to visitors to Europe and Swiss residents travelling in Europe. These include Euro Domino (three- to eight-day passes) and BIJ Wasteels (under 26-year-olds) passes. RailPlus, for seniors, costs SFr. 25 per year and provides a 25 per cent reduction on all rail travel.

A range of Eurail passes allowing travel in 25 countries is available for those with their permanent residence outside Europe, including the Eurailpass, the Eurail Flexipass, the Eurail Selectpass and the Europass.

The Inter-Rail Pass (💻 www.interrailnet.com) is valid for 5, 10 or 22 days or one month and is available to children and adults. It allows rail travel in 30 European countries (including the UK and Ireland) plus Morocco and also provides discounts of up to 50 per cent in the country where it's purchased. Passes for adults cost between SFr. 399 and 1,295, depending on validity and class; children's passes are half price. Youth passes (under 26) cost SFr. 255 to 639 (second class only). Inter-Rail passes are better value than Eurail passes and are available to those who have their permanent residence in Europe, but they must be purchased in your country of residence.

A free Eurail/Inter-Rail timetable is available from offices selling Eurail passes, plus a wide range of brochures and maps.

An excellent book for European rail travellers is *Europe by Train* by Katie Woods (Ebury Press). It covers accommodation, visas, food, sights, customs and even the idiosyncrasies of local transport. *Europe by Eurail* by George and Laverne Ferguson (Globe Pequot) provides tips on how to plan a European tour using a rail pass or other tourist tickets, making day trips from selected base cities. Thomas Cook Publications (UK ☎ 01733-416477, 💻 www.thomas-cookpublishing.com) publishes a wide range of books, guides and maps for train travellers including a *Railpass Guide*, *European Timetable* (includes rail and shipping services), *Rail Map of Europe* and the *Overseas Timetable* (rail, bus and shipping services outside Europe).

TRAINS

The Swiss railway network is one of the most extensive in Europe, with around 5,000km (3,100mi) of track (almost all electrified), nearly 2,000 stations and some 700 tunnels. It includes 2,000km (1,240mi) of private lines operated by some 50 'private' companies – they aren't strictly private as many are run by canton governments. The Swiss federal railway company is usually referred to by its initials, which vary according to the local language: SBB (Schweizerische

Bundesbahnen) in German (and used in this book to refer to the Swiss federal railways), CFF (Chemins de Fer Fédéraux) in French and FFS (Ferrovie Federali Svizzere) in Italian.

The SBB, which celebrated its 160th anniversary in 2007, is renowned for its punctuality (although building or maintenance work and bad weather occasionally delay trains), comfort and speed, the only disadvantage being that the speed of some trains doesn't allow time to admire Switzerland's beauty (if you're sightseeing, make sure you catch a slow train).

Despite frequent fare increases in recent years to try to reduce SBB's deficit, Swiss trains remain inexpensive if you take advantage of offers, excursion fares, family reductions and holiday package deals. Over long distances, trains are cheaper than buses. The Swiss are Europe's most frequent train travellers and average around 1,900km (1,188mi) per year per head of population.

Trains are categorised as local trains (*Regionalzug/Lokalzug, train régional*), fast trains (*Schnellzug, train direct*) and international trains. Fast trains include Intercity (IC) and InterCity Express (ICE), which serve the main Swiss cities; fast regional trains, called RegioExpress, operating in some areas, e.g. between St. Gallen and Chur; S-Bahn (S is short for *schnell* or fast) suburban trains in many areas of Switzerland including Zurich. Eurocity trains (see below) also offer services between Swiss towns. Most Swiss trains consist of first- and second-class carriages.

For travel between Switzerland and the rest of Europe, there are several options:

● Eurocity (EC) trains, which serve over 200 European cities and mostly have sleeping cars and cars with seats that convert into berths (*couchettes*);

● CityNightLine (CNL) sleeper trains to several European destinations;

● French high-speed trains (*Hochgeschwindigkeitsbahn, Train à Grande Vitesse/TGV*) with daily services from Basle, Berne, Geneva, Lausanne/Neuchâtel and Zurich to Paris and southern France, at speeds of up to 320kph (200mph) – Geneva to Paris takes around three-and-a-half hours;

● Cisalpino's *Pendolino* (tilting) trains connecting major Swiss towns with major Italian cities at up to 200kph (120mph);

● German ICE high-speed trains linking Interlaken and Zurich with cities throughout Germany.

As if this weren't enough, Switzerland is building two new high-speed rail tunnels through the Alps to carry heavy goods and passengers – the New Transalpine Railway Project (*Neue Eisenbahnalpentransversalen/NEAT*) is expected to be operational in 2011 at an estimated cost of around SFr. 16bn.

A supplement is payable by all domestic passengers using EC trains and booking (costing SFr. 5) is obligatory for international travel. Booking is optional on IC and many domestic fast trains, though recommended when travelling during holiday periods or over weekends. Bookings can be made from 24 hours to two months in advance (up to three months for compartments in sleeping cars).

In addition to the SBB, there are many small private railways in Switzerland. Among the most interesting, for train enthusiasts and tourists alike, is the Glacier Express, the slowest 'express' in the world (average speed 20mph/12.5mi). It runs from St. Moritz to Zermatt and negotiates 291 bridges and 91 tunnels during its 7.5-hour journey (the Swiss make holes in both their mountains and their cheeses). The Montreux Oberland Bernese (MOB) railway from Montreux to Zweisimmen/Lenk/Lucerne is first class only, with ultra-modern panoramic or 'superpanoramic' express carriages (coaches) and a saloon bar carriage. The Bernina express from Chur to Tirano in Italy, has the highest (2,253m/7,390ft) railway traverse in the Alps and provides a unique and beautiful experience. Information about steam train services is published by Switzerland Tourism (ST), including its brochure *Schweizer Ferien mit Dampf und Nostalgie*.

On most public and private trains carriages (and sometimes the whole train!) can be chartered for special occasions (at a price). Alternatively, you can charter a 'Vista Dome Car' and have it hooked onto most scheduled trains to improve your view of the passing countryside. You can even charter the Orient Express! An excellent book for train buffs is *Switzerland: Rail, Road, Lake* by Anthony Lambert (Bradt Publications).

The following general information apply to Swiss rail services:

- All Swiss Intercity and long-distance trains provide a mobile drinks-and-snacks service, and most have a snack bar and/or restaurant car (some self-service). Restaurant cars are denoted by a crossed fork and knife on timetables.

- The SBB has a 'silent carriage' on each train, where mobile phones, noisy music (with or without headphones) and loud conversation are banned.

- A person or guide dog accompanying a disabled or blind person travels free of charge but needs an SBB pass. The disabled or blind person must be a Swiss resident and have a medical certificate and an official identity card for disabled passengers issued by a canton authority.

- Dogs are permitted to travel in passenger carriages and require a second-class ticket (season tickets are also available), which is also valid in first class. Small dogs – up to 30cm (12in) at the shoulder – travel free when carried in baskets.

- The SBB runs a Junior-Club SBB (🖥 www.magicticket.ch) for children aged 6 to 16, offering reductions on excursions and a bi-annual magazine.

- Rail journeys can be combined with travel on local buses, PostBuses and boats.

- A 'playroom car' for children, denoted by an illustration of a boy and a girl wearing sunglasses on the outside of the carriage, is provided on many routes. Look for the letters 'FA' next to the time on SBB timetables. Playroom cars contain a central play area (free for families with children aged 2 to 12) equipped with a slide, swing, 'fairy-tale' telephones, books and games. They also have a nappy-changing room and folding seats to allow space for prams and push chairs.

Further information about Swiss rail services is available by telephone (☎ 0900 30 03 00 – calls cost SFr. 1.19 per minute) and via the internet (🖳 www.sbb.ch).

Stations

The following facilities can be found at Swiss railway stations:

- Many main railway stations offer a choice of restaurants and snack bars, generally providing good food at reasonable prices.

- Major stations have a 'RailCity' shopping centre with long opening hours, including Sundays and public holidays. Shops in the vicinity of most stations (within around 200m) tend to have long opening times, too.

- Many large railway stations provide wash, shower and brush-up facilities (branded, sadly, 'McClean'), including hair-dryers (there's a fee). Some provide nappy (diaper) changing rooms.

- There are instant passport photograph machines at most stations.

- Park and ride car parks are provided at many railway stations, where you can park from around SFr. 5 per day, depending on the station.

- Wheelchairs for disabled passengers are provided at many railway stations. Most trains have facilities for the storage of wheelchairs and new trains have carriages that accommodate wheelchairs. The SBB publishes a brochure entitled 'Passengers with a Disability' (available only in German). There's also a hotline for disabled travellers (☎ 0800 00 71 02).

- Main railway stations have banks with long opening hours and many smaller stations provide money changing facilities. At many stations you can buy and sell foreign currencies, buy Swiss franc travellers' cheques and cash travellers' cheques.

- Most information regarding the SBB is available in French, German, and Italian at railway stations.

- Bicycles can be hired from many railway stations and transported on trains (see **Bicycle Hire & Transportation** on page 319). Bicycle and moped parking, both covered and uncovered, is provided at most stations.

Information regarding trains (and tickets) is available from information offices (denoted by a blue letter 'i' in a white circle on a blue background) at major stations or the ticket office at smaller stations. Finally, if you want to encourage someone to visit you, you can send them SBB travel gift vouchers.

Luggage

Three items of luggage can be carried on a train without charge – officially with a combined weight of no more than 30kg, although nobody checks or weighs it. However, the SBB has many ways of lightening your load (and taking a load off your mind) when travelling with luggage, including the following.

Unaccompanied Luggage

Provided you have a valid ticket for the same route, luggage can be sent unaccompanied for SFr. 20 per item (SFr. 15 for groups and card holders) and collected at your destination station. Depending on your destination, international luggage can be sent unaccompanied for SFr. 24 to 30 per piece (up to a maximum weight of 25kg). Skis, ski boots or snowboards can be sent for SFr. 10 for each item or a number of items together in a ski bag for SFr. 10 (up to a maximum weight of 25kg). Luggage can be booked in at PostBus depots for delivery to a railway station or airport.

Luggage can also be sent unaccompanied to Switzerland from abroad with a customs declaration form. It's advisable to register your luggage early, at least the day before departure. There may be a storage charge of around SFr. 1 or 2 per day per item, depending on the station. Insurance is available for luggage travelling within Switzerland.

Bicycles

Bicycles can be sent between any two stations in Switzerland for SFr. 16 to 32 provided you have a valid ticket. To send a normal bike internationally costs SFr. 24 to 48, depending on the destination (tandems cannot be sent internationally).

Porters, Trolleys & Lockers

There are porters at some main stations. There's a fixed charge of around SFr. 1 per article and a small tip is customary – one of the few exceptions to the Swiss 'no tipping' rule (see page 383). Many stations have luggage trolleys (at major stations you must pay a returnable deposit of SFr. 2) and luggage lockers in several sizes (e.g. SFr. 5 for a medium-size locker).

Tickets

Tickets (*Fahrkarte*, *billets*) can be purchased online, via your mobile phone (on some routes) and from ticket offices or ticket machines (provided at most stations). You should buy a ticket before boarding a train, but if you don't get the chance to buy a ticket in advance, it's usually possible to purchase one on the train for a surcharge of SFr. 5. However, this isn't the case on short-distance routes, where passengers must validate their tickets – look for the 'eye' symbol (on the side of the train and departure boards) – although sometimes you can buy a ticket from the driver if there's no ticket machine. Most ticket offices are open from around 6am until 7.30pm (even later at major stations).

Single (*einfach*, *aller-simple*) and return (*Retour/hin und zurück*, *aller-retour*) tickets for Swiss destinations can be purchased from touch-screen ticket machines in most stations, which are easy to use and with instructions in several languages including English (touch the button for the desired language). If you wish to pay with cash, make sure that the machine you choose accepts notes and coins, as some accept only cards (machines are clearly marked). All coins except 5 cents are accepted, as well as SFr. 10, 20 and 50 notes, but change is returned only up to SFr. 20; if, for example, you use an SFr. 50 note to pay for an SFr. 20 ticket, you won't receive change! Other methods of payment include REKA cheques, Postcard and credit cards. It's recommended that you use the ticket counter for anything remotely complicated, which will prevent money being wasted on useless tickets, although you can take a ticket bought in error to the counter for a replacement.

Some stations have old-style ticket machines, which aren't touch screen. The instructions for these are as follows:

1. Choose your destination from the list and press the corresponding button.

2. Choose your class, whether you're paying full fare and whether you want a return ticket. Press the buttons next to the required combination.

3. Pay the amount displayed using coins (except for 5 cents) and SFr. 20 notes.

4. Don't forget to retrieve your change from the tray at the bottom!

If you make a mistake, press the *Korrektur/Annulation* button. As above, it's recommended that you use the ticket counter if you're making a 'complicated' journey.

Bookings (reservations) can be made (for SFr. 5) on all IC, ICE, CIS and EC trains and *TGVs* and are obligatory for CIS Cisalpino trains. A second-class ticket can be upgraded to first class on payment of the fare difference.

Information regarding tickets (and trains) is available from information offices (denoted by a blue letter 'i' in a white circle on a blue background) at major stations or the ticket office at smaller stations.

Validating Tickets

In some regions, e.g. Zurich, it's mandatory for passengers to validate a ticket in a special machine (*Entwerter, oblitérateur*), indicated by an eye symbol, before boarding a train. All trains requiring passengers to have a validated ticket before boarding are denoted by the same eye symbol on the side, which is also shown on departure boards.

Failure to buy or validate a ticket can result in an SFr. 80 (minimum) fine if you're discovered during a spot-check, in addition to which you must pay the correct fare. If you omit to buy or validate a ticket but notify the conductor **before** he makes a spot-check, you must pay a surcharge of SFr. 5. Make sure that you don't 'accidentally' travel in a first-class carriage with a second-class ticket, which also incurs a fine.

Discounted Tickets

Many season tickets (*Abonnement*) and other discounted tickets are available in Switzerland. These include tickets for families, the young (16 to 25) and senior citizens, commuters and groups of ten or more, as well as 'ski-day', hiking and cycling tickets and other holiday and excursion tickets. Information is available from the information or ticket office at railway stations (staff usually speak English). A brochure is available from railway stations describing the various season and discounted tickets available.

Half-fare travel card: The best rail offer (possibly in the world) is the half-fare travel card (*Halbtax-Abo, abonnement demi-tarif*), a joint venture of the Swiss transport operators, costing SFr. 150 for one year, SFr. 250 for two years or SFr. 350 for three years. A half-fare travel card for 16-year-olds (who usually pay full price) is available for SFr. 91. Over 2m *Halbtax* cards were sold in 2006. The card entitles the holder to half-fare travel on all SBB trains, PostBuses, selected city buses and trams, and many ferries and cable cars – a total network of around 23,500km (14,688mi). The half-fare travel card can also be used with a junior card (see page 180).

Half-fare travel cards are available at all railway stations and many PostBus depots and travel agents, on production of a passport photo and the fee. You must sign your half-fare travel card below your photograph.

Holders of a half-fare travel card may purchase day cards that provide unlimited travel for a whole day on all SBB trains and PostBuses. Day cards cost SFr. 56 each for second class (SFr. 90 first class), a card providing six days' travel SFr. 280 (SFr. 450 1st class). A child's day card is also available (SFr. 15 for second class and SFr. 30 for first class). As with any other ticket, day cards must be validated before use. People aged under 25 can purchase a card called *Gleis 7, Voie 7* for SFr. 249 which provides half-fare travel before 7pm and free travel after 7pm. A monthly travel card is also available to half-fare travel card holders which converts your half-fare travel card into a general season ticket (see below) for one month.

General season ticket: The general season ticket (*Generalabonnement – GA, abonnement général – AG*), which is purchased by over 316,000 people each year, provides unlimited travel on all SBB trains, PostBuses and other buses and trams in some 35 cities and towns, many private railways and lake steamers. It also includes a 50 per cent reduction for one person on other licensed coach operators, mountain railways and aerial cableways. General season tickets can be extended during a holiday or other long period spent outside Switzerland by depositing them at a station and collecting them on your return.

A general season ticket costs SFr. 2,990 per year second class (SFr. 4,700 first class) if you're over 25, SFr. 2,220 second class (SFr. 3,450 first class) if you're between 16 and 25, SFr. 2,250 second class (SFr. 3,550 first class) if you're a senior citizen, and SFr. 2,150 second class (SFr. 3,400 first class) if you're disabled. Tickets aren't transferable (outside the listed users) and adults require a passport photo. (There are a number of combinations for families – ask ticket office staff for information.) A transferable (impersonal) general season ticket is available for companies and organisations for SFr. 4,800 per year second class (SFr. 7,600 first class). There's even a general season ticket for dogs, which costs SFr. 650 (both first and second class) – no picture required. Although annual season tickets may appear to be expensive, if you do a lot of travelling on public transport they're a bargain. General season tickets cannot be deposited at a station during absences from Switzerland.

Commuter tickets: If you're a regular train commuter, you can buy a weekly, monthly or annual 'point-to-point' season ticket (*Streckenabonnement, abonnement de parcours*). An annual point-to-point season ticket costs around the same as nine monthly tickets. In some cantons the rail network is divided into zones and season tickets are available for a number of zones or the whole network. A photograph is required for an annual season ticket. Multiple journey cards (usually valid for 6 or 12 journeys) can save you time and sometimes money. You can make further savings by combining bus (both PostBuses and local services) and rail journeys. Ask at any railway station.

Other discounts: 'Youth' fares are available for those aged 16 to 25 (30 for full-time students). Discounts are also available on some international routes (see **Rail Passes** on page 183).

BUSES & TRAMS

Two, separate bus services are provided throughout most of Switzerland; the PostBus service and city and suburban bus networks. Together they cover **all** towns and villages in Switzerland. There's also an extensive tram or trolley bus network in all major cities. Like the SBB (Swiss railways), bus companies offer many discounted day, multi-ride and season tickets. There are also international bus services (e.g. Eurolines) to various countries.

Combined bus (PostBus and local buses) and train commuter tickets are available from railway stations, offering large savings compared with the cost of separate bus and train tickets.

The following general information applies to bus and tram travel:

- Trams and buses don't usually operate between around midnight and 5.30am, although major cities have a 'night bus' system for party-goers, shift workers and insomniacs.

- Children under six don't require a ticket when accompanied by an adult. Children from 6 to 16 usually pay a reduced fare. You must generally pay half-fare for dogs and non-collapsible baby carriages; prams usually require an additional full fare.

- School bus and tram passes may be invalid after around 8pm or on Sundays and school holidays.

- A person or guide dog accompanying a disabled or blind person travels free of charge, but a pass is required. The disabled or blind person must be a Swiss resident with a medical certificate and a identity card for disabled passengers issued by the canton authorities.

- Groups of ten or more people are usually given a discount.

- Ticket machines don't always give change, so check before inserting coins. If in doubt, insert the exact fare.

- On many buses and trams you must press a button to open the doors to get on or off (doors are closed by the driver). Trams halt at most stops, although the doors may not open unless you press a button. On buses you must usually request the driver to stop by pressing a stop button when you near your destination. When waiting at a 'request' bus stop, you may need to signal the driver to stop (wave to him).

- In many towns, children up to the age of 16 can travel free and people aged 16 to 25 travel for half-fare with a junior card. (see page 180) and a valid ticket.

- Always check the line number and direction of a tram or bus before boarding. If in doubt ask someone.

PostBus

The PostBus service (*Postauto, Car Postal*), which celebrated its centenary in 2006, covers around 10,450km (6,530mi) of Switzerland's principal roads and provides regular services to over 1,600 localities on its 758 routes. Many remote villages are served only by PostBuses, which carry over 100m passengers a year. PostBuses are painted bright yellow and distinguished by a red stripe and an alp horn motif on their sides. They have a distinctive (real) horn to warn motorists of their approach on mountain roads.

The PostBus service is comfortable, punctual, inexpensive and safe, and employs one of the most modern fleets of buses in the world (safety features include two independent braking systems and a handbrake). PostBus drivers inspire confidence and are among the world's best professional drivers. It's probably the best national bus service provided anywhere in the world.

As its name implies, the main task of the PostBus service is to deliver and collect post. Around one-third of Swiss homes rely on the PostBus service for their post and newspapers, which is one reason why PostBuses have the right of way on all roads. Trailers are often attached to the rear of buses to carry parcels and luggage (in winter a ski trailer is also used).

Like trains, PostBuses also use the eye symbol (see page 192), although on a bus it signifies that a ticket validation machine (*Entwerter, oblitérateur*) is installed on the bus for holders of multi-ride tickets. Passengers without tickets must board at the front of the bus and buy a ticket from the driver. When a bus stop is outside a post office or railway station, you should buy your ticket there to avoid delays on boarding a bus. PostBuses don't automatically stop at all stops, and it's usually necessary to press the stop button to instruct the driver to stop when you want to get off. A stopping sign (*hält an, arrêt*) is illuminated at the front of the bus when it's about to stop. You must usually press another button to open the doors. If you're waiting at a 'request' stop, you will need to flag the bus down (wave to the driver) to make it stop.

The following general information applies to PostBus services:

● Passengers can take hand luggage (no weight limit), although a charge is made for unaccompanied luggage.

● Dogs are carried on PostBuses for half-fare (small dogs in baskets are carried free).

● Bicycles are transported for SFr. 6 inside the bus or in a luggage compartment or trailer (booking is strongly recommended).

● Children under six travel free and children aged 6 to 16 pay half-fare.

● There's a 20 per cent reduction for groups of ten or more.

● Bookings are necessary on some long-distance PostBus routes.

- Journeys may be broken, but tickets must be validated at the start of each journey.

- PostBuses operate weekly bus tours abroad, which include hotel accommodation, full board (all meals), excursions and entrance tickets.

- The half-fare travel card (see page 189) allows half-fare travel on all PostBuses and some local bus services. Other discounts are offered by the tickets described below.

Multi-journey Tickets

A multi-journey ticket (*Mehrfahrtenkarte, carte multicourse*) provides 12 single journeys for the price of ten. Half-fare travel card holders and children under 16 receive a 50 per cent discount. Tickets are transferable and can be used by several people travelling together; they're valid for three years. Tickets are available from PostBus depots and via the internet (🖳 www.sbb.ch).

Route Pass

A route pass (*Streckenabonnement, abonnement de parcours*) is for commuters or anyone who regularly travels the same route (point-to-point). There's a choice of tickets, valid for a week, a month or a year. A seven-day card costs SFr. 35. By purchasing an annual pass you save 25 per cent compared with a monthly pass (i.e. you pay for nine months). An additional saving of around 25 per cent can be gained for those aged from 6 to 25. Passes aren't transferable, require a photograph and must be signed by the holder. Passes can be combined with services operated by other bus companies and are available from PostBus depots.

City Buses & Trams

Most towns and cities in Switzerland are served by local bus services, and the main cities also have tram or trolley bus services. Tickets for both single and multiple journeys must normally be purchased from ticket machines (located at most stops) before boarding. Tickets are also sold at ticket offices, newspaper kiosks and railway stations near bus and tram stops. Tickets can sometimes be purchased from the driver, but a surcharge may be payable if there was a ticket machine (in operation) at the stop where boarding.

The procedure for buying a ticket from a machine is roughly the same throughout Switzerland and instructions on machines and in information leaflets are usually given in English. The stop where you're located may be marked by an arrow or a red spot on a route map, and zones are shown in different colours.

Fare selection buttons are usually colour coded to match the different zones, although in some machines you press the button corresponding to the postcode of your town of destination or simply press the button for your destination. A single arrow denotes a single ticket and two arrows pointing in opposite directions denote a return ticket. Machines usually accept all coins from SFr. 0.10 and some also accept notes, but some don't give change.

In some cities, e.g. Zurich, there are machines that sell tickets for all city transport, including local trains, trams, buses and boats. The procedure for buying tickets from these machines is virtually identical to buying rail tickets (see page 188). The main difference is that there are coloured buttons for the different zones. If you want a day pass, press the button marked with arrows in opposite directions. These machines don't accept banknotes, though some accept credit cards. If you're in doubt about how to use a ticket machine, ask someone to help you; kicking it won't help (but may make you feel better!). In some cities, e.g. Geneva, there are 'rechargeable' tickets, which you can recharge in machines at bus stops.

Tickets are usually valid for both buses and trams, if applicable, and journeys may combine the two modes of transport, provided you travel in one direction only. You can break your journey but must complete the overall journey within the time limit shown on your ticket (e.g. one hour), depending on the number of zones selected. You must validate (time and date stamp) a multi-ride ticket in a machine (*Entwerter*, *oblitérateur*), either before boarding or on board a tram or bus (many trams and buses have a machine inside). If there's no validation machine at the stop where boarding or on board, you should pay the driver and keep your ticket for a future journey.

There are no conductors on buses or trams, but random checks are made by ticket inspectors. If you don't have a valid ticket, you must pay a fine (e.g. SFr. 80 if paid on the spot, more if not) and possibly also the correct fare, depending on the inspector. If you refuse or are unable to pay the fine, you can be arrested (persistent offenders are put in the stocks!).

Journeys on most city bus and tram services can be combined with travel on PostBuses and SBB rail services, with large savings.

Discounted Tickets

There are a variety of discounted city bus and tram tickets available in most regions, including the following:

● Single and multi-ride (e.g. 12 single trips) tickets for different zones, with a time limit to reach your destination, e.g. 30 minutes to two hours, depending on the number of zones. You may change buses or trams but must travel in one direction only.

- Day cards offering unlimited travel within 24 hours on city trams, buses and suburban trains (plus boats and funiculars, if applicable) are available in around 35 towns from around SFr. 8 (the price depends on the number of zones). You must usually sign a day card and it isn't transferable. In some towns a multiple day pass is available, e.g. in Zurich a six-day pass is available (it must be validated before use each day).

- Tickets allowing unlimited travel on city buses and trams are provided for visitors to trade fairs and conventions, as well as guests at some hotels. Ask at the local public transport information office, tourist office or hotel desk.

- 'Green' season tickets (*Umweltschutzabonnement/Umweltpass, abonnement onde verte*) are available in some regions, which allow unlimited travel on all local buses, trams and trains (excluding fast, Intercity and Eurocity trains).

- There are reduced price tickets for students under 30 (with a student identity card), pensioners and the disabled (buses designed for wheelchair users are provided in some cities).

- Monthly and annual season tickets are available for under 25s, pensioners, the disabled and other adults. A monthly pass is available in most cities, allowing unlimited travel on all city transport.

- Family and day tickets are available and the half-fare travel card (see page 189) is valid on most local bus services, where the same conditions apply as for trains and PostBuses.

FERRIES

Over 140 ferries with accommodation for a total of around 60,000 passengers are in service from spring to autumn (April to October) on lakes and rivers throughout Switzerland, including paddle steamers are in service on many Swiss lakes. Regular car and passenger services operate all year round on the main lakes, although services are reduced in winter and bad weather sometimes causes cancellations. In the summer there are round trips including breakfast or lunch, as well as folklore and dinner and dance cruises. Reduced fares are usually offered for groups, school parties and holders of a Swiss Card (see page 182), while holders of an SBB general season ticket (see page 190) or Swiss Pass (see page 181) travel free.

The Swiss Boat Pass (SFr. 50) provides a 50 per cent discount on all boat cruises and is valid for one year on 14 lakes serviced by the Swiss Shipping Company and its partners. The Swiss Family Boat Pass costs SFr. 70 a year and gives parents a 50 per cent discount, while children under 16 travel free (⌨ www.vssu.ch). Boats can be chartered for private cruises on most lakes. Ferry passengers may break journeys without formality.

Car ferry services are provided on lakes Constance, Lucerne (*Vierwaldstättersee*, *lac des Quatre-Cantons*) and Zurich. Passenger ferries of the Köln-Düsseldorf (KD) German Rhine Line operate scheduled services between Basle and points in Germany, France and the Netherlands. Free or reduced price steamer services are available for Eurailpass and Eurail youthpass holders (see **Rail Passes** on page 183).

CABLE CARS & MOUNTAIN RAILWAYS

There are over 700 cog or rack railways, funiculars and aerial cableways in Switzerland, extending over around 1,950km (over 1,220mi). Most operate throughout the year (bad weather excepted) and in winter an additional almost 1,700 ski-lifts (i.e. chair-lifts and T-bars) are in use. Cable cars and mountain railways are generally expensive, particularly those that scale the Jungfraujoch (3,454m/11,332ft) and the Klein Matterhorn in Zermatt (3,884m/12,743ft). It costs SFr. 176.60 to travel from Interlaken to Jungfraujoch full fare, although there are many offers (see 🖥 www.jungfraubahn.ch). Holders of a half-fare travel card (see page 189) and general season tickets can obtain reductions on many cable cars and mountain railways, so don't forget to ask before buying a ticket.

If you plan to travel to the top of a mountain, take sunglasses and a warm pullover and note that the view, which on a clear day can stretch for hundreds of kilometres in each direction, is often disappointing.

AIRLINE SERVICES

Switzerland is well served by airlines, both international and domestic, but no longer has its own international airline – Swiss was taken over by Lufthansa in 2005 (a major blow to Swiss air transport and Swiss pride!), although it retains its Swiss identity (🖥 www.swiss.com).

Although standard air fares to and from Switzerland aren't the most competitive in Europe, a range of reduced fares is available including package tours, APEX, super APEX, PEX, super PEX, Eurobudget and excursion fares and under-12 discounts. The low-cost airline Easyjet (🖥 www.easyjet.com) has daily flights from Basle, Geneva and Zurich to London and Liverpool in the UK. If you're planning a trip abroad during the school holidays, book **well** in advance, particularly if you're going to a popular destination, e.g. London or Paris (the Swiss book months ahead).

Fly + Rail

A 'Fly + Rail' luggage (baggage) service is available, not only for rail travel but also for bus transport. You can check in your luggage at over 100 railway stations and PostBus depots for it to be taken to Basle, Geneva or Zurich airports and on to your final destination.

The Fly + Rail service is available at the following railway stations: Aarau, Adelboden, Arosa, Baden, Basle, Bellinzona, Belp, Berne, Biel/Bienne, Brig, Buchs (SG), Burgdorf, Chur, Davos Dorf/Platz, Engelberg, Fleurier, Frauenfeld, Fribourg, Geneva, Grenchen, Grindelwald, Gstaad, Interlaken Ost/West, Kandersteg, Klosters, Konstanz, La Chaux-de-Fonds, Langenthal, Lausanne, Locarno, Lucerne, Lugano, Montreux, Mürren, Neuchâtel, Olten, Rapperswil, Saas Fee, Sargans, Schaffhausen, Sion, Solothurn, Spiez, St. Gallen, St.Margrethen, St. Moritz, Thun, Wädenswil, Wengen, Wil (SG), Winterthur, Zermatt, Zug and Zurich.

The cost is SFr. 20 per item (up to 32kg or the airline's specification) each way with discounts for Swiss first class passengers and Travel Club members, provided you travel by rail to the airport. Luggage book-in times are listed in a leaflet available from railway stations (you must register your luggage up to 24 hours in advance). Information about the latest check-in times is available from SBB stations. This service isn't available for flights with all airlines. A valid air ticket with a reservation status of 'OK,' a railway ticket and a valid passport (and visa if applicable) must be produced when registering your luggage.

If you're flying with Swiss you can also check in up to 24 hours before your flight departure time and receive your boarding card on the spot. Luggage can also be checked in at foreign airports and collected from an SBB station or PostBus depot for SFr. 20 per item (up to 30kg). An official green address label (obtained before your journey) must be attached to each item of luggage for customs declaration.

Airports

Most international airlines provide scheduled services to and from Switzerland via one of the three 'Swiss' international airports (*Flughafen, aéroport*): Basle-Mulhouse EuroAirport, Geneva-Cointrin and Zurich-Kloten. Basle airport is actually located in France around 5km/3mi (25 minutes) from Basle city centre. It's unnecessary to go through French customs or immigration to enter or leave Switzerland via Basle airport, as the road between Basle city and Basle airport is fenced in all the way. The Basle transport company operates a shuttle bus service from Basle airport to Basle railway station.

Zurich is by far the largest and most modern Swiss airport and is highly rated by international travellers, who have consistently rated it one of the best in the world. Zurich airport has a direct rail connection (every 15 minutes) to Zurich main railway station, taking ten minutes.

Geneva airport is small and provincial in comparison with Zurich, although it has been expanded and modernised in recent years. Its services are stretched to breaking point during the ski season, when it's invaded by thousands of skiers in transit to nearby ski resorts (mostly in France). Geneva airport has a direct rail connection to the main city railway station, taking six minutes.

Besides the three main airports, there are over 40 smaller airfields in Switzerland. Berne, the capital of Switzerland, doesn't have an 'official' international airport, although its airport provides scheduled flights to London, Paris and various destinations in Italy. Berne is also served by regular domestic flights from many other Swiss airports. A PostBus service runs from Berne airport to the city centre. Lugano also has an important regional airport.

The following general information applies to most Swiss airports:

● All major Swiss airports have wheelchairs and ambulance staff to help disabled travellers, and airlines publish brochures for disabled travellers.

● Long- and short-term parking is available at all major airports, including reserved parking for the disabled.

● Both Geneva and Zurich airports have shopping centres open from 8am to 8pm, seven days a week. Internet access is provided in first-class and business-class lounges at Geneva and Zurich airports.

● A welcome surprise at Swiss airports (particularly Zurich) is an ample supply of luggage trolleys, which also allow you to take your luggage up and down escalators.

For flight information contact:

Airport	Telephone Number	Website
Basle-Mulhouse	☎ 061 325 31 11	🖥 www.euroairport.com
Berne	☎ 031 960 21 11	🖥 www.flughafenbern.ch
Geneva	☎ 022 717 71 11	🖥 www.gva.ch
Lugano	☎ 091 610 11 11	🖥 www.lugano-airport.ch
Zurich	☎ 0900 300 313*	🖥 www.zurich-airport.com
* SFr. 1.19 per minute		

Flight information is also available from the Swiss television teletext service. Kuoni Travel publishes a comprehensive *Air Guide* listing the most convenient connections from all Swiss airports to over 260 destinations worldwide. It's available free from Kuoni offices and can be consulted or downloaded on the Kuoni website (🖥 www.kuoni.ch).

TIMETABLES

Swiss timetables are truthful and accurate, meaning that a train or bus due at 8.17am will arrive at or very close to this time. (What else would you expect from the country that invented precision?) In mountainous areas, avalanches and landslides do, however, occasionally upset timetables.

Local bus and train timetables (often sponsored by Swiss banks) are posted in offices, factories and restaurants, are available from post offices, and are delivered free once or twice a year to households in most areas of Switzerland. All services run frequently, particularly during rush hours. Your local public transport company may have a website where you can print out a local timetable. At major airports and railway stations, arrivals (*Ankunft, arrivée*) and departures (*Abfahrt, départ*) are shown on electronic boards. Regional timetables (*Regionalfahrplan, horaire régional*) for both train and bus services are available free of charge from stations and bus depots. A separate timetable is published for trains with restaurant cars.

If you're a frequent traveller on public transport, the official timetable (*Offizielles Kursbuch, indicateur officiel*), published annually at the end of December, is a must. It costs SFr. 16 from any railway information or ticket office (it's also available on CD-ROM for SFr. 16) and includes the following three timetable books:

1   Swiss railways, cableways and ferries;

2   PostBuses;

3   international rail services.

Books 1 and 2 are published annually and the international rail services timetable is published biannually, summer and winter. The international timetable for the second half-year (winter) is sent free on application (a post-free postcard is included in the summer edition). The Swiss railway timetable includes the services of many privately operated railways. All timetables contain information in English.

A timetable is also available via SMS, which is useful when you're en route. Simply send your departure destination station names to ☎ 222 (Orange/ Swisscom Mobile) or ☎ 999 (Sunrise) and you receive a list of the next connections (SFr. 0.60 per SMS).

Rail information can be obtained from the SBB's Rail Service Number (☎ 0900 30 03 00, costing SFr. 1.19 per minute) and from station information offices. An interactive timetable for Swiss trains, ferries and post buses is available via the internet (🖳 www.sbb.ch).

An excellent railway map of Switzerland, including 13 city plans, can be purchased at SBB stations for SFr. 19.80. A variety of free local and regional maps is also published.

TAXIS

Taxis in Switzerland are among the most expensive in the world, with a basic charge of SFr. 6, plus SFr. 3.50 for each kilometre (rates quoted are for Zurich), depending on the area and time of day. There are additional charges for each piece of luggage, e.g. SFr. 5 for a half load and SFr. 10 for a full load, and extra passengers, so it's easy to run up a large bill. In most major cities, including Basle, Berne, Geneva and Zurich, a service charge is included in the fare, although drivers may still expect a tip. Waiting time is charged at around SFr. 63 per hour. Due to an increase in violence, some towns and cities have lowered night taxi rates for women.

Taxis cannot always be stopped in the street but can be hired from taxi ranks at railway stations, airports and hotels, or ordered by telephone. Taxis are usually plentiful – except when it's raining, you have lots of luggage or you're late for an appointment.

In winter, many taxis have ski racks, particularly in ski resorts. When travelling with skis or other large objects, mention it when booking by telephone. Wheelchair-accessible taxis are provided by taxi companies in major cities, most of which have a central telephone number, e.g. ☎ 141 in Geneva and Lausanne.

11.

MOTORING

Swiss motorways and secondary roads are excellent and rate among the best in the world. The total network covers some 70,000km (around 43,500mi), of which around 1,900km (about 1,200mi) are motorways. Switzerland is constantly improving its road system and spends a higher percentage of its motoring tax revenues on its roads than most countries. Nearly every second person in Switzerland owns a car, making it one of the most heavily motorised countries in the world. However, despite the heavy traffic, Switzerland has less fatal accidents (per vehicle) than most other European countries. Although the country has an excellent public transport system, many Swiss prefer to travel by car and vigorously protest against any plans to restrict their freedom.

Traffic density in the major Swiss cities is fast approaching the choking levels already experienced in many other European countries, although generally there are fewer traffic jams, and parking, although a problem, isn't impossible. During rush hours, from around 6.30 to 9am and 4 to 6.30pm Mondays to Fridays, the flow of traffic is naturally slower and any interruptions (roadworks, breakdowns or accidents) can cause huge traffic jams (*Stau, embouteillage*). Town centres are to be avoided during rush hours, particularly Geneva and Zurich.

Motorway travel is generally fast, although it's occasionally slowed to a crawl by road works and the favourite Swiss motor sport of running into the rear of the car in front. Outside rush hours, motoring is usually trouble-free, and driving on secondary roads in country areas is often enjoyable. In winter, many mountain passes are closed due to heavy snowfall from around November to May and vehicles using pass roads that remain open during winter require snow chains (shown on a sign, which also indicates whether a pass is open or closed). Cars are banned in some mountain resorts.

Although Switzerland has some of the most stringent anti-pollution motoring laws in Europe, traffic pollution is a major concern, particularly in large cities. Nevertheless, it's generally lower than in most other western countries.

Information regarding closed roads and passes is available from the Swiss motoring organisations (see page 234), the Swiss television teletext road information service, and the road conditions telephone service number (☎ 163). Signs on motorways show the local radio frequency on which road and traffic bulletins are broadcast. Emergency SOS telephones are located on mountain passes and motorways at 1.6km (1mi) intervals and every 150m in tunnels, where there are also fire extinguishers. Black arrows on white posts at the roadside show the direction of the nearest SOS telephone. The Swiss Bureau for the Prevention of Accidents (see **Accidents** on page 227) publishes safety leaflets for motorists, motorcyclists, cyclists and pedestrians.

CAR IMPORTATION

If you intend to bring a motor vehicle or motorcycle to Switzerland, either temporarily or permanently, you must ensure that you're aware of the latest regulations. Check with the manufacturer's export department, the Swiss importers or the local canton vehicle licensing authority in Switzerland. If you're tempted to buy a tax-free car prior to coming to Switzerland, make sure that it conforms to Swiss regulations. Swiss residents can import one car a year for their personal use with minimum testing and modifications. Any car sold in the EU automatically conforms to Swiss standards and can be imported without modifications.

If you wish to import a car (even temporarily), inform the border customs staff on arrival in Switzerland. It's advisable to enter via a major frontier post (e.g. Basle or Geneva) as smaller frontier posts aren't always equipped to deal with car importation without advance notice. Registration can, however, also be done at customs offices in major cities. You're required to complete a form and show your car documents. The amount of tax and import duty payable and when due, depends on how long you've owned your car, as shown below. Before importing a car, check the documents required with your local Swiss embassy or consulate, or contact the Head Customs Office (*Eidgenössische Zollverwaltung/ EZV, Direction des Douanes*), Monbijoustr. 40, CH-3003 Berne (☎ 031 322 65 11, 🖳 www.zoll.admin.ch).

Cars Owned Less Than Six Months

If you've owned a car for less than six months, you must pay import duty and tax on importing it into Switzerland. You need to provide documentation confirming the value of the vehicle, the country of origin and an EUR1 certificate (if applicable). Clearance can either be done on entry into Switzerland at main border posts or inland in major cities, on authorisation from the border customs office. The customs post issues you with an authorisation (form 15.25) valid for two days, by which time the car must be presented to a customs depot in the interior. Import duty is calculated on the weight and/or engine size of your car, so remove all luggage and non-standard spares before having it weighed. In addition to import duty, you must also pay a 3 per cent statistical charge. You must also pay VAT at 7.6 per cent on presentation of evidence of the car's cost.

Cars Owned Longer Than Six Months

If you've owned a car for **at least six months** and are importing it as part of your personal effects, it's exempt from customs duty and VAT for two years. You're allowed to drive your car in Switzerland for a maximum of one year on foreign registration plates or until they expire if they're only temporary. You're given a permit (*Bewilligung, permis*) that must be produced on demand if you're stopped by the police in Switzerland. The car must be for your personal use only and mustn't be lent, rented or sold to a third party in Switzerland for one year from the date of importation. Ensure that you're legally insured to drive in Switzerland during this period (see **Foreign Registered Vehicles** on page 216).

Around one month after importing a car, you receive a letter from your canton's motor registration office (*Strassenverkehrsamt, office de la circulation routière*), informing you that in one year's time your car will require an official serviceability test (*Fahrzeugkontrolle, contrôle des véhicules à moteur*). If your foreign registration plates are only temporary and aren't renewable, you must have your car tested in order to obtain Swiss registration plates (see **Serviceability Test** on page 209).

There's sometimes a delay in calling up cars for the serviceability test and you may be able to run your car on foreign plates for longer than one year. When your car is called up for the test, it may be expensive to comply with Swiss safety and pollution regulations, and may not be worth the expense – a local garage or motoring organisation can provide a estimate. If you have a right-hand drive car or an old car, it's usually advisable to buy a car in Switzerland before your first year is completed or when your car is called up for test. The authorities may give you just a few weeks notice of the test date and if you decide not to have your car tested you must inform them and export it before the test is due.

After your car passes the test it requires Swiss road tax, insurance and registration plates. **However, you aren't required to pay import duty or tax yet.** You can apply to your motor registration office for deferred duty plates, which are valid for one year and usually renewable for a further year. These plates are distinguished by a red stripe on the right-hand side and display the year and month of expiry in white. Swiss registration plates indicate the canton of residence of the owner (e.g. GE = Geneva, ZH = Zurich) and have both a Swiss flag emblem and the canton insignia on the rear number plate.

After running a car on deferred duty plates for one or two years, you must have it weighed for duty payment. The amount payable also depends on the age and value of the car. You may change your car during the deferred-duty period, but proof of export of your old car must be provided.

Tax-free Importation

If your stay in Switzerland is only temporary and you're domiciled outside Switzerland (e.g. foreign students and businessmen), you may be eligible to buy a duty-free car **in Switzerland** and run it on tax-free 'Z' plates (*Zollschilder, plaques d'immatriculation douanières*) for a maximum of two years. You may need to provide documentary evidence of your status, as most Swiss residence permit holders are considered by the authorities to be domiciled in Switzerland and aren't eligible. Like deferred duty plates, Z plates are initially issued for one year and can be renewed for a second year. They're available from your canton's motor registration office on presentation of a special certificate from a Swiss insurance company. This certificate states that you have valid insurance and that your car has passed the official Swiss serviceability test (see page 209). Insurance may be more expensive with Z plates.

If you're planning to leave Switzerland and take up domicile abroad, you may be entitled to buy a duty-free car in Switzerland and run it on 'Z' plates for up to three months prior to your departure. An emigrating person who **retains** Swiss domicile may take delivery of a duty-free car ten days before departure, but may not re-import it into Switzerland without paying duty and tax.

BUYING A CAR

Cars are cheaper in Switzerland than in many other European countries. In addition, you can obtain a discount of around 10 per cent off the list price of most new cars, even when leasing. If you aren't offered a discount, ask for one. If you're buying a used car from a garage and aren't trading in another vehicle, try to negotiate a reduction, particularly when paying cash. **In Switzerland a car is insured and not the driver, so if you test-drive a car it must be insured – you cannot drive it on your own insurance (see page 214).** If a car has licence plates it should be insured, as you're unable to obtain them without insurance.

New Cars

Making comparisons between new car prices in different countries is often difficult, due to fluctuating exchange rates and the different levels of standard equipment. It's often cheaper to buy a new car from the factory of a European manufacturer or from an exporter in countries which levy high car taxes. This option is worth considering, particularly if you're planning to buy an expensive car. In some countries (e.g. the UK) a tax free car can be purchased up to six months prior to being exported. Personally importing a car from the US is usually much cheaper than buying the same car in Switzerland or elsewhere in Europe, although you must ensure that it conforms to Swiss specifications. Contact manufacturers and exporters directly for information.

Used Cars

Used cars (*Occasionswagen, voiture d'occasion*) in Switzerland are usually good value for money, particularly those over five years old (most Swiss wouldn't be seen dead in an old car unless it's a classic), which are usually in good condition. Nevertheless, if you intend to buy a used car in Switzerland, whether privately or from a garage, check the following:

● that it has passed the official serviceability test (see page 209);

- that it hasn't been involved in a major accident and suffered structural damage. A declaration that it's accident free (*Unfallfrei, sans accident/non-accidenté*) should be obtained in writing;

- that the chassis number tallies with the car registration document (*Fahrzeugausweis, permis de circulation*);

- that the service coupons have been completed and stamped and that servicing has been carried out by an authorised dealer (if under warranty);

- that the price roughly corresponds to that shown in the Touring Club of Switzerland (TCS – see page 234) monthly guide to used car prices issued by the TCS;

- that import tax and duty have been paid (if applicable);

- whether a written guarantee is provided.

When buying a car from a garage, some protection is afforded if it's a member of the Swiss Motor Trade Association (*Autogewerbeverband Schweiz, Association Suisse des Automobilistes,* 🖳 www.agvs.ch). Most garages provide a warranty on used cars, e.g. three months or 4,000km (around 2,500mi). **Second-hand car prices in the more remote parts of Switzerland (e.g. Graubunden or Valais) are generally higher than in the major cities (e.g. Geneva and Zurich).** If you live in a remote area, it's worthwhile comparing prices in national newspapers and used car sites on the internet.

Leasing

If you don't want to pay cash or a large deposit, you can usually lease a new or used car. You're still eligible for a discount on most new cars, which should be offered automatically (if you aren't offered a discount, ask for one). Usually there are no leasing restrictions for foreigners with a B permit (see page 67), although you may not be eligible to lease a car during your first three months in Switzerland. **Bear in mind that the reason there are so many leasing companies is that it's a lucrative way to make money and is generally the most expensive way for an individual to own a car (unless the payments are tax deductible, which they aren't for individuals!).**

On the other hand, interest paid on a car loan, e.g. from your employer or from a bank is tax-deductible, the terms are more transparent and it's usually a lot cheaper. Many leasing contracts have high exit costs, i.e. if you want to cancel the contract early you must pay a higher interest on the time you've had the car, which can amount to several thousand francs. Leasing contracts are also often written in such a way as to avoid the strict rules on consumer credit and may be declared illegal by a court. Before signing a leasing contract, obtain advice from a lawyer or a consumer protection organisation and take out insurance for legal assistance (*Rechtsschutz-Versicherung, protection juridique*) which will pay for a lawyer if there's a problem with the contract.

Most car manufacturers/importers have their own leasing schemes. Shop around as leasing contracts vary considerably from garage to garage, even between those selling the same models. There are also a number of independent leasing companies (*Mietauto/voiture de location*), listed in local phonebooks or on the internet (🖳 www.search.ch or 🖳 www.gelbeseiten.ch are useful for locating them).

SERVICEABILITY TEST

All cars are liable for a stringent official serviceability test (*Motorfahrzeug-kontrolle (MFK), contrôle des véhicules à moteur/expertisé*). New cars are eligible for the test only after they're four years old, unless there's a change of owner or the owner moves to a different canton. The next test is due when the car is seven years old, and thereafter every two years. In practice, tests may be less frequent, as vehicles require testing only when the owner has been officially informed by a test centre. In some cantons there's sometimes a backlog of cars waiting for test and there have been instances of cars not being called up for months after the due date. You can apply to have your car tested earlier than required, for example if you want to sell it.

Many people won't buy a used car that hasn't had a test in the last year, even when it's offered at a bargain price (the Swiss are a suspicious lot!). If the ownership of a used car older than ten years changes after the first year of the test validation period, the new owner must have the car re-tested. However, if ownership doesn't change, the test isn't due until the end of the test period. If you buy an old car that requires testing, it could need expensive repairs. Get the owner or garage to have it tested before you buy it, or failing that, obtain a written undertaking that the owner will pay for any necessary repairs.

If you own an old or imported car which is called up for test, it may be advisable to get a garage to take it in for you or take a mechanic with you. Apart from the fact that their local language ability is probably better than yours, they're usually looked upon more favourably than the general public. If you have any questions regarding the test, it's advisable to discuss them with the testing station in advance. If you have a garage do a pre-test check on your car, don't ask them to repair it to test standard as this could result in unnecessary expense. Get them to take it for the test to find out what (if anything) needs fixing. Essential repairs recommended by a garage may not be the same as those officially required after the test.

You can have the Automobile Club of Switzerland (ACS – see page 234) or the TCS (see page 234) check your car before taking it for the test (in some cantons the TCS is authorised to carry out official serviceability tests). This is advisable, particularly if you plan to register an imported car in Switzerland, as they will tell you what modifications (if any) need to be made. **It can be**

expensive to get a car through the test. For example, a windscreen with a tiny stone chip may need replacing (although this is covered by part or fully comprehensive insurance in Switzerland) and tyres must have at least 1.6 mm of tread over their entire surface. A car without a 'CH' sticker on the back or with no breakdown triangle will also fail. The test is normally completed while you wait and takes around 30 minutes.

The canton test centre is usually located at your canton's motor registration office, the address of which is listed on both your driving licence and car registration document (*Fahrzeugausweis, permis de circulation*). Business hours are usually 7.30am to 4pm, Mondays to Fridays. The test costs around SFr. 60, while a full retest is usually about half this and a minor retest even less. When you apply for a test, you're sent a form which must be completed and returned with your car registration document. If your car fails the serviceability test and you wish to have it repaired at a later date, you can have the registration document stamped 'invalid' and you won't be required to pay road tax or insurance from this date. When you wish to have the car tested again, you can obtain a 'day plate' from the police to take the vehicle to the test centre.

EXHAUST TEST

All Swiss registered cars with a catalytic converter require an exhaust emission test (*Abgastest, test anti-pollution*) every two years, cars without one must be tested annually. The amount of carbon monoxide, carbon dioxide and hydrocarbons emitted by the exhaust mustn't exceed the manufacturer's limits. If they do, adjustments or repairs must be made to the engine, fuel system or exhaust, as necessary. Cars registered in Switzerland before 1st January 1971 are exempt, while older cars registered after this date must have the exhaust test.

A green and white sticker is fixed to the rear or a side window of your car, showing the year and month when the test is next due. The test certificate (*Abgas-Wartungsdokument, fiche d'entretien du systeme antipollution*) must be kept in your car and be produced when asked for by the police. The exhaust emission test costs between SFr. 50 and SFr. 150 and is usually reduced when combined with a service. If you're stopped by the police without a valid exhaust test certificate, you can be fined up to SFr. 200. Vehicle anti-pollution controls in Switzerland are among the strictest in Europe and police have pollution meters to detect cars that exceed pollution levels.

CAR REGISTRATION

In Switzerland a new or used car doesn't have registration plates (*Nummernschild, numéro d'immatriculation*) when purchased. Car registration plates are issued to individuals and when a car is sold they're returned to the issuing canton's motor registration office or transferred to a new car. When you apply to register a car in Switzerland for the first time, you must apply to your canton's motor registration office for registration plates. If you're buying a new or used car from a garage, they usually apply for the registration plates on your behalf and complete the formalities. When applying for Swiss registration plates for the first time, you must provide the following:

- your Swiss or foreign driving licence (before you've completed one year's residence in Switzerland, you must obtain a Swiss driving licence);

- your foreigner's permit (*Ausländerausweis, livret pour étrangers*);

- a certificate of residence (*Wohnsitzbescheinigung, carte d'indigène/ attestation de domicile*), available for a fee of around SFr. 10 to 20 from your community office;

- a certificate from an insurance company confirming that the car has been insured for third-party liability.

A new car must undergo an official test (*Vorführung, contrôle de mise en circulation*) at a canton motor registration office to ensure that it meets Swiss specifications. The test fee (for a car purchased from a Swiss dealer) is about SFr. 50 to 150 and the cost of the car registration document (*Fahrzeugausweis, permis de circulation*) is around SFr. 40 to 60 depending on the canton. The test is arranged by the garage. If you already own a Swiss registered car, your canton's motor registration office requires your existing car's registration document, plus a valid certificate of insurance for the new car from your insurance company.

When changing cantons or leaving Switzerland, registration plates must be returned to your canton's motor registration office (see **Chapter 20**). Notify your canton's motor registration office within 14 days of a change of car or address, a change of canton or when leaving Switzerland. When you register a car or inform your canton's motor registration office of a change, they send you a bill (or a refund) for road tax and the car registration fee, as applicable.

If you're buying a new car and haven't sold your old car, or you intend to run two or more cars but not simultaneously, you can obtain interchangeable registration number plates (*Wechselnummer, plaques interchangeables*) from your canton's motor registration office. This allows you to drive two or more cars on the same insurance and to swap one set of registration plates between them (see **Car Insurance** on page 214). **But note that only the vehicle bearing the interchangeable registration plates can be parked or used on a public road.**

SELLING A CAR

The main points to note when selling a car are:

- If you plan to buy another car, you must retain your registration plates and transfer them to your new car, provided you remain a resident of the same canton. Car registration includes road tax and you're billed for (or reimbursed) the difference when you register a new car. When leaving Switzerland or changing cantons, you must return your licence plates to the issuing canton's motor registration office within 14 days. An application for new plates must be made in your new canton within 14 days of taking up residence.

- Inform your insurance company. Your insurance for a vehicle is cancelled automatically when your registration is cancelled or transferred. It's the responsibility of the new owner of a car to register his ownership with his canton's motor registration office. The seller or buyer is required to have a car's registration document cancelled at his canton's motor registration office. **It isn't advisable to sell your car and give the registration document to the new owner before you've cancelled your registration** – you cannot cancel your insurance until the registration in your name has been cancelled, and the new owner may delay doing this.

- If you're selling your car privately, insist on payment in cash, which is normal practice in Switzerland.

- Include in the receipt that you're selling the car in its present condition (as seen) without a guarantee (*ohne Garantie, sans garantie*), the price paid and the car's kilometre reading. The new owner may ask for a declaration in writing that the car is accident free (*unfallfrei, sans accident/non-accidenté*). This refers to major accidents causing structural damage and not slight knocks.

- The best place to advertise a car for sale is in local newspapers, on free local notice boards, and in the Friday and Saturday editions of major city newspapers. It doesn't matter if you don't live close to a major city, as major city newspapers are distributed throughout Switzerland. Buyers will travel a long way to buy a car that appears to be good value for money.

DRIVING LICENCE

The minimum age for obtaining a driving licence in Switzerland is 18 for a motor car or a motorcycle over 125cc, 16 for a motorcycle of between 50 and 125cc and 14 for a moped (see page 224). Holders of a full foreign driving licence may drive in Switzerland for one year using a foreign or international driving licence. If you or any members of your family hold a foreign driving licence and intend to remain in Switzerland for longer than one year, you must apply for a Swiss driving licence (*Führerschein, permis de conduire*) during your first year in

Switzerland. **If you don't apply during your first year, you aren't allowed to drive after this period until you've passed a Swiss driving test.**

You can apply for a Swiss licence at any time after your arrival, provided you're living in permanent accommodation and not, for example, in a hotel. Most foreigners including EU, Australian and US nationals aren't required to take a practical or written driving test and their driving licence is automatically exchanged for a Swiss one. However, some foreigners including those from Turkey and some African, Asian, Central and South American countries, must pass a practical driving test. If you fail the practical driving test, you're required to take a full Swiss driving test, including a written examination. Some foreign licences, for example licences printed in Arabic or Chinese, must be translated into an official Swiss language or an international licence must be obtained.

If you're required to take a Swiss driving test (see **Learning to Drive** on page 239), you should note that it's more comprehensive than many foreign tests and includes a written examination and the completion of a first-aid course. The written exam may be taken in English and other languages, although according to some reports the English is almost unintelligible and the local language version may be easier – provided of course you can understand it! You're permitted to make just five mistakes in 60 questions. It can take some months to obtain a Swiss driving licence if you fail the written test a few times, **during which period you aren't permitted to drive in Switzerland.**

To apply for a Swiss driving licence you need to:

● Obtain an application form from your canton's motor registration office.

● Arrange a sight test (around SFr. 20) with your doctor or an approved optician (listed on the back of the application form). The optician will complete a section on the back of the form after the test is completed. The sight test is valid for six months. You require some form of official identification, e.g. a passport or identity card.

● Provide one to three colour passport photographs (approximately 35 by 45 mm and not older than 12 months), as requested by the canton authority. These can be obtained from photo booths at most railway stations.

● Complete the application form and take it to your canton's motor registration office (the address is listed on the back of the form) with the following:

    – your foreign driving licence and if applicable, an international driving licence;

    – your Swiss residence permit;

    – the completed application form, including the eye test report;

    – one to three passport photographs;

– a police certificate (*Strafregisterauszug, certificate de bonne conduite*), if applicable. This certificate is required in some cantons and is available from your canton's foreigners' police (*Fremdenpolizei, police des étrangers*) for around SFr. 20.

Your Swiss driving licence (similar to a credit card) is sent to you around one week later with a bill and is valid for life. The cost varies wildly depending on your canton of residence (e.g. Basle SFr. 140). The driving licence doesn't show your address and therefore doesn't need to be re-issued every time you move home. If you move to a different canton you only have to inform the canton motoring authority in writing of your new address and of the number of the driving licence.

DRIVING ABROAD

An international driving licence is required if you plan to drive in some countries. This may vary depending on which driving licence(s) you hold. Check with a Swiss motoring organisation (see page 234). An international driving licence is obtainable from the ACS or TCS and canton motor registration offices for SFr. 30 to 50 and is valid for three years. You must provide your passport, a Swiss or foreign driving licence, a passport-size photograph and the fee. A translation of your Swiss or foreign driving licence is required for some countries and is obtainable from Swiss motoring organisations or canton motor registration offices for SFr. 30. Holders of a car driving licence can ride a motorcycle of up to 50cc in Switzerland without a special licence. For motorcycles over 50cc, you must have a motorcycle licence.

CAR INSURANCE

The following categories of car insurance are available in Switzerland:

● **Third-party** (*Haftpflicht, responsibilité civile*) – Third-party insurance includes passenger cover and is compulsory in all cantons.

● **Part comprehensive** (*Teilkasko, casco partielle*) – This is known in some countries as third-party, fire and theft. It includes cover against fire, natural hazards (e.g. rocks falling on your car), theft, broken glass (e.g. windscreen) and damage caused by a collision with animals (for example a collision with a deer is possible on some country roads, which incidentally, must be reported to the local police). You can usually choose to pay an excess (*Selbstbehalt, franchise*), for example the first SFr. 500 to 2,000 of a claim, in order to reduce your premium. **Part comprehensive insurance is compulsory in some cantons.**

● **Full comprehensive** (*Vollkasko/Kollisionskasko, casco intégral (complète)/ assurance tous risques*) – This type of insurance covers all risks including self-inflicted damage to your own car. You can choose to pay an excess (*Selbstbehalt, franchise*) in order to reduce your premium. It also covers high fliers against collisions with aircraft. It's usually compulsory for leasing and credit purchase contracts.

If you take out third-party insurance with a Swiss insurance company and wish to increase your cover to full comprehensive later, you aren't required to do this through your third-party insurance company, but may shop around for the best deal. Separate passenger insurance is unnecessary as passengers are automatically covered by all Swiss motor insurance policies. However, extra passenger cover (*Insassen Versicherung, assurance passager/accidents des occupants*) is available for a small extra charge, providing higher financial cover for passengers and including the owner-driver, which third-party doesn't. Swiss motor insurance always includes a green card (available free on request), which extends your insurance to most European countries.

The cost of motor insurance in Switzerland is high and varies considerably between insurance companies. Your foreign no-claims bonus is usually valid in Switzerland, but you must provide written evidence from your present or previous insurance company (not just an insurance renewal notice). The no-claims bonus in Switzerland is a maximum of 70 per cent and is more generous than in many other countries. However, it may vary for third-party and full comprehensive insurance and there isn't a no-claims discount on the part comprehensive part of your insurance. Claims are calculated in 'steps' (*Bonusstufen/ étapes de bonification*) or percentages according to the number of years with no claims. It's usually 10 per cent after one year (or 'step'), 20 per cent after two years (or two 'steps'), 25 per cent after three years and an additional 5 per cent a year up to a maximum of 70 per cent after 12 years. After a claim you usually lose two steps (20 per cent) or two years' no-claims bonus. Accident prone drivers can, however, find themselves paying up to 170 per cent (the maximum) **above** the basic premium.

Inexperienced, young or accident prone drivers, must usually pay an extra excess (*franchise*). Drivers under 25 must pay a 20 per cent loading or the first SFr. 500 of a claim and inexperienced drivers (holders of a licence for less than two years) must pay the first SFr. 500 of a claim. The extra premium for full comprehensive insurance for young or inexperienced drivers can be from SFr. 300 to 3,000, depending on the car. Your type of permit (see **Chapter 3**) may also influence the cost of car insurance. B and C permit holders usually pay the standard rate, but L permit holders and those on short-term contracts may need to pay up to double and **in advance**. Shop around for an insurance policy and ask companies whether they have higher premiums for foreigners, as not all do. If you're staying in Switzerland for a short period only, check whether you can take out a fixed period policy or terminate your insurance at short notice without penalty.

Most insurance companies try to tie you to a five or ten-year contract, which you cannot cancel unless your premium is increased (which happens frequently) or you change vehicles. You can, however, tell your insurance broker that you want a shorter term or request that the contract can be cancelled at the end of each year (usually with a notice period of three months). If you want to change companies, you must notify your insurance company in writing by registered letter (your new insurance company will be happy to do this for you).

Some employers may have an arrangement with a car insurance company, whereby employees are offered a discount. Ask your colleagues for their advice and shop around. Motor insurance premiums are valid for a full calendar year from January to December. If you take out a policy in mid-year, you may be billed to the end of the year only. Many companies send out bills in advance with 30 days to pay, so that payment is received before the start of the new insurance period.

If you own two or more cars, you need only insure the most expensive one, provided you (or your family members) intend to drive only one car at a time. If this is the case, contact your insurance company and ask them for am interchangeable registration number (*Wechselnummer, plaques interchangeables*) for the vehicles involved. There's an extra insurance charge of around SFr. 100 a year. Registration plates can be fitted with a quick release mount, so that they can be easily swapped between cars. This also means that you pay road tax (see below) only on the most expensive car, as only one car can be on the road at a time. An interchangeable number cannot be swapped between a car and a motorcycle. **If you insure two cars in the same name, you can claim a no-claims bonus for one car only and you must pay the full premium for the other.**

If you're going to be out of Switzerland for at least 30 days but less than one year, you can save a proportion of your car insurance and road tax. To qualify you must remove your car plates, return them with the registration document to your canton's motor registration office, and inform your insurance company. Upon your return, notify your insurance agent, who authorises you to reclaim your licence plates from your canton's motor registration office. A car mustn't be driven or parked on a public road without registration plates. Some people garage their cars for around three months during winter, preferring to use public transport when road conditions are bad. Due to the fees and effort involved, it isn't worthwhile taking a car off the road (and reclaiming insurance and road tax payments) for a period of less than three months.

For an extra premium of around SFr. 90 a year, your insurance company will cover your legal costs (*Rechtsschutz, protection juridique*) arising from road accidents. A special federal insurance (*Bundesversicherung, assurance fédérale*) scheme covers victims of hit-and-run accidents (see page 227).

Foreign Registered Vehicles

It isn't mandatory for cars insured in an EU country to have an international insurance green card (*Internationale Versicherungskarte für Motorfahrzeuge, carte internationale d'Assurance automobile/carte verte*) for Switzerland. Motorists insured in an EU country are covered for third-party insurance in most EU countries plus Liechtenstein, Norway and Switzerland. Most insurance companies in Western Europe provide a 'free' green card, which extends your normal domestic insurance cover to other western European countries (although it doesn't always include Switzerland).

This doesn't include the UK, where you can usually obtain a green card for a maximum of three months and it's expensive. A green card must be signed to be valid and in some countries, e.g. the UK, all drivers must sign it, not just the car owner. Your insurance cover may be invalid if you drive in Switzerland with a foreign insurance policy stating that you're a resident of another country, when you're actually resident in Switzerland. Contact your insurance company to find out your legal position.

If you bring a foreign-registered car to Switzerland, you may need a new insurance policy, which can be either a special European insurance policy (expensive) or insurance with a Swiss company. Some Swiss insurance companies (e.g. Zürich-Versicherungen) insure a foreign registered car, but usually for a limited period only, e.g. one year.

ROAD TAX

Road tax (*Verkehrssteuer, impôt sur la circulation*) rates in Switzerland vary considerably from canton to canton. It's calculated on the engine size (CC), power (DIN-PS) or the weight of your car, depending on your canton of residence. (Canton Ticino are the exception, where they charge a basic premium of around SFr. 150 and add the DIN-PS figure, times the weight of the car, divided by 800 – creating these calculations keeps thousands of civil servants in work.) This means you can usually expect to pay around SFr. 180 for a car with an engine size up to 1,079cc; SFr. 200 for a car with an engine size of 1,080cc to 1,276cc and SFr. 230 for a car with a engine size of 1,277cc to 1,472cc.

When you register a car with your canton's motor registration office, the road tax bill is sent with your car registration document. A refund is possible if you leave Switzerland, change cantons or take your car off the road for more than 30 days (see **Car Insurance** on page 214). If you have two or more cars using the same registration number, you must pay road tax only on the most expensive one, as only one vehicle can be on a public road at a time.

An additional motorway tax of SFr. 40 applies to all vehicles up to 3.5 tonnes using Swiss motorways (see **Motorway Tax** on page 77).

GENERAL ROAD RULES

The following general road rules may help you adjust to driving in Switzerland:

- The Swiss drive on the right-hand side of the road.

- All motorists must carry a red breakdown triangle. It must be stowed inside the car within reach of the drivers seat, not in the boot, as this may be damaged and jammed shut in an accident. If you have an accident or breakdown, the triangle must be placed at the edge of the road at least 50 metres behind the car on secondary roads and at least 150 metres on 'roads with fast traffic', e.g. motorways.

- Swiss traffic regulations state that you **should** carry first-aid equipment and some chalk (to mark the position of vehicles in case of an accident!). In many European countries it's mandatory to carry a fire extinguisher and a first-aid kit (see **Driving Abroad** on page 214). If you witness an accident, you must stop and render assistance and give evidence if required. Only give medical assistance when absolutely necessary and when qualified (see also **Accidents** on page 227).

- In towns you may be faced with a bewildering array of signs, traffic lights and road markings. If in doubt about who has priority, always give way (yield) to trams, buses plus all traffic coming from your RIGHT. All drivers must give way to police cars, ambulances and fire engines in emergencies (with disco lights and wailing sounds) and trams and buses, e.g. leaving stops. On secondary roads **without** priority signs (a yellow diamond on a white background, used throughout most of Europe) you must give way to vehicles coming from your RIGHT. **Failure to observe this rule is the cause of many accidents.** The priority to the right rule usually also applies in car parks. If you're ever in doubt about who has the right of way, it's generally wise to give way. As the Swiss say 'fairness above all' (*Fairness vor allem, fair-play avant tout*) – particularly when confronted by a 28-tonne truck (might is right!).

- On roundabouts (traffic circles), vehicles on the roundabout have priority and not those entering it, who are faced with a give way sign. Traffic flows anti-clockwise around roundabouts and not clockwise as in the UK and other countries driving on the left.

- The wearing of seatbelts is **compulsory** and includes passengers in rear seats when seatbelts are fitted. In the event of an accident, a Swiss insurance company **isn't obliged** to pay the whole cost of damages when it 'appears' those injured weren't using their seatbelts (benefits may be reduced by up to 50 per cent). Children under the age of 12 may ride in the front of a car, but only when it's impossible for them to ride in the back, e.g. it's already full of under 12-year-olds. Children under seven must occupy a special child's seat, even in the rear of a car. If you're apprehended with a child under seven who isn't in a child's seat, your licence may be confiscated for several months. Although generally extremely law-abiding, around 20 per cent of Swiss drivers don't always fasten their seatbelts, although you can be fined for not doing so. The Swiss Bureau for the Prevention of Accidents (see **Accidents** on page 227) publishes a brochure entitled *Auto-Kindersitze* (in German), which compares the different types of baby seats and boosters available for babies and children, plus a general brochure regarding seatbelts.

- Don't drive in bus, taxi or cycle lanes unless it's necessary to avoid a stationary vehicle or obstruction and give priority to authorised users. Bus drivers get irate if you drive in their lanes and you can be fined for doing so. Be sure to keep clear of tram lines and outside the restricted area shown by a line.

- Dipped (low beam) headlights must be used in tunnels, fog, snowstorms, heavy rain and when visibility is reduced to less than 200 metres. While it isn't mandatory to have the light on in daytime, the Swiss government advise to do so because of safety reasons. It's illegal to drive on parking (side) lights at any time, although many people do it. Front fog or spot lights must be fitted in pairs at a regulation height and should be used only when visibility is less than 50 metres. Rear fog lamps are officially permitted on the offside only (to prevent following vehicles mistaking two fog lamps for brake lights) and although many cars have two, only the offside lamp should be fitted with a bulb. Unfortunately, many Swiss drivers don't know what fog lamps are for and use them when visibility is good (or forget to turn them off), but fail to use them in fog.

- **Note that headlight flashing has a different meaning in different countries.** In some countries it means 'after you' (generally also in Switzerland) and in others 'get out of my ******* way. (It may also mean 'I am driving a new car and haven't yet worked out what all the switches are for'.) A vehicle's hazard warning lights (both indicators simultaneously) may be used to warn other drivers of an obstruction, e.g. an accident or a traffic jam.

- The Swiss are obsessed with amber flashing lights, which are usually a warning to proceed with caution, for example for roadworks, non-functioning traffic lights and to indicate special speed restrictions, particularly on motorways. Many crossroads and junctions have flashing amber traffic lights outside rush hours. Flashing amber lights also operate in conjunction with normal traffic lights, as a warning to watch for cyclists and pedestrians when turning right at junctions.

- You may notice that many traffic lights have an uncanny habit of changing to green when you approach them, particularly during off-peak hours. This isn't magic or a result of your magnetic personality, but due to sensors installed in the road that change the lights to green when no other traffic has priority.

- When two vehicles meet on a narrow mountain road, the ascending vehicle has priority – the other must give way or reverse, as necessary. Postbuses always have right of way irrespective of direction and their drivers sound their horns to announce their approach to blind corners and narrow turns. When the road is too narrow to pass, postbus drivers have the authority to give other road users instructions regarding reversing or pulling over to one side.

- On-the-spot fines can be imposed for traffic offences such as minor speeding; not being in possession of your car documents; not removing your ignition key when leaving a vehicle unattended; not using dipped (low beam) headlights at night, in tunnels or in poor visibility; and parking infringements. Non-resident foreigners must pay fines on the spot. Residents who are unable to pay on the spot are given a giro payment form, payable within ten days. A fine of over SFr. 50 (for any offence) is recorded for posterity on your canton register. It pays not to contest a fixed fine unless you have a cast-iron defence, because if you lose the case the eventual fine will be much higher.

- Many motorists seem to have an aversion to driving in the right-hand lane on a three-lane motorway, which in effect, reduces the motorway to two lanes. Motorists should signal before overtaking **and** when moving back into an inside lane after overtaking, e.g. on a motorway. If you drive a right-hand drive car, take extra care when overtaking – the most dangerous manoeuvre in motoring.

- There are regulations in some cantons and towns requiring motorists to switch off their engines when waiting at traffic lights or railway crossings, where there may be a sign instructing you to do so. Public notices carry slogans such as 'For purer air – switch off engine' (*Für bessere Luft – Motor abstellen*) or 'Cut your motor' (*Coupez le Moteur*), but you can be fined for not switching off your engine. When stopped in tunnels, e.g. due to a breakdown, accident or traffic jam, you **must** switch off your engine (carbon monoxide poisoning can drastically shorten your life expectancy).

- Approach a railway level crossing slowly and **STOP**:
  - as soon as the barrier or half-barrier starts to fall;
  - as soon as the red warning lights are on or are flashing;
  - in any case when a train approaches.

A heavy vehicle that's slowing traffic is required to stop at the '300 metre' sign before closed railway crossings, to allow other vehicles to pass it.

- Be particularly wary of moped (*Motorfahrrad/Mofa, vélomoteur*) riders and cyclists. It isn't always easy to see them, particularly when they're hidden by the blind spots of a car or are riding at night without lights. Many moped riders seem to have a death wish and tragically many (mostly teenagers) lose their lives annually in Switzerland (maybe 14 years of age is too young to let them loose on the roads?). They constantly pull out into traffic or turn without looking or signalling. **When overtaking mopeds or cyclists, ALWAYS give them a wide. . . WIDE berth.** If you knock them off their bikes, you may have difficulty convincing the police that it wasn't your fault.

● Drive slowly when passing a stationary tram or bus, particularly a school bus. Where passengers must cross a road to reach a pedestrian path, for example from a tram stop in the middle of the road, motorists must stop and give way.

● A 'CH' (from the Latin *Confoederatio Helvetica*) nationality plate (sticker) must be affixed to the rear of a Swiss-registered car when motoring abroad. Drivers of foreign-registered cars in Switzerland must have the appropriate nationality plate affixed to the rear of their car. You can be fined on the spot for not displaying it, although it isn't often enforced judging by the number of cars without them (maybe German and Italian-registered cars are exempt?). Cars must show only the correct nationality plate and not an assortment.

● If you need to wear glasses or contact lenses when motoring, it's noted on your Swiss driving licence and you must always wear them. You must also carry a spare pair of glasses or contact lenses when driving.

● **It's illegal to use a mobile telephone when driving in Switzerland (unless it's a hands-free phone), for which you can be fined SFr. 100.**

● A roof rack load may be a maximum of 50kg (110lb) for vehicles registered after January 1st 1980 and 10 per cent of a vehicle's unladen weight for vehicles registered before this date.

● Trailers registered in Switzerland may be up 2.1m (6.9ft) wide and 6m (19.7ft) long (tow-bar included). Trailers registered abroad may be up to 2.2m (7.2ft) wide and 7m (23ft) long, but they aren't permitted to travel on Swiss mountain passes. A special permit must be obtained at Swiss border posts. If a towing vehicle has insufficient power to pull a trailer or caravan up an incline in heavy traffic, a journey over mountain passes mustn't be attempted. When towing a caravan or trailer of up to 1,000kg (2,204lb) in weight, you're restricted to 80kph (50mph) on motorways and 60kph (37mph) on all other roads (except where lower speed restrictions apply).

● A *Handbook of Swiss Traffic Regulations* is available for SFr. 12 from canton motor registration offices and customs offices. It's recommended reading for all motorists and is available in English, French, German, Italian and Spanish.

SWISS DRIVERS

The most popular Swiss motor sport is a public-road variation of stock car racing, commonly referred to as 'tail-gating' or 'shunting'. The rules of tail-gating are relatively simple: drivers are required to get as close as possible to the car in front **without** making contact, e.g. smashing into its rear. Unfortunately (as with all motor 'sports') there's an element of risk involved, which in this case is exacerbated by the low level of skill of the average participant, many of whom have yet to master the art of stopping at 120kph (or often faster) within a few car lengths. This results in quite a few collisions, often in motorway tunnels and always during rush hours.

A tailgater usually sits a few metres (centimetres?) from your bumper and tries to push you along irrespective of traffic density, road and weather conditions, or the prevailing speed limit. There's no solution, short of moving out of his way, which is often impossible (if you could move out of the way, there would be no 'fun' in doing it). Flashing your rear fog lamp or warning lights usually has no effect and braking can be disastrous – nothing deters the habitual tailgater. Sudden stopping and braking are allowed only **in an emergency** and motorists have been successfully sued for damages by someone who has run into the back of them, **because they stopped for no apparent reason.** Always try to leave a large gap between your vehicle and the vehicle in front. This isn't just to allow you more time to stop, should the vehicles in front decide to come together, but also to give the inevitable tailgater behind you more time to stop. **The closer the car behind you, the further you should be from the vehicle in front.**

The majority of motorists in Switzerland (and many other countries) drive much too close to the vehicle in front and have little idea of stopping distances. The *Handbook of Swiss Traffic Regulations* (see above) states that the safe stopping distance (including thinking distance) is **45m (147ft)** at 60kph (37mph), which increases to a massive **144m (472ft)** at 120kph (74mph). These stopping distances are on dry roads with good visibility and are greatly increased on wet or icy roads. **Although these distances may be generous, they aren't stupid.** If further proof is needed of how dangerous and widespread tail-gating is, simply check the statistics on the number of 'concertina' (multiple car) accidents in Switzerland, particularly on motorways and in tunnels.

The Swiss have a few other motoring idiosyncrasies, one of which is an aversion to using their handbrakes, even when stopped on a hill (they would rather burn their clutch out). Don't get too close as they're likely to roll back into you (it's all part of the racing image, as a good getaway is all important). Other common habits are a tendency to drive in the middle of the road on country lanes and sudden braking when approaching a 50kph (31mph) or other speed restriction (which can be annoying). In general, Swiss drivers are above average (average is bad) and no worse than most other European drivers. However, some foreigners consider Swiss drivers to be more aggressive and impolite than motorists in some other countries (e.g. the UK and the US). They are, for example, often reluctant to give way to a motorist waiting to pull out into traffic, and on motorways many drivers remain in the overtaking lane and cut across at the last moment when they want to take an exit. Swiss motorists are, however, usually law abiding (except with regard to speed limits), observe parking restrictions (more than most other European motorists) and are kind to animals.

Don't be too discouraged by the tailgaters and road hogs. Driving in Switzerland is often a pleasant experience, particularly when using country roads, which are relatively traffic-free outside rush hours. If you come from a country where traffic drives on the left, most people quickly get used to driving on the 'wrong' side of the road. Just take it easy at first, particularly in winter, and bear in mind that there may be other motorists around just as confused as you are.

WINTER DRIVING

Winter driving in Switzerland needn't be a survival course. Most motorists fit snow tyres (*Schneereifen/Winterreifen, pneus neige*), which although not compulsory help make winter driving safer. If you have an accident on snow in a vehicle that isn't fitted with snow tyres, you may be considered to be at fault if the other vehicles involved have snow tyres, irrespective of other circumstances. In some rural areas, roads aren't cleared of snow, in which case snow tyres may be a necessity. In towns, many roads are salted or gritted in winter, although some cantons have cut down on the use of salt because of its corrosive and anti-environmental properties. Due to the risk of corrosion, many motorists change to steel wheels in winter, rather than fit snow tyres to their expensive alloy wheels (assuming you could buy snow tyres in the correct size). Shop around for the best buys in winter tyres and steel wheels, as prices vary considerably.

It's necessary or even compulsory to fit snow chains (*Schneeketten, chaîne à neige*) on a vehicle's driving wheels in some areas, particularly on mountains roads and passes (see below). When chains are necessary, it's indicated by a road sign; **ignore it at your peril**. Buy good quality snow chains and practice putting them on and removing them **before** you get stuck in the snow – even getting the container undone can be a trial with cold numb fingers, let alone fitting them. Studded tyres (spikes) may be used on vehicles up to 3.5 tonnes from 1st November to 31st March. Vehicles with studs are restricted to 80kph (50mph) and aren't permitted to use motorways.

Winter driving courses are held in all areas of Switzerland, where motorists can learn how to drive on snow and ice (don't, however, expect to compete with Scandinavian rally drivers after a day's tuition). The cost is between SFr. 300 and 500 and courses usually last a whole day (drivers aged between 18 and 29 usually receive a reduction of SFr. 100 at Swiss motoring organisations). It isn't necessary to use your own car, as you can hire (rent) one from the centre (better than wrecking your own). If you use your own car, you can take out special insurance cover for around SFr. 15 to 20 a day, which is usually included in the course fee. Contact your canton's motor registration office or Swiss motoring organisations for more information. The Swiss Conference for Road Traffic Safety (*Schweiz. Konferenz für Sicherheit im Strassenverkehr, Conférence Suisse de sécurité dans le Trafic Routier*) subsidises advanced and special driving courses, e.g. anti-skid courses, for both motorists and motorcyclists throughout Switzerland.

Most rural roads are lined with two-metre high poles, which mark the edges of the road when there's heavy snow.

Skis carried on ski roof racks should have their curved front ends facing towards the rear of the car.

Take it easy in winter. In poor road conditions you will notice that most Swiss slow down considerably and even the habitual tailgaters leave a larger gap than usual between them and the car in front. Even a light snow fall can be treacherous, particularly on an icy road. When road conditions are bad, allow two to three times longer than usual to reach your destination.

MOUNTAIN PASSES

Snow chains must be fitted to all vehicles crossing mountain passes in winter (even in summer, freak snow storms can make roads treacherous). Always check in advance whether a pass is open, especially if using the pass means making a detour. A sign on the approach road indicates whether a pass is open (*offen*, *ouvert*) or closed (*geschlossen*, *fermé*) and whether chains are necessary.

The following mountain passes are open year round, although opening times may be reduced in winter (e.g. from 7am to 6 or 9pm): Bernina, Brünig, Flüela, Forclaz, Julier, Maloja, Mosses, Ofen (Il Fuorn), Pillon and Simplon. The following passes are open for part of the year: Oberalp, San Bernadino, Susten, Umbrail, St. Gotthard and Splügen open from May to November; Furka, Great St. Bernhard, Grimsel and Klausen open from May to October; Albula open from June to November; and Lukmanier open fromApril to December. The Great St. Bernard, St. Gotthard and San Bernadino passes have alternative road tunnels open all year round. There's a toll of from around SFr. 30 (depending on your car's wheelbase) to use the Great St. Bernard road tunnel between Bourg St. Pierre and Aosta (Etroubles) in Italy. The status (open/closed) of Swiss alpine tunnels and passes is given on Swiss television teletext and the road report service (☎ 163).

MOTORCYCLES

Switzerland is a great country for bike enthusiasts and its clean mountain air, excellent roads, beautiful scenery and generally good weather (from spring to autumn) make it a Mecca for bikers.

Mopeds

The following rules apply to riders of mopeds (*Motorfahrrad/Mofa*, *vélomoteur*) up to 50cc:

● you must be at least 14 years old;

● permission must be obtained from a parent if the rider is aged below 18;

● you must have an eye test and pass a written road rules test;

● a licence plate (*Kontrollschild*, *plaque*) must be obtained and/or a *vignette* from your community, which includes road tax and third-party insurance. The cost varies considerably (e.g. from SFr. 50 to 70 a year) depending on your canton of residence and is renewable annually by 31st May. Insurance is also available from Swiss motoring organisations.

● a lock must be fitted which blocks a wheel or the steering, or a cable or chain lock must be used;

● a crash helmet must be worn.

An application for a licence must be made to your canton's motor registration office with the following:

● your Swiss residence permit;

● two photographs;

● a completed application form, available from your community.

The maximum permitted speed for a moped is 30kph (19mph). Motorists with a car licence (Swiss or foreign) may ride a moped without passing a test or obtaining a special licence. Theft insurance can be taken out separately and breakdown assistance is available from Swiss motoring organisations for around SFr. 45 a year. Swiss motoring organisations also run motorcycle instruction courses.

Many moped riders are killed each year in Switzerland, mostly teenagers. If you have a child with a moped, it's important to impress upon him the need to take care (particularly in winter) and not take unnecessary risks, e.g. always observe traffic signals, signal before making a manoeuvre and **WEAR A CRASH HELMET** (some riders don't bother, although it's against the law). Car drivers often cannot see or avoid moped riders, particularly when they're riding at night without lights or when they dart out of a side street without looking. **Mopeds in the wrong hands can and do KILL!**

Motorcycles 50 to 125cc

The following rules are applicable to riders of motorcycles (*Motorrad*, *moto*) between 50 and 125cc:

- you must be at least 16 years old to ride a 50 cc motorcycle, and 18 to ride a 125 cc bike;

- you must attend eight hours of traffic theory and pass a practical test;

- a crash helmet must be worn;

- dipped (low beam) headlights must be used at all times;

- you must have valid third-party insurance;

- you must always carry your insurance certificate and driving licence.

The same application form is used to apply for a motorcycle licence as for a car driving licence and includes an eye test. After you pass the written road rules test, a provisional licence is issued for three months. This can be extended for a further two months, after which a practical test must be taken.

If you already have a car licence, you don't need to take a road rules or practical test, but you must still take a traffic theory course of at least eight hours.

Standard Motorcycles

The following rules are applicable to riders of standard motorcycles (*Motorrad*, *moto*) over 125cc:

- you must be at least least 25 years old or have held a motorcycle licence (for a motorcycle between 50 and 125cc) for at least two years;

- you must attend 12 hours of traffic theory (6 hours if you've already passed the test for motorcycles up to 125cc) and pass a practical test;

- a crash helmet must be worn;

- dipped (low beam) headlights must be used at all times;

- you must have valid third-party insurance;

- you must always carry your insurance certificate and driving licence.

For all licences you must have had an eye test, attended a first aid course and passed a road rules test before you can apply for a provisional driving licence.

CAR DOCUMENTS

The following documents must be carried when driving:

● driving licence (Swiss if held);

● vehicle registration document;

● exhaust test certificate (Swiss-registered cars only);

● your insurance certificate and green card (international motor insurance certificate) if applicable. Motorists must also carry their insurance certificate or green card when driving outside Switzerland.

● you should have a European accident report form (*Europäisches Unfallprotokoll, rapport européen des accidents routiers*), although it isn't compulsory. This is usually provided by insurance companies.

If you're stopped by the police and are unable to produce your car documents, you can be fined on the spot. It's advisable to make a copy of all your car documents and keep them in a safe place.

ACCIDENTS

If you're involved in an car accident (*Verkehrsunfall/Autounfall, accident d'auto*) in Switzerland, the procedure is as follows:

1 Stop immediately. Place a warning triangle at the edge of the road at least 50 metres behind your car on secondary roads or 150 metres on fast roads, e.g. motorways. If possible, a triangle should be placed in both directions. If necessary, for example when the road is partly or totally blocked, switch on your car's hazard warning lights and dipped (low beam) headlights and direct traffic around the hazard. In bad visibility, at night, or in a blind spot, try to warn oncoming traffic of the danger, e.g. with a torch or by waving a warning triangle. **Motorists who witness an accident are required by law to stop and render assistance.**

2 If anyone is injured, immediately call a doctor or ambulance (dial ☎ 144 in most areas), the fire brigade (dial ☎ 118) if someone is trapped or oil or chemicals have been spilled, and the police (dial ☎ 117). **If someone has been injured more than superficially the police MUST be summoned.** Don't move an injured person unless absolutely necessary to save him from further injury and don't leave him alone except to call an ambulance. Cover him with a blanket or coat to keep him warm. The REGA helicopter service (see page 135) is available for the evacuation of seriously injured people (☎ 1414 in an emergency situation).

3 If there are no injuries and damage to vehicles or property isn't serious, it's unnecessary to call the police to the accident scene, which may result in

someone being fined for a driving offence. If you and any other driver(s) involved aren't willing to let your insurance companies deal with the matter, then you're at liberty to call the police. For anything other than a minor accident it's advisable to call the police, as it will be too late to try to sort out who was at fault afterwards. **It's advisable to report any minor accident to the police within 24 hours to avoid any repercussions later (if someone else reports it and you don't, you could find yourself in trouble and can even end up losing your licence for a period!).**

4   If the other driver has obviously been drinking or appears incapable of driving, call the police. In all cases you mustn't say anything that could be interpreted as an admission of guilt (even if you're as guilty as hell!). Apparently admitting responsibility for an accident, either verbally or in writing, **can release your insurance company from responsibility under your policy**. You must say nothing or only that your insurance company will deal with any claims, and let the police and insurance companies decide who was at fault.

5   If either you or the other driver(s) involved decide to call the police, don't move your vehicle or allow other vehicles to be moved. If it's necessary to move vehicles to clear the road, mark their positions with chalk (have you ever tried writing on snow or ice with chalk?). Alternatively take photographs of the accident scene if a camera is available or make a drawing showing the positions of all vehicles involved before moving them (there's a space for this on the insurance accident report form).

6   Check whether there are any witnesses to the accident and take their names and addresses, particularly noting those who support **your** version of what happened. Note down the registration numbers of all vehicles involved and their drivers' names, addresses and insurance details. Give any other drivers involved your name, address and insurance details, if requested.

7   If you're detained by the police, you will have no right to contact anyone or to have legal representation. If you're travelling with a passenger, ask him to contact anyone necessary as soon as you realise you're going to be detained. **Don't sign a statement, particularly one written in a foreign language, unless you're CERTAIN you understand and agree with every word.**

8   If you've caused material damage, you must inform the owner of the damaged property as soon as possible. If you cannot reach him, contact the nearest police station (this also applies to damage caused to other vehicles when parking).

9   Complete the accident report form (*Europäisches Unfallprotokoll, rapport européen des accidents routiers*) provided by your insurance company as soon as possible after the accident and send it to your insurance company,

even if you weren't at fault. **Don't forget to sign it.** If you have an accident, obtain another accident form as soon as possible (accidents usually happen in threes!).

Hit-and-run Accidents

If you're the victim of a hit-and-run accident, report it to the local canton police immediately, preferably before driving your car away (if possible). They will inspect your car and take photographs and paint samples. This isn't just to help them catch the culprit, but to enable you to make a claim on a special federal insurance (*Bundesversicherung*, *assurance fédérale*) covering hit-and-run accidents. You or your insurance company must pay the first SFr. 1,000 of a claim and the federal insurance will pay the rest.

DRINKING, DRUGS & DRIVING

As you're no doubt aware, driving, drugs and drinking don't mix – an estimated 20 per cent of Swiss road deaths are a result of drunken driving. In Switzerland, you're no longer considered fit to drive when your blood alcohol concentration exceeds 50mg of alcohol per 100ml of blood, although if you cause an accident you can still be fined if you've been drinking, even when below the legal limit. The law regarding drunken driving is strict. If convicted you lose your licence for a long period (at least a year), receive a heavy fine (several thousand Swiss francs) and may even be imprisoned. To ensure that they have the same impact on everybody, fines are usually calculated as a percentage of the offender's salary. Anything more than one beer or a glass of wine may be too much for some people. Random breath tests can be carried out by the police at any time.

Also driving under the influence of illegal drugs is strictly forbidden and the police are allowed to conduct tests if they have any suspicions. If you test positive for illegal drugs, a blood sample is taken and analysed, and if you fail it you lose your driving licence for at least three months.

If you have an accident while under the influence of alcohol or drugs it can be very expensive. Your car, accident and health insurance may all be nullified. This means you must pay your own (and any third party's) car repairs, medical expenses and other damages. **Anyone who holds a driving licence and travels in a car with a drunken or drugged driver is held equally responsible under Swiss law.**

CAR THEFT

Car theft is relatively rare in Switzerland, so rare in fact that there are officially no cars stolen at all in some years. One reflection of the low rate of car theft is that until recently it was unusual for cars to be fitted with an alarm or engine immobiliser in Switzerland. However, thefts of articles from cars is on the increase in Swiss towns (many trusting Swiss make it easy for thieves by leaving their car windows open and the keys in the ignition!). Don't take any unnecessary risks and always lock your car and stow any valuables in the boot or out of sight, particularly when parking overnight in a public place.

Outside Switzerland car theft is rife. When visiting some of Switzerland's neighbouring countries (particularly Italy) you'd be well advised to have foolproof theft insurance and have your car fitted with every anti-theft device on the market. This is particularly important if you own a car that's particularly desirable to car thieves. For complete peace of mind, you're better off using public transport or hiring a car.

PETROL

In 2007, unleaded (*Bleifrei*, *sans plomb*) petrol cost from around SFr. 1.70 a litre, 'super plus' unleaded around SFr. 1.75 and diesel about SFr. 1.70 a litre. Leaded petrol is no longer available but large petrol stations sell an additive that allows unleaded fuel to be used in older cars. Unleaded petrol is 95 octane and super plus unleaded is 98 octane. The price of petrol generally varies from SFr. 0.10 to 0.20 a litre, with motorway petrol stations the most expensive and supermarkets the cheapest.

Most large petrol stations are open from around 6am until 10 or midnight. When paying at self-service petrol stations, either tell the cashier your pump number or hand him the receipt issued by the pump (if applicable). Outside normal business hours, many petrol stations have automatic pumps accepting SFr. 10 and 20 notes. Petrol pumps may also accept credit cards, Reka cheques and credit cards issued by oil companies. **Not all petrol stations accept credit cards and some may just accept certain kinds, which may not include the major ones.**

In Switzerland you're allowed to carry spare petrol in plastic cans, up to a maximum quantity of 25 litres. **Note that many countries have restrictions on how much petrol you're allowed to carry in your car (other than in the petrol tank) and some ban plastic petrol cans.** For more information check with a motoring organisation (see page 234).

GARAGES

Garages in Switzerland are generally open from 7am to 6.30pm and most close for lunch between noon and 1pm. Servicing and repairs are expensive (particularly in major towns), but the quality of work is generally of a high standard. You may find that smaller garages (not unqualified back street places, but reputable garages who guarantee their work) are cheaper than main dealers.

If you require a major repair job or service and are able to drive your car, it may pay you to have it done outside Switzerland. Similarly, if you require new tyres or a new exhaust, they may be cheaper in one of Switzerland's neighbouring countries.

Most garages, including all main dealers, provide a replacement car (*Ersatzwagen, véhicule de remplacement*) for around SFr. 50 a day, while your car is being serviced. Some garages supply a free car when you have a service done and charge for petrol only. If you're a member of a Swiss motoring organisation such as the TCS, you can have your car tested for around SFr. 60 and receive an accurate estimate of any necessary repairs.

SPEED LIMITS

The following speed limits are in force throughout Switzerland:

Motorways	120kph (75mph)
Dual-carriageways	100kph (62mph)
Country Roads	80kph (50mph)
Towns	50 or 60kph (31 or 37mph) – 50kph if not sign-posted
Residential Roads	30kph (18mph) or as sign-posted (sometimes 30 or 40kph is indicated for sharp bends)

Some cantons have introduced controversial temporary speed limits (coupled with intensified speed checks) of 100kph (62mph) for cars and 70kph for trucks and cars towing caravans on certain stretches of motorways in July and August, in an attempt to reduce 'summer smog'. In some cities, e.g. Zurich and Basle, 'blue' zones have been established where speed limits have been reduced to 30kph (20mph). Roads in blue zones are liberally dotted with 'sleeping policemen' (speed bumps) and other obstacles to slow traffic.

When towing a caravan or trailer, you're restricted to 80kph (50mph) on motorways and 60kph (37mph) on all other roads. Mobile radar traps and laser detectors (more accurate than radar) are regularly set-up around the country, in addition to permanent photographic radar traps. If you're caught speeding, the police may send you a souvenir picture of your car number plate, with the fine (*Busse/Strafe, amende*). Cameras are also positioned at major intersections to photograph the registration numbers of cars driving through red lights. Fines for many motoring offences were sharply increased in recent years.

Swiss law requires motorists to adapt their speed to the weather, visibility and road conditions. In particular, you must be able to come to a full stop within the distance you can see. This means that you can be fined for speeding, for example at night or in bad weather, even if you were driving within the actual speed limit.

Speeding fines depend on the speed above the legal speed limit, and for serious offences, the offender's number of previous motoring convictions. For marginal speeding 1 to 5kmh above the limit the fine is SFr. 40, except on motorways where it's SFr. 20. Fines for driving more than 5kmh above the speed limit depend on where the offence was committed, e.g. town centre, town suburb or country road/motorway. Fines for 6 to 10kmh above the limit are from SFr. 60 to 120; for 11 to 15kmh above the limit SFr. 120 to 250; for 16 to 20kmh above the limit SFr. 180 to 240; and for 21 to 25kmh above the limit SFr. 260 to 1,000 (SFr. 260 on a motorway). If you're caught doing over 15kmh above the speed limit in a town centre, over 20kmh in a suburb or on a country road or over 25kmh on a motorway, you must appear in court, will be heavily fined (e.g. SFr. 500 to 1,000) and could also lose your licence for a period.

If you're stopped by the police for marginal speeding (where a fixed penalty applies), fines can be paid on the spot or by giro payment within ten days; they **must** be paid on the spot if you're a foreign visitor, although if you're unable to pay they won't usually impound your car. Fitting and using radar warning devices is illegal in Switzerland and in most other European countries. You're forbidden to drive on motorways in the fast lane unless you're overtaking, and where sign-posted, below a minimum speed limit (you can be fined for doing so). Switzerland doesn't have a licence points system where driving licences are 'endorsed' (stamped) when you commit an offence, but nevertheless an accumulation of offences (not just for speeding) can result in a driving ban.

Many Swiss motorists have a complete disregard for speed limits, particularly during rush hours on motorways. The police could have a field day any time they wanted, although police cars are rarely seen on motorways (although they also use unmarked cars), except when attending accidents. Motorists tend to drive faster in southern Switzerland and are generally less disciplined than motorists in the north (it must be something to do with the proximity to France and Italy).

ROAD MAPS

Road maps (*Strassenkarte, carte routière*) are available from various sources:

● Good free maps of Switzerland are available from city tourist information offices, car hire (rental) offices and many Swiss banks. Switzerland Tourism offices sell a good map of Switzerland for SFr. 1.

● An excellent road map of Switzerland is available from offices of the Zurich insurance company.

● A detailed Swiss road map book entitled *Auto Schweiz (Suisse)* is published by Kümmerly + Frey, containing 35 town plans (it's also available without the town plans).

- The ACS and TCS Swiss motoring organisations produce many Swiss road maps.

- Free local town maps are available from many tourist information offices. More detailed maps are available from bookshops, news agencies, kiosks and railway station booking offices. Local village maps can usually be obtained from community offices.

Unfortunately Switzerland doesn't have any large-scale maps for rural areas containing a comprehensive street index, but internet maps and GPS devices are good alternatives.

CAR HIRE

Major international car hire (rental) companies (e.g. Avis, Budget, Europcar and Hertz) are represented in most cities in Switzerland and at international airports (offices are open from around 6.30am until 11pm). Cars can also be hired from local garages and car hire offices in most towns. Look under *Autovermietungen/Mietwagen*, *location de voitures* in the telephone directory or on the internet. Hire cars in Switzerland have a registration plate with a V (for *vermietet* or hired) after the number.

Car hire is generally **very** expensive in Switzerland and around double the cost in many other European countries and up to three times the rate in the US. Hire costs vary considerably between companies, particularly over longer periods (weekly and monthly rates are lower). Hiring a car from an airport is the most expensive, as are one-way hires. Older cars can be hired from many garages at lower rates than those charged by the multinational companies. In winter, hire cars are fitted with winter tyres and usually supplied with snow chains and ski racks at no extra charge. Hire cars can be ordered with a portable telephone, a luggage rack and child seats (for an extra charge).

In addition to standard saloon cars, you can hire a four-wheel-drive car, estate (station wagon), minibus, luxury car, armoured limousine or a convertible, often with a choice of manual or automatic gearbox. Minibuses accessible to wheelchairs can also be hired, e.g. from Hertz. In some cities, e.g. Geneva, electric cars with a limited range can be hired from Avis, Hertz and Sixt-Alsa. Vans and pick-ups are available from the major hire companies by the hour, half-day or day, or from smaller local companies (which are cheaper than the major companies). When you have your car serviced or repaired, most garages will hire you a car for a nominal sum or even lend you one.

To hire a car in Switzerland you require a valid Swiss, European or international driving licence, which must have been held for a minimum of one year. The minimum age of a driver must usually be 20 or 21 and can be as high as 25 for some categories of cars. It's usually necessary to have a credit card to hire a car in Switzerland. **Don't be late returning a car as it can be expensive.**

One way to reduce the cost of car hire in Switzerland is to hire a car through the US office of an international car hire company and pay by credit card. This is a legitimate practice and can save you up to 50 per cent on local rates. The US freephone (800) numbers of hire companies, such as Alamo, Avis, Budget and Hertz can be obtained from international directory enquiries and must be prefixed by the international access number.

Mobility Car Sharing is a more affordable solution for the occasional driver. With Mobility you pay an annual subscription of SFr. 290 or SFr. 190 when combined with a half-fare travel card, a *Streckenabonnement* of the Swiss federal railway, a *Generalabonnement*, or a Migros membership card. You can reserve a car from some 350 railway stations (or from 1,000 Mobility stations in total) and are charged a low rate based on the time used and the kilometres travelled. For more information contact Mobility CarSharing Schweiz, Gütschstrasse 2, CH-6000 Lucerne 7 (☎ 0848 824 812, 💻 www.mobility.ch). Mobility members also receive a 30 to 35 per cent discount on Avis and Hertz car hire in Switzerland and a 10 per cent discount in Europe.

MOTORING ORGANISATIONS

There are three Swiss motoring organisations:

- **Automobile Club of Switzerland/ACS** (*Automobil Club der Schweiz, Automobile Club Suisse*) – Wasserwerkgasse 39, PO Box, CH-3000 Berne 13 (☎ 031 328 31 11, 💻 www.acs.ch);

- **Touring Club of Switzerland/TCS** (*Touring Club der Schweiz, Touring Club de Suisse*) – ch. de Blandonnet 4, PO Box 820, CH-1214 Vernier (☎ 0844 888 111, 💻 www.tcs.ch);

- **Transport Club of Switzerland/VCS** (*Verkehrs-Club der Schweiz, Association Suisse des Transports*) – Lagerstr. 41, CH-3360 Herzogenbuch-see (☎ 0848 611 611, 💻 www.verkehrsclub.ch).

The organisations have offices in all major cities and large towns. There are few essential differences between the services provided by the two largest Swiss motoring organisations, the ACS and TCS, although charges vary. The services provided by the VCS are more limited. The annual membership fee is SFr. 120 for one vehicle (VCS SFr. 60). In general, membership for the first year is noticeably cheaper compared to the following years. There are reduced fees for spouses and juniors, and company membership is also possible.

The ACS and the TCS (and, to a lesser extent, the VCS) provide a wide range of services, which may include official control and pre-control serviceability tests; estimation of repair costs; verification of repairs and bills;

guarantee claims; holiday luggage and travel insurance; car, motorcycle and cycle insurance; travel bureau and ticket office services; hotel reductions; valuations of used cars; legal and technical advice; advice on buying cars; running cost estimates (per km); tyres and car accessories; customs' documents; information about road conditions; tourist information; road maps and tourist guides; free national and canton newspapers; international driving licences; and translations of Swiss driving licences.

Members of Swiss motoring organisations who break down anywhere in Switzerland can call service telephone number ☎ 140 (24-hour service, SFr. 0.20 per call) for free help; non-members can also obtain assistance, but it can be expensive. Emergency SOS roadside telephones (painted orange) are provided throughout Switzerland on motorways, mountain passes and in tunnels. Black arrows on white posts at the side of motorways show the direction of the nearest telephone (situated every 1.6km/1mi). Keep your membership card in your car and quote your number when calling for help. In Switzerland, membership includes the breakdown patrol service, towing to a garage, or transportation of your car to your home garage. In addition, when necessary, the cost of a taxi to the nearest bus or rail station, a taxi home or a hotel room will be paid. Swiss motoring organisations have reciprocal arrangements with motoring organisations in most European countries.

All Swiss motoring organisations provide a comprehensive international travel insurance policy, called a 'protection letter' (*Schutzbrief, livret*), which covers most travel accident possibilities. If you have a car accident or a breakdown abroad, the 'protection letter' insurance pays for hotel and medical costs, car hire and essential repairs, or transportation of your car back to Switzerland. This insurance is valid irrespective of the mode of transport used and can be taken out with the TCS for Europe (including Russia) and the Mediterranean countries or the whole world. The VCS insurance covers only Europe and the Mediterranean countries, while ACS offer world-wide cover only. Insurance costs from around SFr. 80 to 150 a year, depending on the motoring organisation and whether you have European or world-wide cover.

'Protection letters' also cover car hire (vouchers for Avis or Hertz), repairs, emergency medical attention, legal aid, technical survey and police fines (resulting from an accident). The 'protection letter', which must be signed, and your identity card (*Ausweiskarte, carte d'authentification*), should be kept in a safe place. The TCS 'protection letter' also covers holiday or travel cancellation fees, or fees incurred by curtailment of a holiday when caused by an emergency. The insurance provided by the 'protection letter' is much cheaper than most holiday travel insurance, **but you should ensure that it includes all your travel insurance requirements.**

Legal expenses insurance (*Rechtsschutz, protection juridique*), covering legal costs in the event of an accident, is available from Swiss motoring organisations but is usually cheaper from Swiss motor insurance companies.

The ACS or TCS can also help you when you're locked out of your car.

PARKING

Parking in Swiss towns can be a problem, particularly on-street parking. In most towns there are many public and multi-storey car parks, indicated by the sign of a white 'P' on a blue background. In cities there are also hundreds of parking meters, but they usually all seem to be constantly occupied, particularly on Saturdays. In some cities, e.g. Berne, there are signs that direct you to a car park with free places. Parking in towns costs SFr. 2 to 3 per hour. Parking in a centrally located city car park costs at least SFr. 2 an hour and 24 hours can cost SFr. 25 or more. Geneva introduced an obligatory parking sticker for the central area in an effort to reduce traffic pollution. Cheaper parking is often available not far from city centres and some city shopping centres allow a period of free parking, e.g. three hours. You may prefer to drive to a convenient railway station or a park and ride (P+R) area, where bus or train connections are available to city centres. A 'P+R' parking ticket may also include the cost of the bus or tram journey to and from the local town centre. P+R parking at railway stations costs from SFr. 2 to 15 per day (average SFr. 4) and monthly rates are available for commuters (typically a 50 per cent reduction).

If you park in a multi-storey car park, make a note of the level and space number where you park as it can take a long time to find your car if you have no idea where to start looking! Tear-off slips showing the parking level (*Geschoss/Stockwerk*, *étage*) are sometimes provided at lifts in multi-storey car parks. On entering most car parks you take a ticket from an automatic dispenser and must pay **before** collecting your car, either at a cash desk (*Kasse/Caisse*) or via a machine, which may accept both coins, notes and credit cards. **You cannot pay at the exit.** After paying you usually have around 15 minutes to exit, where you insert your ticket in the slot of the exit machine (in the direction shown by the arrow on the ticket). In some ski resorts, parking in a multi-storey car park is free for skiers or anyone using the ski lifts. You must stamp your car park ticket in a machine, usually at the station above the car park level, in order to exit from the car park without paying. **Headlights should be used in all underground and badly lit garages.**

Swiss companies don't usually provide employees with free parking facilities in large cities and towns. Outside main towns, free parking is usually available at or near offices or factories. Disabled motorists are provided with free or reserved parking spaces in most towns, shopping centres and at airports, but must display an official disabled motorist badge inside their windscreen (some city car parks also have spaces reserved for women near the exit). Regular drivers for the disabled can also obtain special parking permits in some cities. Apart from off-street parking, e.g. multi-storey car parks, the following kinds of on-street parking are provided in most towns:

● **parking meters**, where the maximum permitted parking period varies from 15 minutes to ten hours. Meter-feeding is illegal and you must vacate the parking space when the meter time expires. Meters usually accept a combination of 50 cent and one franc coins. The costs varies, e.g. SFr. 1 per hour in a city centre and SFr. 0.50 outside. Most meters are in use from 7am to 7pm, Mondays to Fridays and from 7am to 4pm on Saturdays (check the meter to be sure), and some are free during lunch periods, e.g. noon to 2pm. Meters at railway stations may be in use 24 hours a day.

● **white zones**, indicated by white road markings and a sign, permit free unlimited parking;

● **blue zones** (*Blaue Zone, zone bleue*), indicated by blue road markings, require a parking disc (*Parkscheibe, disque de stationnement*) to be displayed behind your car windscreen. EU-compatible parking discs are available free from Swiss motoring organisations, police stations, banks, hotels, insurance offices, kiosks and tourist offices. Motor accessory shops and garages also sell them for a few francs. The parking disc must be set to the next half or full hour and then allows one hour's parking from that time. For example, if you arrive at 9.50am you set your parking disc on 10am and can leave the car in the parking space until 11am. If you arrive at 10.05 am you set the car to 10.30 am and are allowed to use the parking space until 11.30am. Free parking is also permitted from 6pm until 9am the next day. In some towns, it's possible to purchase a permanent pass from your local traffic office or some police stations, valid for extended parking in a blue zone. However, it's normally valid only in your local postcode area.

● **pay and display** parking areas, where you must buy a parking ticket (showing the parking expiry time) from a ticket machine and display it behind your car windscreen. These areas include both on and off-street parking areas and may include park and ride (P+R) car parks, e.g. at railway stations. There may be a maximum parking period of around two hours in town centres.

The attitude towards illegal parking is much stricter in Switzerland than in most other European countries, although the Swiss still seem to park anywhere in the cities. You're forbidden to park on footpaths (even with one or two wheels) anywhere in Switzerland, unless sign-posted and marked otherwise (in some towns parking spaces include part of the footpath, shown by a line).

You can be fined for parking illegally in a private parking area. Parking illegally in reserved car parking spaces can result in a heavy fine, e.g. SFr. 100 (private parking spaces may be reserved by local residents and aren't used during business hours only). Private parking spaces are sacred in Switzerland and **very** expensive. For minor parking offences in some car parks, e.g. exceeding the permitted parking time by up to half an hour, you may be fined SFr. 10, which must be inserted in the envelope provided and deposited in a special box at the exit. Official parking fines are high, e.g. SFr. 40 for exceeding the allowed/paid time by up to two hours, SFr. 60 from two to four hours and SFr.

100 for four to ten hours. In some towns you can be fined for parking facing the wrong way, i.e. you must be able to pull out directly into the flow of traffic on the same side of the road as you're parked. If you receive a parking ticket, it's usually thoughtfully accompanied by a giro payment form (*Einzahlungsschein, bulletin de versement*) and is payable within ten days. You're sent a reminder letter if you don't pay a fine on time and it may be increased as a consequence.

Be careful where you park your car in the mountains, particularly during spring when the snow is melting and the weather is wet and/or stormy. It isn't unknown for falling rocks (even small ones) to make large dents in cars.

PEDESTRIAN ROAD RULES

The following road rules apply to pedestrians in Switzerland:

- Motorists **must** stop for a pedestrian waiting at a pedestrian crossing if the pedestrian shows by any action his intention to cross the road. However, you should still take extra care when using pedestrian crossings in Switzerland as Swiss motorists aren't fond of stopping. If you come from a country where motorists routinely approach pedestrian crossings with caution and stop when pedestrians are waiting, **take extra care** (some 18 per cent of Swiss road fatalities are pedestrians).

- Pedestrians are forbidden to cross a road within 50 metres of a pedestrian crossing, bridge or subway (pedestrian underpass).

- Teach your children the green cross code: look **left**, look **right**, look **left** again, before crossing the road (remember that traffic drives on the **RIGHT** hand side of the road). In school, children are taught to stop, look, listen and walk.

- Pedestrians must wait for a green light before crossing the road at a pedestrian crossing with pedestrian lights, irrespective of whether there's any traffic. You can be fined for jay walking, i.e. crossing the road where it's prohibited or against a red pedestrian light.

- Pedestrians must use footpaths where they are provided or may use a bicycle path when there's no footpath. Where there's no footpath or bicycle path, you must walk on the left side of the road facing the oncoming traffic.

MOTORING ABROAD

When motoring abroad **NEVER** assume that the rules, regulations and driving habits are the same as in Switzerland. Always take your Swiss (or foreign) driving licence, car registration and insurance documents (e.g. green card), and bear in mind such things as breakdown insurance, essential spares, and security for your car and belongings. Check that your car complies with local laws and that you have the necessary equipment, such as a warning triangle(s), first-aid kit, reflective vest and fire extinguisher. If in doubt, check the latest laws and regulations with a Swiss motoring organisation.

The most dangerous European countries for motorists vary depending on which newspapers or magazines you read and whose statistics they use. However, it's undeniable that the likelihood of having an accident is much higher in some countries. Driving in some European cities is totally chaotic, a bit like fun fair bumper cars without the fun, and nerve-wracking at the best of times. It's no way to spend a relaxing holiday. If in doubt about your ability to cope with the stress or the risks involved, you'd be wiser to fly or take a train.

LEARNING TO DRIVE

The following points are applicable to learner drivers in Switzerland:

● You must be at least 18 years old.

● You must have attended a first-aid-course (see below) and passed a written road rules test which can be taken in English and other foreign languages. There are 50 questions in each of the ten possible examinations (one is randomly chosen for you). A booklet containing the 850 possible questions of the basic theory examination (in German, French and Italian) is available from your canton's motor registration office. Once you've passed the test you can apply for a provisional driving licence.

● You must attend eight hours of compulsory traffic theory (costing for example around SFr. 240 at Migros Club School). This cannot be done before the road rules test has been passed.

● You must display an L plate (white L on a blue background) at the rear of your car.

● You aren't permitted on busy roads, including motorways, until you're deemed proficient enough (usually after a few months).

● A fee of around SFr. 250 is payable (depending on your canton), which includes the cost of the provisional driving licence, the test fee (written and practical) and a book of the rules of the road.

● You must always be accompanied by a qualified driver who has held a full driving licence for at least three years.

● It isn't compulsory to take driving lessons with a driving school (*Fahrschule*, *auto-école*) before obtaining your licence. Nevertheless it's advisable as the instructors know the standard demanded by examiners. Instruction is available in most languages. Reckon on around 20 to 30 hours of instruction costing from around SFr. 85 an hour (plus a one-off insurance fee of about SFr. 80).

● You must complete a 10-hour first-aid course (*Nothelferkurs*, *cours de premier secours*) at a federally approved institute, e.g. the Migros Club School (see **Day & Evening Classes** on page 312) or a motoring organisation.

In some cantons, the practical driving test can be taken only three times. After the third failure you must see a psychologist who decides if you're psychologically fit to drive (many 'qualified' drivers would immediately be confined to a padded cell if they had to take this test!). On the recommendation of the psychologist you may take the test a fourth **and final time**. In other cantons, (e.g. Zurich), after the 3rd failure of the practical exam, you're put into a special, smaller class where you can receive the personal attention required to pass the exam. Swiss motoring organisations run 'refresher' courses for senior citizens (aged 55 plus). If you're over 70 years old you need confirmation from your GP annually that you're still fit to drive.

The driving licence for motorcycles and cars (categories A and B) is issued on probation for the first three years, and only after further training (theoretical and practical tests) do you receive a definitive licence – yet another reason to have your foreign licence converted before you've lived in Switzerland for a year.

USEFUL TELEPHONE NUMBERS

Keep the following telephone numbers handy in case of need:

Number	Service
☎ 117	Police (emergencies only)
☎ 118	Fire (emergencies only)
☎ 144	Ambulance (emergencies only)
☎ 1414	Rega Helicopter Rescue
☎ 140	Vehicle Breakdown (SFr. 0.20 per call)
☎ 163	Road Reports (recorded information)

The above telephone numbers can be dialled from anywhere within Switzerland and are manned or provide recorded information (in the local language: French, German or Italian) 24 hours a day. See also **Emergency Numbers** on page 135.

12.

HEALTH

Switzerland spends around 11 per cent of its GDP, over SFr. 50,000bn per year, on health, which is one of the highest percentages in the OECD. Although Swiss health insurance is expensive (only North Americans spend more on health care) and becoming more so every year, the country's health services are among the best in the world. Switzerland has a wealth of modern hospitals, excellent doctors (the highest ratio of doctors to patients in the world) and highly trained nurses, employing the latest equipment and medical techniques. There are generally no waiting lists for operations or hospital beds and the standard of treatment is second to none. If you must get sick, you could hardly choose a better place – provided of course that you're insured or can afford to pay the bill!

Two yardsticks used to measure the quality of healthcare worldwide are the infant mortality rate and life expectancy, and Switzerland has one of the lowest infant mortality rates in the world (around four deaths in the first year for every thousand live births) and its life expectancy of nearly 84 for women and 79 for men is exceeded only by Iceland, Japan, France and Spain.

Nevertheless, the famous Swiss air isn't always as fresh as the guidebooks would have you believe. Despite strenuous efforts to reduce pollution, impure air and high ozone levels in summer in the major Swiss cities are causing health problems (mainly respiratory ailments and allergies), particularly among children. (However, compared with what passes for fresh air in most countries, Swiss city air is pure oxygen.) Pollution is also caused by smokers, as Switzerland rates highly in the world smoking league (per head of population) and has a particularly high proportion of young women smokers. The main causes of death in Switzerland are cardiovascular disease (around 37 per cent) and cancer (some 26 per cent). You can safely drink the water in Switzerland, but the wine and beer taste much better.

The Swiss are prominent in the lucrative 'immortality' business, which includes plastic surgery, rejuvenation and regeneration clinics, spa treatment centres and therapies by the dozen. Cellular rejuvenation (a snip at around US$10,000) is especially popular, although patients are injected with live sheep cells – Switzerland abounds with geriatrics prancing around like spring lambs. Complementary medicine is also popular in Switzerland (particularly homeopathy) and is usually paid for by Swiss health insurance.

Hay fever sufferers can obtain the daily pollen count (*Pollenbericht*, *pollen bulletin*) between March and July via the Swiss television teletext service and daily newspapers.

EMERGENCIES

The emergency medical services in Switzerland are among the best in the world. Keep a record of the telephone numbers of your doctor and local emergency hospital and other emergency telephone numbers (see page 133) near your telephone. Emergency first-aid information is available at the back of all telephone directories in French, German and Italian. If you're unsure who to call, dial the police on 117, who will tell you who to contact or will contact the appropriate service for you. The action to take in a medical 'emergency' (*Notfall*, *urgence*) depends on the degree of urgency and may include one of the following:

- Call ☎ 144 for an ambulance. Most ambulances are equipped with cardiac equipment, and 'cardiomobiles' are provided for emergency heart cases. Details of the Swiss air rescue service (REGA) can be found on page 134.

- If you're able, you can go to the emergency treatment centre (*Notfalldienst*, *service d'urgence*) of a hospital or to an emergency clinic (*Pikett-Dienst*, *permanence*) for minor casualties in French-speaking Switzerland. You may need to show proof of health insurance. Non-Swiss residents without insurance and no means to pay may be turned away, although this is unlikely and won't happen in a life or death situation.

- Call your family or personal doctor. Outside surgery hours an answering machine gives you the telephone number of the doctor on call.

In major cities a telephone number is provided where a doctor is available to advise you on medical and psychiatric emergencies. Call the operator on ☎ 111 and ask for the emergency medical service (*Ärztlicher Notfalldienst/ Zentrale Örtliche Notfalldienst*, *médecin de service/médecin de jour*). The operator keeps a list of doctors, dentists, pharmacies and veterinarians who are on call 24 hours a day. Doctors and dentists are categorised by speciality, location and the languages spoken.

If you have an existing medical problem that cannot easily be seen or recognised, e.g. a heart condition, diabetes, a severe allergy (e.g. penicillin), epilepsy or a rare blood group, you may be interested in Medic-Alert. Medic-Alert members wear an internationally recognised identification bracelet or necklace emblem with your medical problem, membership number and a telephone number engraved on the back. When you're unable to speak for yourself, doctors, police or anyone providing aid can obtain immediate vital medical information from anywhere in the world by telephoning a 24-hour emergency number. Medic-Alert is a non-profit registered charity. Members pay for the cost of the emblem and a small annual fee. For more information contact the Medic-Alert Foundation, 1 Bridge Wharf, 156 Caledonian Road, London N1 9UU, UK (☎ 0800-581420, 💻 www.medicalert.co.uk).

ACCIDENTS

If you have an accident resulting in an injury, either to yourself or to a third party, inform the following, as necessary:

- your family doctor or another doctor (if treatment is necessary);

- the police (contacting the police within 24 hours may be compulsory);

- your accident insurance company (who will send you a form to complete);

- your employer.

If you have an accident at work, report it to your manager as soon as possible. If you work more than eight hours per week and have an accident outside work, you should inform your employer, as he must provide you with accident insurance (see page 266).

An accident report form must be completed for all accidents where medical treatment is necessary and which result in a claim on your accident insurance. As a general rule, Swiss accident or health insurance policies pay for medical treatment only when the patient remains in Switzerland. Journeys abroad while undergoing a course of treatment as the result of an accident may require the consent of your insurance company. The length of time during which you remain on full pay after an accident usually depends on your length of service (see **Salary Insurance** on page 260).

For information on how to prevent and avoid accidents (road, sport, household, garden and leisure), contact the Swiss Bureau for the Prevention of Accidents (*Schweiz. Beratungsstelle für Unfallverhütung*, *Bureau suisse de prévention des accidents*), Laupenstr. 11, CH-3008 Berne (☎ 031 390 22 22, 🖥 www.bfu.ch). The bureau publishes numerous free leaflets and a magazine, which is available on subscription.

DOCTORS

There are excellent doctors (*Arzt, médecin*) everywhere in Switzerland, many of whom speak reasonable or good English. Many embassies in Switzerland maintain a list of English-speaking doctors (or doctors speaking their national language) in their area, and your employer or colleagues may be able to recommend someone. Doctors are listed in telephone directories under *Ärzte*, *médecin* and their speciality. General practitioners (GPs) or family doctors are listed under *Allgemeine Medizin or médecin général*. A list of doctors can be found on 🖥 www.doktor.ch (in German only). Most doctors list both their surgery and home telephone numbers. A zero with a diagonal line through it alongside a telephone number signifies a 24-hour answering service. Many major cities operate an emergency medical service (*Ärztlicher Notfalldienst, médecin de service*), where a list of doctors is kept, categorised by speciality, location and languages spoken.

If you're working or studying in Switzerland it's mandatory to have health insurance (see page 262), which may determine or restrict your choice of doctor. Otherwise, you may usually go to any doctor anywhere, although each canton has different rules and procedures. An appointment must usually be made before visiting a doctor (except in 'emergencies').

Most surgeries are closed on one day or afternoon a week and many doctors hold Saturday morning surgeries. Be prepared to wait anything up to an hour past your appointment time (the only time your doctor will be punctual is when you're late!). Doctors in Switzerland make house calls only *in extremis*.

Many doctors' surgeries in Switzerland are equipped to do simple tests (e.g. blood and urine), take X-rays and carry out most out-patient treatment performed in a clinic or small hospital. This is particularly so in villages and remote areas, where the nearest clinic or hospital may be some distance away. Your doctor is able to give advice or provide information on all aspects of health or medical care, including blood donations, home medical equipment and counselling, but there are specialists for many fields of medicine which in many other countries are treated or dealt with by a general practitioner (GP). These include children's illnesses, internal disorders and maternity-related problems.

It isn't always necessary to be referred to a specialist by your family doctor and you're usually free to make an appointment directly with, for example, an eye specialist, gynaecologist or orthopaedic surgeon. If in doubt, ask your health insurance company for advice. Note, however, that there may be a long waiting list for an appointment with a specialist if you aren't an urgent case and your GP may be able to make an earlier appointment.

Specialists in Switzerland are usually free to charge what they like and their fees are significantly higher than family doctors'. Hospitals and doctors generally have different charge rates, as follows (lowest rate first):

● patients who have health insurance cover within the canton;

● patients who have health insurance cover in another canton;

● private patients who don't belong to a Swiss health fund or Swiss health insurance scheme.

If you go to your doctor for treatment of an injury as the result of an accident, e.g. skiing, you must inform your accident insurance company within a few days. If you work over eight hours a week, treatment is free as you're covered by compulsory accident insurance (see page 266).

When you receive a bill from your doctor, you should pay it within the period specified (usually 30 days) and send it to your health fund or insurance company. A health fund (see page 269) usually reimburses up to 90 per cent of the cost. If you send your health fund your bank account details (bank name, branch and account number) or post office account number, they pay refunds directly into your account and advise you when payment has been made. You should scrutinise all bills carefully, as it isn't unknown for doctors to overcharge.

Keep all receipts for health treatment. If your family's total health bills (including dental bills) that **aren't** covered by health insurance amount to 5 per cent or more of your annual income, you're able to offset the cost against your income tax bill.

Your doctor usually sends you a bill for each illness within a three-month period. If you're forced to visit different doctors (e.g. when your doctor is sick or doing military service) for the same illness, the bills should be sent to your health fund together. If you change doctors of your own accord during a course of treatment, you must pay twice.

MEDICINES

Medicines prescribed by a doctor are obtained from a chemist's (*Apotheke*, *pharmacie*) denoted by the sign of a green cross on a white background. In most cities, several chemists' are open until late evening (e.g. 10pm) and some provide a 24-hour service on certain days or even seven days a week. Ask the telephone operator (111) for the address. At least one 'duty' chemist's (pharmacy) is open outside normal opening hours in all areas (a list is published in local newspapers and posted on chemists' doors) for the emergency dispensing of drugs and medicines. A list of all 'duty' chemists is available on the internet (⌨ www.sos-apotheke.ch).

Switzerland has some of the highest prices in Europe for prescribed medicines, some 50 per cent higher than the EU average. As with various other items, many medicines are sold much cheaper (e.g. less than 50 per cent of the Swiss price) in Switzerland's neighbouring countries, particularly France and Italy. **Note that a surcharge (e.g. SFr. 30 in Lucerne) is made on medicines purchased outside normal opening hours.**

If there isn't a chemist's in the village where your doctor practises, he usually supplies medicines from his own supplies. If he doesn't have them in stock he writes a prescription. Some medicines, e.g. herbal and homeopathic medicines, aren't recognised by a health fund and you must pay the full cost for them. Usually your doctor tells you when this is the case and he may offer to prescribe an alternative.

Medicines are prescribed in the following four ways:

- once only when the prescription is filled;

- one repeat dose without the need for a second prescription;

- repeat doses as often as necessary within a three-month period;

- repeat doses for up to a year (e.g. for birth control pills).

Chemists are permitted to charge a fee for providing advice (irrespective of whether they actually proffer any advice or simply hand you the medication) and another fee for keeping your details on their computer. These fees were introduced to compensate chemists for a reduction of margins on medication in 2001 and are covered by health insurance.

Most health insurance companies issue a credit-card-size insurance card that you show at the chemist's together with the prescription from your doctor. The chemist takes your insurance number and details and invoices the health insurance company directly. The company sends you an invoice for the annual excess and/or the 10 per cent you must pay yourself.

Some health insurance companies – usually the ones with the lowest premiums – don't automatically pay chemists but require members to pay for medication and send the invoice to them for a refund.

If you have a long-term prescription, it's cheaper and more convenient to have your medication delivered to your home. Zur Rose Versandapotheke AG, Steckborn, Postfach 117, CH-8501 Frauenfeld, ☎ 0848 842 842, 🖳 www.zur-rose.ch) is a company that provides this service in co-operation with health insurance companies.

Non-prescription medicines can be purchased from a chemist's or a drug store (*Drogerie, droguerie*) and are expensive. A drug store also stocks cosmetics, toiletries, cleaning supplies and a few unexpected items, such as alcohol (official recognition of its medicinal qualities perhaps?). A health food shop (*Reformhaus, magasin de produits diététiques*) sells health foods, diet foods and eternal-life/virility/youth pills and elixirs, for which the Swiss are famous.

HOSPITALS & CLINICS

Most Swiss towns have a hospital (*Krankenhaus/Spital, hôpital*) or clinic sign-posted by a sign showing a white 'H' on a blue background. Hospitals are listed in telephone directories under *Spitäler, hôpitaux*. Depending on the canton and region of Switzerland, hospitals may be designated as cantonal, 'zonal', regional or specialised or a private clinic-hospital. A cantonal or general hospital (*Kantonsspital, hôpital cantonal*) is the largest and best equipped, with the most experienced staff. Clinics are usually private and treatment there isn't generally covered by a health fund or medical insurance, unless specifically stated in your policy. In French-speaking Switzerland there are emergency clinics (*Pikett-Dienst, permanence*) providing 24-hour treatment for minor accidents and 'emergencies' (there are also 24-hour emergency dental clinics).

Except for emergency treatment, you may be admitted to a hospital or clinic only after consultation with a doctor. Normally you're admitted to a hospital in your own canton (or zone in a city), unless specialist surgery or treatment is necessary that's unavailable there. Children are usually treated in a dedicated ward, well stocked with games, toys, books and other children. Children who require long-term hospitalisation may, depending on their health, be given school lessons in hospital.

Your choice of hospital and type of accommodation also depend on your level of health insurance cover (see page 262). Many doctors treat patients only at certain hospitals and you may have to choose between having your usual doctor or specialist attend you, or treatment in a particular hospital. Patients with standard cover are accommodated in a general ward (two to four beds), those with half-private cover in a two-bed ward and those with private cover in a private room. Patients without private or half-private insurance are usually unable to choose their doctor – this may be important as not all doctors speak good English. Nurses may not speak English, particularly in French- and Italian-speaking areas.

If you're a non-resident and aren't a member of a health fund or don't have Swiss medical insurance, hospitals usually require a deposit on your admittance (they aren't taking any chances on your survival!). The deposit may range from SFr. 2,000 to 10,000 and depends on whether you're resident in the canton where the hospital is located, elsewhere in Switzerland or abroad. The actual cost of treatment is calculated later and you receive a rebate or a bill for the difference (usually they overestimate the cost). In some private clinics, foreign patients must make deposits of up to SFr. 50,000 on admission!

Hospital visiting times vary according to whether you're in a private, half-private or general ward (no prize for guessing which patients have the longest visiting hours) and are shown in telephone directories. In private clinics there may be no restrictions on visiting.

A publication entitled *Private Hospitals Switzerland* (there are over 100) and a brochure giving details of convalescence homes and hotels are available from Switzerland Tourism (see page 299). Information is also available from Private Hospitals Switzerland (Privatkliniken Schweiz, Cliniques Privées Suisses), Worbstrasse 52, PO Box, CH-3074 Muri-Berne (☎ 031 380 85 98, 🖳 www. privatehospitals.ch).

CHILDBIRTH

Childbirth in Switzerland usually takes place in a hospital, where a stay of three to five days is usual. The father is usually encouraged to attend the birth, unless difficulties are expected or he looks as if he's about to faint (or worse). You can also have a baby at home. Ask your family doctor or obstetrician for information and advice.

Maternity costs (in a general ward) are fully covered by the basic Swiss health insurance (see **Health Insurance** on page 269). Some private clinics are covered by health fund insurance (private hospital cover) but cover may not cover the cost of delivery by caesarean. Ask for a list of charges in advance. You may choose a gynaecologist in advance (if you don't, one is assigned at the hospital) and you can usually request an English-speaking midwife.

Foreigners giving birth in a Swiss hospital must bring the following papers with them on admittance:

● passport;

● Swiss residence permit;

● *marriage licence or divorce papers;

● *birth certificates of both parents.

*   These may not be necessary, but check in advance.

When a Swiss national gives birth in a Swiss hospital, she must provide a name or names for both sexes in advance, **from an approved list of names**. Although the approved list of names may not apply to foreigners, you may need to show that the name you choose is normal in your country (although how do you do that is another question!). See also **Births & Deaths** on page 254.

You must notify your health insurance company of your new arrival, as babies must be insured within three months of their birth (it can be done in advance from the expected month of birth, but if you give birth prematurely, don't forget to inform your health insurance company.) Notify your employer of the birth and check that child allowance (see page 55) is paid with your salary.

Most communities provide a free post-natal nursing service (*Säuglingss chwester, nurse*). The nurse visits you at home, usually once only, and you may take your child to the nurse's clinic for regular check-ups during the following year. The nurse is an excellent source of information on all baby health matters but may not speak English. The nurse provides a certificate if you breastfeed your child, for which many communities pay an allowance. Switzerland has a comprehensive vaccination programme for babies and children of all ages.

Your local community may present you with a toy for your child, and around ten cantons pay a birth allowance, e.g. SFr. 600 to 1,500. Expect to be inundated with advertisements for everything from baby food and toys to banks offering to make a donation of SFr. 20 to 50 if you open a savings account for your child. Baby changing facilities are provided in some public toilets and by most department stores in cities.

Useful publications for new mothers and parents in Switzerland include *Mothering Matters*, a bi-monthly newsletter (🖳 www.mmjournal.com) and *The New Stork Times*, a magazine published ten times a year (🖳 www.thestork.ch).

DENTISTS

There are excellent dentists (*Zahnarzt, dentiste*) everywhere in Switzerland, many of whom speak reasonable or good English. Many embassies keep a list of English-speaking dentists (or dentists speaking their national language) in their area and your employer or colleagues may be able to recommend someone. Dentists are listed in telephone directories under *Zahnärzte, dentistes*. A zero with a diagonal line through it alongside a telephone number indicates a 24-hour answering service. Some dentists have Saturday morning surgeries. Most major cities have a dental emergency telephone number, where a list of dentists is kept, categorised by speciality, location and the languages spoken. In some areas, e.g. Geneva, there are 24-hour emergency dental clinics. Call the telephone operator on ☎ 111 for information.

Many family dentists in Switzerland are qualified to perform specialised treatment, e.g. periodontal work, which is carried out by a specialist in many countries.

Switzerland's annual consumption of over 11kg of chocolate per head annually is the world's highest and ensures that dentists (and Swiss chocolate manufacturers) remain financially healthy – especially as dental treatment is expensive, e.g. over SFr. 5,000 to straighten a child's teeth isn't unusual. Fees are calculated according to a points system and you're entitled to an itemised bill. Dental treatment is cheaper in all Switzerland's neighbouring countries and may be even lower in your home country – even the US, home of the million-dollar smile, is cheaper! This option, although less convenient, may be worth considering if you're faced with expensive treatment (see also **Dental Insurance** on page 269). You should, in any case, obtain a detailed written estimate before committing yourself to an expensive course of treatment.

OPTICIANS

The optician or optometrist (*Optiker*, *opticien*) business is competitive in Switzerland. Prices for spectacles and contact lenses aren't fixed, as they are for many other professional services, so it's wise to compare costs before committing yourself to a large bill. The prices charged for most services, e.g. spectacles, lenses, and hard and soft contact lenses, vary considerably and are usually higher than in most other European countries. Disposable and extended-wear soft contact lenses are also widely available.

You may go to an oculist or eye specialist (*Augenarzt*, *occuliste*) for an eye test. An oculist can usually make a more thorough test of your eyesight than an optician and is able to test for certain diseases which can be diagnosed from eye abnormalities, for example diabetes and certain types of cancer. The costs are covered by most medical insurance.

HOME CARE SERVICES

Most communities operate a home nursing service for house-bound invalids, the cost (e.g. SFr. 25 per hour) depending on the patient's or family's income. You can join a housekeeping and nursing service association (*Haus- und Krankenpflegeverein*, *société des aides familiales et des soins à domicile*) such as Spitex, Belpstrasse 24, PO Box 329, 3000 Bern 14 (☎ 031 381 22 81, 🖳 www.spitexch.ch), which reduces the cost of home nursing and household help. Free services, such as blood pressure checks, may be provided for members.

Many communities provide families with a cleaning and general household service (including cooking) when the main carer (mother or father) is ill. The service is cheaper if you're a member of a housekeeping and nursing service association (see above). Most health insurance companies offer an optional premium to cover the cost of home help when a carer is ill for more than a few days. The cost of a stand-in mother/housekeeper is tax deductible. For information contact your community.

Pro Senectute provides help for the elderly, including social and community work and homecare, e.g. home help, cleaning services, mobile mending and laundry, meals-on-wheels, pedicure, transport and home visits. The charge for services varies with the canton and is usually the actual cost incurred (those on low incomes may be partly or fully reimbursed). Foreigners are treated the same as Swiss, except that they must have five years' continuous residence in Switzerland to qualify for financial support. For information contact Sozialberatung Pro Senectute, Lavaterstr. 60, PO Box, CH-8027 Zurich (☎ 044 283 89 89, 💻 www.pro-senectute.ch).

The Red Cross and local nursing societies provide nursing services and the rental of apparatus for the sick and disabled.

SPAS

There are some 20 spas or thermal baths (*Bad/Kurort*, *station thermale*) in Switzerland, which, although called *Bad* in German, are good for you and provide therapeutic and medicinal benefits. Spa treatment is recommended for a number of illnesses, including the alleviation of arthritic and rheumatic pains. The cost may be covered by your health fund when treatment is prescribed by a doctor. Most spas can be visited on an 'outpatient' basis. Day tickets usually have a time limit of around two hours. The usual maximum immersion time is 20 to 30 minutes, followed by a rest period (reclining chairs are provided) of about the same duration.

A *Swiss Spa Guide* is published by the Swiss Spa Association, listing the facilities and accommodation provided at major Swiss spas, and containing general information in English, French and German. It's available free from Schweizer Heilbäder, Avenue des Bains 22, 1400 Yverdon-les-Bains (☎ 024 420 15 21, 💻 www.heilbad.org). Switzerland Tourism also publishes a brochure about Swiss spas in French and German entitled *Wellbeing*.

COUNSELLING & SOCIAL SERVICES

All cantons in Switzerland provide counselling (*Beratung*, *conseil*) and assistance for certain health and social problems. These include drug addiction, alcoholism (Alcoholics Anonymous), compulsive gambling, attempted suicide and psychiatric problems, youth-related problems, battered children and women, marriage problems, and rape. Many cantons have a telephone number where children can obtain confidential help, e.g. in cases of physical or sexual abuse. Counsellors provide advice and help for sufferers of various diseases (e.g. multiple sclerosis and muscular dystrophy) and the disabled (e.g. the blind and deaf). They also help critically and terminally ill patients and their families to come to terms with their situation. The Samaritans (*Die dargebotene Hand, la main tendue*) also provide a free telephone counselling service in times of personal crisis (☎ 143). In times of need there's **always** someone to turn to and all services are confidential. In major towns, counselling is usually available for foreigners in their own language. If you need help desperately, someone speaking your language will be found.

Many cantons publish a handbook of counselling centres. Contact your canton's health service (*Kantonsärztlicher Dienst des Gesundheitsdepartment, service médical cantonal*) or ask your family doctor for advice. The website 🖳 www.infoset.ch provides information (in German and French) about addiction therapy in Switzerland.

In an attempt to combat one of the highest per capita rates of drug addiction in Europe, some cantons treat drug addiction as a social rather than a criminal problem and provide medical support, social workers, methadone treatment, and free or inexpensive food and drink, syringes and accommodation. Free drugs are provided for registered addicts in some cities (e.g. Basle and Zurich) in a controlled programme to help them kick their habit. In a move to combat AIDS (see below), local authorities in some Swiss cities provide free needles and a 'fixing' room for drug addicts' use, with a nurse on hand.

AIDS & HIV

Switzerland has one of the highest per capita levels of AIDS cases in Europe, particularly among people aged 35 to 54. As part of the Swiss campaign against AIDS (it's naive slogan is 'Love Life, Stop AIDS'), many supermarkets and department stores (e.g. Coop and Migros) stock condoms (*Präservative, préservatifs*) in their cosmetics sections. Condom dispensing machines have been installed in some schools and in many public toilets, and there's a national telephone helpline (☎ 044 477 11 11) and website (🖳 www.aids.ch).

All cases of AIDS and HIV-positive blood tests in Switzerland must be reported to the federal authorities, although patients' names aren't published.

BIRTHS & DEATHS

Births and deaths in Switzerland must be reported to your local registrar's office (*Zivilstandamt, bureau de l'état civil*). In the case of a birth, registration is carried out by the hospital where the child is born. However, if you have a child at home or in a different community from where you live, you must complete the registration yourself within three days. (If a child is born en route to the hospital, there will be an exciting legal wrangle to decide its community of birth.) Ask the registrar's office for information. A Swiss birth certificate (*Geburtsschein, acte de naissance*) is issued automatically.

In the event of the death of a Swiss resident, all interested parties must be notified. A doctor provides a certificate specifying the cause of death – make around ten copies as they're required by banks, insurance companies and various other institutions. A death certificate may be required before probate can be granted for a will. A body can be buried or cremated in Switzerland or the body or ashes can be sent to another country. In some cantons (e.g. Geneva) burial is free in your local commune. **Note that burial land in Switzerland is recycled after 25 years, when graves are excavated and the land reused for further burials.** For more information contact your local community office.

Births and deaths should be reported to your local consulate or embassy, for example to obtain a national birth certificate, passport and social security number for a child.

13.

INSURANCE

Switzerland isn't exactly a nation of gamblers, a fact reflected by the amount the average Swiss household spends on insurance (*Versicherung, assurance*), which at an average of around SFr. 40 per day (excluding car insurance) is the highest in the world. The Swiss don't care to take any chances, particularly when they can insure against them – they spend some SFr. 35bn a year on life insurance premiums alone!

The Swiss government and Swiss law provide for various obligatory federal and employer insurance schemes. (The Swiss government spends around a quarter of its budget on social security and other insurance schemes.) These include the following, for which premiums are obligatory for all employees in Switzerland and automatically deducted from your gross monthly salary by your employer:

● **Old age & survivors' insurance** (*Eidgenössische Alters- und Hinterlassen versicherung/AHV, Assurance-Vieillesse et Survivants fédérale/AVS*) and **disability insurance** (*Invalidenversicherung/IV, Assurance Invalidité/AI*), abbreviated below to the English acronyms OASI and DI respectively in order to avoid confusion, the contribution for all employees being 5.05 per cent of their gross monthly salary;

● **Company pension** (*Berufliche Vorsorge/BVG, prévoyance professionelle/LPP*) – Contributions vary from around 5.5 to 11 per cent of your gross monthly salary, depending on your age and your employer's pension fund.

● **Accident insurance** (*Unfallversicherung, assurance accidents*) – Occupational accident insurance is non-contributory (paid for by your employer). Private accident insurance contributions vary with your employer from nothing (non-contributory) to around 2 per cent of your gross monthly salary.

● **Unemployment insurance** (*Arbeitslosenversicherung, assurance chômage*) – Contributions for all employees is 1 per cent of your gross monthly salary up to SFr. 8,900 per month.

● **Maternity insurance** (*Mutterschaftsversicherung, assurance maternité*) – Employed and self-employed women receive 80 per cent of their salary (up to SFr. 172 per day) for 14 weeks after giving birth.

● **Health insurance** (*Krankenversicherung, assurance maladie*) – compulsory for everyone except foreign diplomats;

● **Third-party insurance** (*Haftpflichtversicherung, assurance responsibilité civile*) – obligatory for motor vehicles (see page 208), motorcycles, bicycles and some sports;

● **House contents insurance** (*Hausratsversicherung, assurance ménage*) – obligatory in most cantons;

Other insurance may also be obligatory depending on your age, canton of residence or employer. The most common types of optional insurance available in Switzerland are the following:

● public liability insurance;

● salary insurance;

● comprehensive car insurance (see page 208) – third-party motor insurance being obligatory;

● breakdown insurance for cars, motorcycles and bicycles (see page 227);

● dental insurance;

● life & annuity insurance;

● private pension;

● personal effects insurance;

● travel insurance.

Details of these types of insurance can be found below, except where indicated.

In all matters regarding insurance you're responsible for ensuring that you and your family are legally insured in Switzerland. If you wish to make a claim against your insurance or a third party is claiming against you, you'd be wise to report the matter to the police within 24 hours, which may in some cases be a legal requirement, e.g. if you set fire to a rented apartment. Obtain legal advice for anything other than a minor claim. Swiss law may be different from that in your home country or your previous country of residence and may also vary from canton to canton. (As an additional warning that disaster can strike at any time, some insurance companies provide policyholders with an emergency telephone number for use at nights and weekends.) It's wise to follow the example of the Swiss and make sure you're covered against most disasters. Regrettably you cannot insure yourself against being uninsured or sue your insurance agent for giving you bad advice!

It's particularly important to ensure that your family has full health insurance during the period between leaving your last country of residence and obtaining new health insurance in Switzerland. This is particularly important if you're covered by a company health insurance policy that terminates on the day you leave your present employment. One way to do this is to take out a travel or holiday insurance policy, although this could be inadequate, particularly if a serious illness for which you aren't covered is diagnosed in the interim period. If possible, it's better to extend your present health insurance policy. If you come to live in Switzerland, health insurance starts on the day you enter the country, even if you choose your insurance company a few weeks later. Of course, this also means that your premiums start from your first day in the country.

INSURANCE COMPANIES

Insurance is one of Switzerland's major businesses and there are numerous insurance companies to choose from, many of which provide a range of insurance services, while others specialise in certain fields only. The major insurance companies have offices or agents throughout Switzerland, including most small towns. Telephone insurance companies (such as Züritel) have been introduced in recent years and usually offer lower premiums than traditional agents. All Swiss insurance companies provide a free analysis of your family's insurance needs, and your Swiss bank may also provide independent advice (although they usually have a deal with an insurance company). Obtain a few quotations before signing a contract and ask the advice of your colleagues and friends (but don't believe everything they tell you!).

In most cities you can find English-speaking independent financial advisers or insurance brokers who can help you obtain appropriate cover with the best companies. Before choosing an adviser, ask whether he has experience dealing with expatriates, as your needs might be different from those of a Swiss family who never leave the country. A good financial adviser or broker can also assist you if you need to make a claim.

INSURANCE CONTRACTS

Read all insurance contracts before signing them. If you cannot obtain an English translation and you don't understand everything, ask a friend or colleague to translate a contract or take legal advice. Most insurance companies have English-speaking representatives and some provide information and an English translation of policies.

Most insurance policies run for the calendar year (1st January to 31st December). If you take out, change or cancel a policy during the year, you're billed or reimbursed the balance to the end of the year. All insurance policy premiums should be paid punctually, as late payment may affect your benefits or a claim (although, if this is so, it should be noted in your policy). **While most policies have what looks like a fixed term, e.g. three years, they're still renewed automatically by another year if you don't give notice three months before the end of the term.**

SOCIAL SECURITY SYSTEM

Switzerland has a three-part social security system for all employees, called the 'three-pillar' system (*Drei-Säulen-Konzept, système des trois piliers*), consisting of:

1   compulsory federal old age and survivors' insurance and disability insurance, which is the Swiss federal social security pension scheme;

2   compulsory private company pension funds for employees;

3   voluntary tax-deductible private pension savings and life insurance.

The aim of the federal social security system is to guarantee employees at least a subsistence income on retirement or in case of disability. To receive a full state pension you must contribute for the maximum number of years, which is 44. A full state pension and company pension bring your pension to around 60 per cent of your final salary.

OLD AGE & SURVIVORS' INSURANCE

The federal old age and survivors' insurance (OASI) and disability insurance (DI) are the Swiss federal social security pension scheme (*Staatliche Vorsorge*, *prévoyance sociale*). It's the first part of the three-part social security system and is referred to as 'pillar one'. OASI and DI include the following:

● a retirement pension for a single person or a couple;

● a supplementary pension for a younger wife;

● a child's pension for the child of the beneficiary of a retirement pension;

● a widow's pension or gratuity (a widower can claim a pension only if he has children under 18);

● an orphan's single pension (one parent deceased) or double pension (both parents deceased);

● long-term treatment and all associated costs for the disabled;

● an invalidity pension for a disabled person;

● a disability allowance for those requiring full-time personal supervision (to qualify for a disability pension, contributions must have been paid for one year);

● appliances for a disabled person.

All employees in Switzerland contribute to OASI/DI from 1st January of the year following their 17th birthday until the official age of retirement until the official retirement age of 65 for men and 64 for women, or until the actual age of retirement if later. Non-employed people contribute from 1st January of the year following their 20th birthday. This includes all 'leisured foreigners' (the idle rich), who are assessed on their assets, i.e. capital, investment income or pension, and income from annuities. If your spouse works and you don't, you're automatically included in his/her contributions. Contributions and qualifying years are also allocated to your pension for the time spent looking after children aged under 16.

If you retire before the official retirement age, you must continue to make OASI contributions until the official retirement age. If you earn above a certain sum after the official age of retirement, you must also continue to pay OASI, although this won't increase your pension above the maximum amount when you finally retire. Pensions are adjusted, usually every two years, in line with the wage and price index. Complementary benefits are payable to foreigners with low incomes who have lived continuously in Switzerland for at least 15 years.

If you defer receipt of your pension for one to five years, the following increases are paid:

No. of Years	Increase
1	5.2%
2	10.8%
3	17.1%
4	24.0%
5	31.5%

When your salary includes income 'in kind', for example board and lodging or a car, the value is added to your salary and OASI/DI is payable on the total sum.

Employees pay OASI/DI at 5.05 per cent of their monthly gross income and employers pay the same amount. The total of 10.1 per cent includes 8.4 per cent for OASI (old age and survivors' insurance), 1.4 per cent for DI (disability insurance) and 0.3 per cent for *APG/EO* (salary compensation insurance for the loss of earnings incurred during military service or women's military corps, Red Cross and civil defence service). If you're self-employed, your contributions depend on your income and are between 5.1 per cent and the maximum of 9.5 per cent if you earn over SFr. 53,100 a year. The minimum monthly contribution is SFr. 445.

Everyone who pays OASI/DI receives an insurance certificate (*Versicherungsausweis/AHV-IV, certificat d'assurance/AVS-AI*). The certificate contains your personal insurance number and the number of the OASI/DI compensation office (*Ausgleichskasse, caisse de compensation*) that has opened an account in your name (addresses are listed on the last two pages in telephone directories). Make a note of this number and keep both it and the certificate in a safe place. If you change jobs, you must give your insurance certificate to your new employer so that he can register you with the local OASI/DI compensation office.

The pension you receive on retirement depends on your average annual contributions and the number of years you've contributed. The minimum annual full pension in 2007 was SFr. 13,260 (SFr. 1,105 per month) for a single person and SFr. 19,920 (SFr. 1,660 per month) for a couple. The maximum full pension in 2007 was SFr. 26,520 a year (SFr. 2,210 a month) for a single person and SFr. 39,780 a year (SFr. 3,315 a month) for a married couple (a married couple's pension is divided into two equal portions and paid separately to each individual). A full pension is paid only when you've contributed for at least 44 years.

Foreigners qualify for a reduced pension after contributions have been paid for one year. Switzerland has bilateral agreements with over 20 countries including all western European countries, Canada and the US. If you qualify for a Swiss pension and live in one of these countries, you're entitled to receive it; if you live anywhere else, you aren't. Contributions to OASI/DI aren't transferable to foreign national insurance schemes and aren't refundable if your country of domicile has a bilateral agreement with Switzerland. If a bilateral agreement isn't applicable and you aren't entitled to a pension under Swiss law, your OASI/DI contributions are refunded when you leave Switzerland.

If you live in Switzerland for a short period only, you may be exempt from paying OASI/DI, particularly if your country of origin has a bilateral agreement with Switzerland regarding pension contributions. To qualify you must usually be transferred to Switzerland by your employer for a maximum of 24 months and must remain covered by your home country's social security system. Non-working spouses and employees of international organisations (e.g. the United Nations) and diplomatic missions are exempt from paying OASI/DI.

As in most developed countries, Switzerland has too few employed people to pay the pensions of the increasing number of retirees. The over 65 population is expected to double in the next 50 years to around 40 per cent of the population, which will cause social costs to explode. The Swiss government is studying ways to avoid this and one of the proposals is to increase the official retirement age.

For further information contact the Federal Office for Social Insurance (Bundesamt für Sozialversicherungen, Office Fédéral des Assurances Sociales), Effingerstr. 20, CH-3003 Berne (☎ 031 322 90 11, 🖳 www.ahv.admin.ch) or the Central Compensation Office (Zentrale Ausgleichsstelle, Centrale de compensation), ave. Edmond-Vaucher 18, CH-1203 Geneva (☎ 022 795 91 11 🖳 www.avs-ai-international.ch).

COMPANY PENSION

A company pension fund (*Berufliche Vorsorge/BVG*, *prévoyance professionelle/LPP*) is a compulsory contributory pension scheme for employees. It's the second part of the Swiss social security system and is called 'pillar two'. All employees earning over SFr. 19,890 a year and over 17 years of age must be members of a company pension fund, which may be run by the company, a professional association or an insurance company. The maximum insured salary in 2007 was SFr. 79,560. From this amount, SFr. 23,205 is deducted, and the remainder, SFr. 56,355, is the insured sum.

Self-employed people aren't required to belong to a company pension fund and can choose to pay higher tax-deductible private pension contributions to compensate for the lack of a company pension (see **Private Pension** below).

From 1st January after your 17th birthday until the age of 24, contributions are lower as only accident, death and disability are covered. From 1st January of the year following your 24th birthday, contributions are increased to include retirement benefits. Total contributions to a company pension fund increase from around 7 to around 18 per cent, depending on your salary, age, sex and the particular fund, approximately as shown below:

Age	Contribution
25 to 34	7%
35 to 44	10%
45 to 54	15%
55 to 65	18%

Depending on the employer, contributions are increased by between 3 to 4 per cent to cover additional premiums for risk insurance and a security fund. Of the total pension fund premium, your employer pays at least 50 per cent, meaning that the amount you pay varies from around 5 to 11 per cent of your gross salary.

The benefits paid on retirement depend upon your accrued fund assets. The fund provides retirement, survivor's and disability pensions. A widow's pension is 60 per cent of the disability or retirement pension, and an orphan's and children's pension 20 per cent.

If you join a company after the age of 24, you may have the option of paying a lump sum into the pension fund or of paying higher monthly contributions in order to qualify for a larger pension.

If you change your employer, the accrued amount you've paid (plus interest) is credited to your new employer's pension scheme. Employees who change employers also receive the employer's contributions plus accrued interest.

In a move designed to encourage home ownership, employees may withdraw money from their company pension fund to buy a home in Switzerland, pay off an existing mortgage, or pay for renovations or alterations. The money must be used for their primary residence. Until the age of 50 the total accrued sum can be withdrawn, after which you can withdraw the total sum that was accrued when you reached the age of 50 or half the total sum currently accrued, whichever is the higher. You can repay money to your pension fund at any time in order to restore your pension. If you sell your primary residence and don't buy another, you must pay back any money withdrawn.

A cash payment of the accrued capital is possible only under the following circumstances:

● when you leave Switzerland for good. However, due to a bilateral agreement between Switzerland and the EU, there are restrictions on how much EU citizens can withdraw in cash from their pension fund when they move to an EU country. In the case of EU citizens leaving Switzerland, the equivalent of the compulsory minimum pension capital must remain in a vested benefits account in Switzerland up to the Swiss age of retirement. Any capital exceeding the compulsory minimum sum can be withdrawn.

● when you become self-employed (your local OASI/DI office must provide proof so that your pension fund recognises you as self-employed);

● when the total sum accrued is less than one year's pension payments.

Pensions are indexed to the cost of living. Your company pension fund rules are detailed in your employment terms (see **Chapter 2**) or in a separate document and you receive regular pension fund statements from your employer or fund.

For more information contact the federal department for social security (Bundesamt für Sozialversicherung, Office fédéral des assurances sociales/Fondation institution supplétive LPP), Effingerstrasse 20, CH-3003 Berne (☎ 031 322 90 11, 🖳 www.bsv.admin.ch).

PRIVATE PENSION

The federal and company pension schemes (see above) are equal to a maximum of 60 per cent of earnings (for those who have worked in Switzerland their whole working life!). To supplement these and bring your pension closer to your final salary, you can contribute to a private pension fund (*Alterssparheft, caisse privée de prévoyance-vieillesse*) and receive tax relief on your contributions (up to a limited amount). This is the third part of the Swiss social security system, called 'pillar three' (*Selbstvorsorge, épargne personelle*).

If you're a member of a company pension fund, you may pay up to 8 per cent of the maximum average 'pensionable' salary, which was SFr. 6,365 a year in 2007, tax-free into a private pension fund or a special bank account. If you aren't a member of a company pension fund, you may save up to 20 per cent of your annual income tax-free, up to a maximum of SFr. 31,824.

You can receive the benefits of a private pension scheme up to five years before the Swiss retirement age of 65 (men) or 64 (women), although you must pay a reduced rate of tax on a portion of the amount. A private pension can also be redeemed in the following circumstances:

- if you become an invalid;

- if you leave Switzerland permanently;

- if you become self-employed (after being an employee);

- if you join another pension scheme.

The interest paid by banks on private pension savings in Switzerland is around 1 to 1.5 per cent. There are no bank charges or bank taxes. You might find it worthwhile to compare the interest on a private pension fund in Switzerland with that paid in other countries. However, you should take care which currency you choose, as your savings could be considerably reduced if the currency is devalued (and you may have to pay tax on the interest).

ACCIDENT INSURANCE

There are two categories of mandatory accident insurance (*Unfallversicherung, assurance accidents*) for employees in Switzerland:

- **Occupational accident insurance** (*Betriebsunfallversicherung, assurance accidents professionels*) – compulsory and paid by your employer, covering accidents or illness at work and accidents that occur when travelling to and from work, or when travelling on company business. One of the best known accident insurance companies is SUVA or CNA (*Schweizerische Unfallversicherungsanstalt/SUVA, Caisse nationale suisse d'assurance en cas d'accidents/CNA*, 💻 www.suva.ch).

- **Non-occupational accident insurance** (*Nichtbetriebsunfallversicherung, assurance accidents non-professionels*) – compulsory for all employees who work over eight hours per week and all part-time employees who make OASI/DI contributions. An employer may pay the whole cost of non-occupational accident insurance or pass some or all of the cost on to employees. The portion payable by the employee is a maximum of around 2 per cent of his gross monthly salary up to SFr. 106,800 per year/SFr. 8,900 per month in 2007 (SFr. 126,000 per year/SFr. 10,550 per month in 2008). Where applicable, your contribution is deducted from your salary at source.

If you work less than eight hours a week, you usually have only occupational accident insurance (but you're covered for other accidents by your health insurance) unless you make OASI/DI contributions. Accident insurance paid by employers includes only employees and not family members. **Ensure that your**

family is covered by private accident insurance, which can be combined with a health fund insurance; otherwise you must pay the full cost of any treatment yourself. The self-employed, who obviously don't benefit from occupational accident insurance, are covered for accidents by their health insurance and may contribute to a private accident insurance scheme.

Accident insurance allows for a total disability pension of 80 per cent of your annual salary and, in the event of death, a survivor's pension of up to 70 per cent of your annual salary. If you engage in dangerous or high-risk pursuits, you should check whether your accident insurance has any exclusion clauses. Skiing and most sports accidents are, however, fully covered by non-occupational accident insurance.

You must usually make a claim on your accident insurance within three months of an accident. If you fail to meet this deadline, you must either pay the bill yourself or make a claim on your health insurance.

When medical treatment is necessary abroad as the result of an accident, you're refunded a maximum of double the costs that would have been incurred in Switzerland.

SALARY INSURANCE

Many companies provide salary (or salary continuation) insurance (*Salärausfall versicherung/Salärlosenversicherung, assurance salaire*), which provides sick pay (*Taggeld, indemnité journalière*) in the event of illness or an accident, although it may cover you for a limited period only (usually 720 days). Employees usually pay part of the premium, e.g. 50 per cent of contributions; some employers pay the whole salary insurance premium and others pass the whole cost on to you. The percentage payable by the employee is a maximum of around 2 per cent of his gross monthly salary, usually up to a maximum limit. Salary insurance also applies to part-time employees who have been employed for three months or longer.

Your salary is usually paid in full during the first month of an illness or accident. After the first month, you're normally paid 100 per cent or 90 per cent of your salary for up to two years, though the amount may be 80 per cent for single employees and 85 per cent for married employees with no children.

If the company has no insurance, the period for which you're entitled to sick pay depends on your length of service and may be calculated as a percentage of your hourly rate. The minimum period is usually three weeks in your first year of service.

UNEMPLOYMENT INSURANCE

Unemployment insurance (*Arbeitslosenversicherung/ALV, assurance chômage*) is compulsory for all employees. Your contribution, deducted at source from your gross monthly salary, is 1 per cent up to a salary of SFr. 106,800 per year (SFr. 8,900 per month). Your employer's contribution is also 1 per cent, making a total contribution for unemployment insurance of 2 per cent. Unemployment insurance is often included with OASI/DI on your salary statement.

Unemployment benefits are paid when you're on short time or when an employer is unable to pay your wages, e.g. he has gone bankrupt, as well as when you're unemployed. Part-time employees are also entitled to unemployment benefits when wholly or partly unemployed. Unemployment benefits provide for retraining, further education and schemes for the unemployed.

To qualify for unemployment benefits, you must have worked and contributed in Switzerland for at least 12 months during the previous two years. You must register within a few days of losing your job or of your employer being unable to pay you.

The amount of benefits paid depend on your previous salary and marital status, and may also depend on whether you were made redundant or were fired or resigned voluntarily (not advisable if you wish to receive unemployment benefits!). Unemployed people with a family and the disabled receive a higher percentage of their previous salary (up to a maximum salary of SFr. 106,800 per year or SFr. 8,900 per month) than single people who aren't disabled. Lower benefits are paid if you resigned from your job, unless you can prove that your working conditions were intolerable (which is extremely difficult). Additional payments are made to cover children's allowances and educational costs, as prescribed by Swiss law. The length of time you receive unemployment benefits depends on your length of prior employment.

When you're unemployed you must report monthly to your local employment office (*Arbeitsamt, office du travail*). The payment of benefits depends on your seeking employment, with the help of the employment office and your community, although you may restrict your job hunting to the area where you live and the field or profession in which you're qualified. You should apply in writing for around ten suitable jobs each month and the authorities may ask to see your letters and any replies.

You're obliged to accept any reasonable job offered you by the employment office; if you're a brain surgeon you won't be offered a job as a waiter or waitress! If you're offered a job with a lower salary than the amount you receive in unemployment benefits, you must accept it, although you're compensated by the employment office for one year.

Benefits are paid only while you live in Switzerland, except for benefit for non-payment of your salary by an employer, e.g. when he has gone bankrupt, which is paid even if you've already left Switzerland. If you leave Switzerland before the benefit period has ended, no further monthly payments or lump sum payments are made. If your residence permit expires before the benefit period has elapsed, it's extended on application. Employees of foreign embassies, missions and international organisations who don't pay OASI/DI or unemployment insurance aren't eligible for unemployment benefits. Additional information can be obtained from your local employment office.

If you're unemployed and no longer entitled to unemployment benefits, your residence permit may be cancelled. When your entitlement to federal unemployment benefits has expired, you're dependent on supplemental canton programmes, which vary with the canton. Under federal law, those earning below a certain amount (which varies from canton to canton) per year are eligible for public welfare (such as rent assistance), and cantons and communities also provide financial assistance to families whose income falls below a minimum figure, e.g. around SFr. 18,000 a year in Zurich.

Employers in Switzerland aren't required to make redundancy payments. Irrespective of how long you've been employed, you're entitled only to the notice period stated in your employment contract or conditions, or payment in lieu of notice. Executive positions may, however, provide for a cash payment (a 'golden handshake') if you're sacked or made redundant.

HEALTH INSURANCE

Basic health insurance (*Krankenversicherung, assurance maladie*) is compulsory for everyone living in Switzerland for three months or more, with the exception of foreign diplomats and employees of international organisations. Foreigners must obtain health insurance within three months of their arrival in Switzerland and babies must be insured within three months of their birth.

Some large companies have their own health insurance schemes offering advantageous conditions and reduced premiums for employees and their families. If you're a member of a health insurance scheme sponsored by your employer or a professional association, your premium may be deducted at source from your salary. Private health insurance premiums may be paid annually, quarterly or monthly, by giro payment or by standing order from a bank or post office account. Your employer may pay part or all of the cost of your health insurance, although this isn't usual.

Health insurance (*Krankenversicherung, assurance maladie*) in Switzerland can be taken out with a health fund (*Krankenkasse, caisse maladie*) or a private health insurance company. Health funds, of which there are over 100 in Switzerland, are of the mutual benefit or friendly society type and mostly non-profit organisations. They try to exert some control over doctors' and hospital fees, and are the cheapest form of health insurance in Switzerland. It's important to shop around as costs vary considerably between the cheapest and most expensive insurance companies in different cantons (you can do this on the internet at 🖳 www.comparis.ch). The premiums of those with low incomes are subsidised by cantons, although you must usually make an application.

All companies must offer identical basic cover as prescribed by law, which includes treatment by doctors, chiropractors, midwives and certain other practitioners (e.g. nurses and physiotherapists) when treatment is approved by a doctor; medication and laboratory tests; dental treatment necessary as the result of an accident or illness; hospitalisation in a general ward; and emergency treatment abroad. Existing conditions cannot be excluded from the basic cover (including pregnancy).

Hospital treatment in a general ward is usually restricted by health funds to hospitals in your canton of residence, although you can choose to pay extra to be hospitalised in a public hospital outside your canton of residence and for a half-private (two-bed) or private room. A health fund pays for treatment in a private clinic only when similar treatment isn't available locally in a general hospital.

A private health insurance scheme usually includes half-private or private hospital cover as standard, and may include medical services and medicines that aren't covered by a health fund.

Standard cover (e.g. a general hospital ward) from a health fund usually costs between SFr. 200 and 400 per month for an adult, depending on the insurer and where you live. Premiums have been increasing in leaps and bounds in recent years, particularly private and half-private hospital cover (which can double your premium), although steps have been taken to curb increases. Premiums for private and half-private cover can be reduced by payment of an excess or deductible (*selbstbehalt, franchise*). The minimum compulsory excess is SFr. 300 per year for adults (zero for children), although you can choose to pay up to SFr. 2,500. Patients must pay 10 per cent of all non-hospital costs (treatment, medicines, etc.) above the excess.

Standard cover is valid worldwide and pays a maximum of twice what the same treatment would cost in Switzerland, which could be a problem in the US, where it's advisable to take out supplementary cover or travel health insurance. However, under the bilateral treaties between Switzerland and the EU, Swiss and EU citizens travelling to an EU country receive only the cover which is compulsory in that country (which may be different from Switzerland and where additional charges may apply). It's therefore advisable to have additional travel insurance, which can be obtained from many Swiss insurers for an annual premium of approximately SFr. 160 for a family. Swiss and EU citizens should carry the European Health Insurance Card/EHIC (obtainable from your Swiss insurance company) when travelling to an EU country in order for medical costs to be charged to the Swiss insurance system directly. Without the form you may need to pay doctors' or hospital fees yourself and apply for a refund from your insurance company – usually a time-consuming process!

If you're working in Switzerland for less than three months (e.g. on a contract basis) and aren't covered by Swiss compulsory health insurance, you need an international health insurance policy. These usually offer members a choice of premiums: to cover average health costs or to provide cover in countries with high medical costs, which usually includes Switzerland. Besides the usual doctors' and hospital fees, claims can generally be made for body scans, convalescence, home nursing, outpatient treatment, health checks and surgical appliances. With an international health insurance policy, you may be able to renew your cover annually, irrespective of your age, which could be important. If you have a foreign health policy, ask your insurance company what it will cost for cover in Switzerland.

The following general points apply to most health insurance policies in Switzerland:

- You must enrol your spouse and children as members, as they aren't automatically covered by your membership.

- Private medical and extra dental cover (and other optional benefits) may become effective only after a qualifying period of around three months. This period may be waived if you can prove membership of another insurance scheme (Swiss or foreign) with the same or a higher level of cover.

- If you're forced to visit different doctors (e.g. when your doctor is sick or doing military service) for the same illness, the bills should be sent to your health fund together. If you change doctors of your own accord during a course of treatment, you can claim for only one doctor's bills.

- If you wish to see a complementary medical practitioner, you must usually be referred by your doctor (unless you're a private patient and pay the bill yourself). Your health fund may pay all or part of the cost of acupuncture treatment, an osteopath or chiropractor, massage (**not** the sort provided in 'massage' parlours), Chinese medicine, homeopathy, anthroposophic medicine, neural therapy, spa treatment, a chiropodist or witch doctor. Check with your fund what percentage of the bill (if any) they pay, before committing yourself to a course of treatment and a large bill.

- All bills, particularly those received for treatment outside Switzerland, must include **precise** details of treatment and prescriptions received. **Terms such as 'consultation' or 'dental treatment' are insufficient.** It's helpful if bills are written in a language intelligible to your health fund, for example English, French, German or Italian.

- There are no restrictions on changing insurance companies, although the cancellation period for basic insurance is three months (if premiums are increased, a policy can be terminated with one month's notice) and policies can be terminated only on 30th June and 31st December (in writing by registered post). However, a policy with a higher deductible than the legal minimum can only be cancelled on 31st December. If you're planning to change your health insurance company, ensure that no important benefits are lost. If you change your health insurance company, it's advisable to inform your old company if you have any outstanding bills for which they're liable.

- If you're leaving Switzerland, you must cancel your insurance in writing and give at least one month's notice. **When leaving Switzerland, you should**

ensure that you have continuous medical insurance. Note, however that if you're elderly or have a poor health record, you may find it difficult or impossible to obtain health insurance in some countries at an affordable price.

Checklist

When comparing costs and the level of cover provided by different health insurance schemes, the following points should be considered:

- Are discounts available for families?

- Is private, half-private and general hospital cover available (as applicable)? Are private and half-private rooms available in local hospitals? What are the costs? Is there a limit on the time you can spend in hospital? What are the restrictions regarding hospitalisation in a canton other than your canton of residence?

- Is dental cover available? What exactly does it include? Can it be extended to include extra treatment? (Dental insurance usually contains numerous limitations and doesn't cover cosmetic dental treatment.)

- Are accidents, e.g. sports injuries, automatically covered or can they be excluded? Note that it may be to your advantage to exclude them, as employees in Switzerland are automatically covered by their employer's obligatory accident insurance and car accidents are usually covered by Swiss motor insurance. Those with accident insurance can reduce their premiums by up to 10 per cent by omitting accident insurance from a health insurance policy, though as a general rule health insurance includes cover for accidents.

- What emergency ambulance or other transport fees are covered?

- What is the qualification period for benefits and services?

- What level of cover is provided in the rest of Europe and/or the rest of the world? What are the limitations?

- Are all medicines covered for 90 per cent of their cost or are there restrictions?

- Does the insurance company issue an insurance card that enables chemists to bill the company directly?

- Are convalescent homes or spa treatments covered when prescribed by a doctor?

- What are the restrictions on complementary medicine, e.g. chiropractic, osteopathy, naturopathy, massage and acupuncture? Are they covered? Must a doctor make a referral?

- Are extra costs likely and, if so, what for?

- Are spectacles or contact lenses covered and, if so, how much can be claimed and how frequently? Some Swiss health funds allow you to claim for a new pair of spectacles every two or three years.

- Is the provision and repair of artificial limbs and other essential health aids covered?

HOME CONTENTS INSURANCE

In most cantons it's mandatory to take out house contents insurance (*Hausratsversicherung/Haushaltversicherung*, *assurance ménage*) covering your belongings against hazards such as fire, flood, gas explosion and theft. House contents insurance is inexpensive, at around SFr. 200 per year for cover totalling some SFr. 50,000, or about SFr. 4 for each SFr. 1,000 of cover. Most house contents insurance policies cover the cost of replacing items at their replacement cost ('new for old') and **not** their second-hand value (except bicycles, skis and snowboards, although you can include 'new for old' cover for these items for a small additional fee). House contents insurance **doesn't** include accidental damage caused by you or members of your family to your belongings. It may also exclude accidental damage to fixtures or fittings (e.g. baths, wash basins, electrical fittings and apparatus), which can be covered by a private liability insurance policy (see below). A supplement may be payable to cover special window glass, which is expensive to replace.

Take care that you don't under-insure your house contents and that you periodically reassess their value and adjust your insurance premium accordingly. Alternatively, you can arrange to have your insurance cover automatically increased annually by a fixed percentage or amount by your insurance company. If you make a claim and the assessor discovers that you're under-insured, the amount due is reduced by the percentage by which you're under-insured. For example, if you're insured for SFr. 50,000 and you're found to be under-insured by 20 per cent, your claim totalling SFr. 5,000 is reduced to SFr. 4,000. Keep a list of all major possessions and receipts.

Insurance companies provide you with a free estimate based on the number of rooms in your home, the number of occupants and whether you have expensive possessions or worthless junk. Don't forget to mention any particularly valuable items, e.g. the family jewels or antique collection. House contents insurance can be combined with private liability insurance (see below).

PUBLIC LIABILITY INSURANCE

It's customary in Switzerland to have public (sometimes called 'private') liability insurance (*Privathaftpflichtversicherung, assurance responsibilité civile*). To take an everyday example, if your soap slips out of your hand and jumps out of the window while you're taking a shower, and your neighbour slips on it and breaks his neck, he (or his widow) will sue you for millions of francs. With public liability insurance you can shower in blissful security (but watch that soap!). If you set fire to your rented apartment, your landlord will claim against your liability insurance (if you don't have insurance, the authorities will lock you up and throw away the key). The cost is around SFr. 100 per year for cover of SFr. 5m (which is the recommended cover). For some claims you may be required to pay the first SFr. 100 to 200.

Public liability insurance, which can be combined with house contents insurance (see above), covers all members of a family and includes damage done or caused by your children and pets (for example if your dog or child bites someone). Where damage is due to severe negligence, benefits may be reduced. Check whether it covers you against accidental damage to your apartment's fixtures and fittings. Some sports accidents aren't covered by public liability insurance, for example if you accidentally strike your opponent with your squash racket, he cannot claim against your liability insurance to have his teeth fixed (but he can claim against his accident insurance).

DENTAL INSURANCE

Basic dental insurance (*Zahnarztversicherung, assurance dentaire*) can be taken out as a supplement to Swiss health insurance. Health funds and health insurance companies offer dental cover or extra dental cover for an additional premium, although there are many limitations and cosmetic treatment is excluded. It's unusual to have full dental insurance in Switzerland as the cost is prohibitive. A dental inspection is usually required before you're accepted as a reasonable risk. Dental treatment can be **very** expensive in Switzerland (you don't always receive gold fillings, but even black ones cost the earth!) and you should obtain an estimate before committing yourself to a large bill.

If you or your children require expensive cosmetic dental treatment, e.g. crowns, bridges, braces and false teeth, it's usually cheaper to have the treatment outside Switzerland, as dental costs are lower in all of Switzerland's neighbouring countries. Alternatively, ask your dentist if he can reduce the cost by reducing the work involved. This may be possible, as Swiss dentists usually strive for perfection, e.g. when straightening a child's teeth. It could be a lot cheaper to settle for something more characterful.

In primary and (sometimes) secondary school, children receive a free annual dental inspection from a school-appointed dentist. An estimate is provided for any dental treatment required and communities may pay a percentage of bills for low-income families. Your health insurance company may also pay a percentage, if your child is insured for dental treatment. The amount payable by your health insurance for a particular treatment is fixed and depends on your level of dental insurance; a list of the amounts refunded is available from health insurance companies.

There are usually no restrictions on where (either in Switzerland or abroad) you obtain dental treatment, although you must provide your health insurance company with a detailed itemised bill. You can use a health insurance form to pay your dental bill, although most people pay their dental bills directly (after pawning the family jewels and taking out a second mortgage) and then send the bill to their health insurance company for a refund.

LIFE & ANNUITY INSURANCE

Swiss 'life' policies are usually for life **insurance** and not, as for example in the UK, for **assurance**. (Assurance is a policy which covers an eventuality which is certain to occur sooner or later, e.g. your death – unless the Swiss invent an immortality drug; thus a life assurance policy is valid until you die. An **insurance** policy covers a risk that **may** happen but isn't a certainty, for example an accident (unless you're **very** accident prone).

Some Swiss companies provide free life insurance (*Lebensversicherung, assurance vie*) as an employment benefit, although it may be accident life insurance only. You can take out a life insurance or endowment policy with numerous Swiss and foreign insurance companies.

In Switzerland a life insurance policy is generally valid until you're 70 years old, depending on the company. If you die before you're 70 they pay up, but if you live longer than 70 years they pay nothing. Health insurance companies work closely with the medical profession to ensure that you don't die before you're 70 and even sponsor fitness courses to keep people fit and healthy so they live to a ripe old age (and they rake in the profits). A life insurance policy is useful as security for a bank loan and can be limited to cover the period of the loan (some lenders insist upon it).

PERSONAL EFFECTS INSURANCE

You can take out personal effects insurance (*Diebstahlversicherung, assurance vol*) to cover your belongings when travelling or when you're away from your main home (e.g. in a second home). This can be included in your house contents insurance. The cost is around SFr. 80 a year for cover of SFr. 2,000. Some companies may require you to pay the first 10 per cent or SFr. 200 of a claim.

TRAVEL INSURANCE

Travel insurance (*Reiseversicherung, assurance voyage*) is available from insurance companies, travel agents, airports and railway stations in Switzerland. A peculiarly Swiss phenomenon is the protection letter (*Schutzbrief, livret*), a comprehensive travel insurance policy, available from the Swiss motoring organisations (see page 227). It covers most travel and holiday emergencies and is valid irrespective of the mode of transport used. Short-term holiday insurance is also provided by Swiss railways (SBB).

Carefully check the level of travel insurance you require. For example, you may want to insure against the loss of your deposit or holiday cancellation, the loss or theft of money, personal effects and baggage, health treatment and accidents, and damage or injury you cause to third parties. **Travel insurance usually excludes high-risk sports such as skiing and jet-skiing.** You must never admit liability and never pay out a cent without written permission from your insurers.

If you belong to a Swiss health fund or health insurance scheme, you're usually covered for health treatment worldwide costing up to twice as much as treatment in Switzerland.

14.

FINANCE

Switzerland is one of the wealthiest countries in the world, with one of the world's highest gross domestic products (GDPs) per head (around US$33,000) – the Swiss are the richest people in Europe in terms of average personal wealth. Swiss banks and financial institutions are renowned for their efficiency and security, and Zurich is one of the world's major financial centres and Switzerland the world capital of private banking.

Financially, Switzerland is the safest country in the world and it has traditionally been a favourite bolt-hole for 'hot' money. The world-famous (- infamous) secrecy surrounding Swiss numbered bank accounts extends to all customer accounts, and heavy fines and even imprisonment can result for employees who breach this confidentiality. The Swiss have, however, succumbed to international pressure in recent years and introduced tougher rules to combat money laundering. This hasn't stopped some critics labelling Swiss banks 'launderettes' and 'mafia' money is allegedly still flooding into the country.

Competition for your money is fierce in Switzerland, and financial services are provided by numerous Swiss and foreign banks, investment brokers, post offices and even railway station booking offices.

One of the surprising things about the Swiss is that they don't usually pay bills with cheques or credit cards and use cash more than anywhere else in the developed world. When you arrive in Switzerland to take up residence or employment, ensure that you have sufficient cash, travellers' cheques, credit cards, luncheon vouchers, gold and diamonds to last at least until your first pay day, which may be up to two months after your arrival. During this period you will find an international credit card useful.

This chapter contains information about currency, banking, tax and the cost of living; see **Chapter 13** for information regarding company and private pension schemes, and life and annuity insurance.

IMPORTING & EXPORTING MONEY

Switzerland has no currency restrictions. You may bring in or take out as much money as you wish, in any currency. The major Swiss banks change practically all foreign banknotes without batting an eyelid and may even exchange coins, although at a lower rate than banknotes. Banks give a higher exchange rate for travellers' cheques than for banknotes. The most popular foreign currencies can be changed to Swiss francs via machines at airports and major railway stations. The big banks (UBS and Crédit Suisse) charge a fee of SFr. 5 for cash currency exchanges if you don't have a bank account with them. The Coop Bank and Migros Bank and many canton banks don't charge such fees and often offer better exchange rates. Many Swiss hotels and shops accept and change foreign currency, but usually at a less favourable exchange rate than banks.

The Swiss franc exchange rate (*Wechselkurs, taux de change*) against most European and major international currencies is listed in banks and daily newspapers. Most Swiss banks sell palladium, platinum, gold and silver (bars and coins), which are a good investment – particularly when the world's stock markets are in a panic. Swiss gold coins are a favourite gift from Swiss godparents to their godchildren (in fact most people are happy to receive them).

Many railway stations provide a money-changing service, which is particularly handy for 'spur of the moment' trips abroad. Major SBB stations have change bureaux (with extended opening hours) where you can buy or sell foreign currencies at favourable rates, buy and cash travellers' cheques, and obtain a cash advance on credit cards. In over 300 smaller stations, you can buy currency and travellers' cheques in the most popular foreign currencies. Railway station offices are open during normal railway booking office hours from around 6am until 7.30pm, including weekends, and are open even later at major stations. The SBB and Swiss Post are also representatives of Western Union in Switzerland, and will send or receive (by telegraphic transfer) cash in as little as ten minutes, although fees are **very** high. When sending money abroad, you may receive a better exchange rate from a post office than a bank.

SWISS CURRENCY

The unit of Swiss currency is the Swiss franc (*Frank, franc*), considered by many to be the most stable currency in the world. The Swiss franc has been allowed to float on the foreign exchange markets since 1973, since when it has increased in value against the US$ and GB£ by over 250 per cent (which naturally has **nothing** whatsoever to do with why foreigners are so eager to work in Switzerland!). More recently, however, the Swiss franc has lost some value in comparison with the euro.

The Swiss franc is divided into 100 cents (*Rappen, centime*) and Swiss coins are minted in 5, 10, 20 and 50 cents and 1, 2 and 5 francs. Banknotes are printed in denominations of 10, 20, 50, 100, 200, 500 and 1,000 francs. New high-tech banknotes with a wide range of security features have been introduced and are allegedly 'virtually impossible' to counterfeit. The new notes contain five visible safety features plus a second level detectable by special equipment and a third level known only to the central bank. **Nevertheless, you should beware of counterfeit banknotes, some of which are made with sophisticated colour laser copiers.**

The Swiss franc is usually written as SFr. (as in this book). When writing figures in Switzerland, a quotation mark (') is used to separate units of millions, thousands and hundreds, and a comma (,) to denote cents, e.g. 1'500'485,34 is one million, five hundred thousand, four hundred and eighty five francs and 34 cents – a nice healthy bank balance! Values below one franc are written as a percentage of a franc rather than in cents, e.g. 0,75 is seventy-five cents (note that in this book they're written in the standard English format, with a point instead of a comma, e.g. SFr. 0.75).

BANKS

If there's one place in Switzerland where you can be sure of a warm welcome, it's a Swiss bank (unless you plan to rob it!). It will probably come as no surprise to you that there are **lots** of banks in Switzerland (around 600), although many have closed in recent years or been swallowed up by the major banks. Switzerland is one of the most 'over-banked' countries in the world and in addition to the two major banks (USB is Switzerland's largest bank, followed by Crédit Suisse), which have branches in most towns, there are many smaller regional, canton, loan and savings banks, plus private (mainly portfolio management) and foreign banks (around 150).

If you do a lot of travelling abroad, you may find that the comprehensive range of services provided by the major Swiss banks is more suited to your needs than those of foreign banks. The major banks are more likely to have staff who speak English and other foreign languages, and they can provide statements and other documentation in English and other non-Swiss languages. The major Swiss banks also offer 24-hour telephone and internet banking.

In a small country town or village, there's usually a branch of one of the local banks (e.g. Raiffeisenbank, Banque Raiffeisen) and a post office, but not a branch of a major bank. Local banks usually provide a more personal service, may offer cheaper loans and mortgages than the major banks and (in most cantons) provide a guarantee for deposits. Many Swiss prefer using canton banks.

The following points apply to most Swiss banks:

● All bills can be paid through your bank. Simply send the payment forms to your bank with a completed payment advice form, provided free by your bank on request, or drop them in your bank's post box using the free envelopes provided and your bank makes a payment order (*Zahlungsauftrag, ordre de paiement*). This method of payment is free and has the advantage that your payments (or the total payment) are recorded on your monthly bank statement. Alternatively you can pay your bills at a post office (see page 119).

● Internet banking is provided by most Swiss banks and is usually free.

● Buying stocks and bonds in Switzerland is normally done through a bank and not through a stockbroker. Most banks post the latest Swiss share prices in all branches and some have computer enquiry systems where information is displayed on a screen.

● You can open a foreign currency account with any Swiss bank, although no interest is paid. If you receive a transfer from abroad, make sure that it's deposited in the correct account.

● All correspondence from the major Swiss banks can be requested in English and certain other non-Swiss official languages, in addition to French, German and Italian. **Note that banks charge the postage for each item of post**

sent to you – SFr. 1.00 or 0.85, depending on whether you choose 'A' or 'B' class post.

● Many banks offer extra interest to students or youths aged, for example, from 16 to 20. This costs the banks very little as most students are broke, but all banks know that you need to 'get 'em while they're young', as few people change banks (which is why some banks offer to open a savings account for your new baby with a free deposit of SFr. 25 or 50).

● An account holder can create a joint account by giving his spouse (or anyone else) signatory authority. A joint account can be for two or more people. You can specify whether cheques and withdrawal slips need to be signed by any joint account holder or require all account holders' signatures.

● At the end of the year (or more frequently, depending on your bank) you receive a statement listing all bank charges, interest paid or earned and the taxes, e.g. federal withholding tax (see page 290), deducted during the previous year. Keep this in a safe place: when you complete your income tax return you can reclaim the withholding tax, and any interest paid is tax deductible.

● The charge for standing orders from a salary account is around SFr. 15 a year. Standing orders are paid automatically, provided there are sufficient funds in the account to cover them. If you have insufficient funds in your account, your bank may not pay your standing order payments (*Dauerauftrag, ordre permanent*) **and may not inform you of this**.

● If an American citizen wishes to hold US securities in a Swiss account, he must sign a form stating that either the Swiss bank is allowed to inform the IRS about the account or that on the sale of the securities a withholding tax of 31 per cent of the profits or capital gains will be levied. All other citizens must sign a statement to the effect that they aren't American citizens and have no tax liabilities in the US.

All major Swiss banks produce numerous free brochures and booklets (many in English) describing their services and containing interesting and useful information. The major banks also publish newsletters in English and other foreign languages, which are sent free to customers.

Opening Hours

Normal bank opening hours are from 8 or 8.30am to 4.30 or 4.45pm Mondays to Fridays, with no closure over the lunch period in cities and large towns. Most banks are open late, e.g. until 5.30 or 6.30pm, on one day a week depending on the bank and its location. In cities, a few banks have extended opening hours during the week and are open on Saturdays from around 9am to 4pm. In large shopping centres (*Einkaufszentrum, centre commercial*) most banks are open until 5pm on Saturdays and major banks are also open on Saturdays in many tourist areas.

There are no general opening hours for country or village banks, which may be closed on Monday mornings and Wednesday afternoons and open on Saturday mornings. They usually close for lunch, which may extend from 11.45am until 2pm, but often remain open until 5.30pm, Mondays to Fridays. Banks at Swiss airports and major SBB stations are open from around 6.30 or 7am until 6.30pm (10.30pm at airports).

In major cities there are 24-hour automated banking centres, where you can purchase foreign currencies, change foreign currency into Swiss francs, buy travellers' cheques and gold, change Swiss banknotes and coins, and rent safety deposit boxes. You can also obtain 24-hour telephone customer advice, and stock market and general banking information via computer terminals. These services are provided in addition to the usual automatic banking facilities, such as cash withdrawals, deposits and checking account balances.

Opening an Account

One of your first acts in Switzerland should be to open a bank account. Simply go to the bank of your choice and tell them you're living or working in Switzerland and wish to open a salary account (*Salärkonto/Lohnkonto, compte salaire*) or current account (*Girokonto, compte courant/chèque*). Some companies have a preferential arrangement with a particular bank, which may result in lower bank charges for employees. Current accounts in Swiss francs and foreign currencies are available to all residents. Banks offer a range of other accounts, including a variety of savings accounts providing higher interest rates than a salary or current account. Migros bank (🖳 www.migrosbank.ch), owned by Switzerland's largest supermarket chain (which also owns Globus and OfficeWorld), usually pays 0.25 to 0.5 per cent higher interest than most other banks.

After opening an account, don't forget to give the details to your employer (or you won't be paid). Your salary is normally paid by your employer directly into your bank or post office account. Your monthly salary statement is sent to your home address or given to you at work. You may need to wait up to two months for your first pay cheque, although this is unusual; check with your employers. If necessary they may give you an advance on your salary.

Bank statements are usually issued monthly (optionally daily, weekly or quarterly), interest is paid on deposits and an overdraft facility is available. With a salary account, as well as a monthly or quarterly statement, you receive confirmation of payment of standing orders and cheques (debit advice), and a credit advice for payments made into your account other than your salary. Bank charges are levied annually, plus postal and other charges. **Note that if you ask your bank to retain your post for collection, fees can be astronomical.**

You don't receive a cheque book with any account, but an account card containing your encoded account information.

There are considerable differences in bank fees, for example UBS and Crédit Suisse are more expensive for accounts with relatively small balances, although if the balance averages over SFr. 10,000 fees are reduced. Some banks charge if you don't maintain a minimum balance. If you have less than SFr. 10,000 in your UBS account, you pay SFr. 0.30 for payments to a Swiss bank account and SFr. 5 for payments to accounts outside Switzerland. The smaller banks, such as canton banks, Migros and Coop bank, usually have lower fees. **Note that if you pay a cheque drawn on a non-Swiss bank into your Swiss bank account, it may take weeks to be cleared and is expensive.**

Account Cards

Most banks issue account cards (*Bankkarte*, *carte bancaire*) which can be used at any branch to withdraw cash and carry out other transactions over the counter, and to withdraw up to SFr. 5,000 per day from cash dispensing machines or 'automated teller machines' (ATMs). When using your account card over the counter, identification must be provided, e.g. your Swiss residence permit, passport or driving licence. Account cards can also be used to make deposits (*Anzahlung*, *acompte*) or payments via machines (envelopes are provided), check account balances, order forms, and print a mini-statement and balance. They can also be used in foreign currency machines. Account cards are issued free to salary and current account holders.

LOANS & OVERDRAFTS

Interest rates for borrowers are low in Switzerland, but so is the interest paid on deposits. Some banks won't give foreigners with a B permit an unsecured loan (*Darlehen*, *emprunt/prêt*) during their first year in Switzerland and you're generally unable to obtain any loan or an overdraft (*Kontoüberziehung*, *dépassement de crédit*) until you've been in Switzerland at least three months.

The net interest margin charged by most Swiss banks is among the lowest in the world, although you should still shop around for the best deal. Interest rates vary considerably with the bank, the loan amount and the period of the loan. Don't neglect smaller banks, as it isn't always necessary to have an account with a bank in order to obtain a loan. Ask friends and colleagues for their advice. Some insurance companies also provide loans. If you have collateral, e.g. Swiss property or insurance, or can get someone to stand as a guarantor for a loan, you may be eligible for a loan at the (lower) mortgage interest rate. Some banks require you to take out a life insurance policy for the duration of a loan.

It's usually easier to obtain an overdraft than a loan, particularly during your first year in Switzerland, although credit may be a limited, e.g. to SFr. 10,000.

The overdraft interest rate is usually a few percentage points higher than the mortgage rate, but much lower than the rate for a standard loan. Some banks allow salary or personal account holders an automatic overdraft equal to one month's net salary without making special arrangements, for which the current overdraft rate applies. Some banks insure overdrafts free against customers being unable to repay them. If you have a hire purchase (credit) agreement, e.g. for a car, a bank won't usually give you a loan or overdraft, but they may offer to pay off the outstanding debt with a loan.

Borrowing from private loan companies, which advertise in some newspapers and magazines, is expensive, as interest rates are high. **Use them only as a last resort when all other means have been exhausted.** Even private loan companies may require you, as a foreigner, to find a homeowner or Swiss citizen to act as a guarantor (in which case you'd be better advised to borrow from a bank).

CREDIT CARDS

Most large Swiss businesses accept major international credit cards, although they don't always advertise this fact. Credit cards aren't so readily accepted by small businesses, for whom the commission charge can be prohibitive. The Swiss generally mistrust plastic money and prefer payment in cash, gold or diamonds. You can apply for certain credit cards, such as a MasterCard or Visa, through your bank. 'Gold' cards (with a higher spending limit and greater pose value) are available, but require a higher annual fee plus an 'entrance' fee, although the annual fee may be reduced by 50 per cent if you spend, for example, SFr. 7,500 during a year and may be waived altogether if you spend SFr. 15,000 per year. (Special edition cards are issued with colourful designs by Swiss artists, for which there's an extra fee.) Some credit cards provide free travel and accidental death insurance when travel costs are paid with the card. Before obtaining a card, compare the costs and benefits provided, particularly the interest rates charged.

Major department stores issue their own credit or 'account' cards, e.g. Globus, Jelmoli and Manor. Some store cards allow credit, whereby the account balance may be repaid over a period of time, although interest rates are usually **very** high.

Many foreigners can obtain an international credit card in a country other than Switzerland (or can retain existing foreign credit cards) and be billed in the currency of that country. You may, however, find it more convenient and cheaper to be billed in Swiss francs than in a foreign currency, where you must wait for the bill from outside Switzerland and payments vary with exchange rate fluctuations.

If you lose a bank or credit card, report it immediately to the issuing office, when your liability is usually limited to SFr. 100. Even if you don't like credit cards and shun any form of credit, they do have their uses, such as no deposits on car hire, no prepaying hotel bills, safety and security, and above all, convenience.

VALUE ADDED TAX

Goods and services are subject to value added tax (*Mehrwertsteuer/MWSt*, *taxe sur la valeur ajoutée/TVA*) but Switzerland's low standard rate of just 7.6 per cent compares favourably with the average of over 15 per cent in EU countries.

Certain products and services are exempt from VAT, including postal services, healthcare, social security, sport and cultural activities, insurance, current-account transactions and the export of goods. VAT applies to other goods and services at the following rates:

Rate	Applicability
2.4% (reduced)	Food and drinks (excluding alcoholic drinks and cooked meals); meat; cereals; plants, seeds and flowers; some basic farming supplies; mains water; medicines; books, newspapers, magazines and other printed matter
3.6% (hotel rate)	Hotel and other accommodation;
7.6% (standard rate)	All goods and services not listed above.

Most prices in Switzerland are quoted inclusive of VAT. Companies and sole traders (the self-employed) must register and add VAT to their bills when their annual exceeds SFr. 75,000.

INCOME TAX

The rate of income tax (*Einkommenssteuer*, *impôt sur le revenu*) levied in Switzerland varies between around 15 and 35 per cent, which is good news for many foreigners, particularly those from most other European countries, and especially single people, although rates are rising faster than in most other developed countries. Income tax is levied by the federal government (direct federal tax) and by cantons and communities (see below). Each of the 26 Swiss cantons is autonomous as far as taxes are concerned, which makes it impossible to provide comprehensive figures here, although some examples are given below. If you want to check the tax rates in a particular area, contact a local tax adviser (*Steuerberater*, *fiduciaire*), who will usually be able to provide you with a comparison between rates in different cantons and communities.

Income tax consists of the following taxes:

● **Federal tax** (*Direkte Bundessteuer*, *impôt fédéral direct*) – levied at between 1 and 5 per cent depending on your income and comprising around 20 per cent of your total tax bill. It's assessed differently from canton and community taxes and entered on a separate tax form, sent with your community and canton tax forms. The deductions allowed against federal tax, based on your net annual salary, aren't the same as for canton and community taxes.

- **Canton & community taxes** (*Staatssteuer/Kantonssteuer, impôt cantonale* and *Gemeindesteuer, impôt communal*) comprise by far the major part of your total tax bill. Generally, the richer the community, the lower its tax rate.

- **Fire service tax** (*Feuerwehrsteuer, taxe d'exemption au service de feu*) is paid by all community residents who aren't active members of the local fire service. It may be calculated as a percentage of your basic tax value (see **Tax Calculation** on page 290) or may be a fixed sum (e.g. SFr. 100 per year), depending on your canton.

- **Church tax** (*Kirchensteuer, impôt écclésiastique*) is calculated as a percentage of your basic tax value and is payable by all who pay direct tax, but can be reclaimed by those who aren't registered as members of an official Swiss religion (see page 80). The amount payable varies from community to community depending on your canton and church, and may be up to 20 per cent of your basic tax value.

Canton and community taxes together comprise around 80 per cent of your tax liability.

Tax rates are progressive – the more you earn the more tax you pay – and vary according to whether you're married and how many children you have, as well as where you live. Married couples and their children under 18 are assessed jointly. A divorced or legally separated person is assessed separately. Unmarried couples often delay getting married in Switzerland because their joint income would put them in a higher tax bracket.

The tax amounts shown in the table below are for a married man without children and are based on 2006 tax rates:

Canton	Annual Income		
	SFr. 50,000	SFr. 100,000	SFr. 200,000
Basle	SFr. 3,850	SFr. 16,016	SFr. 50,527
Berne	SFr. 3,532	SFr. 14,637	SFr. 48,171
Fribourg	SFr. 3,624	SFr. 14,775	SFr. 48,685
Geneva	SFr. 832	SFr. 12,589	SFr. 47,878
Ticino	SFr. 1,357	SFr. 10,912	SFr. 44,283
Zug	SFr. 1,207	SFr. 7,210	SFr. 29,263
Zurich	SFr. 2,396	SFr. 10,702	SFr. 39,536

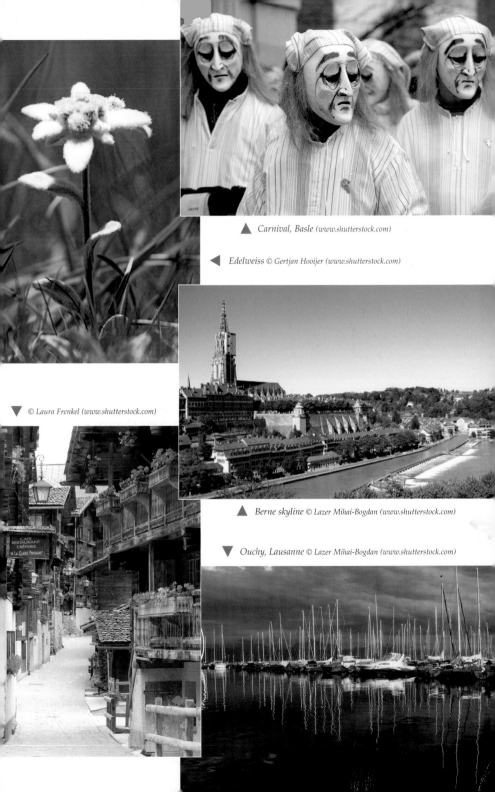

▲ *Carnival, Basle (www.shutterstock.com)*

◀ *Edelweiss © Gertjan Hooijer (www.shutterstock.com)*

▼ *© Laura Frenkel (www.shutterstock.com)*

▲ *Berne skyline © Lazer Mihai-Bogdan (www.shutterstock.com)*

▼ *Ouchy, Lausanne © Lazer Mihai-Bogdan (www.shutterstock.com)*

▲ *Mountain Goat (www.bigstockphoto.com)*

◀ *Lugano © Elpis Ioannidis (www.shutterstock.com)*

▼ *© Bateleur (www.shutterstock.com)*

▲ *© Olga Shelego (www.shutterstock.com)*

▼ *Mount Rigi © Roth (www.shutterstock.com)*

▲ Lake Lugano © Daniela Mangiuca (www.shutterstock.com)

© Antonio Jorge Nunes (www.shutterstock.com) ▶

▼ Emmental © Ronald Sumners
(www.shutterstock.com)

▲ Berne © mqmCA (www.shutterstock.com)

▼ © photobank CH (www.shutterstock.com)

Geneva © Kheng Guan Toh (www.shutterstock.com)

Sion, Valais © Alexy Drozdetskiy (www.shutterstock.com)

© Gertjan Hooijer (www.shutterstock.com)

Rumine Palace, Lausanne
© Lazer Mihai-Bogdan (www.shutterstock.com)

Ascona, Lake Maggiore
© Stephen Beaumont (www.shutterstock.com)

When they start working in Switzerland, foreigners usually pay direct (withholding) income tax (*Quellensteuer, impôt à la source*), which is deducted from their salaries by employers and generally settles their income tax liability. This may result, however, in foreigners paying a higher tax rate than the Swiss. Note the following exceptions:

● If you're married to a Swiss citizen, you don't need to pay direct income tax.

● If you work in Switzerland and live in another country (e.g. Austria, France, Germany or Italy), you must usually pay income and other taxes in the country where you're resident.

If you pay direct tax, you should be aware of anything which entitles you to a refund such as mortgage interest. You should write to your canton's tax authorities requesting a reduction of your tax liability if you have interest expenses such as credit cards, car loans, mortgages or child support payments, whether in Switzerland or another country (a letter documenting the expenses and requesting a refund will suffice). Most cantons require the letter to be received by 31st March of the year following the tax year for which you're claiming.

Some cantons don't require foreigners to pay direct income tax when they earn above a certain amount (e.g. SFr. 120,000 per year), or when their cantons of residence and employment are different, although foreigners without a C permit must pay direct income tax in most cantons irrespective of their income level. You're always subject to tax in your canton of residence and not your canton of employment if they're different (this is a constant source of conflict between Geneva and Vaud as thousands of residents of Vaud work in Geneva but pay no taxes there).

Foreigners paying direct income tax aren't generally required to file a tax return, although it's usually necessary if your gross earnings exceed SFr. 120,000 per year and/or you have considerable assets (such as property and investments), either in Switzerland or abroad.

When a foreigner obtains a C permit after five or ten years (see page 65), he automatically ceases to pay direct income tax and must complete an income tax return every one or two years and pay tax annually.

Non-employed foreigners can choose to be taxed on a fixed basis (*Pauschalbesteuerung, forfait fiscal*) in many cantons, where assessment is made according to a person's 'lifestyle'. In the cantons of Geneva and Vaud, the assessment is based on five times the annual (theoretical) rental of the person's accommodation (including a garage) or around 3 to 7 per cent of the property's value. To qualify for this scheme, which may not be advantageous to those whose only income is a pension or annuity, you must officially spend a minimum of 180 days a year in Switzerland and have a net wealth of at least SFr. 2m and a minimum taxable income of SFr. 300,000.

In addition to Swiss taxes, you may be liable for taxes in your home country. Citizens of most countries are exempt from paying taxes in their home country when they spend a minimum amount of time abroad, e.g. one year, although US nationals remain subject to US income tax while living abroad. **It's your responsibility to familiarise yourself with the tax laws in your home country or country of domicile.** If you're in doubt about your tax liability in your home country, contact your nearest embassy or consulate in Switzerland. US citizens can obtain a copy of the *Tax Guide for US Citizens and Resident Aliens* from American Consulates or from ▣ www.irs.gov/publications – go to Publication 54.

Tax Deductions

The following list is a rough guide to the deductions you can make from your gross salary when calculating your taxable income. Note that deductions are different for federal and canton/community taxes.

- obligatory insurance contributions such as federal old age and survivor's insurance, disability insurance, accident insurance, health insurance and unemployment insurance and contributions to a company pension fund. Most obligatory insurance contributions (see **Chapter 13**) are deducted from your gross salary by your employer.

- premiums for optional insurance such as life insurance, a private pension, accident insurance and sickness insurance, up to a maximum amount;

- business expenses, e.g. car expenses (including travel to and from your place of work), entertainment (if not paid or reimbursed by your employer), employment-related education and books;

- interest charges on mortgages, loans and overdrafts;

- medical expenses for your family that aren't reimbursed by an insurance policy and which total 5 per cent or more of your annual income (in some cantons all medical expenses are deductible);

- study costs, if not reimbursed by your employer;

- donations to recognised charities up to a maximum amount.

Standard allowances are permitted on many items, without proof of expenditure. Personal allowances vary according to your circumstances, e.g. single or married, divorced or widowed, and the number of children or dependants you have. Allowances vary from canton to canton.

Tax Calculation

Your canton/community income tax assessment is based on a 'basic tax value' (*ordentliche Steuer/einfache Steuer*, *impôt de base*), calculated from your taxable income after all deductions have been made. The basic tax value is derived from tables produced by each canton and is different for single and married people. A simple example of a tax calculation for federal and canton/community taxes is shown below:

Net annual salary	SFr. 100,000
Deductions	(SFr. 12,000)
Taxable income	SFr. 88,000
Basic tax value	SFr. 6,000
Canton tax (120% of basic tax value)	SFr. 7,200
*Community tax rate (120% of basic tax value)	SFr. 7,200
Parish church tax (20% of basic tax value)	SFr. 1,200
Community fire tax	SFr. 100
Total Canton/Community Tax	SFr. 15,700

* Calculated from tables provided by your community tax office.

Income Tax Return

If you don't pay direct income tax, you must complete an income tax return annually. Note that in some cantons, foreigners with a B permit paying direct income tax and earning above a certain amount, e.g. SFr. 120,000 a year, must complete a tax return. The forms are sent to you by your community tax office, usually in January, and must usually be completed and returned by 31st March. If necessary, ask for a delay in completing the return, which should be a formality as it takes months to process them all.

It's advisable to contact a tax accountant (*Steuerberater, conseil fiscal/fiduciaire*), your local tax office (*Steueramt, service des contributions*) or your bank for help in completing your tax return. Apart from language problems and the tax knowledge necessary, a pile of forms must be completed. For most people it simply isn't worth the effort doing it themselves, particularly as a tax accountant may charge 'only' a few hundred francs to complete a simple tax return. If you need information regarding your tax return or any correspondence from your local tax office, it's better to go in person than to telephone. Take someone with you if you don't speak the local language. The tax authorities want to know about all your sources of income, including the following:

- salary, commission or any other form of employment income, including allowances in cash or kind;

- professional or business income (net of expenses);

- pensions and annuities;

- income from property (real estate) and the estimated rental value of your property (net of estimated maintenance costs);

- dividends and interest from investments in Swiss or foreign securities, receivables or deposits, royalties and licence and similar fees;

- interest you've paid on debts, loans or mortgages and on late tax payments (these can all be claimed).

Taxable income usually includes your total income from all sources and all net assets **worldwide**, excluding property. If part of your income is taxed abroad in a country with a double-taxation treaty with Switzerland, you won't be required to pay Swiss tax on that amount. However, your Swiss tax rate (basic tax value) may be assessed on your total worldwide income, including the portion on which you've already paid tax. Despite the name, a double-taxation treaty is designed to **prevent** you paying double taxes and not to ensure that you pay twice. Income derived from property outside Switzerland is exempt from Swiss tax, but may be taxed abroad. For information, contact the Swiss Federal Tax Office, Section for International Fiscal Law and Double-Taxation Matters, Eigerstrasse 65, CH-3003 Berne (🖳 www.estv.admin.ch).

If you pay direct income tax, you can request a tax review (by completing an income tax return) if you think you've paid too much tax. **Note, however, that there's the possibility that instead of giving you a rebate, the tax authorities will 'invite' you to pay additional tax.** Anyone can lodge an appeal against their tax assessment. If your tax status changes in the first year after completing a tax return, e.g. due to the birth of a child, marriage or a large change in income, you can ask to have an intermediate assessment instead of waiting until the end of the tax period. If your spouse starts working, an intermediate assessment is obligatory. Tax for a period of less than a year is assessed on a pro rata basis.

All Swiss taxes must be paid when changing cantons or before leaving Switzerland.

Tax Bill

Income tax for Swiss, foreigners with a C permit and others who aren't eligible to pay direct income tax is payable annually. Nearly all cantons have now switched to a system whereby tax is based on the income of the preceding year and an assessment is made annually. If you have no income record in

Switzerland, you receive a provisional assessment until a full tax period has passed, when the difference between what you've paid and your actual tax bill is payable (or, if you've paid too much, refunded). The Swiss don't call it a tax **demand**, but an 'invitation to pay' – if you decline the invitation, they lock you up!

Your tax bill (*Steuerrechnung*, *prélèvement fiscale*) usually comes in two parts: one for federal tax, one for canton and community taxes.

Federal Tax

Federal tax bills are payable by 1st March annually. If you don't pay your bill by the due date, you can be charged interest on any outstanding sum. In practice it may be possible to pay your tax bill, or part of it, a month or two late without paying interest (but don't count on it). If you aren't going to be able to pay your tax bill on time, it's advisable to inform your community tax office (so they won't think that you have absconded).

Canton & Community Taxes

You usually receive your canton and community tax bills for the current year a few weeks after filing your tax return. **Note that the dates tax is due can be different for federal, canton and community taxes.** In some cantons, canton tax is due before the end of the current tax year and it's up to you to estimate the amount in order to pay it on time. When you pay late, interest at around 5 per cent is charged. If you pay a bill early, the tax office pays you interest, which is usually higher than if you'd left the money in a savings account (and the interest isn't taxable). Payment slips for advance payments are available at tax offices. If you prefer to pay your tax bill monthly or quarterly, inform your tax office and they will send you the appropriate payment advices. If you receive a late assessment and bill for tax, you may be given an extra month or two to pay it. In this case your tax bill may consist of various parts, payable at different times.

FEDERAL WITHHOLDING TAX

A federal withholding tax (*Verrechnungssteuer*, *impôt anticipé*) of 35 per cent is deducted directly from investment income, which includes all interest on bank balances in Switzerland. This tax is intended for businesses and although it's automatically deducted by all banks from the interest on deposits, it's reclaimable by individuals paying Swiss income tax, provided they declare their assets. You may, however, be liable for wealth tax on your assets (see below). If you pay direct income tax, federal withholding tax can be reclaimed for the preceding three years via a form available from your community office. If you declare and pay tax annually, a claim should be made on your income tax return.

You can choose to have federal withholding tax repaid in cash or into a bank or post office account, or deducted from your next tax bill, when you will be paid interest on the amount due.

WEALTH TAX

A wealth tax (*Vermögenssteuer*, *impôt sur la fortune*) is levied by all cantons on those with a high net wealth. The rate is progressive and varies with the canton and community where you live, but is usually between 0.25 and 1 per cent of the net value of your assets. Where applicable, wealth tax is paid with your canton and community taxes.

PROPERTY TAX

Some cantons impose a property tax (instead of or in addition to wealth tax), which can range from 0.03 and 0.3 per cent of the taxable value of your property.

CAPITAL GAINS TAX

Capital gains tax is levied on property (real estate) but not on other assets, and depends on the amount of profit made and the length of ownership. As with income tax, rates vary from canton to canton. Capital gains are usually taxed separately and not with general income.

INHERITANCE & GIFT TAX

There are no federal estate, inheritance or gift taxes in Switzerland, but these taxes are levied by most cantons. Rates in most cantons are low compared with those in many other western European countries, particularly if the deceased was domiciled in Switzerland at the time of death. Rates for inheritance tax vary considerably with the canton and the relationship of the beneficiary to the deceased or donor. Generally, relatives (particularly the spouse and children) of the deceased pay lower rates of inheritance tax than non-related beneficiaries. For example, in many cantons, the spouse and children of a deceased who was a resident taxpayer are exempt from inheritance tax and in some cantons, for example Basle and Berne, only on unrelated beneficiaries are taxed. Canton Schwyz has no inheritance or gift tax.

Given the complexity of inheritance tax rules and the wide differences between rates in different cantons, you're advised to take advice from a tax professional, preferably one with knowledge of inheritance tax in your home country.

WILLS

It's an unfortunate fact of life that you're unable to take all those lovely Swiss francs with you when you make your final exit. All adults should therefore make a will (*Testament/testament*) irrespective of how large or small their assets.

In general, all valid wills made in accordance with the law of the place of execution are recognised in Switzerland, both under the Hague convention, to which Switzerland is a signatory, and under the Swiss Private International Law Act 1987. It's possible to make two wills, one relating to Swiss property and another for foreign property (which is always advisable).

If you live in Switzerland and wish your will to be interpreted under Swiss law, you can state this and that you've abandoned your previous domicile. If you don't want your estate to be subject to Swiss law, you're usually eligible to state in your will that it's to be interpreted under the law of another country. This depends on your and your spouse's nationality and your ties with that country. A foreigner who also holds Swiss nationality **must** make his will under Swiss law if he's resident in Switzerland. If your estate comes under Swiss law, your dependants may be subject to Swiss inheritance laws. **Swiss law is restrictive regarding the distribution of property and the identity of heirs, and the estate is divided according to the number of children, who may receive the lion's share of the spoils.** You might not be too concerned about this (wherever you end up), but your other dependants might be!

In order to avoid being subject to Swiss inheritance tax (see above) and inheritance laws, you must establish your domicile in another country. Note, however, that foreigners living in Switzerland with a C permit are usually considered under Swiss federal and private international law to be domiciled in Switzerland. Take advice from an expert before establishing or changing your domicile to Switzerland or any other country.

Making a will in Switzerland is simple: it must be hand-written, state your full name, and be dated and signed. No witnesses are required. However, to ensure that its contents comply with Swiss law, it's advisable to obtain legal advice.

Keep a copy of your will(s) in a safe place and another copy with your solicitor or the executor of your estate. Don't leave your will in a safe deposit box, which in the event of your death will be sealed for a period under Swiss law. You should keep information regarding bank accounts and insurance policies with your will(s) – but don't forget to tell someone where they are.

If you die while working in Switzerland and have more than five years' service, your salary is usually paid for an extra month or two (maybe the Swiss, who all go to heaven, have access to ATMs there?).

COST OF LIVING

No doubt you'd like to know how far your Swiss francs are likely to stretch and how many (if any) you will have left after paying your bills. First the good news.

As you're probably aware, Switzerland has one of the world's highest standards of living, its per capita income and purchasing power is among the highest in the world, and executive salaries are among the highest in Europe. (On the other hand, well over 200,000 people receive social assistance, and Caritas estimates that up to five times this number live on or below the official Swiss poverty line, defined as an income of around SFr. 2,500 a month for a single person.) Switzerland also generally has low taxes and a very low inflation rate – in mid-2007 it was just 0.5 per cent.

The bad news is that Switzerland has one of the highest costs of living in Europe, and Swiss cities, particularly Zurich and Geneva, are among the most expensive in the world. The prices of some goods are unnecessarily high thanks to Switzerland's cartels and anti-competitive practices. The average price of many goods and services in Switzerland is up to 40 per cent higher than in EU countries and up to 60 per cent higher than in the US. However, prices of many goods and services (e.g. most retail goods, government-fixed prices such as hospital, postal and railway charges, insurance premiums and credit costs) are monitored and controlled by the office of the Price Controller to prevent unjustifiable price increases. If you wish to make comparisons, the UBS bank publishes a free annual booklet in English entitled *Prices and Earnings Around the World*.

Food in Switzerland is 25 to 50 per cent more expensive than in most EU countries and North America (Switzerland's food prices are exceeded worldwide only by Tokyo's), so your food bill will almost certainly be higher, although the actual difference in your food bill will depend on what you eat and where you lived before coming to Switzerland. Around SFr. 600 should feed two adults for a month in most areas, excluding fillet steak, caviar and alcohol (living in Switzerland provides an excellent incentive to cut down on all those expensive, rich foods).

Despite the high price of food, the cost of living in Switzerland needn't be astronomical. If you shop wisely, compare prices and services before buying, and don't live too extravagantly, you may be pleasantly surprised at how little you can live on (provided you don't want to buy a house). In fact, with the notable exception of housing, many people find that the cost of living in Switzerland isn't as high as they expected. Shopping abroad (see page 358), particularly for expensive purchases and food, can help reduce your living costs considerably. When possible, many foreigners choose to live in a neighbouring country (where the cost of living is significantly lower) and commute to their jobs in Switzerland.

A list of the approximate **minimum** monthly expenses for an average single person, couple and family of four is shown in the table below (the numbers after some of the items refer to the notes below). When calculating your cost of living, remember to deduct the appropriate percentage for income tax and obligatory insurance deductions from your gross salary.

ITEM	MONTHLY COSTS		
	Single	Couple	Family of Four
Housing (1)	SFr. 1,000	SFr. 1,500	SFr. 2,000
Food (2)	SFr. 400	SFr. 600	SFr. 800
Utilities (3)	SFr. 200	SFr. 250	SFr. 300
Leisure (4)	SFr. 400	SFr. 450	SFr. 500
Car (5)	SFr. 250	SFr. 250	SFr. 250
Travel	SFr. 100	SFr. 150	SFr. 200
Insurance (6)	SFr. 450	SFr. 700	SFr. 900
Clothing	SFr. 100	SFr. 200	SFr. 300
TOTAL	SFr. 2,900	SFr. 4,100	SFr. 5,250

1. Rent or mortgage payments for a modern or modernised apartment or house in an average small town or suburb, excluding major cities and other high-cost areas. The properties envisaged are a studio or one-bedroom apartment for a single person, a two-bedroom property for a couple, and a three-bedroom property for a couple with two children. **Note that in some cities, e.g. Geneva and Zurich, housing can cost double or treble these amounts.**

2. Doesn't include luxuries or alcohol.

3. Includes electricity, gas, water, telephone, cable or satellite TV, and heating and air-conditioning costs.

4. Includes all entertainment, dining out, sports and holiday expenses, plus newspapers and magazines.

5. Includes running costs for an average family car, plus third-party insurance, annual taxes, petrol, servicing and repairs, but excludes depreciation and credit costs.

6. Includes standard Swiss health insurance (but not expensive international health insurance), household (building and contents), third-party liability, travel, car breakdown and life insurance.

15.

LEISURE

This is how Switzerland was described in a travel book published in 1928: "North of Italy among the Alps, is Switzerland; it's a small state with no language of its own, producing little but goats and some timber; but possessing considerable wealth because of the large numbers of visitors who arrive every year for climbing or sight-seeing."

Some 80 years later, not surprisingly, a few things have changed (there are fewer goats and trees). However, Switzerland still has immense wealth and catering for visitors has developed into a very profitable tourist industry. Tourism is Switzerland's third largest industry, employing 240,000 people directly or indirectly and earning around SFr. 22bn annually (5 per cent of the GDP). Many people in mountain areas rely on tourism for a livelihood.

Leisure activities and entertainment in Switzerland are of the high standard and diversity you would expect from a country that celebrated 220 years of tourism in 2007 (and its 700th anniversary in 1991) and is credited with having invented tourism. It offers a huge variety of entertainment, sports (see **Chapter 16**) and pastimes and is blessed with a wealth of natural beauty hardly matched anywhere in the world in such a small area. The majority of tourists come to Switzerland to participate in outdoor sports, e.g. skiing and hiking, and not, for example, to savour the night life (which although lively enough for most people, may disappoint the international jet set). If you want to avoid road traffic and its ever-attendant pollution, visit one of Switzerland's delightful car-free Alpine resorts: Bettmeralp, Braunwald, Mürren, Riederalp, Rigi-Kaltbad, Saas-Fee, Stoss, Wengen and Zermatt.

Switzerland is a small country and no matter where you live you can regard the whole country as your playground. Due to excellent road and rail connections, a huge area is accessible for day excursions and anywhere in Switzerland (and many neighbouring countries) is within easy reach for a weekend trip. The maximum distance from east to west is only 348km (216mi) and from north to south it's just 220km (137mi).

Information regarding local events and entertainment is available from tourist offices and local newspapers. In most cities there are magazines or newspapers devoted to entertainment, e.g. Panorama and Scoop in French-speaking Switzerland. Free weekly or monthly programmes are published by tourist offices in all major cities and tourist centres. Many city newspapers publish free weekly magazines or supplements containing a comprehensive programme of local events and entertainment. Other useful sources of information are the monthly English-language magazines GT Magazine (🖥 www.genevanews.com) and Swiss News (🖥 www.swissnews.ch), plus Revue Switzerland (🖥 www.revue.ch), which is published in a combination of English French, German, Italian and Spanish. The latest entertainment information can also be obtained from the Swiss television teletext service and Switzerland Tourism (ST – see below).

The main aim of this chapter, and indeed the purpose of the whole book, is to provide information which isn't found in standard guide books. General tourist information is available in many excellent Swiss guide books including the

Michelin *Green Guide to Switzerland, Lonely Planet Switzerland* and *The Rough Guide to Switzerland* (see **Appendix B** for a list).

TOURIST OFFICES

There are tourist offices in all Swiss cities and tourist areas, where English-speaking staff can provide you with a wealth of information and also find you a hotel room. They're open daily, including Saturdays and Sundays, in most major cities and tourist centres. Telephone the tourist office or consult a guide book to find the exact business hours. In major towns, reduced opening hours are in operation during winter, while in smaller towns and resorts tourist offices close for lunch and may open during the winter **or** summer season only. Services provided by tourist offices include local information, hotel reservations, local and city tours, excursions, congresses, car hire (rental), guides and hostesses, and train and bus information. In some towns, walking audio tours (with free map) are available for a small fee.

Switzerland Tourism (ST/*Schweiz Tourismus, Suisse Tourisme*) is a mine of information and in addition to promoting tourism its aim is the further understanding of Switzerland's special political, cultural and economic characteristics, in close co-operation with the regional tourist promotion boards. ST has offices in many countries including Australia, Austria, Belgium, Brazil, Canada, China, Egypt, France, Germany, Hong Kong, India, Israel, Italy, Japan, the Netherlands, Spain, Sweden, Taiwan, the UAE, the UK and the US. It produces over 100 publications (one in over 30 languages) totalling around 4m copies and distributes many more. ST is continually revising, updating and replacing its publications, and therefore some of the brochures mentioned in this book may no longer be available – contact ST's toll-free call centre (☎ 0800 100 200 30) or the website (🖥 www.myswitzerland.com) for information.

Whatever you'd like to know, ST provides you with the information directly or gives you the name of someone who can help you. They answer telephone enquiries and send information by post, including an annual booklet entitled *Events in Switzerland*, listing music, theatre and film, folklore, public festivals, sports events, exhibitions, fairs, markets and congresses. ST is Switzerland's ambassador of tourism and in contrast to the sometimes frosty reception from Swiss embassies, particularly when enquiring about employment in Switzerland, they're a paragon of co-operation and friendliness. The head office is Switzerland Tourism, PO Box 695, CH-8027 Zurich (☎ 0800 100 200 30, 🖥 www.myswitzerland.com).

HOTELS

All Swiss hotels are comfortable, clean and efficient. The standard of hotel accommodation and service is excellent; whether a luxury 5-star hotel or a humble pension, it's almost impossible to find a bad hotel in Switzerland (the Dolder Grand in Zurich was chosen as the world's best hotel by the US trade journal Conde Nast Traveler in 1998). Not surprisingly, Swiss hotels and hotel training schools provide the best training for hotel staff in the world. Swiss hotels are, however, **very** expensive (the Royal Suite in the Hotel President Wilson in Geneva costs over SFr. 20,000 a night!), particularly in major cities, and the most expensive in Europe (the average is over SFr. 200 per night!). Prices vary considerably depending on the standard, location, season (low, middle or high) and the amenities provided. The following table can be used as a **rough** guide:

Class	Rating	Price Range
Luxury	5 star	SFr. 250 to 500+
First	4 star	SFr. 100 to 250
Middle	3 star	SFr. 75 to 150
Comfortable	2 star	SFr. 50 to 100
Simple	1 star	SFr. 40 to 80

The prices quoted above are **per person, per night**, sharing a double room with bath (prices are usually quoted per person and not per room in Switzerland). There's usually no charge for children up to six years old when sharing their parents' room and reductions for older children are usually provided, e.g. 50 per cent for those aged 6 to 12 and 30 per cent for those aged 13 to 16. Continental breakfast is often included in the cost and a British or American style cooked breakfast, sometimes buffet style (self-service), is provided in many first class hotels (although it may be an extra). Many hotels with restaurants offer half-board (breakfast and dinner) or full-board (breakfast, lunch and dinner) on favourable terms. A hotel Garni (similar to a hostal) provides bed and breakfast and beverages, but no meals.

Inexpensive accommodation, e.g. small one-star hotels and pensions, is usually difficult to find in the main cities. Outside major cities it isn't necessary to pay a fortune. A guide to over 240 'simple & cosy' hotels is available from Swiss Budget Hotels, Case postale 153, CH-1860 Aigle (☎ toll-free 0848 805 508, 🖳 www.rooms.ch). Their hotel accommodation varies from dormitory beds at SFr. 30 per night up to the most expensive rooms at around SFr. 150 per person, per night. They produce a booklet (available from the website) listing inexpensive hotels, inns and pensions for an average of around SFr. 60 per night (including breakfast but without a bath or shower). See also **Youth Hostels** on page 305. Many hotels in Switzerland have special rates for senior citizens and children. Most people should be able to find something to suit their budget and taste among the 6,000 hotels and boarding houses in Switzerland, offering a total of over 250,000 beds.

The *Swiss Hotel Guide* (*Schweizer Hotelführer, Guide Suisse des Hôtels*) is published annually by the Swiss Hotel Association (SHA), and is available free from them (see address below) and ST offices. It contains the addresses, telephone/fax numbers, opening dates, room rates and amenities of over 2,500 hotels, guesthouses and pensions, including hotels with special facilities for the disabled. It also lists restaurants, spas and climatic resorts. The SHA also publish brochures for senior citizens, a list of hotels with special facilities for families and information about country inns. For more information contact Hotelleriesuisse, Monbijoustr. 130, PO Box, CH-3007 Berne (☎ 031 370 41 11, 🖳 www.swisshotels.ch).

Holidays tailored specially for pensioners are organised by Pro Senectute Schweiz, Lavaterstr. 60, PO Box, CH-8027 Zurich (☎ 044 283 89 89, 🖳 www. pro-senectute.ch). Information about hotels with special facilities for the disabled is available from Procap, Reisen für Menschen mit Handicap, Froburgstr. 4, CH-4601 Olten SO (☎ 062 206 88 30, 🖳 www.procap.ch). They also produce holiday catalogues for disabled people and city guides for the disabled for 26 Swiss towns and cities.

In most Swiss cities and resorts, the local tourist office will find you a hotel room for a fee of around SFr. 2. They may also provide brochures and information regarding youth accommodation, hotels catering especially for children, and hotels with swimming pools and sports facilities. Residential hotels and one-room hotel apartments are available for longer stays. Hotel apartments in cities aren't often rented for less than six months, due to the difficulty of finding replacement tenants, particularly in winter. In mountain resorts, many hotels close for the summer months or close between the end of the summer season and the start of the winter season, e.g. October to November. If you want a room in a top class hotel during an international convention or fair, or in a city or popular resort (particularly during school holidays), you should book well in advance.

In addition to hotels, bed and breakfast (*Zimmer zu vermieten, chambre à louer*) accommodation is available throughout Switzerland, particularly in small towns and villages in tourist areas. Local tourist offices may maintain a list of rooms to let in private homes. An excellent resource is *Bed and Breakfast Switzerland* published by Nicole Neyroud, Rue du Village 38, CH-1802 Corseaux (☎ 021 923 67 41, 🖳 www.bnb.ch).

SELF-CATERING ACCOMMODATION

You can find self-catering accommodation, e.g. apartments and chalets, in all holiday areas in Switzerland. Chalets and apartments can be rented through agencies or direct from owners. An apartment is generally much cheaper than a hotel room, you have more privacy and freedom, and you're able to prepare your own meals. Standards, while generally high, vary considerably, and paying a high price doesn't always guarantee a good location or a well furnished apartment (most look wonderful in brochures).

Most holiday apartments are, however, comfortable and all are spotlessly clean. Apartments are generally well-equipped with bed linen, towels, cooking utensils, crockery and cutlery, although there may be an extra charge for bed linen. Some basic food stuffs (e.g. salt and sugar) and such essentials as toilet paper and soap may be provided, but don't count on it. Most people take essential foods and supplies with them, and buy fresh food on arrival. Shops in holiday areas may be open for a period on Sundays, particularly in ski resorts during the winter season.

You're normally required to do your own daily cleaning as apartments aren't serviced unless part of a large private chalet or a hotel apartment complex, when chambermaids are provided. Don't overdo the cleaning as you must usually pay for an apartment to be cleaned on your departure. Apartments are normally let on a weekly basis from Saturday to Saturday. You're required to move out by around noon on your last day, when a veritable army of cleaning ladies march in.

Apartments are best rented from the owners and not through agents. Write to the tourist office of the town or village where you wish to stay. Tourist offices usually send you a list of apartments with prices and a map showing their location. The location is of particular importance if you're going to be skiing, as you will want to know how far the apartment is from the nearest ski lift; generally the nearer apartments are to ski lifts, the more expensive they are. Other aspects that influence the rental cost are the size, amenities, general quality and the season. Budget for around SFr. 150 to 250 per person, per week, for a four-bed apartment in high season, and up to 50 per cent less during the low season.

If you obtain a list of apartments from the tourist office, you must contact the owner or agent directly to find out the availability and further details, and to make a booking. **Book well in advance for public and school holiday periods, e.g. three to six months in winter.** You may need to pay a deposit or the full cost in advance. Check whether there are any extras for cleaning or breakages (sometimes included in the rent). In most ski resorts, landlords collect a small visitor's tax (*Kurtaxe, taxe de séjour*), which may amount to a few francs per adult, per day.

In summer you can usually find an apartment on the spot without any trouble, particularly in resorts catering mainly for winter sports fans. Chalets and apartments can also be rented from many agents in Switzerland including the Automobile Club of Switzerland (ACS), Wasserwerkgasse 39, CH-3000 Berne 13 (☎ 031 328 31 11, 🖳 www.acs.ch); Interhome (Schweiz), Sägereistr. 20, CH-8152 Glattbrugg/Zurich (☎ 0800 84 88 88, 🖳 www.interhome.ch); 🖳 www.vacanca.com; and 🖳 www.holiday-home.ch. One way to enjoy a relatively inexpensive self-catering holiday in Switzerland is to exchange your home abroad with someone who lives in Switzerland. For further information contact

International Home Exchange, Fair Tours, PO Box 615, CH-9001 St. Gallen (⌨ www.gn.apc.org/fairtours).

CARAVANNING & CAMPING

Switzerland has around 400 camping and caravan (trailer) sites, graded from one to five stars depending on their amenities, location and other factors. Many are open all year round. The cost varies and averages around SFr. 20 per night for a family of four. Campers must have an international camping carnet, available from Swiss camping associations (see below). Permission is required to park or camp on private property or anywhere outside official camping sites. Caravans can be hired in most areas of Switzerland.

For detailed information about campsites, contact the Swiss Camping and Caravanning Federation (Schweizerischer Camping und Caravanning Verband, Fédération Suisse de Camping et de Caravanning, PO Box, CH-4009 Basle, ☎ 061 302 26 26, ⌨ www.sccv.ch). They publish handbooks, which are available from bookshops in Switzerland, listing all Swiss campsites and their facilities. See also ⌨ www.camping.ch and ⌨ www.camping-switzerland.ch. The Touring Club of Switzerland (TCS) publish the *TCS Camping Guide*, available from TCS offices and bookshops (⌨ www.tcs.ch). In addition to listing campsites in Switzerland, it also lists sites in France, Italy and Spain, including a section on naturist camp sites for those wishing to save on laundry bills. A list of campsites is also available from ST offices.

YOUTH HOSTELS

If you're travelling on a tight budget, one way to stretch your precious financial resources is to stay in youth hostels, of which there are around 60 in Switzerland. Youth hostel accommodation is open to all, although members under seven years of age must be accompanied by an adult. All youth hostels provide separate dormitories for men and women and hot showers, and some provide cooking facilities, a laundry and an inexpensive restaurant. The cost of accommodation at most youth hostels ranges from around SFr. 20 to over SFr. 40 per night (average SFr. 25 to 35) and includes a cotton sleeping bag or bed linen.

You don't need to be a member of the Swiss Youth Hostels (SYH) to stay in one, although membership provides reduced prices and an international membership card. Membership costs SFr. 22 for those aged under 18 and SFr. 33 for those over 18. Family membership is also available for SFr. 44 (parents and children aged up to 18) and group leaders' membership for groups of ten or more (SFr. 55). **To avoid disappointment you're advised to book at least five days in advance and in February, July, August and holiday periods, pre-booking is usually essential.** Youth hostels require guests to remain quiet until

7am and they don't allow alcohol on the premises. Smoking is restricted to designated rooms only.

For more information contact Swiss Youth Hostels/SYH (*Schweizer Jugendherbergen, Auberges de Jeunesse Suisses*), Schaffhauserstr. 14, CH-8042 Zurich (☎ 044 360 14 14, 🖳 www.youthhostels.ch). The SYH publish a free 'Know How' map showing hostel locations and listing their facilities and a free booklet entitled *Downtown Switzerland*. Youth hostel information is also available from ST who publish a free Swiss Hostel Guide. ByeBye Holiday & Travel (☎ 0848 333 330, 🖳 www.byebye.ch), organises trekking, adventure, culture and education tours, as well as flights for youth hostellers. STA Travel (Ankerstr. 112, PO Box, CH-8026 Zurich, ☎ 058 450 40 40, 🖳 www.statravel.ch), provides information for travellers aged from 16 to 35 and has offices in all major Swiss cities and towns.

MUSEUMS & ART GALLERIES

Switzerland has some 950 museums, art galleries, gardens and zoos (Basle and Zurich zoos are world-famous and offer family and individual annual season tickets for regular visitors). Art treasures are housed in two National Museums in Zurich and at the Château de Prangins (near Nyon, Vaud), and in historical museums in Basle, Berne, Geneva and Zurich. Most museums are closed on Mondays and on public holidays, which is unfortunately standard practice in Europe. Admission is usually free on Sundays (first Sunday a month in Geneva). Many museums close during lunch periods and opening times vary hugely, so check in advance. Some exhibitions make reductions for foreigners on production of a passport and reduced-price local transport tickets are often available for visitors to trade exhibitions.

Lists of museums, zoological gardens and botanical gardens are available from ST offices and 🖳 www.museums.ch, and museum lovers may also be interested in the *Swiss Museum Guide* available from Swiss bookshops. All tourist information offices provide information about local attractions. An annual (SFr. 111, adult; SFr. 202, family) Swiss Museums Passport is available from tourist information offices and is valid at over 420 museums throughout the country. The Michelin *Green Guide to Switzerland* includes a list of the major museums, sights, tourist attractions and summer cable-cars and chair-lifts, including costs and opening times. News about exhibitions and fairs can be obtained from the telephone service number ☎ 1600 (SFr. 0.50 basic fee plus per minute).

CINEMAS

Around 325 cinemas (*Kino, cinéma*) throughout Switzerland show English-language films in the original language with German and French subtitles.

Cinema listings in German-language newspapers show the original soundtrack language (first upper-case letter) and the subtitle languages (lower-case letters). For example, E/d/f denotes a film with English as the original soundtrack language with German (*Deutsch*) and French (*français*) subtitles, F/d denotes French language with German subtitles. In the French-speaking region of Switzerland, films are usually shown in French without subtitles and not in the original language. In French-speaking areas, '*v.o.*' denotes *version originale* (original language version). Programmes are shown on street posters in major cities.

Age restrictions vary from six years for Walt Disney type films to 9, 12 and 16 years for other films. In some cantons, cinemas must advertise the suitable age limit, but don't always enforce it when children are accompanied by an adult. Otherwise, for children accompanied by adults, the age restriction may be two years below the suitable age limit, e.g. in Basle if the general unaccompanied age limit is 12, then a child accompanied by an adult must be aged at least ten to see the movie. It isn't unusual for children (or adults) who look younger than their years to be asked for proof of their age, e.g. a school identity card.

Most cinemas accept telephone reservations and provide season tickets. You can also purchase 'Movie Cards' or other membership-type cards for most cinemas. These allow holders to purchase subsidised tickets, make advance bookings online and provide other benefits. Ask at your favourite theatre for information. Film festivals are held in major cities, when cinemas show films non-stop (24 hours a day) for a number of days and offer reduced admission prices. There are private film clubs in the main cities showing old classics.

THEATRE, OPERA & BALLET

Switzerland has many excellent theatres (around 150) and thriving opera houses, including many small theatres and troupes, with performances in French, German, Italian and other languages. In major cities, amateur English-language theatre companies periodically stage plays, and incidentally, are always on the lookout for new talent (see **Appendix A**). English and American repertory companies occasionally tour Switzerland (programmes are available from tourist information offices). **Tickets for ballet and opera are in high demand, so apply well in advance** (tickets can be purchased by subscription).

An annual calendar of music, theatre and dance events is available free from ST offices. A Swiss cultural magazine *Konzert & Theater* is available on subscription from Konzert & Theater, Museumstr. 1, PO Box 463, CH-9004 St. Gallen (☎ 071 242 05 05, 🖳 www.sinfonieorchestersg.ch, 🖳 www.theater sg.ch).

Switzerland has a surprising number of travelling circuses (over 25), including the world-famous Circus Knie (the Swiss National Circus), which tours from March to November (🖳 www.knie.ch).

CONCERTS

Classical concerts, music festivals and solo concerts by international musicians and performers, are held regularly throughout Switzerland. Many Swiss international music festivals, from orchestral, choral and opera to jazz and rock, are world renowned. Season tickets are usually available for a whole season of classical performances or a selection of performances may be chosen from a prepared list. Although they aren't world-renowned, Basle, Geneva and Zurich all have excellent orchestras. Free organ and choral concerts are performed in churches throughout the year and free outdoor concerts are staged in summer. Look for announcements in local newspapers or ask at your local tourist office.

The easiest place to purchase tickets for concerts and other events is from TicketCorner (☎ 0900 800 800 at SFr. 1.19 per minute, 🖳 www.ticketcorner. com). Tickets are also available at some department stores, music shops, and bookshops, most notably Manor department stores. **Ticket prices in Switzerland are generally high and can be astronomical for 'superstars'.**

For the musically talented there are musical (classical and brass bands) and choral societies in most towns and villages, and national orchestras for the really gifted (around 35 large professional orchestras). Those who cannot sing or play a musical instrument can join a yodelling group! A list of all major concerts and music festivals in Switzerland is provided in the ST brochure, *Events in Switzerland*.

SOCIAL CLUBS

There are many social clubs and organisations in Switzerland, catering for both foreigners and Swiss. These include Ambassador clubs, American Women's and Men's Clubs, Anglo-Swiss clubs, Business Clubs, International Men's and Women's clubs, Kiwani Clubs, Lion and Lioness Clubs, and Rotary Clubs. Expatriates from many countries have their own clubs in major cities (ask at your local embassy or consulate in Switzerland – see **Appendix A**). Many social clubs organise activities and pastimes such as chess, whist, art, music, sports activities and outings, and theatre and cinema visits.

If you wish to integrate into your local community or Swiss society in general, one of the best ways is to join a Swiss club. Most communities publish a calendar of local sports and social events. A list of social clubs and organisations for English-speaking foreigners is contained in **Appendix A**.

DISCOTHEQUES & NIGHT-CLUBS

There are discotheques and night-clubs in all major Swiss towns and cities, although they're generally expensive. The entrance fee for discos, irrespective of whether they have a drinks licence, is usually between SFr. 10 and 30 (it sometimes includes a 'free' drink). When available, drinks are **very** expensive.

Although most Swiss aren't night owls, there are jazz and night clubs, bars, cabarets and discotheques open until between 2am and 6am in the major cities. Many clubs are private and don't admit casual visitors unless accompanied by a member. At weekends in the major cities, it isn't uncommon to have 'after-hours parties' lasting until noon the following day. The Swiss are also known for rave-type parties that are held throughout the year, with house/techno and other youth-orientated music. Keep a lookout for posters in cities.

CASINOS

Until recently, you could only play Boule, a sort of simplified roulette, in the 13 'B license' Swiss casinos in Bad Ragaz, Crans, Courrendlin, Davos, Fribourg, Interlaken, Locarno, Mendrisio, Meyrin by Geneva, Pfäffikon, Schaffhausen, St. Moritz and Zermatt. However, in a historic vote on the 7th March 1993, the Swiss voted to remove the long-standing ban on 'real' casinos to aid the declining tourist industry and bolster government coffers. After much debate, seven 'A licenses' (GrandCasino) were allocated in spring 2005 to Baden, Basle EuroAirport, Berne, Lucerne, Lugano, Montreux and St. Gallen.

'A license' casinos can offer unlimited betting with no jackpot limit, while gamblers at 'B license' casinos are allowed to bet a maximum of SFr. 5 only, with a maximum jackpot of just SFr. 5,000. The new GrandCasinos (along with the smaller, B license ones) are expected to take in SFr. 769m a year, with SFr. 370m going to social security and a further SFr. 54m to the cantons.

Before the introduction of the GrandCasinos, all the big Swiss gambling money flowed over the border into the strategically placed casinos surrounding Switzerland, which reap 25 times the revenue of the Swiss 'B License' casinos. These include casinos at Aix-les-Bains, Evian and Divonne (France), Campione D'Italia (Italy), Bregenz (Austria) Konstanz and Lindau (Germany).

BARS & CAFES

Bars and cafés abound throughout Switzerland, which, like most European countries, has sensible licensing laws. Most bars and local restaurants (i.e. bars providing food) are open from morning to midnight, including Sundays. Hot food, snacks and excellent coffee are usually available. There are also many English and Irish-style pubs where you can buy English, Irish and other foreign beers. Local Swiss beers and wines are generally good and imported beverages are widely available (local **hell** beer won't kill you, it just means light beer). Spirits and cocktails are outrageously expensive, particularly in hotels. Good local mineral waters are available everywhere. Bear in mind that some tea-rooms and cafés **don't sell alcohol**. In bars, a choice of non-alcoholic drinks should be available at prices below the cheapest alcoholic drink, although this isn't always the case (non-alcoholic wines and beers are also usually available).

In Swiss bars you don't pay for each drink as it's served, except in crowded tourist haunts or a pub with English bar service. You usually receive a total bill at the end of the evening (the system is designed to help you drive home, as the size of the bill has an immediate sobering effect). While on the subject of drinking and driving, the law is **very** strict in Switzerland and penalties are severe (see page 229). If you have more than one or two small drinks you would be well advised to hitch a ride with a sober friend or use public transport. The legal age for drinking beer and wine in public places in Switzerland is 16, and 18 for spirits and alcopops. Most cafés, bars and local restaurants provide free local newspapers and magazines, a common practice in continental Europe.

A popular card game named Jass, remotely similar to bridge and requiring a special deck of cards, can be played in most bars and local restaurants. Most local bars have a family or regulars' table (*Stammtisch, table des habitués*), reserved for regular customers. It's usually denoted by a huge ashtray and you may be asked to move if you sit there. Like restaurants, most bars and cafés close on one or two days a week (*Ruhetag, jour de repos*), usually posted on the door.

RESTAURANTS

There are around 29,000 restaurants in Switzerland, approximately one for every 250 inhabitants and one on top of every mountain. Restaurants in Switzerland invariably provide good food and service, although there's little original Swiss cooking on offer apart from fondue, raclette and rösti, and most serve international cuisine. Like most continental Europeans, the Swiss take their food seriously and the main meal of the day is usually eaten at midday (lunchtime). Unlike in some countries, it isn't usually necessary to have a meal in a Swiss restaurant and you can order a snack or a drink only.

All restaurants are obliged by law to display their menu and prices outside. A good meal for two with a modest bottle of wine costs around SFr. 60 to 90 in an average restaurant (about the same price as in most northern European countries). Of course you can easily pay up to SFr. 200 a head if you want the best and the cost of wine can be astronomical. In many expensive restaurants, nouvelle cuisine is fashionable, consisting of tiny portions artfully arranged on large plates – if you're starving, eat at a local bar. All restaurants offer a variety of house wines (*Offener Wein, vin ouvert*), which can be ordered by the deci-litre (but it's still expensive). Swiss restaurants and hotel bills include a service charge of 15 per cent, designed to cut out tipping (the price you see on the menu is the price you pay). Don't be concerned about not leaving a tip or leaving a few small coins only, as the waiter won't abuse you or spill soup over you on your return.

Most restaurants offer a daily menu (*Tagesmenu, menu du jour*) at lunchtime, usually from noon to 2pm. It includes a choice of meals with soup or salad (and sometimes a dessert) and costs from around SFr. 14. Dinner in a local restaurant or bar is usually served from 7 to 10pm. Many restaurants offer half-portions for children or have a children's menu. Mövenpick restaurants are particularly good for children and offer a choice of menus, and McDonalds has branches in most major cities and large towns (you can also hire restaurants for children's parties). Many department stores have good value for money restaurants. If you like a glass of wine or a beer with your meal, avoid alcohol free (*Alkoholfrei, sans alcool*) restaurants (e.g. Migros), tea-rooms and cafés.

Exotic foreign restaurants, which in Switzerland includes most foreign restaurants, aren't as common as in many other European countries and can be expensive. Most foreign cuisine is, however, available in the major cities. It's advisable to make a reservation for the more expensive or more popular restaurants, particularly during lunchtimes, on Friday and Saturday evenings, and at anytime for parties of four or more people.

In most bars and local restaurants you're given cash register receipts for each item ordered, which are totalled when you request your bill. Sliced bread is usually provided free with a meal, but bread rolls usually cost extra. If your waiter or waitress is going off duty, don't be surprised if you're asked to pay half-way through your meal.

Most restaurants close on one or two days a week (*Ruhetag, jour de repos*), which is usually posted on the restaurant door. Many bars and restaurants have a private room that can be used (usually free) for a club meeting or social function, provided you buy coffee or other drinks. The continental game of skittles (*Kegelbahn, jeu de quilles*) can be played in some restaurants. Among the best Swiss restaurant guides are the Michelin *Schweiz Red Guide* and the *Gault-Millau Guide Schweiz*. You can also find Swiss restaurants on 🖥 www. restaurants.ch.

Smoking

Smoking is currently permitted in restaurants in Switzerland, except in Canton Ticino, although most cantons are revising their laws regarding smoking in public places. In 2007, residents of Basle were pushing for a referendum to ban smoking in all workplaces, which would include restaurants and bars. The federal health commission has decided to propose a law to protect people from secondhand smoke so new legislation regarding smoking is expected. In the meantime, the healthy majority (some 70 per cent of the Swiss population) can locate non-smoking restaurants at 🖥 www.eatsmokefree.ch and 🖥 www.rauch freigeniessen.ch.

LIBRARIES

Most public libraries in cities and large towns have books in English, French, German and Italian. Opening times vary but are usually around 9am to 6.30pm from Mondays to Fridays and 9am to 4pm on Saturdays. Smaller libraries may open on only one or two days a week and opening hours may be reduced during the summer holiday period. Most large towns and cities have a central library (*Zentralbibliothek, bibliothèque centrale*) with a large selection of English-language books, and most universities also have libraries that are open to the public. Library membership is usually free or a nominal charge is made, for example SFr. 10 for ten years. In addition, it's common to pay a fee for each item borrowed, e.g. SFr. 1 per book (four weeks) and SFr. 4 per DVD (two weeks).

Private libraries are fairly common in major cities, some of which have a large collection of English-language books, magazines and newspapers. The American library in Geneva is the second largest English reading library on the continent, with around 17,000 titles. It's usually necessary to pay an annual membership fee to join a private library. The Federation of American Women's Clubs Overseas (see **Appendix A**) run English-language libraries in most major Swiss cities, which are open to non-members for a small subscription fee.

FOREST HUTS

Most communities have their own forest hut (*Waldhütte, cabane*), which can be hired for social events (e.g. parties). The fee is usually from SFr. 75 to 140 per day or night for a community resident or double this for a non-resident. The rent varies depending on the community and the amenities provided. In some huts, glasses, crockery and cutlery are provided besides electricity, running water and toilets, while others are more basic.

Forest huts are an excellent place to hold a party at any time of the year (in winter you can usually build a log fire). You can make as much noise as you like, as there are no neighbours to call the police at 10pm. It's also unnecessary to invite your neighbours and you don't need to worry about your guests spilling red wine on the carpet (there isn't one) or setting fire to the furniture (the community, on the other hand, won't be too happy if you burn down their hut!). You're required to clean the hut after your party or pay to have it cleaned. Book early, particularly for weekends and holiday periods.

If you're sick of cooking and don't fancy catering to an army of ravenous guests, party catering services are available, e.g. from Migros, Coop and Mövenpick, who can also provide staff. They provide both hot and cold buffet food and deliver it to the forest hut or your home. A personal touch can be provided by a metre or two of bread with a personal message, courtesy of Migros and other bakers.

DAY & EVENING CLASSES

Adult day and evening classes are run by various organisations in all Swiss cities and large towns. The largest is the Migros Club School (*Migros Klubschule, école club Migros*, 🖳 www.klubschule.ch), funded by the Migros supermarket and department store chain. It has ten regional co-operatives who operate over 50 centres in major cities and towns throughout Switzerland. Over 300 different subjects are taught, including foreign languages and local language courses for foreigners (about 50 per cent of total classes), handicrafts, hobbies and sports (around 40 per cent), and further education, e.g. computer studies and typing (some 10 per cent). Migros schools publish regional programmes containing a list of all local clubs (available free from Migros clubs and stores).

Other companies and organisations providing day and evening classes include Coop Leisure Centres (*Coop-Freizeit-Center, centre de loisirs Coop*) and the People's High School (*Volkshochschule, université populaire*), both of which hold classes in general education, geography, culture and languages. The Federation of American Women's Clubs Overseas and other expatriate organisations also organise day and evening classes in many subjects, and some organisations provide classes for children (e.g. English), particularly during school holidays.

Adult further education programmes are published in many areas (often delivered free to local residents) and include all courses organised by local training and education centres. Local newspapers also contain details of evening and day courses. Many communities publish an annual programme of events, including day and evening classes, and tourist offices may also be able to provide you with information. Many cantons publish a list of local adult education centres. Swiss universities organise non-residential courses and special language courses during their summer recess. See **Further Education** on page 173 and **Language Schools** on page 173.

16.

SPORTS

S ports facilities in Switzerland are excellent. Among the most popular sports are skiing and other winter sports, hiking, cycling, mountaineering, tennis, squash and swimming. Most water (sailing, windsurfing, water-skiing) and aerial sports (hang-gliding, ballooning, flying) also have many devotees. Participation in some sports is expensive, although costs can be reduced through the purchase of season tickets, annual membership or by joining a club. Switzerland Tourism (ST/*Schweiz Tourismus, Suisse Tourisme*) can provide information about practically any sport and the appropriate contact name and address – see page 301. Various publications are available from tourist offices promoting special sports events and listing local sports venues.

The Swiss Olympic Association (Schweiz. Olympischer Verband, Association Olympique Suisse, PO Box 606, CH-3000 Berne, ☎ 031 359 71 11, 🖳 www. swissolympic.ch) publishes a monthly magazine, *Swiss Sport*. Many cantons and cities publish comprehensive booklets listing local sports organisations, facilities and classes. Sports results are announced on the telephone service number ☎ 164 (SFr. 0.50 basic fee plus 0.50 per minute) and on the Swiss television teletext service. Leaflets containing information about how to prevent and avoid sports accidents and injuries, e.g. cycling, hiking, skiing, football and watersports, are available from the Swiss Bureau for the Prevention of Accidents (see **Accidents** on page 227).

AERIAL SPORTS

The Alps are ideal for aerial sports (particularly gliding, hang-gliding, paragliding and hot-air ballooning), due to the updrafts and the low density of air traffic (apart from all the gliders, hang-gliders and balloons). Hang-gliding has become increasingly popular in Switzerland in recent years and there are over 20 hang-gliding schools. To obtain a glider pilot's licence you must make 40 flights in five different areas. For more information contact the Swiss Hang-Gliding Association (Schweiz. Hängegleiter-Verband, Association Suisse de Vol Libre), Seefeldstr. 224, CH-8008 Zurich (☎ 01 387 46 80, 🖳 www.shv-fsvl.ch).

Paragliding (*Gleitschirm, parapente*) entails jumping off steep mountain slopes with a parachute. There are over 20,000 registered 'pilots' in Switzerland and around 40 schools, and the sport even has its own magazine, *Swiss Glider*. Participants must have the proper equipment and complete an approved course of instruction lasting 20 half days, after which (if they survive) they receive a proficiency certificate and are permitted to go solo. For more information about paragliding contact the Swiss Hang-Gliding Association (address above). Ballooning has a small but dedicated band of followers. Participation is generally limited to the wealthy due to the high cost of balloons. A flight in a balloon is a marvellous experience, particularly over the Alps. There is, however, no guarantee of distance or duration, and trips are dependent on wind conditions and the skill of your pilot. A list of ballooning clubs is available from ST.

Light aircraft and gliders (sailplanes) can be hired (rented) with or without an instructor from most small airfields in Switzerland (provided you have a pilot's licence!). There are around 60 gliding clubs in Switzerland. Freefall parachuting (sky-diving) flights can be made from most private airfields in Switzerland; however, it's expensive and costs can run to over SFr. 7,000 for training and equipment. Information regarding free-fall parachuting, para-gliding, gliding and flying is available from ST and the Aero-Club of Switzerland (Aero-Club der Schweiz, Aéro Club de Suisse) Lidostr. 5, CH-6006 Lucerne (☎ 041 375 01 01, 🖥 www.aeroclub.ch). A special weather report for aerial sports is provided on Swiss television teletext.

Before taking up the above sports, you're advised to make sure that you have adequate health, accident and life insurance (see **Chapter 13**) and that your affairs are in order.

CYCLING

Cycling is popular in Switzerland, not only as a means of transport or a serious sport, but also as a relaxing pastime for the whole family. The weather from spring through to autumn is usually fine for cycling, mainly dry and warm and generally not too hot. There are over 6,000km (3,700mi) of marked bicycle paths in country areas. These include the 'Cycling in Switzerland network' which was officially opened in 1998, consisting of nine national cycle routes covering a total of over 3,300km (2,050mi) of cycle paths (maps are available from ST and railway stations, or visit 🖥 www.cycling-in-switzerland.ch).

In Switzerland, serious cyclists abound; cycle racing also has a huge following and races are organised at every level. The *Tour de Suisse* is Switzerland's premier race, held in June over a 1,600km (1,000mi) route, and one of Europe's major events. For information contact the Swiss Cycling Federation (Schweiz. Radfahrer-Bund, Fédération Cycliste Suisse), Haus des Sportes, Talgutzentrum 27, CH-3063 Ittigen (☎ 031 359 72 33, 🖥 www.cycling.ch). Information about cycling can also be obtained from 🖥 www.kettenrad.ch, 🖥 www.tourenguide.ch and 🖥 www.veloland.ch.

For the recreational cyclist, a standard bicycle (*Fahrrad, vélo/bicyclette*) can be purchased for SFr. 800 to 1,000 (cheaper bikes are also available); shop around for the best buy (a professional racing bicycle can cost many thousands of francs). If you're feeling particularly energetic you can buy a 21-speed mountain bike and go cycling in the Alps (some resorts have special mountain bike trails). Mountain bikes are currently all the rage and cost from around SFr. 1,000 for a good basic bike and many thousands for a top quality machine.

Apart from cycling to work, which many people do from spring to autumn, cycling is an excellent way to explore the countryside at your leisure and get some fresh air and exercise at the same time. Special cycling maps (*Velokarte, itinéraire pour cyclistes*) are produced by the Traffic Association of Switzerland (scale 1:50) and are available from bookshops everywhere. A *Bicycling in*

Switzerland booklet is available from ST, plus many regional cycling guides containing recommended one-day trips. Swiss motoring organisations also provide maps and books containing cycling tours (also have a look at 🖳 www. tourenguide.ch). **Note that mountain bikes are banned on many hiking paths due to the dangers and inconvenience to hikers, and cross-country 'off-piste' cycling is also prohibited in some areas to protect plant and wildlife.** However, downhill cycling is a popular summer sport in ski resorts, where you can usually transport your bike on ski lifts.

Before a bicycle can be used on public roads it must be licensed at your local post office, bicycle shop or Migros store. The licence costs around SFr. 5 a year, depending on your canton of residence, and is valid until 31st May of the following year (the license includes third party insurance). When you licence a bicycle, you receive a self-adhesive *vignette* (*Kontrollschild, plaque d'immatriculation*) showing your canton initials, year and licence number, and a licence card, which must be signed and kept in a safe place. When you buy a bicycle in Switzerland you're given a small aluminium licence plate. This must be fastened vertically to your rear mudguard or rear frame, where it's easily visible, and your self-adhesive *vignette* affixed to it. In subsequent years you receive a new *vignette* and licence card when you buy your licence. Bicycle breakdown assistance and theft insurance is available from Swiss motoring organisations (see page 234).

Important Notes

- All cyclists should be familiar with the road rules for cyclists contained in the *Handbook of Swiss Traffic Regulations*, available for around SFr. 12 from canton motor registration offices.

- Take **particular** care on busy roads and don't allow your children onto public roads until they're experienced riders. Children aren't permitted to cycle on a public road until they're aged seven and attending primary school; kindergarten doesn't count, even when a child is already seven. Bicycles aren't permitted on motorways.

- If you cycle in cities you should wear reflective clothing, protective head gear and a smog mask. It isn't necessary to wear expensive sports clothing when cycling, although a light crash helmet is advisable, particularly for children. Head injuries are the main cause of death in bicycle accidents, most of which don't involve accidents with vehicles, but are a result of colliding with fixed objects or falls. Always buy a quality helmet that has been subjected to rigorous testing and approved by a safety organisation.

- Children up to the age of seven can be carried on the back of an adult's bicycle in a specially designed chair. Riders must be aged over 16.

- Bicycles must be fitted with an anti-theft device blocking a wheel or the steering. A basic locking device is already fitted to bicycles purchased in Switzerland and you can buy a more secure steel cable or chain with a lock from bicycle accessory shops and supermarkets, e.g. Migros. **Note, however, that no devices are foolproof and some people take a wheel with them when leaving their bike unattended!** If your bicycle is stolen contact the local police.

- Where special cycle tracks or lanes are provided, they must be used. Unfortunately there aren't many off-road cycle lanes in cities and towns, and you often take your life into your hands when venturing onto main roads, particularly during rush hours.

- You aren't permitted to ride on footpaths unless sign-posted otherwise or two abreast on roads. Being pulled along by a moped (*Motorfahrrad/Mofa*, *vélomoteur*) is illegal and dangerous, and riding with your hands off the handlebars or feet off the pedals is also prohibited.

- If you import a bicycle, it must conform to Swiss safety standards. These include front and rear reflectors, front and rear lamps, pedal reflectors, bell, mudguards, front and rear brakes, and good tyres. Off-road bikes, e.g. some racing and mountain bikes, cannot be used on public roads (unless road legal), except when riding to and from race venues.

- Take drinks, first-aid kit, tool kit and a puncture repair outfit when on a long cycling trip.

- Take care not to get your wheels stuck in tram or railway lines.

Bicycle Hire & Transportation

Bicycles can be hired (rented) from over 100 Swiss railway stations and returned to any other participating station (see ⌨ www.rentabike.ch.) Bookings should be made by 6pm the previous day or a week in advance for groups. You can choose from a country bike, mountain bike or children's bike, the fees for which are shown below:

- half-day (until/after 12.30), returning to the station where you hired the bike: SFr. 23 (SFr. 18 for children under 16 and holders of a Swiss rail general season ticket or half-fare card);

- one day, returning to the station where you hired the bike: SFr. 31 (SFr. 26 for children under 16, etc. as above);

- one day, returning to a different station from where you hired the bike: SFr. 38 (SFr. 33 for children under 16, etc. as above).

With a junior card (see page 180) children's bikes are free. A country bike can also be fitted with a free child's seat, but you need to book. Bicycles can be left at any participating station for SFr. 7, which is waived if you hire a bike for more than a day. Further information is provided in a brochure available from railway stations, which includes suggested routes. Bicycles can be hired from cycle shops in many towns, and mountain bikes are available in some mountain resorts for around SFr. 50 per day. At many stations you can borrow a helmet.

You can transport your bicycle between any two stations for SFr. 16 per day, except for certain Eurocity and S-Bahn trains during peak periods. You must load and unload it yourself and have a valid ticket for the same destination (Intercity and fast trains excluded). Bicycles sent by train in Switzerland can be insured for SFr. 5 per SFr. 500 value. Using the train allows you to cycle one way and return by train (or vice versa). Swiss federal railways (Schweizerische Bundesbahnen/ SBB) offer many special cycling tours and trips, and 'rail bicycle' brochures are available from railway stations. The SBB also publish a book entitled *40 Bicycle Tours* (with the train).

In some cities you can hire a bicycle (or even a skateboard, kickboard, or electrobike!) for free. All you need to do is show personal identification and pay a deposit of SFr. 20. Further information is available from 🖥 www.bernrollt.ch.

FISHING

Fishing facilities in Switzerland are superb. There are a huge variety of well-stocked waters totalling some 133,000hectares (330,000acres) of lakes and 32,000km (20,000mi) of running water; enough to keep even the keenest of anglers busy for a few weeks. Lakes and mountain streams are stocked annually with trout, grayling and pike. You must buy a fishing permit for rivers and some lakes. which are usually available for a day, week or month from the local tourist office or the area council office (*Bezirksamt, administration de district*). You can obtain an annual permit for your own canton and monthly permits for other cantons. Fishing licences for non-residents of a canton can be expensive, although there are some unrestricted waters which don't require a permit. Contact the local area council office or local tourist office for information.

The fishing season and rules and regulations regarding the permitted size of fish which can be taken vary from canton to canton, so check before planning a trip. Angling competitions are organised in many areas. For more information contact the Swiss Angling Association (Schweiz. Fischerei-Verband, Association Suisse des Pêcheurs – 🖥 www.sfv-fsp.ch).

GOLF

There are some 80 golf courses (9 and 18 holes) in Switzerland with more planned, plus mini-golf courses. However, Switzerland has just one public golf course, the Executive Golf de Chessel between Aigle and the Lake of Geneva (there are also public driving ranges in some areas). Golf is an elitist and expensive sport in Switzerland and it's almost impossible to join a city club without excellent contacts and a low handicap (the waiting list for membership of some clubs is longer than the average expatriate's stay in Switzerland). The average joining fee for an 18-hole club is SFr. 20,000 to 25,000 and annual fees are an additional SFr. 2,500 a year. Members of foreign and other Swiss golf clubs can usually play at town clubs from Mondays to Fridays on production of a membership or handicap card. Green fees are from around SFr. 100 in urban areas and from SFr. 60 to over SFr. 100 in rural areas. Your best bet may be to play at a mountain resort course, where you can play golf in beautiful scenery (at around 1,500 metres) without being a member.

Many cities and resorts have indoor practice centres, where you can have a video analysis of your swing. Switzerland also has the world's largest indoor golf club ($1,500m^2/16,146ft^2$) at Zumikon, Zurich. Crazy golf (golf obstacle course) is played in many areas. It's taken seriously and competitions (even Swiss championships) are organised. For more information contact the Swiss Golf Association (Schweiz. Golfverband, Association Suisse de Golf), Place de la Croix-Blanche 19, CH-1066 Epalinges (☎ 021 785 70 00, 💻 www.asg.ch). An excellent *Official Guide to Golf Courses in Switzerland* is available from ST. Many hotels offer special golf packages; for information, contact the Swiss Golf Hotels Group, Bahnhofstr. 8, PO Box, 7304 Maienfeld (☎ 081 300 44 22, 💻 www.swissgolfhotels.ch).

HIKING

Switzerland is a hiker's paradise with over 31,000km (over 19,000mi) of marked main routes, including ten national hiking routes each covering a distance of 200 to 400km (around 125 to 250mi), and some 400 secondary routes. The country boasts a grand total of over 60,000km (37,500mi) of hiking trails in some of the most beautiful scenery in the world. The Swiss are keen hikers and infants to pensioners can be seen everywhere in their hiking gear. Although the main hiking season is from around May to September, hiking in Switzerland isn't just a summer sport. Most winter sports resorts keep several hiking trails open for walkers throughout the winter – a total of some 4,600km (1,800mi). It's fun walking in the snow and the weather can be quite hot in the mountains in winter (you will also be hot after walking for a few kilometres).

Many local communities and walking clubs organise walks (*Volksmarsch*, *marche populaire*). There's a small fee (around SFr. 3) and a medal for any survivors (you will have earned it by the time you reach the top of the Matterhorn!). A complete programme of hikes organised by local walking clubs is available from the Federation of Swiss Hiking Trails (Schweizer Wanderwege, Fédération Suisse de Tourisme Pédestre), Monbijoustrasse 61, PO Box, CH-3000 Berne 23 (☎ 031 370 10 20, 💻 www.swisshiking.ch), who publish a bimonthly magazine (*Wander-Revue, Revue Sentiers*) for hikers, available in French and German editions. Membership of the Federation of Swiss Hiking Trails costs from around SFr. 15 to 50 a year, depending on your canton of residence. Guided hiking tours are organised in many resorts and the Swiss Alpine Club (SAC) organises excursions for experienced hikers (see **Mountaineering & Caving** on page 326). Contact ST and local tourist offices for information. Orienteering is also a popular sport in Switzerland.

Many mountain resorts have a tourist information telephone number, where the latest information is recorded about local weather conditions, cable-cars and other mountain transport services, and the condition of hiking paths. Numbers are listed in telephone directories. The weather forecast is also available on service telephone number ☎ 162 (SFr. 0.50 basic fee plus 0.50 per minute) and on Swiss television teletext. See also **Climate** on page 366.

An abundance of wild mountain flowers are in bloom in the Alps from around May to August, July usually being the best month. Many mountain areas have alpine gardens and guides to the local flora and fauna can be purchased from tourist offices. **Note that many plants are protected and you're forbidden to pick or uproot them (offenders can be fined).**

Signs

Hiking paths (*Wanderweg, chemin pédestre*) are indicated by yellow metal signs showing the altitude and destination and often the approximate time required to reach it. Times are based on a walking speed of 4.2km (2.6mi) an hour on well surfaced flat land, which is generous enough for anyone but a tortoise – provided of course you don't get lost. They sometimes show the distance to the destination. Mountain paths (*Bergweg, sentier de montagne*) are marked by yellow signs with a red and white tip or arrow point. Where there are no signposts, routes are marked with yellow arrows or diamond-shaped signs on trees, rocks, posts and buildings (part of the challenge is trying to find the path). Signs may also be in canton colours. Some areas have hiking paths for those confined to wheelchairs. Always stick to marked paths, particularly in difficult terrain.

To commemorate Switzerland's 700th anniversary in 1991, the Swiss created the 'Swiss Path' (*Weg der Schweiz, la voie Suisse*) around lake Uri (part of the lake of Lucerne) at a cost of SFr. 12m. Each canton was responsible for a stretch of the 35km (22mi) trail, which takes around 12 hours to negotiate (it's usually a two-day hike). A Swiss Path train pass can be purchased from anywhere in Switzerland and a plan of the walk is available in English for around SFr. 5.

Books & Maps

You should plan a walk using a good map, for example Swiss ordnance survey maps (*Landeskarte der Schweiz, carte nationale de la Suisse*). These excellent maps are produced in both 1:25 and 1:50 sizes and sold at stationers, railway stations, and shops in walking and climbing areas. Special hiking maps (*Wanderwegkarte, carte des chemins pédestres*) can also be purchased from most bookshops. A good general book on hiking is *Walking Switzerland: The Swiss Way* by Marcia & Philip Lieberman (Cordee). It includes all the necessary advice required (unless you plan an assault on the north face of the Eiger) and includes a selection of walks. An excellent book of selected hikes of varying degrees of difficulty is the *Grosser Wander-Atlas der Schweiz* (Kümmerly + Frey). It contains summer, winter and town walks, cross-country skiing tracks, and excellent maps showing the gradients of walks (or how far you will fall if you don't take care). Another good book is the TCS *Grosse Freizeit und Ferienbuch* (Kümmerly + Frey), which not only includes hikes but also lists cycling tours, natural and cultural experiences, and paddle trips on rivers and lakes.

Free hiking brochures are produced by various organisations, including the post office, Swiss motoring organisations and Swiss banks. ST publish a series of hiking brochures, entitled *Switzerland Step by Step*, each containing 100 walks. They include town to town, mountain passes, and lake and panorama walks. Local hiking maps are available in all areas from shops and tourist and community offices. Plans showing local hiking paths are also displayed at many railway stations. Many areas have a **hiking pass**, available from most railway stations and tourist offices, with suggested walking tours. See also **Appendix B** for a list of hiking books.

Emergencies

If someone is seriously injured, don't move him unless it's absolutely necessary to protect him from further injury. Keep him warm and seek help as soon as possible. The alpine SOS consists of a series of six signals evenly spaced over one minute (one every ten seconds) and then a repetition of six more after a minute's pause. The signals may consist of either six blasts on a whistle, six loud shouts, six flashes of a torch or six swings of an article of clothing (attached to a stick if possible) swung in a semi-circle from the ground. The reply to an emergency signal is three repeats of the visual or acoustic signal a minute, at one-minute intervals.

Standing upright with both arms stretched above your head signals a request for a rescue helicopter. Holding one arm up with the other arm held down at your side indicates that a rescue helicopter isn't required. The Swiss REGA helicopter service (see page 135) is the ambulance of the Alps and all SAC huts have radio telephones that can be used to summon a helicopter. If you need to call REGA (☎ 1414) for a rescue helicopter, you should provide the following information:

● your name, location of telephone and telephone number;

● what has happened where;

- number of patients and their approximate injuries;

- location – give exact details, e.g. map co-ordinates;

- town, name and birth date of the injured person (it isn't essential to revive an unconscious patient and ask him);

- weather conditions and landing possibilities in the accident area;

- any helicopter obstructions in the accident area, e.g. pylons, cables and power lines.

Some resorts, e.g. Sion and Zermatt, provide a local helicopter rescue service. If you're going hiking with visitors to Switzerland, make sure that they have adequate accident insurance (see page 266), including helicopter rescue. The cost of a rescue party or helicopter and medical treatment can be very expensive. If you work in Switzerland, you're covered for accidents by your compulsory employee, non-occupational, accident insurance.

General Information

The following notes may help you survive a stroll in the mountains:

- If you're going to take up hiking seriously, a good pair of walking shoes or boots is mandatory (available from most Swiss shoe and sports shops). Always wear proper walking shoes or boots where the terrain is rough. Modern walking boots are light and comfortable and are available from shoe and sports shops. Wearing two pairs of socks can help prevent blisters. Break in a new pair of boots on some **gentle** hikes before setting out on a marathon hike around Switzerland.

- Don't over-exert yourself, particularly at high altitudes where the air is thinner. Mountain sickness usually occurs only above 4,000m/13,000ft, but can also happen at lower altitudes. A few words of warning for those who aren't particularly fit; take it easy and set a slow pace. It's easy to over-exert yourself and underestimate the duration or degree of difficulty of a hike. Start slowly and build up to those weekend marathons. If you're unfit, use chair-lifts and cable-cars to get to high altitudes.

- **Don't attempt a major hike alone as it's too dangerous.** Notify someone about your route, destination and estimated time of return, and give them a mobile phone number on which you can be contacted or call for help is necessary (but bear in mind that reception is impossible in some areas!). Check the conditions along your route and the times of any public transport connections (set out early to avoid missing the last cable-car or bus). Take into account the time required for both ascents and descents. If you're unable to return by the time expected, let somebody know – if the rescue service is summoned in error, you may have to pay. If you realise that you're unable to reach your destination, for example due to tiredness or bad weather, turn back in good time or take a shorter route. If you're caught in a heavy storm, descend as quickly as possible or seek protection, e.g. in an SAC hut.

- Check the weather forecast, usually obtainable from the local tourist office. Generally the higher the altitude, the more unpredictable the weather, even for Swiss meteorologists.

- Hiking, even in lowland areas, can be dangerous, so don't take any unnecessary risks. There are enough natural hazards including bad weather, rock-falls, avalanches, rough terrain, snow and ice, and wet grass, without adding to them.

- Don't walk on closed tracks at any time (they're sign-posted). This is particularly important in the spring when there may be the danger of avalanches or rockfalls. Tracks are sometimes closed due to forestry work or army exercises. If you're in doubt about a particular route, ask in advance at the local tourist office. **Note that if the Swiss signpost anything as dangerous (*Gefahr/Lebensgefahr, danger*), you can bet it is!**

- Wear loose fitting clothes and not, for example, tight jeans, which can become uncomfortable when you get warmed up. Shorts are excellent in hot weather. Lightweight cotton trousers are comfortable unless it's cold. You can wear your shorts underneath your trousers and remove your trousers when you've warmed up.

- Take a warm pullover, gloves (in winter) and a raincoat or large umbrella (an excellent plastic raincoat is sold at main post offices). Mountain weather can change suddenly and even in summer it's sometimes cold at high altitudes. A first-aid kit (for cuts and grazes), compass, identification, maps, small torch/flashlight, a Swiss army knife and a mobile phone may also come in handy. A pair of binoculars are handy for spotting wildlife (or hikers having fun in the bushes). Take a rucksack to carry all your survival rations. A 35 to 40-litre capacity rucksack is best for day trips or a 65-litre capacity for longer hikes.

- Take sun protection, for example a hat, sunglasses, and sun and barrier cream, as you burn more easily at high altitude due to the thinner air. Use a total sunblock cream on your lips, nose and eyelids, and take a scarf or handkerchief to protect your neck from the sun. You may also need to protect yourself against ticks and mosquitoes in some areas. Take a water bottle. This is much appreciated when you discover that the mountain restaurant that was just around the corner is still miles away because you took the wrong turn (there's a restaurant on top of every mountain in Switzerland).

- Beware of wild animals that appear ill or unnaturally friendly as they may have rabies (see **Pets** on page 375).

- If you're gathering mushrooms, always present them to your local official 'mushroom inspector', for checking, as some species are deadly poisonous (a number of people die each year from eating poisonous mushrooms or toadstools). **There's usually a limit to the amount of mushrooms which can be picked per person per day, e.g. 1 to 3kg (2.2 to 6.6lb).**

- Don't take young children on difficult hikes unless you enjoy carrying them. Impress upon children the importance of not wandering off on their own. If you lose anyone, particularly children, seek help as soon as possible and before nightfall. It's advisable to equip children with a loud whistle, some warm clothing and a mobile phone (provided they are old enough to use it), in case they get lost.

- Hikers are asked to observe the Swiss Nature Society's green rules:

  - Take care not to damage trees, flowers and bushes.

  - Leave animals in peace (dogs mustn't be allowed to disturb farm animals).

  - Be careful with fire and never start a fire in a forbidden area.

  - Watch where you walk and keep to the paths.

  - Don't litter the countryside.

  - Think of others.

  - Close all gates after use.

MOUNTAINEERING & CAVING

Those who find hiking a bit tame might like to try mountaineering, rock-climbing or caving (subterranean mountaineering), all of which are extremely popular in Switzerland. Switzerland has over 100 peaks of around 4,000m/13,000ft, which provide even the experts with plenty of challenges (usually consisting of trying to climb them all in one day!). If you're an inexperienced climber, you would be well advised to join an alpine club before heading for the mountains. Contact the Swiss Alpine Club (Schweizer Alpen-Club, Club Alpin Suisse/SAC) Monbijoustr. 61, CH-3000 Berne 23 (☎ 031 370 18 18, 💻 www.sac-cas.ch) for information. The SAC maintain over 150 climber's mountain huts throughout Switzerland, listed in a book entitled simply *Huts (Hütten der Schweizer Alpen)*.

Unless you're an experienced climber, you need to hire a registered guide, particularly when climbing glaciers (don't, however, follow your guide too closely – if he falls down a crevice it isn't necessary to go with him). There are mountaineering schools (around 32 in total) in all the main climbing areas of

Switzerland. Contact the Swiss Federation of Mountain Sport Schools (Verband Bergsportschulen Schweiz, Ecole Suisse d'Alpinisme), co. Borter Meichtry AG Marketing & Management Support, PO Box 400, Kantonsstrasse 55, CH- 3930 Visp (☎ 027 948 13 45, 🖥 www.bergsportschulen.ch) for information. Guides are available at all mountaineering schools and in many smaller resorts. If you find a guide other than through a recognised school or club, ensure that he's qualified and registered. A good map is important – Swiss ordnance survey maps (*Landeskarte der Schweiz, carte nationale de la Suisse*) are the best and available in both 1:25 and 1:50 sizes from stationery stores, railway stations and shops in climbing areas.

Scores of climbers are killed each year in Switzerland, many of whom are inexperienced and reckless. Many more owe their survival to rescuers who risk their own lives to rescue them. Before taking up mountaineering, it's advisable to visit the alpine museum and graveyard in Zermatt (interesting even if you aren't planning to take up residence). Over 500 climbers have died attempting to climb (or descend) the Matterhorn. If this doesn't succeed in bringing you to your senses, all that remains is to wish you the best of luck.

It's extremely foolish – not to mention highly dangerous – to venture off into the mountains without an experienced guide, proper preparation, excellent physical condition, sufficient training, the appropriate equipment and accident insurance.

Mountain walking shouldn't be confused with hiking as it's generally done at much higher altitudes and in more difficult terrain. It can be dangerous for the inexperienced and should be approached with much the same degree of caution and preparation as mountaineering. A free brochure entitled *Safer Mountain Walking (Bergwandern-Mit Sicherheit mehr Spass, la sécurité lors des radonnées en montagne)* containing advice about how to avoid accidents, fitness tips and safety rules, is available from Schweizerische Beratungsstelle für Unfall-verhütung, Laupenstr. 11, CH-3008 Berne (☎ 031 390 22 22, 🖥 www. bfu.ch). Rega, the Swiss helicopter rescue service (see page 135), has the job of rescuing climbers who get stuck on mountains and also provides safety guidelines for mountaineers. See also **Emergencies** on page 244.

RACKET SPORTS

There are excellent facilities in Switzerland for most racket sports, particularly tennis and squash. There are two main types of racket clubs; sports centres open to anyone and private clubs. Sports centres require no membership or membership fees and anyone can book a court. Private clubs usually have high membership fees running into thousands of francs a year, although court fees are low or non-existent. Some private clubs are fairly exclusive and it's difficult to join unless you're introduced by a member and are wealthy.

Tennis is the most popular racket sport in Switzerland and there's an abundance of covered and outdoor tennis centres. Courts are more expensive in winter (see below). Tennis centres have coaches available for both private and group lessons. Many communities also have outdoor courts, often floodlit, for which fixed weekly bookings are taken for the whole summer season.

Clubs catering exclusively for squash are rare, although most tennis centres have a number of squash courts, a total of over 600 in some 175 centres throughout Switzerland. The standard of squash isn't high due to the general lack of top coaching and top competition, although it's continually improving. Rackets and balls can be hired from most squash clubs for squash or racketball (a simpler version of the game).

Some tennis centres also provide badminton courts, which, due to their rarity, are fairly solidly booked on most weekday evenings (they're usually easier to book at weekends). Most badminton centres have clubs entitling members to play free of charge or on reserved courts at fixed times.

Typical peak-hour evening court hire costs are:

| Sport | Typical Costs per Hour | |
	Winter	Summer
Tennis	SFr. 30 to 55	SFr. 20 to 52
Badminton	SFr. 18 to 35	SFr. 16 to 27
Table Tennis	SFr. 10 to 20	SFr. 10 to 20
Squash	SFr. 20 to 35	SFr. 20 to 35

Court costs are usually cheaper before 5pm and at weekends. Costs can be further reduced by paying for a fixed number of periods (e.g. 5 or 10) or reserving a court for a fixed time each week throughout the season. **Note that you must cancel a booked court 24 hours in advance, otherwise you must pay for it if it isn't re-booked.**

Many clubs provide 'free' saunas and whirl-pools, and solariums are often available for a small extra cost. Racket clubs sometimes have a resident masseur. Most public racket clubs have a restaurant (possibly alcohol-free) or snack bar and some have swimming pools. A free list and map of local tennis and squash centres is available from many clubs. Some hotels have their own tennis and squash courts and organise coaching holidays throughout the year. Information is available from racket clubs, travel agents and resorts.

Most racket centres run fee-paying clubs allowing members to play free of charge or at a reduced cost at certain times, and to participate in club competitions. League and knockout competitions are organised, both within clubs and nationally, through affiliation to Swiss sports federations. In order to play in inter-club competitions, competitors must be registered with the national federation for their sport (fees include accident insurance). There's a full programme of local and national league competitions for all racket sports.

To find the racket clubs in your area, enquire at your local community or tourist office, or contact the Swiss national associations:

- Badminton – ☎ 031 359 72 55, 🖥 www.swiss-badminton.ch;

- Squash – ☎ 043 377 70 03, 🖥 www.squash.ch;

- Tennis – ☎ 032 344 07 07, 🖥 www.mytennis.ch.

Table tennis is a sport that's rarely played socially in Switzerland. Normally you must be a member of a club, although you can play casually at hotels, swimming pools and youth clubs. Membership of a table tennis club is usually divided into 'active' (those representing the club in leagues and competitions) and 'passive' members (those playing socially only). Costs vary but it's an inexpensive sport with little equipment necessary. Typical annual club fees are from SFr. 100 to 150 for active membership.

RUNNING

Competitive running has a strong following in Switzerland, although jogging isn't very popular judging by the lack of joggers puffing their way up and down the hills. For serious competitive runners, a free annual booklet is produced by the Swiss Light Athletics Federation (Schweiz. Leichtathletik-verband, Fédération Suisse d'Athlétisme), Haus des Sports, PO Box 606, CH-3000 Bern 22 (☎ 031 359 73 00, 🖥 www.swiss-athletics.ch). It contains a complete list of running events throughout Switzerland and is available from sports shops or the above address.

For those who like to combine running and exercises there are around 500 planned courses (*Vita-Parcours*) throughout Switzerland, sponsored by the Zurich Life Insurance Company. Courses consist of a route of 3 to 4km, with an exercise stop every few hundred metres to keep you in good shape (or kill you if you're in poor shape). Contact the Stiftung Vita Pacours (🖥 www.vitaparcours. ch) for a complete list of courses. Many communities organise local runs (*Volkslauf, course populaire*) of around 10km (6mi), where all competitors receive a commemorative medal for finishing the course. Contact your local tourist office or community office for details of local races.

SKIING & SNOWBOARDING

A book about living in Switzerland would hardly be complete without a 'few' words about skiing. Skiing is Switzerland's national sport and some 40 per cent of the population ski or snowboard regularly, including many foreigners, plus another 2m visitors. Wherever you live you won't be far from the ski slopes, although in some areas the nearest facilities may be in a neighbouring country. Switzerland has around 200 ski resorts, most of which are located in attractive mountain villages. However, although Switzerland has largely resisted the temptation to construct purpose-built resorts in virgin areas, it has, like other countries, damaged its mountain environment by over development (the Alps are the world's most environmentally-threatened mountain range).

There are two main types of skiing in Switzerland: alpine or downhill (*Alpin*) and cross-country (*Langlauf/Ski-Wandern, ski de fond/ski nordique*). Many downhill skiers look down on cross-country skiing as boring and lacking in excitement. This may be because it's too much like hard work to most of them, although it would be fair to say that if it's excitement and exhilaration that you're after, downhill skiing is hard to beat.

Although originally thought of as a sport for those who are too clumsy to master the art of skiing, snowboarding is extremely popular, especially with teenagers. While snowboarders can use the same pistes as skiers, many winter sport resorts have special snowboarding schools and half-pipes (barrel-run).

The skiing season in Switzerland lasts from December to April in most resorts and from November to May in resorts at around 2,000 to 3,000 metres, although it's possible to ski the whole year round on mountains with glaciers.

Alpine Skiing

Alpine or downhill skiing as well as snowboarding are expensive sports, particularly for families. The cost of equipping a family of four is around SFr. 4,800 for equipment and clothing (about SFr. 1,200 each). If you're a beginner, it's advisable to hire snowboarding or ski equipment (e.g. skis/board, poles, boots) or buy second-hand equipment until you're addicted, which, if it doesn't frighten you to death, can happen on your first day on the slopes. However, bear in mind that many a would-be skier has invested a lot of money in new equipment, only to find they don't like skiing. Most sports shops have pre-season and end of season sales of ski equipment.

Ski-lift passes can cost over SFr. 50 a day for an adult in a top Swiss resort and skiing in some resorts, particularly at weekends (Sundays are worst), entails a lot of time-consuming and 'expensive' queuing. In many resorts you can buy a limited area ski-lift pass or a half-day pass, e.g. from noon, which is cheaper than buying a day pass for a whole area (you often need to be an Olympian to ski a large area in one day). You can buy a ski-lift pass in most resorts for almost any number of days or for the whole season. Generally, the longer the period covered by a pass, the cheaper the daily cost. In bad weather conditions, which is quite often, many runs are closed and there's usually no compensating reduction or refund in the price of ski-lift passes.

It's advisable to leave the top resorts to the experts and frequent some of the smaller, cheaper areas, until you are sufficiently skilled and fit enough to take full advantage of the more difficult runs. That isn't to say that the bigger, more expensive resorts, don't provide good value for money. A top resort may offer up to ten times the number of lifts and prepared runs (*pistes*) than a small resort, while charging 'only' an extra 25 to 75 per cent for a ski-lift pass. A day's skiing for a family of four, including the cost of travel, ski-lift passes and food and drinks, costs around SFr. 250 in an average resort, but can be much higher.

In many areas, local coach companies organise day trips to ski resorts (usually on Sundays) and make stops in local towns to pick up skiers. They're reasonably priced and include a ski-lift pass. Swiss railways also offer special day-trip excursions which include a ski-lift pass (*Snow'n'Rail*). All large and many smaller resorts provide baby-sitting services or a ski nursery school, although most ski schools won't accept children below the age of three. Ask ST for information (see page 301) or contact resort tourist offices directly (many have websites).

Accommodation in ski resorts is more expensive during holiday periods (Christmas, New Year and Easter), when the pistes are **very** crowded. During public and school holiday periods, the crowds of schoolchildren may drive you crazy, both on and off-piste, particularly when queuing for ski-lifts (Swiss children aren't taught to queue and are born queue jumpers). Some resorts provide floodlit pistes in the evenings (information is available from ST), but make sure that you check what time the lights go out or you could find yourself skiing in the dark.

It's unlikely, but not impossible, to have your ski equipment stolen in Switzerland, although it's common in some of Switzerland's neighbouring countries. **Take good care of your expensive equipment wherever you are, and when you must leave it unattended, mix your skis and poles with those of your friends** (most people won't ski with odd skis and poles!). The price of new skis purchased in Switzerland often includes a year's insurance against theft or damage, or you can insure them separately for around SFr. 20 a year.

Learning to Ski or Snowboard

If you're a newcomer to downhill skiing, it's worthwhile enrolling in a ski school for a week or two to learn the basics – and it's much safer than simply launching yourself off the nearest mountain, particularly for other skiers. Good skiing is all about style and technique, and the value of good coaching cannot be over-emphasised. Private and group lessons are available in all resorts, for toddlers to senior citizens. ST publish an *Index of Swiss Ski Schools* (see also 🖳 www. snowsports.ch). Many of the ski schools also provide snowboarding classes.

Don't let the 'experts' talk you into buying or hiring long skis. They usually have little or no idea what it's like to learn to ski (particularly as an adult), as most could ski before they could walk. **Putting a beginner on long skis is like putting a learner driver behind the wheel of a grand prix car.** If you're a complete beginner, you may like to try the French short ski (*Kurzski, ski-évolutif/ski moderne*) method of instruction using progressively longer skis. As a learning method for adults it's highly recommended by both former pupils and experts alike. As a beginner you want to be able to turn easily and you **don't** want to go fast. Short skis provide both of these advantages, plus better balance, and allow beginners to start learning parallel turns immediately. Adult beginners start on skis of around one metre in length and usually progress to 1.6 metre skis within a week, by which time most are making 'passable' parallel turns.

The main drawback is that the *ski-évolutif* method isn't taught in many resorts outside France (try Migros Club Schools in Switzerland – see **Day & Evening Classes** on page 312). A similar method is widely taught in North America, where it's called the graduated length method (GLM). The traditionalists in Switzerland and Austria don't usually teach the *ski-évolutif* method, mainly because the locals learn to ski while 'in the womb'.

Buy yourself a good skiing book. The Sunday Times book *We Learned to Ski* (Collins) is an excellent choice, not only for beginners but for any skier. It's expertly researched and written and cannot be too highly recommended. According to the experts, it's the best book ever written about learning to ski.

Ski Exercises

It's advisable to perform some special ski exercises for a few weeks before taking to the pistes. This helps to increase your general flexibility and strength, and prepares your body for the unique demands of skiing. It also ensures that you don't ache quite so much after a day on the pistes. Special ski exercise classes are held in most cities and towns in Switzerland and shown on TV. Most ski books also contain recommended exercises. **Remember, grossly unfit skiers are a danger to everyone – not least themselves.**

Insurance

Check that your family and visitors are fully insured for ski accidents, including helicopter rescue (see page 135). If you live and work in Switzerland, you're covered for ski accidents by your compulsory employee, non-occupational, accident insurance, but this doesn't include family members. See also **Chapter 13**.

Piste Plan

Always obtain a piste plan on arrival in a resort and check the connecting runs, so as not to get lost or take the wrong runs. In Switzerland runs are graded as follows: blue = easy, red = intermediate and black = difficult. In Austria and France there are green-graded runs for beginners. Unfortunately plans aren't always easy to read. There's sometimes a lot of walking between lifts and what appears on the plan to be the top of a lift, may turn out to be the bottom. Without a piste plan it's possible to end up by mistake on one of those dreaded 'north face of the Eiger' blackest-of-black runs. A piste plan also helps beginners avoid T-bars when skiing on their own, although they can be shared with another skier. Swiss resorts have mostly T-bars and few button (single tow) or chair-lifts.

Clothing

Besides proper ski clothes (jacket, trousers and gloves), long johns, thermal underwear, silk inner gloves, silk socks, scarves and woollen hats may be necessary. These may not sound too fashionable or glamorous, but are more welcome than the latest ski-wear fashions on freezing cold days – if you ski badly, you look like an idiot no matter what you're wearing! A one-piece ski suit is best for beginners, as it keeps out the snow when you fall on your behind. Lightweight clothes and gloves can be worn on warmer days (gloves should always be worn to protect your hands from injury). Après ski boots with non-slip rubber soles, e.g. moon boots, are essential and inexpensive.

Skin & Eye Protection

Your skin and eyes need protection from the sun and glare when skiing (snow blindness is rare, but not unknown). When skiing in bright sunlight, special ski sunglasses with side protection or mirror lenses are best. Buy the best you can afford. A loop connected to sunglasses and hung around your neck helps prevent their loss in a fall and is also handy to use to hang them up when you aren't wearing them. However, don't wear dark sunglasses or goggles that inhibit your vision in poor visibility, e.g. when it's snowing, as it makes it's difficult to see the bumps and dips. You can have a nasty accident if you hit an unseen bump (or a fellow skier) at speed.

It's easy to get sunburnt at high altitudes, even in winter. Use a total block-out cream for your lips, nose, ears and the rest of your face, even when it doesn't appear particularly bright. Apply often and liberally, particularly to lips.

Safety

Safety is of paramount importance in any sport, but it's particularly important when skiing, where the possibility of injury is ever present (one in every ten participants suffers some sort of injury). In recent years, skiing-related deaths and serious injuries have increased considerably as slopes have become more crowded and skiers have looked further afield for more daring and dangerous thrills. Around 15 skiers die annually in Switzerland and a further 5,500 are seriously injured. **Accident insurance (see page 266) is essential when**

skiing anywhere! Safety brochures for skiers are available from the Swiss Bureau for the Prevention of Accidents (see **Accidents** on page 227).

Equipment

While it's unnecessary to wear the latest ski fashions, it's important to have suitable, secure and safe equipment – particularly bindings and boots. Although the latest high-tech bindings are a great help in avoiding injuries, the correct settings are vital. They should be set so that in the event of a fall, you part company with your skis before your leg (or part thereof) parts company with your body. Beginners' bindings must be set so that they release fairly easily, but not so easily that they open each time a turn is attempted. Have your skis and bindings serviced each season by a qualified ski mechanic (any ski shop can do this). If you're using hired or second-hand skis, double check that the bindings are set correctly and that they release freely in all directions. If you aren't entirely happy with hired equipment, never hesitate to request adjustments or an exchange. Young children should wear safety helmets at all times as soon as they're able to use normal pistes and lifts.

Ability & Injuries

Try to ski with people of the same standard as yourself or with an experienced skier who's willing to ski at your pace, and don't be in too much of a hurry to tackle those black runs. Stop skiing and rest when you feel tired. A sure sign is when you keep falling over for no apparent reason. Most accidents happen when skiers are tired. If you injure yourself, particularly a knee, stop skiing and seek medical advice as soon as possible. If you attempt to ski with an injury or before an injury has had time to heal, you risk aggravating it and doing permanent damage. **It's better to ride down in the cable-car than on a stretcher!**

Weather

Unless you're an expert skier, it's best to avoid skiing in bad weather and in poor snow conditions. When snow cover is poor or runs are icy, the danger of injury increases dramatically, particularly for beginners and intermediates who often find it difficult or impossible to control their skis. It also isn't much fun unless you're a fanatic!

Avalanche Warnings

NEVER ignore avalanche warnings (*Lawinengefahr*, *danger d'avalanches*), denoted by black and yellow flags or signs and warning lights, or attempt to ski on closed (*gesperrt*, *barré*) pistes or anywhere there's a danger of avalanches (reports are issued at tourist offices). Avalanches on open pistes are extremely rare as the overloaded slopes overlooking pistes are blasted with explosives to remove excess snow. Don't ski or snowboard off-piste unless you're an experienced skier, and in an unfamiliar area you should hire an experienced local guide.

Each year around 25 skiers and snowboarders are killed in avalanches in the Alps, usually when skiing off-piste (although in recent years there have been a number of disasters involving chalets situated directly below mountains). You can buy a small radio transmitter, e.g. an avalanche transceiver, that helps rescuers locate you if you're buried in an avalanche (some also have a flashing light system). They're expensive, although sensible off-piste skiers consider their lives are worth the cost (most guides insist upon them). You can also wear an ABS air balloon rucksack, which can be inflated like a car air-bag to protect you in the event of an avalanche (although experts are undecided about their effectiveness). **Never ski off-piste on your own.** Avalanche bulletins are given on the Swiss television teletext service and a special telephone service is also provided on service number ☎ 187 (SFr. 0.50 basic fee plus 0.50 per minute) and the internet (🖳 www.slf.ch) for ski tourers. Skiers who cause avalanches can be billed for the cost of rescue, damage to property and clean-up operations.

Restricted Areas

Only ski or snowboard where it's permitted. In some areas off-piste skiing is forbidden to protect plants and the wildlife habitat. Many animals are hibernating in winter and others need to preserve their precious reserves of fat to survive the winter. You won't help their chances of survival by frightening them. Trees are planted in many areas to help prevent avalanches and are easily destroyed by careless skiers. Some areas, which are sign-posted, are designated as conservation areas for flora and fauna, and you can be fined for skiing there.

The Highway Code for Skiers & Snowboarders

As the ski slopes become more crowded, the possibility of colliding with a fellow skier has increased dramatically. Snowboarders have a reputation of being ruthless and leaving a trace of fallen skiers behind when speeding down the piste – snowboarders use a different line from skiers and need to take particular care. Happily, the result of most clashes is just a few bruises and dented pride, nevertheless the danger of serious injury is ever present. You cannot always protect yourself from the lunatic fringe. e.g. the crazy novice who skis way beyond his limits and the equally loony 'expert' who skis at reckless speeds with a total disregard for other skiers. Serious head injuries can often be prevented by wearing a helmet – many ski schools make them compulsory for children. The following guidelines from the International Ski Federation's (FIS) Code of Conduct for skiers may help you avoid an accident:

- **Respect for others** – A skier or snowboarder must behave in such a way that he neither endangers nor prejudices others.

- **Control of speed & skiing** – A skier or snowboarder must adapt his speed and way of skiing to his own personal ability, and to the prevailing conditions of terrain and weather.

- **Control of direction** – A skier or snowboarder coming from above, whose dominant position allows him a choice of paths, must take a direction which assures the safety of the skier below.

- **Overtaking** – A skier or snowboarder should always leave a wide enough margin for the overtaken skier or snowboarder to make his turn.

- **Crossing the piste** – A skier or snowboarder entering or crossing a piste must look up and down to make sure that he can do so without danger to himself or to others. The same applies after stopping.

- **Stopping on the piste** – Unless absolutely necessary, a skier or snowboarder must avoid making a stop on the piste, particularly in narrow passages or where visibility is restricted. If a skier or snowboarder falls, he must clear the piste as soon as possible.

- **Climbing** - A climbing skier or snowboarder must keep to the side of the piste and in bad visibility, keep off the piste altogether. The same goes for a skier or snowboarder descending on foot.

If you're hit by a reckless skier or snowboarder you can sue for damages or can equally be sued if you cause an accident. There's no foolproof way of avoiding accidents (apart from avoiding skiing altogether). Obey the FIS code (see above) and make sure that you're well insured for both accidents and private liability (see **Chapter 13**). If you're involved in an accident or collision you should do the following:

- obtain the names and addresses (local and permanent) of all people involved and any witnesses;

- report the accident to the local police within 24 hours. This is essential if you wish to make a claim against an insurance policy or a third party;

- make notes and diagrams of the accident scene while it's still fresh in your mind;

- notify your insurers as soon as possible and forward any documentation to them.

If you suspect any equipment was at fault, e.g. a ski binding, retain it (provided it wasn't hired) and note the precise type, size, adjustments and nature of the fault. If you work in Switzerland, your compulsory accident insurance covers you against ski accidents. However, it doesn't include cover for accidents caused by you, for which you need private liability insurance (see page 274) with an minimum insured sum of SFr. 2m.

The Swiss Commission for the Prevention of Accidents on Ski-Runs and Cross-Country Trails (SKUS), Laupenstrasse 11, CH-3001 Berne (☎ 031 390 22 30, 🖳 www.skus.ch), publish a booklet in English entitled *Guidelines for the Conduct of Skiers and Snowboarders*.

Snow & Weather Conditions

Information on alpine snow and weather conditions is provided on TV teletext on most stations during the skiing season. The DRS (Swiss German television service) provides the most comprehensive service. It lists resorts by area and gives snow depth (village and top station), the type of snow, piste conditions and whether the runs down to the village are open. It's updated twice a week on Mondays and Thursdays. The ARD/ZDF (German TV) service includes the major resorts in Austria, France, Germany, Italy and Switzerland. French teletext is unobtainable via a Swiss TV due to the different teletext system used in France. The Eurosport satellite channel provides regular snow reports for major resorts, although not on teletext. Snow conditions are also available via the internet (🖳 www.skiinfo.ch).

It's important to check the snow conditions. When snow cover is poor, many runs are closed, particularly those down to the valley or bottom station, and you must endure a lot of queuing and walking between lifts. Many resorts have installed snow-making machinery on runs and are able to guarantee that a limited number of runs are open. However, when snow conditions are bad in most areas, the overcrowding is horrendous. Many ski resorts have a special ski information telephone number (*Schnee- und Pistenbericht, bulletin d'enneigement*) where the latest information is recorded including snow conditions, condition and number of runs open, local weather and the number of lifts in operation. Numbers are listed in telephone directories (see page 132).

Before you set out or plan a day or weekend skiing trip, it's wise to check the weather forecast, as it isn't much fun skiing in a blizzard, rain, freezing cold or bad visibility. Swiss weather forecasting is usually highly accurate and one of the best weather forecasts is provided by the Swiss television teletext service.

Ski Clubs

You may find that it's worthwhile joining a ski club affiliated to the Swiss-Ski Federation, Haus des Skisports, Worbstr. 52, PO Box 478, CH-3074 Muri b.

Berne (☎ 031 950 61 11, 🖥 www.swiss-ski.ch). This usually entitles you to an Swiss-Ski booklet; skiing insurance; ski-lift vouchers; hotel and other discounts; membership of your local canton ski association; and a subscription to the Swiss-Ski magazine (in German), the official organ of Swiss-Ski.

All towns, most villages and many companies have their own ski clubs, and in some cities there are also international ski clubs for expatriates. Groups of ten or more skiers usually receive a reduction of around SFr. 5 per person off the cost of an individual day pass. A schedule of Swiss downhill skiing, cross-country and skating races (*Terminkalender Breitensport, calendrier du ski populaire*) is published annually by the Swiss-Ski Federation (see above).

Cross-country Skiing

Cross-country skiing (*Ski-Langlauf/Ski-Wandern, ski de fond/ski nordique*) doesn't have the glamorous jet-set image of alpine skiing, but nevertheless it's a popular sport in Switzerland. It appeals to both young and old, particularly those whose idea of fun is a million miles away from hurtling down a hill at 100kph (62mph), with a thousand metre drop on one side and a glacier on the other. Cross-country skiing can be enjoyed at any pace and over any distance, and therefore has great attractions for both those who aren't very fit and keen athletes. It can be exhilarating, particularly if you make the effort to learn the correct technique and persevere beyond the beginner's stage. It's also rates highly as a total body workout and is claimed by many to be one of the best of all forms of exercise.

Compared with alpine skiing, cross-country skiing has the advantages of cheaper equipment, lower costs, fewer broken bones **and** no queues. No expensive ski-lift passes are necessary, although skiers must buy a SFr. 100 annual Cross-Country Pass entitling them to use over 5,500km (3,500mi) of tracks throughout Switzerland (🖥 www.loipen-schweiz.ch). Alternately, a local seasonal card can be purchased for around SFr. 35 or a day pass for SFr. 6 per day. Children (under 16) ski for free. Essential equipment costs as little as SFr. 500 for skis, bindings, poles, boots and gloves. No special clothing is necessary apart from gloves and boots, provided you have a warm pullover and tracksuit. You can, of course, buy more expensive equipment and special clothing.

Prepared cross-country trails (classical as well as skating style), usually consisting of two sets of tracks (*Langlauf-Loipen, pistes de ski de fond*), are laid on specially prepared and sign-posted routes, where you ski in the direction of the arrows. There are cross-country ski trails in most winter ski resorts in Switzerland, Austria and Germany, although there are fewer in France and Italy. You can enjoy cross-country skiing anywhere there's sufficient snow, although using prepared trails is easier than making your own, as is usually done in Scandinavia. The total number of kilometres of cross-country trails open in Swiss resorts is shown on the Swiss television teletext service. Many resorts have floodlit tracks for night skiing.

An annual booklet published by Swiss-Ski, *Langlauf, Ski de fond*, is a must for all keen cross-country skiers. It contains information on all aspects of cross-country skiing (in English, French and German), a complete list of all Swiss cross-country skiing circuits, and race information. It's available from most sports shops or by post from Swiss-Ski (see page 337).

SKI VARIATIONS & OTHER WINTER SPORTS

When you're bored with all those 'easy' black pistes, you might like to try something different For information on the following winter sports, contact ST (see page 301).

- **Bob-sleighing** – This is for the really brave or completely loony sensation-seeker (the famous Cresta run in St. Moritz is the world's fastest and most dangerous). Ladies aren't allowed to participate – unless they masquerade as men!

- **Curling** – Curling is a bit like lawn bowls on ice, except that the 'balls' (called rocks) are flat with a handle on top. Curling rinks are usually located indoors, although some resorts have outdoor rinks.

- **Dog sledding & horse racing** – Dog sledding and horse racing are popular in some resorts, although they generally aren't for novices.

- **Freestyle skiing** – A winter sport for circus acrobats and high-board divers. Involves doing a triple somersault on skis – among other things. For the brave and **very** accomplished skier. Spectacular but can be dangerous if you land on your head.

- **Heli-skiing** – No, you aren't pulled along by a helicopter, but are deposited by it in inaccessible places at around 4,000m (ca. 13,000ft) from where you ski home (or get lost). For proficient off-piste skiers only. Heli-skiers in Switzerland must be accompanied by a licensed mountain guide.

- **Ice hockey** – A popular sport in Switzerland with both competitors (five leagues) and spectators. If only the Swiss could come up with a decent national team!

- **Ice skating** – Many towns and winter holiday resorts have outdoor ice rinks open from around October to April. There are also some 90 indoor rinks, many of which are open all year round. **Take extra care when skating on natural ponds and always observe warning signs. Rescue equipment (long poles) and alarms are usually prominently displayed.**

- **Luge** – A single seat, feet-first toboggan used on a bob-sleigh run at break-neck speeds. Skeleton is a head-first (kamikaze position) version of the luge, hence the name.

- **Mono-skiing** – Mono-skiing equipment consists of one wide ski with two normal ski bindings side by side. Skiers use normal ski poles and wear ski boots. Usually requires good skiing ability, although it might appeal to those who have difficulty distinguishing between their left and right feet (see also **Snow surfing** below).

- **Off-piste skiing** – Off-piste skiing in deep powder snow is what most advanced skiers dream about. It can be dangerous and aspirants should be able to handle black runs **with confidence**. See also **Avalanche Warnings** on page 334.

- **Ski-bobbing** – This is similar to bicycling on snow and sometimes called snow-biking. Provides plenty of exhilarating, down-to-earth thrills. Ski-bobs can be hired in over 70 resorts, some of which have specially marked runs. However, some resorts ban them owing to the danger to skiers.

- **Ski hang-gliding & paragliding** – If jumping out of an aeroplane or off a mountain with a parachute or hang-glider (while wearing skis) is your idea of fun, these sports may appeal to you.

- **Ski-joring** – Skiers are pulled along by galloping horses at hair-raising speeds. An old 'sport' which is quite rare these days (mad horses and even madder skiers being in short supply).

- **Ski touring** – This involves walking uphill and skiing downhill. Requires good off-piste skiing ability, excellent physical condition and special skis (skins) and equipment. Should never be attempted without a guide.

- **Snow rafting** – Participants sit in a rubber boat (or rubber tube), while it rockets down pistes at 100kph. It's best attempted on controlled and segregated slopes, where there are no trees or other obstacles (such as people). A dangerous 'sport' which is banned in many resorts.

- **Speed skiing** – For skiers who never got to lesson three – how to turn. Ski at up to 200kph/124mph (if you dare). Popular in France (enough said).

- **Telemark skiing** – The Swiss Telemark Ski Association (💻 www.telemark. ch) was founded in 1989, since when it has enjoyed increasing popularity. Telemark is characterised by 'bending down', which is enabled by the free heel and the mobile shoe, dropping the knee and lifting the heel. Courses are provided in the larger ski resorts, but bear in mind that it isn't easy to learn.

- **Tobogganing & sledding** – Many resorts have special runs reserved for tobogganing, while in others, runs may also be open to skiers. Great fun for children, both young and old (i.e. adults). Sometimes runs are floodlit during the evening. A brochure is available from ST listing runs of up to 11km/7mph.

Some of the above sports are limited to a small number of resorts or are restricted to particular pistes or areas. If they don't provide enough challenges, you can always try skiing down the Matterhorn as a Japanese Kamikaze skier did in 1985 (he survived). Another Japanese (who else?) skied (he actually fell most of the way) down Mount Everest with a parachute, which was supposed to slow him down. He also lived to tell the tale and they even made a film of it – otherwise nobody would have believed it!

SWIMMING

There are heated indoor (*Hallenbad, piscine couverte*) and outdoor (*Freibad, piscine en plein air*) swimming pools in most Swiss towns, a total of around 1,000 when both public and hotel swimming pools are included (most hotel pools are open to non-residents for a small fee). Most towns and villages catering for winter sports and summer hiking have indoor swimming pools. The entrance fee is usually from around SFr. 5 and facilities may include wave machines, saunas, solariums, table tennis, mini-golf and games areas. You can also swim at over 170 locations in Swiss lakes (*Strandbad, piscine naturelle*) from around June to September (the water temperature for the largest lakes is listed on Swiss television teletext). There are even a few areas set aside for nude sunbathing, although men and women are usually segregated and all are hidden from prying eyes.

There are a number of large indoor swimming centres and water parks in Switzerland containing hot water pools, sulphur baths, thermal whirlpools, connecting indoor and outdoor pools, wave machines, huge water slides, solariums and saunas (some have mixed saunas). Swimming centres have restaurants and are open daily from around 10am to 10pm. The entrance fee is high, e.g. SFr. 25 for just four hours, although they make a pleasant change from the local pool for a special day out. Spas throughout Switzerland (see page 253) have hot-spring pools where you may swim gently or relax in the water. Children aren't, however, always admitted. Most swimming pools and clubs organise swimming lessons (all levels from beginner to fish) and run life-saving courses.

WATERSPORTS

All watersports including sailing, windsurfing, water-skiing, rowing, canoeing and subaquatic sports are popular in Switzerland. This is hardly surprising as the country has over 1,600 natural lakes (totalling some 13,355,100km^2 or 330,000 acres) and 32,000km (20,000mi) of rivers. Boats and equipment can be hired on most lakes and rescue services are provided, although they aren't usually free. Instruction is available for most watersports on major lakes and in holiday centres. There is unfortunately one small problem with sailing and windsurfing in Switzerland: a lack of wind, particularly in summer.

Being landlocked hasn't held Switzerland back in the world yachting arena, and the Swiss have won the prized America's Cup on two occasions: in Auckland in 2003 and in Valencia in 2007. The Geneva-based 'Alinghi' team, made up of sailors from some 20 countries, is considered to be one of the world's best.

Rowing and canoeing are possible on most lakes and rivers. The Rotsee lake near Lucerne is the most famous Swiss rowing venue and provides one of the most beautiful courses in the world. Wetsuits are recommended for windsurfing, water-skiing and subaquatic sports, even during the summer. White-water rafting is an exciting and popular sport and is taught and practised in many areas. Those who like something even more adventurous (and even wetter) might wish to try canyoning, which involves sliding down water channels (or ice channels) on your bottom.

You must pass a written test before you can use a motorboat with a motor size of 6kW (7.5 PS) or a sailing boat with a sail area of over 15m^2 (161ft^2). Boats must usually have a mooring and cannot be stored at home except in a garage. Sailing and windsurfing weather and the summer water temperature of the major lakes is provided on Swiss television teletext service. Information regarding river rafting, kayaks and sailing schools is available from ST. **Be sure to observe all warning signs on lakes and rivers!**

OTHER SPORTS

The following is a selection of other sports that attract a popular following in Switzerland:

Athletics

Most Swiss towns and villages have local athletics clubs and organise local competitions and sports days.

Ballet & Jazz Ballet

Hardly sports, but nonetheless excellent exercise. Dance, training and exercise classes are provided in many towns throughout Switzerland and are also organised by gymnasiums. Jazz ballet classes are also organised by Migros Club Schools (see **Day & Evening Classes** on page 312).

Billiards & Snooker

Many hotels, bars and sports clubs have billiard or snooker tables and there are a few billiards' clubs in the larger towns. English-style snooker isn't played in public clubs in Switzerland.

Bungee Jumping

If your idea of fun is jumping out of a cable car or a hot-air balloon with an elastic rope attached to your body to prevent you merging with the landscape, then bungee jumping may be just what you're looking for.

Darts

Not really a sport, darts can be played at any of the Pickwick chain of pubs (🖳 www.pickwick.ch) in Switzerland and other English- and Irish-style pubs.

Football

Between mid-July and mid-June, the ten football (soccer) clubs in the first division (Super League) play each other at home and away twice. The team finishing top is crowned champion, while the bottom team moves down to the second division (Challenge League) and the team finishing ninth has to beat the team that finished second in the Challenge League to stay in the Super League. The Challenge League consists of 18 teams. Most major Swiss cities and towns have either a first or second division football team. Many are professional and of a similar standard to teams in the English or German second or third divisions. Most towns and villages have amateur football clubs for all ages and standards.

Gymnasiums & Health Clubs

There are gymnasiums and health clubs in most towns with tonnes of expensive bone-jarring, muscle-wrenching apparatus. Costs are around SFr. 100 a month or SFr. 1,000 a year, although they can be reduced by taking advantage of off-peak reductions. Many first class hotels have fitness rooms.

Gymnastics

An extremely popular sport in Switzerland and gymnastic clubs abound in all areas, even in small towns and villages.

Handball

Played indoors on a pitch similar to a five-a-side football pitch. Handball players pass the ball around by hand and attempt to throw it into a small goal.

Hockey

Called land hockey to avoid confusion with the more popular ice hockey.

Horse Riding

Popular but expensive. There are around 380 riding schools and equestrian centres in Switzerland. Hiring a horse from a farm is cheaper, but tuition isn't usually provided. Some resorts organise cross-country riding holidays.

Martial Arts

Kung Fu, Judo and Karate are taught and practised in most towns. There are around 320 judo clubs in Switzerland. Timid children are sometimes encouraged to learn judo to combat school bullies.

Roller Skating & Skate-boarding

Rinks are provided in many towns and sometimes winter ice skating rinks are used for roller skating in summer.

Rugby

A surprisingly popular sport in Switzerland, where there are clubs in all the major cities (yet another 'habit' they picked up from the British – along with skiing).

Shooting

Shooting ranges abound in Switzerland and shooting is particularly popular on Sunday mornings to prevent you having a lay-in. Annual target shooting is compulsory for all Swiss men as part of their military service. Most towns and villages have a local shooting federation which organises local competitions. Crossbow shooting is also popular.

Ten-pin Bowling

Ten-pin bowling centres can be found in all major Swiss cities. Ten-pin bowling and skittles (*Kegelbahn, jeu de quilles*) are also played in some hotels and restaurants.

Swiss Sports

The Swiss also have their own Alpine sports, which are usually incomprehensible to anyone but a Swiss mountain man. These include stone throwing (*Steinstossen* or *Steinwerfen, le lancer de la pierre*), traditional Swiss wrestling (*Schwingen, la lutte à la calotte*) and the strangest of all, *Hornussen*. In *Hornussen* a puck-like plastic object (the *Hornuss*) is placed at the tip of a curved rail planted in the soil. The striker hits the *Hornuss* with a whip-like cane around two metres in length, while the catchers (strategically placed in the field) attempt to bat it away with large wooden boards on poles before it hits the ground. *Hornussen* isn't expected to become an Olympic sport in the near future.

Miscellaneous

Many foreign sports and pastimes have a group of expatriate fanatics in Switzerland including cricket, American football, baseball, boccia, boules, croquet, polo and softball. For more information enquire at community and tourist offices, embassies and consulates, and social clubs (see **Appendix A**).

SPORT FOR THE DISABLED

Switzerland has an extensive sports programme for the disabled, organised by the Swiss Association for Handicapped Sport (*Plusport Behindertenspor Schweiz, Sport Handicap Suisse*) Chriesbaumstr. 6, CH-8604 Volketswil (☎ 044 908 45 00, 💻 www.plusport.ch).

17.

SHOPPING

Shopping in Switzerland is among the best in the world, although you may sometimes wonder whether all Swiss are millionaires and just what they do with all those gold watches, diamond necklaces and fur coats. Actually millionaires make up only half the population of Switzerland – the rest are foreigners. Joking aside, it has been conservatively estimated that Switzerland has some 100,000 millionaires (including many foreigners) and the highest level of per capita accumulated wealth in the world. There are, however, a few shops that cater to the needs of poor foreigners and English is spoken in most major towns and tourist areas.

There's generally no bargaining in Switzerland, although if you plan to spend a lot of money in one store you might ask for a discount (except in department stores and supermarkets). Value added tax (VAT) is always included and there are no hidden extras: the advertised price is the price you pay. Swiss shopkeepers are usually scrupulously honest and most shops exchange goods or give refunds without question. The Swiss customer is highly critical and demands top quality, durability, after sales service and value for money – all features of most Swiss products. Although prices may be higher than in many other countries, goods may be of superior quality and therefore comparisons aren't always valid. Most Swiss shops accept euros and may also accept other major foreign currencies.

Cartels are common and aren't illegal unless shown to be harmful. Consequently, the prices of some goods and services can be up to 50 per cent higher than in most EU countries, which makes shopping in Switzerland's neighbouring countries rewarding. Sales and prices of most goods in Switzerland are strictly regulated and prices for branded goods are fixed to protect small shop owners. Stores can, however, sell branded goods under their own name at lower prices or sell goods at reduced prices during official sales, e.g. in January and July. Many Swiss prefer to shop in their local village or town and happily pay higher prices in return for the convenience of shopping locally. There are large indoor shopping centres in all areas where you can do all your shopping under one roof, and cities and most large towns usually have a traffic-free shopping street or town centre. Many Swiss manufacturers provide factory shops where you may shop at generous discounts, although opening hours are limited and some shops are only open one day a week or month.

Most shops hold sales (*Sonderverkauf/Ausverkauf, soldes*) in January and July, when goods are available at bargain prices and if you plan to have a shopping spree, it's definitely worth waiting for the sales. Around Christmas time, storage areas are provided in many towns, where shoppers may leave their purchases free of charge (while they buy more). Some major cities, e.g. Zurich, produce monthly shopping guides. Finally, don't panic if you're pounced on by an army of shop assistants – it's just the natives way of being friendly. If you don't want their help, tell them that you're just looking and hopefully they will go away.

For those who aren't used to buying articles with metric measures and continental sizes, a list of comparative weights and measures are included in **Appendix D**. American Women's Clubs (see **Appendix A**) and other women's clubs are an excellent source of shopping information, particularly for those hard to find imported foods.

SHOPPING HOURS

Shopping hours in Switzerland are usually from around 8 or 9am to 6.30 or 6.45pm Tuesdays to Fridays and from 8am to between 4 and 6pm on Saturdays. On Mondays many shops close in the morning and open from between 1 and 2pm until around 6.30 or 6.45pm, although some are closed all day. Many towns have late night shopping until 8 or 9pm on Wednesday, Thursday or Friday (in Zurich shops stay open until 8pm from Mondays to Fridays); larger shopping centres also have extended shopping hours. In smaller towns, all shops and businesses close for lunch, e.g. from noon until 2pm. Local shops, for example those located in villages, close for a half or full day a week and may close earlier on a Saturday, e.g. 2pm. It's customary for certain businesses to be closed on the same day, for example most hairdressers (*Coiffeur*) are closed on Mondays and pharmacies (*Apotheke, pharmacie*) on Thursdays. Shops generally close at 4 or 5pm the day before a public holiday, even when it's a late shopping day.

All shops are closed on Sundays except bakeries, some of which open from around 10am to noon. However, a recent law allows stores to open on six Sundays or official holidays a year (stores are often open on a few Sundays before Christmas). Geneva and Zurich airports have shopping centres open from 8am to 8pm daily and some motorway (*Autobahn, autoroute*) shopping centres are open every day of the year, with the possible exception of Christmas day. In and around most main railway stations (*Hauptbahnhof, gare centrale*) in the main cities you can find shops with extended opening times (e.g. 7am to 10pm), including Sundays and public holidays. Grocery stores near border crossings are usually open on Sundays and shops in many holiday resorts (including special tourist areas of some major cities) are open on Sundays and public holidays throughout the season. At Christmas time, many major stores hold shopping evenings exclusively for the disabled.

SHOPPING CENTRES & MARKETS

There are many large modern indoor shopping centres (*Einkaufszentrum, centre commercial*) in Switzerland. These may contain over 100 shops including supermarkets, department stores, furniture stores, restaurants, banks and a post office, plus many of the small specialist shops you'd expect to find in an average town. The main attractions, in addition to the wide choice of shops, are protection from inclement weather and free parking, meaning you can simply wheel your purchases to your car (parking is expensive and difficult in most city and town centres, particularly on Saturdays). To encourage the use of public tranport, some shopping centres charge a small fee for parking, perhaps offering the first hour free. Most banks are open on Saturdays in shopping centres. Shopping centre stores periodically issue books of discount coupons *Einkaufsbon/ Bezugsschein, bon d'achat*) to attract customers.

Most towns have markets on various days of the week, with Wednesdays and Saturdays the most popular. These vary from fruit and vegetable markets to flea/curiosity (second-hand goods) markets. In major cities there are markets on most days of the week. Food markets usually open around 6am and may close as early as 11am, while curiosity markets often operate from 10am to 4pm or even until 9pm in summer. Check with local tourist and information offices.

SUPERMARKETS

Many foreign foods can be found in local supermarkets (*Supermarkt, supermarché*) if you look hard enough, but don't overlook the many delicious local foods on offer. One of the advantages of living in central Europe is being able to sample the bewildering choice of continental food and beverages on offer. Don't despair if you cannot find your favourite food as there are many other delicacies available. The German, French and Italian-speaking parts of Switzerland all offer excellent regional and ethnic specialities. Most department stores sell imported foods, particularly Globus, Jelmoli and Manor (see **Department & Chain Stores** below) and all major towns have a variety of delicatessens and imported food shops. A number of companies import American and British foods and advertise in the English-language press in Switzerland (e.g. Taste of America – 💻 www.tasteofamerica.ch).

Among the best value-for-money supermarkets are Aldi, Carrefour, Coop, Denner Discount (particularly for wine, beer, cigarettes and perfumes), Lidl, Migros and Pick Pay, all of which have branches throughout Switzerland. Prices in village shops are generally higher than in supermarkets, although many villages have a reasonably priced Volg store. Migros, one of the largest companies in Switzerland, has the lowest prices. It also has the most outlets and accounts for some 24 per cent of the food sector. The Coop has around 21 per cent of the food market (but a slightly larger share of the non-food market than Migros). Migros **doesn't** sell spirits, wine or tobacco, unless it's a rural branch that has a special licence. Migros and the Coop operate mobile shops in some areas (ask your neighbours or at your local branch).

In common with many countries, most supermarkets in Switzerland provide only small plastic carrier bags, and charge from SFr. 0.20 to 0.40 for larger, more sturdy bags. Copy the Swiss and take a bag with you when shopping. Some supermarkets provide free boxes. Supermarket trolleys require a deposit of SFr. 1 or 2, which ensures that most customers return them to a collection point rather than abandoning them in the car park (or taking them home). Items such as tea and coffee contain stamps on their labels, which can be collected and exchanged for books, pictures and games (etc.) when you've collected 'a few million'. Stamp catalogues can be obtained from manufacturers (addresses are printed on labels).

Migros offers regular customers a client reward scheme whereby you receive a client 'cumulus' card (*Cumulus-Karte, carte cumulus*) and earn one point for each franc spent. Every three months you receive a booklet with special discount offers and vouchers worth SFr. 0.01 per point collected, so effectively you receive 1 per cent discount on your purchases. The Coop has a similar scheme called 'Supercard' where you collect points and benefit from discounts on specific articles.

Most supermarkets have a coffee bean grinding machine for their customers' use. If you live in a farming community, you can buy unpasteurised milk from your local dairy by the bucket full (you supply the container). It's cheaper than buying milk by the carton from a supermarket, but it should be boiled before use. Many farms sell potatoes and other vegetables in bulk and allow you to pick your own fruit during the harvest season.

Supermarkets sell beer, soft drinks and mineral water by the crate, where you pay a deposit on the crate and bottles, which are usually returnable. Many people also have drinks delivered to their homes, rather than struggle home with heavy crates from the supermarket. Ask your neighbours about deliveries.

See also **Shopping Abroad** on page 357 and **Home Shopping** on page 356.

DEPARTMENT & CHAIN STORES

Switzerland has many excellent department (*Warenhaus, grand magasin*) and chain stores. One of the most famous and exclusive Swiss department stores is Globus, part of a group which includes Herren Globus (menswear), Interio (home furnishings and furniture) and Office World – all of which are now owned by Migros. Manor and Jelmoli (including Innovation and Grand Passage) are department store chains with outlets in most Swiss cities and large towns. Manor are noted for their own-label, high quality, value-for-money clothes. Other department stores include Coop City, Bon Genie and Loeb (Berne).

Jumbo, a do-it-yourself (DIY) and hardware store chain, also merits a special mention. Besides selling hardware and household goods, Jumbo also stock motoring accessories, bicycles and skis at competitive prices (plus food in some stores). Other DIY and hardware chains include Coop Bau und Hobby, Hornbach and Obi. One of the largest discount houses for TV, video, hi-fi, photographic, computer and household goods is Eschenmoser. They publish a comprehensive catalogue and have sales in January and July at their stores in Basle, Berne and Zurich. Media Markt is a good source for inexpensive CDs and electronic equipment, while Inter Discount operate a large chain of stores selling hi-fi, video, photographic, radio, computer and other electronic equipment at competitive prices. Shop around for electronic and computer equipment, as prices for similar items can vary considerably; don't forget to compare the guarantee period, which can vary from six months to two years.

Many department stores (e.g. Globus, Jelmoli, Loeb and Manor) provide account cards (store cards), some of which double as credit cards where the account balance can be repaid over a period. Card holders may take advantage of special offers and discounts. Some account cards can be used in other franchised stores and businesses, e.g. Globus and the Jelmoli J-Card. Some stores don't give a foreigner an account card until he has a C permit (see **Chapter 3**). Department stores and many smaller shops provide a free gift-wrapping service, particularly at Christmas time, and will deliver goods locally or send them by post (both within Switzerland and world-wide). Some stores have a 'Mister Minit' department, where on-the-spot shoe repairs, key cutting and engraving is done.

Migros (🖳 www.migros.ch) deserve a special mention for the high quality and range of its products (mostly own brand) and services, plus a reputation for limiting price increases. Migros stores come in three sizes, denoted by the number of Ms displayed outside:

M	Food store only
MM	Food and household goods, sometimes a restaurant
MMM	Complete department store selling food, household goods, furniture, clothes, hi-fi, electrical goods; sports equipment and often has a restaurant

Migros (plus some other stores) provide discounts on all purchases on the opening day of a new branch and on special anniversaries, plus many special offers. They also operate DIY stores, a travel agency, book and record stores (Ex Libris), petrol stations and banking services (M-Bank, with ATMs in its supermarkets called M-Bancolinos), among other things. In addition to the M-card (Migros bank), Migros accepts credit and debit cards and Postcards (see page 122). Except for the M-card, the same applies to the Coop (🖳 www. coop.ch), which operates a bank, furniture stores (TopTip), electronics stores (Inter Discount) and other ventures.

NEWSPAPERS, MAGAZINES & BOOKS

You may not have been much of a newspaper (*Zeitung, journal*), magazine (*Magazin/Zeitschrift, revue/périodique*) or book (*Buch, livre*) reader at home, but not being able to obtain your favourite English-language reading can be an unexpected deprivation abroad. However, newsagents in Switzerland probably stock the widest selection of foreign newspapers in the world, although British and American newspapers and magazines are expensive. If you enjoy reading, it's advisable to stock up on magazines and books before your arrival and during holidays abroad. However, a large saving can be made by taking out subscriptions to magazines and newspapers.

British and other European newspapers are sold at kiosks in most large towns. British daily newspapers are usually on sale at most railway stations the day after publication and at main railway stations and international airports on the day of publication. If you're hooked on British Sunday newspapers, they're available at many main railway stations and airports from around 11am on Sundays. To save a wasted journey, telephone first, as they sometimes don't arrive – if they aren't at your local railway station, they're usually also unavailable at airports. **Note, however, that they are very expensive.**

Major foreign European newspapers are available on the day of issue in Basle, Geneva and Zurich and perhaps a day later in other cities. Some English-language daily newspapers are widely available on the day of publication including *USA Today*, *International Herald Tribune* (printed in Zurich) and the *Wall Street Journal Europe* (printed in Frankfurt). Many English and foreign newspapers produce weekly editions including the British *International Express*, *Guardian Weekly* and *Weekly Telegraph*.

Many foreign newspapers can be purchased on subscription at a large saving on kiosk prices. When sent airmail from within Europe, e.g. from the UK, they usually arrive a few days after publication.

English-language monthly magazines published in Switzerland include *Swiss News*, and the *'Hello'* magazines of Basle, Berne and Zurich. Quarterlies include *AIR Magazine* and *Inside Switzerland*. **Note also that most major international newspapers are available online, although you may need to subscribe in order to view or print them.**

There are no national newspapers in Switzerland, but a wide variety of regional daily newspapers (around 130), weekly newspapers (over 380) and some 2,000 magazines, plus professional and specialist journals. Most cantons have an official daily or weekly newspaper or booklet containing a wealth of local information. It includes announcements of job vacancies, local and official events, meetings, church services, plus advertisements for houses and apartments (for rent and sale), small advertisements, restaurants and entertainment. A number of unsolicited free newspapers are delivered to homes.

There are many excellent English-language bookshops in Switzerland (such as those advertising in this book!) including all the major cities, although the selection may be a bit limited when compared with a major bookshop in the UK or the US. However, most order any English-language book in print at no extra cost. A small selection of English-language paperbacks is also usually available in Swiss bookshops and at news kiosks.

FURNITURE

Furniture (*Möbel*, *meubles*) in Switzerland is generally quite expensive compared with many other European countries. There is, however, a huge choice and the quality is invariably good. Exclusive modern and traditional furniture is available everywhere, although not everyone can afford the exclusive prices.

Cheaper options offering good quality, modern furniture (usually for home assembly) and home furnishings include Ikea (💻 www.ikea.com/ms/de_CH) with eight stores around the country; Interio (💻 www.interio.ch), part of the Migros group and also with eight stores in Switzerland; Migros (💻 www.migros.ch) with particularly good value furniture, especially for quality leather suites; Manor (💻 www.manor.ch); and numerous other 'Wohngaleries' and 'Wohnboutiques' selling household accessories.

One of the largest furniture store chains in Switzerland is Möbel Pfister (💻 www.mobelpfister.ch), which has its flagship store in Suhr (Aargau) in northern Switzerland and branches throughout the country. They offer a huge choice with a wide quality and price range. If you need carpets at reasonable prices, Möbel Pfister sell large-sized remnants (*Restposten*, *surplus*) at bargain prices – typically 50 per cent reduction. Most carpet shops and department stores also offer their remnants for sale cheaply.

A rare exception to fixed prices in Switzerland is when you're buying a large quantity of furniture. Don't be reticent about asking for a reduction, as many stores will give you a 10 to 20 per cent discount. Considerable savings can also be made on furniture when shopping abroad (see page 357).

HOUSEHOLD GOODS

Large appliances such as cookers and refrigerators are usually provided in rented accommodation, although not always in French-speaking areas. Dishwashers are sometimes installed and private washing machines are rare. **When looking for kitchen units or appliances such as a refrigerator, washing machine or dishwasher, note that the standard Swiss unit width isn't the same as in other countries.** The standard width of kitchen appliances in Switzerland is 5cm less than across the rest of Europe (to reduce foreign competition) and consequently domestic prices for dishwashers, washing machines and dryers are much higher than the European average. If you can tailor your kitchen to accommodate foreign appliances, you can save a lot of money by buying them abroad. However, check the latest Swiss safety regulations before shipping these items to Switzerland or buying them abroad, as they may need expensive modifications.

If you already own small household appliances, it's worthwhile bringing them to Switzerland as usually all that's required is a change of plug (but check first). If you're coming from a country with a 110/115V electricity supply, e.g. the US, then you need a lot of expensive transformers (see page 104). Don't bring a TV to Switzerland without checking its compatibility first, as TVs from the UK, France and the US won't work (see page 142). Smaller appliances such as vacuum cleaners, grills, toasters and electric irons aren't expensive in Switzerland and are of excellent quality.

If you need kitchen measuring equipment and cannot cope with decimal measures, you need to bring your own measuring scales, jugs, cups and thermometers. Foreign pillow sizes, e.g. British and American, aren't the same as in Switzerland and the Swiss use duvets and not blankets to keep warm in winter (besides central heating).

LAUNDRY & DRY CLEANING

All towns and shopping centres have dry cleaners (*Chemische Reinigung*, *nettoyage à sec/chimique*), most of which do minor clothes repairs, invisible mending, alterations and dyeing. **Note that express cleaning may mean a few days rather than hours, even at an outlet where cleaning is done on the premises.** You usually pay in advance and it's quite expensive (better to buy washable clothes), particularly for leather and suede. Cleaning by the kilogramme with no pressing is possible in some places and much cheaper.

If you live near the French border it might be worthwhile taking your clothes to a French dry cleaner. Not only can they do the job much quicker (usually 24 hours) but they also charge considerably less.

There are self-service launderettes (*Wäscherei*, *blanchisserie*) in major towns and cities, but they're expensive at around SFr. 10 to wash and dry a 5kg load. They are, however, rare in smaller towns, as (communal) washing machines are provided in most rented accommodation (the Swiss don't usually wash their dirty linen in public).

SECOND-HAND BARGAINS

Switzerland has an active second-hand (*gebraucht*, *occasion*) market, particularly in antiques, motor cars, gold and gem stones, although asking prices are generally higher than in other countries. There's a local second-hand furniture and junk store (*Brockenhaus*, *broccante*) in most towns, and many also have a Salvation Army (*Heilsarmee*, *armée du salut*) shop. These usually have restricted opening hours. Second-hand clothes shops are popular. The Seefeld district in Zurich has numerous factory shops offering designer clothes at a fraction of the original price and shops offering clothes of humbler (and cheaper) pedigree are available in many areas.

You can find second-hand stores and flea markets on the internet (🖳 www.fundgrube.ch) and there's always eBay (🖳 www.ebay.ch). There are special weekly newspapers in some areas devoted to bargain hunters, for example *Fundgrueb* and *Inseratenmarkt* in German-speaking areas, and *Aux Trouvailles* in French-speaking areas. Advertising is usually free, as advertisements are financed by newspaper sales, although you must buy a copy to insert an advertisement.

The classified advertisements in local newspapers and adverts on shopping centre, supermarket and company bulletin boards, may also prove fruitful. Many expatriate clubs (see **Appendix A**) and large companies publish monthly magazines or newsletters containing small ads., where everything from furniture to household apparatus and cars are advertised for sale. Sales are held in many towns and villages, e.g. for children's clothes and toys, usually in autumn and spring.

HOME SHOPPING

Home shopping is fairly popular in Switzerland and you can expect to receive some unsolicited mail-order catalogues with your junk mail. A few large chain stores also publish mail-order catalogues, for example Ackermann and Jelmoli. Beware of some mail-order companies (e.g. selling CDs and books) who offer attractive gifts to members as an inducement to recruit new members. Prices are often high, particularly when compared with the special offers available in many shops, and it's costly to resign your membership – whether you've received any benefits or not. **Make sure you know what you're signing.**

Many major stores abroad publish catalogues and send goods anywhere in the world, for example Fortnum & Masons, Habitat and Harrods in the UK. Many provide account facilities or payment can be made by international credit cards. Although many foreign mail-order companies won't send goods abroad, there's nothing to stop you obtaining catalogues from friends or relatives and ordering through them. Buying goods mail-order from the US can result in large savings, even after paying postage and VAT. Most mail-order companies also have websites where you can order catalogues and goods.

INTERNET

Shopping via the internet has taken off in a big way in recent years and is now the fastest-growing form of retailing. Many Swiss companies offer internet shopping, but the real benefit comes when shopping abroad, when savings can be made on a wide range of products (you can buy virtually anything via the internet). However, when comparing prices take into account shipping costs, insurance, duty and VAT. Shopping on the internet is usually very secure and even safer than shopping by phone or mail-order (in many cases the trader never even sees your credit card details). To find companies or products via the internet, simply use a search engine (🖳 www.search.ch for Swiss websites).

Online grocery shopping is provided by Coop (🖳 www.coop.ch) and Migros (Le Shop), probably the best online shop in Switzerland (🖳 www.le-shop.ch). It offers everything from fresh produce to alcohol, including imported products from around the world. They offer a monthly billing service, next day delivery via the post, and a flat SFr. 12 delivery fee anywhere in Switzerland. Other good Swiss internet sites include ▣ www.directmedia.ch, which sell CDs, movies and videogames online, and ▣ www.dvdone.ch, where you can rent a selection of DVDs for less than a video store post-free (if you order at least four) – and you can keep them for a whole week!

If you purchase a small item by post from outside Switzerland, you may have to pay VAT (*MWSt*, *TVA*) of 7.6 per cent on delivery or at the post office on collection. Goods sent from EU countries (usually above a minimum value) should be free of local value added tax (see **Shopping Abroad** below). Gift parcels from abroad that don't exceed SFr. 100 in value are exempt from VAT, but must be clearly marked in customs declarations.

When you purchase a large item abroad and have it shipped to Switzerland by air freight, you should have it sent to your nearest airport. The receiving freight company will notify you when it has arrived. You must provide them with details of the contents and cost (an invoice copy) so that they can clear the goods through customs. They will deliver the goods to you with the bill for VAT and freight, payable on the spot, unless you make alternative arrangements.

The cost of air freight within Europe or even from North America is usually reasonable, however, the delivery and handling charges from a Swiss airport to your home can be as high as the air freight costs to Switzerland! If possible, it's a lot cheaper to collect goods yourself after they've been cleared through customs. **Ensure that goods sent by air freight are fully insured.** It's sometimes better to have goods sent by post (excluding local taxes), rather than importing them personally, when it's often a long process to obtain a refund.

SHOPPING ABROAD

Shopping abroad makes a pleasant change from all those boring Swiss shops full of diamond necklaces, gold watches and *haute couture* fashions. It can also save you a lot of money and makes a enjoyable day out for the family. Don't forget your passports or identity cards, car documents, dog's vaccination documents and euros. Most shops in border towns gladly accept Swiss francs, but usually at a lower exchange rate than a bank.

Many foreigners and Swiss, particularly those living in border areas (e.g. Basle, Geneva and Lugano), take advantage of the generally lower prices outside Switzerland and do their weekly shopping abroad. Almost half the residents of Geneva (one-third of whom are foreigners) regularly do the bulk of their shopping in France and overall around one-third of Swiss residents regularly shop abroad. Germany, France and Italy all have a lower cost of living than Switzerland (although salaries are also much lower). A combination of lower prices, a favourable exchange rate and low Swiss VAT, mean that savings of a third or more can be made on many items. Many foodstuffs (and wine) are up to 50 per cent cheaper in France, Germany and Italy (overall savings are around 30 per cent). This means that if you spend SFr. 200 a week on groceries and alcohol in Switzerland, you can save up to SFr. 3,000 or more a year by shopping abroad! However, the strong euro and high petrol prices are a deterrent for some shoppers. **Note that in all countries except Germany there are minimum purchase levels, below which you're unable to reclaim local VAT.**

Prices in Germany are lower for most goods and you often save around 25 to 30 per cent after paying Swiss VAT and receiving the German VAT refund. The best buys in Germany include electrical, electronic and photographic equipment; household appliances; computers and software; DVDs and videos; optical goods and services; furniture; sporting goods; car parts, servicing and accessories; alcohol; and meat products. Buying a car abroad, e.g. in Germany or Italy, can also yield large savings.

On weekdays, shopping hours are much the same as in Switzerland, except on Wednesdays, when shops usually close at 1pm. In many German towns bordering Switzerland, most shops are open until 6pm on Saturdays especially to cater for the influx of shoppers from Switzerland. **Note, however, that prices may be slightly higher in border towns than in larger inland German cities.**

Of course, not everything is cheaper abroad and it's wise to compare prices and quality before buying. Bear in mind that if you buy goods that are faulty or need repair, you may have to return them to the place of purchase, which could be a hassle with customs paperwork. When buying goods outside Switzerland on which you intend to reclaim the foreign VAT, the procedure is as follows:

1 Obtain a receipt for your purchase and tell the shop assistant that you'd like a form to reclaim the tax. The shop completes the tax reclaim form (*Ausfuhrschein/Zollschein, fiche d'exportation/feuille d'exportation*) and enters the tax rate and total amount to be refunded. Write your name and your Swiss address on the form. If you wish to claim your tax refund by post, check that the vendor will reimburse the tax by post.

2 Have the form stamped by a customs official in the country of purchase before entering Switzerland. The official might want proof that you don't live in the country, e.g. a Swiss residence permit. **If you're flying back to Switzerland with your purchases, e.g. from the UK, you may need to carry them as hand luggage in order to have your tax reclaim form stamped.**

3 At the Swiss customs post, present your receipt to the official and tell him what you've purchased. He determines the import duty and Swiss VAT to be paid, if any. Swiss customs officials sometimes query your country of residence, so make sure you have your Swiss residence permit handy.

4 To reclaim the VAT, return the form in person to the vendor or send it by post (keep a copy of the receipt and tax form). This must usually be done within a limited period, e.g. six months for goods purchased in Germany.

Some shops in border areas deliver goods to your home in Switzerland within a certain radius, in which case you won't pay local VAT but may be charged for delivery. For expensive purchases, a shop may send someone to accompany you to the border and return your local tax on the spot, on receipt of the stamped tax reclaim form.

DUTY-FREE ALLOWANCES

The Swiss customs regulations allow duty-free purchases up to SFr. 300 with the following restrictions (amounts per person, per day):

- 1 l/kg of butter and cream;

- 4 l/kg of oil, shortening and margarine;

- 5 l/kg of milk, cheese, yoghurt and other dairy products;

- 2.5 kg of eggs;

- 20 kgs of any vegetables or fruit;

- 2.5kg of potatoes (including crisps!);

- 20kg of flour or flour-based products (bread, cakes etc);

- 3.5kg of meat and meat products. This may include a maximum of 500g of fresh or frozen meat (oxen, sheep, lamb, horses, goats, kids and pigs).

People over 17 years can also import the following:

- 2 litres of wine or champagne under 15 deg. proof **and** 1 litre of alcohol over 15 deg. proof (if you import more than one litre, duty on the excess amount is likely to equal or exceed its cost);

- 200 cigarettes **or** 50 cigars **or** 250g of pipe tobacco (doubled for visitors domiciled outside Europe).

There are regulations prohibiting the importation of meats from certain countries and occasional restrictions on the import of some meats due to an outbreak of swine fever or foot and mouth disease. If in doubt, check with the Federal Veterinary Office, Schwarzenburgstr. 155, CH-3003 Berne (☎ 031 323 30 33, 🖳 www.bvet.admin.ch). On no account may you exceed the limit on meat imports.

General Information

- The total value of duty-free goods permitted is SFr. 300. At the Swiss border you must declare what you've purchased and, if asked, produce receipts to verify the place of origin and the price paid. When you exceed the permitted tax-free limit, you're liable to pay VAT of 7.6 per cent on **ALL** your purchases, including the duty-free allowance.

- Customs duty on goods imported above the duty-free allowance is calculated by weight, depending on the category of goods. This is payable in addition to the 7.6 per cent VAT.

- Duty-free goods and petrol can also be purchased in the town of Samnaun (Graubünden). La Cure, a village on the Swiss-French border in the Jura hills above Nyon, also harbours a duty-free 'shop' (*Bar de la Dôle*).

- Never attempt to import illegal goods. Don't agree to bring a parcel into Switzerland or to deliver a parcel in another country, without knowing exactly what it contains. A popular con trick is to ask someone to post a parcel in Switzerland (usually to a *poste restante* address) or to leave a parcel at a railway station or restaurant. **THE PARCEL USUALLY CONTAINS ILLEGAL DRUGS!**

Swiss customs officials are usually reasonable and flexible and unless you're a big-time smuggler, treat you fairly. See general **Customs** notes on page 76 and ▣ www.ch.ch (go to 'Individuals' and follow the links to 'State and Law' and then 'Customs Duties').

EMERGENCY RATIONS

All residents of Switzerland are requested to keep an emergency food supply (*Notvorrat, provisions de secours*) in their nuclear shelter. The food supply includes 1 to 2kg per person of sugar, rice or pasta, oil or fat, protein rich food, carbohydrate rich food and food of your choice (if the bombs don't get you the food will!). To this must be added drinks (two litres a day), fuel, cleaning materials, assorted extras such as medicines, rubbish sacks, spirit stove (for cooking), methylated spirits and iron tablets. Don't forget essentials such as baby food, nappies (diapers), diabetic treatments, drugs and vitamin tablets. Washing powder is also one of the essential requirements, although most shelters have no running water and no toilet facilities. You should take a radio (although reception may be impossible). Most Swiss also keep a good supply of wine in their shelters (they plan to go out with a party!).

The necessary foods are listed in a pamphlet called *Household Reserves*, available from your community or from the Bundesamt für wirtschaftliche Landesversorgung, Belpstr. 53, CH-3003 Berne (☎ 031 322 21 56, ▣ www.bwl. admin.ch). Foods can be stored only for a limited period and must be replaced periodically (see pamphlet).

RECEIPTS

When shopping in Switzerland, always insist on a receipt (*Quittung/Kassenbon*, *quittance*) and retain it until you've left the store or reached home. This isn't just in case you need to return or exchange goods, which may be impossible without the receipt, but also to verify that you've paid if an automatic alarm sounds as you're leaving the shop or any other questions arise. When you buy a large object which cannot be wrapped, a sticker should be attached as visible evidence of purchase, in addition to your receipt. In supermarkets, the cashier usually sticks your receipt to goods with sticky tape.

It's advisable to keep receipts and records of all major purchases made while resident in Switzerland, particularly if your stay is for a limited period only. This may save you time and money when you finally leave Switzerland and are required to declare your belongings in your new country of residence.

CONSUMER ASSOCIATIONS

The independent Swiss Consumer Association provides free product information and legal advice, and publishes books and monthly or bimonthly magazines in local languages, available on subscription and from news kiosks. The association has three main offices, serving the main language regions of Switzerland, plus local advisers in many areas.

- **French** – Fédération Romande des Consommateurs, rue de Genève 7, PO Box 6151, CH-1002 Lausanne (☎ 021 312 80 06 or ☎ 0900 575 105 for advice and information, SFr. 2.13 per minute, 🖳 www.frc.ch).

- **German** – Stiftung für Konsumentenschutz, Monbijoustr. 61, PO Box, CH-3000 Berne 23 (☎ 031 370 24 24 or ☎ 0900 900 440 for advice, SFr. 2.10 per minute, 🖳 www.konsumentenschutz.ch).

- **Italian** – L'Associazone Consumatrici della Svizzera Italiana, via Polar 46, PO Box 165, CH-6932 Breganzona (☎ 091 922 97 55, 🖳 www.acsi.ch).

Another publication worthy of special mention is *Ktipp*, a German-language consumer magazine which is one of the best-selling subscription publications in Switzerland. It costs SFr. 31.50 a year (20 issues), or SFr. 58 for two years from K-Tipp, Wolfbachstr. 15, PO Box 431, CH-8024 Zurich (☎ 044 266 17 17, 🖳 www.ktipp.ch).

18.

ODDS & ENDS

This chapter contains miscellaneous information. Most of the topics covered are of general interest to anyone living and working in Switzerland, although not all subjects are of vital importance. However, buried among the trivia are some fascinating snippets of information.

ALARMS

There are various alarms for the Swiss population in times of peace (*Alarmierung der Bevölkerung in Friedenszeiten, alarme de la population en temps de paix*), with which all residents of Switzerland should be familiar. When alarms are to be tested, announcements are made in the communities concerned. The famous Swiss underground shelter plays an important role in Switzerland's civil defence system and all new houses built in Switzerland must have one. (Maybe they have a master plan to arise from their bolt-holes after the radiation has dispersed and conquer what's left of the world?

The following information is provided at the back of Swiss telephone directories, where it's listed in French, German and Italian. Some communities and cantons may have additional alarm signals.

General Alarm

The general alarm (*allgemeiner Alarm, alarme général*) is a continuous oscillating high frequency tone for one minute. Information is broadcast on radio DRS (frequency 103) and local radio in the Swiss national and other languages, including English. Instructions is given by the authorities on what action to take. Inform your neighbours (or ask them what's going on).

Radioactivity Alarm

The radioactivity alarm (*Strahlenalarm, alarme radioactivité*) is an interrupted oscillating high frequency tone for two minutes. Signifies **IMMEDIATE DANGER**. Close all doors and windows and seek shelter **IMMEDIATELY** in the nearest nuclear shelter. Take emergency rations with you if they aren't already stored in your shelter, plus a transistor radio and listen for further instructions (if you can hear anything in your bunker).

Water Alarm

The water alarm (*Wasseralarm, alarme eau*) is an interrupted low frequency tone for six minutes. Warning of a danger of floods in the local area. Listen to local radio and TV for information. If you're in the danger area, evacuate **IMMEDIATELY** and seek out high ground. There may also be local regulations concerning water alarms.

All Clear

The all clear (*ende der gefahr*, *fin du danger*) is announced via radio, TV and loudspeaker vehicles.

BUSINESS HOURS

The usual business hours (*Geschäftsstunden*, *heures de bureau*) for offices (not shops or factories) vary, but are generally from 8 to noon and 1.30 or 2pm to 5 or 6pm, Mondays to Fridays. Many businesses close for lunch, which may extend from 11.30 or noon to 2pm, and most are closed on Saturdays. Switchboards may be unmanned at lunchtimes, during which telephones may be unanswered or be connected to an answering machine. Government offices are usually open from around 8 to 11.45am and from 2 to 4pm.

CHILDREN

There are various laws in Switzerland governing the behaviour of children in public places. Children under 16 years old, which is the legal age of sexual consent in Switzerland, aren't permitted in public places after 10pm. unless accompanied by an adult. Those under 16 aren't allowed in bars, night clubs or casinos. Switzerland is generally a very safe place for children, although they should be informed of the dangers of 'talking to strangers'.

CITIZENSHIP

Obtaining Swiss citizenship (*Schweizer Nationalität/Schweizer Staatsbürger*, *nationalité suisse/citoyen suisse*) isn't easy and the application process is long-winded. Following your application, an 18-month investigation is carried out to determine whether you're suitable. If you survive the inquisition you must then pass a general knowledge quiz on Switzerland – failure to answer correctly means no lovely red Swiss passport (as a consolation, a tasty chocolate Swiss passport is available from sweet shops).

To qualify for Swiss citizenship, a foreigner who isn't married to a Swiss citizen must be a resident of Switzerland for 12 years, including three of the last five years, in order to qualify for Swiss citizenship. The number of years spent in

Switzerland between the ages of 10 to 20 count double. A foreigner married to a Swiss citizen must have been married three years and have been living in Switzerland for five years, and is eligible for simplified citizenship (*erleichterte Einbürgerung, naturalization facilitée*), which in practice means a quicker citizenship process. A child born to a foreigner in Switzerland has the right of Swiss citizenship only when his parents are married and one is a Swiss citizen.

Foreigners who take Swiss citizenship no longer automatically lose the nationality of their country of origin, as dual nationality is now accepted (at least by the Swiss).

CLIMATE

It's almost impossible to give a general description of the Swiss climate, as it varies considerably from region to region (like the Swiss people themselves). Probably no country in Europe has such diverse weather conditions in such a small area.

The Alps, extending from east to west, form a major weather division between the north and south of Switzerland, and separate weather forecasts are usually given for each area. The climate north of the Alps is continental with hot summers and cold winters, although prolonged periods when the temperature is below freezing are rare during daytime (unless you live on top of a mountain). At high altitudes, it's frequently warm during the day at any time of the year, although cold at night, even in summer. In winter it usually snows everywhere at some time (even in the lowlands), but it generally thaws by spring, except above 2,000m (6,561ft). Many areas often experience heavy fog and mist, caused by temperature inversions, particularly in autumn. In winter, storms are apt to cause avalanches, mudslides, rockfalls and floods in some areas.

In Ticino, south of the Alps, a mild Mediterranean climate prevails and even in winter it's significantly warmer here than elsewhere in Switzerland. Spring and autumn are usually mild and fine in most areas, although it can be dull and wet in some regions. Spring in Ticino is particularly warm and pleasant. Generally Switzerland has more rainfall than most other regions of Europe (although Valais is particularly dry) and the country is noted for its low humidity and lack of wind. Most areas suffer occasionally from the *foehn*, a warm oppressive south wind often blamed for headaches, fatigue, vertigo, bad tempers and other minor irritating complaints. You can even buy a gadget to ease its unpleasant effects. High ozone levels caused by summer smog are becoming more common and creating health hazards in some areas.

The daily weather forecast in winter includes the snow limit (*Schneegrenze, limite d'enneigement*), which is the lowest level (in metres) where snow will fall and where freezing point will occur (*Nullgradgrenze, limite du degré zéro*). Generally Swiss weather forecasts are surprisingly accurate. Average afternoon temperatures in Centigrade and Fahrenheit (in brackets) are:

Location	Spring	Summer	Autumn	Winter
Geneva	14 (58)	25 (77)	14 (58)	4 (40)
Lugano	17 (63)	28 (83)	17 (63)	6 (43)
Zurich	12 (53)	22 (71)	11 (52)	0 (32)

The Swiss weather forecast is available by telephone in the local language (162, SFr. 0.50 per call plus 0.50 per minute), via the Swiss television teletext service and in daily newspapers. The pollen count (*Pollenbericht, indice de pollen*) is reported from March to July on the Swiss television teletext service and in daily newspapers. Daily weather reports for around 25 Swiss resorts are displayed at major railway stations. The weather in major European cities is also given on Swiss television teletext. Avalanche bulletins are given on telephone service number ☎ 187 (SFr. 0.50 basic fee plus 0.50 per minute). Weather forecasts are also available via numerous websites such as 🖳 www.meteoschweiz.ch and 🖳 www.wetter.ch.

CRIME

Compared with other western countries, Switzerland has a low crime rate. Violent crime remains relatively rare, with some 75 murders committed (plus another 129 attempted) in 2005. About half of these murders were linked to domestic violence. However, there's been a steady increase in assaults in recent years, particularly among young men and teenage boys, and the number of rapes on women doubled between 1995 and 2005. Negligence is the cause of many thefts, with mopeds and bicycles being the main target (over 70,000 are stolen each year!). The Swiss are too trusting for their own good and often leave doors, windows and even safes open for their friendly neighbourhood thief (if you're a crook, you shouldn't be reading this).

Switzerland has a growing drug problem and the open drug scene in some cities (e.g. Zurich) is conspicuous in a country where cleanliness and order abound. Most of the recent increase in crime and violence (and burglaries) is associated with drug dealers (many of whom are foreigners) and addicts. Zurich and other Swiss cities have been losing the drug war for many years. Many observers put the blame on Switzerland's tolerant attitude towards drug addicts, which some claim acerbates the problem and serves to attract foreign addicts. The use of hard drugs is one of the few problems that Switzerland has on the same scale as other European countries. Nearly 50 per cent of crimes in Switzerland are committed by foreigners and Swiss prisons contain a high proportion of foreigners, although many are non-residents who come to Switzerland simply to commit crimes. Prison overcrowding is widespread and a growing problem.

Like most countries, Switzerland has professional thieves who do a good business breaking into private houses and apartments. Don't leave cash, cheques, credit cards, passports, jewellery and other valuables lying around or even hidden in your home (the crooks know **all** the hiding places). Good locks help but don't keep the professionals out (they drill them out). It's better to keep your valuables in a safety deposit box (costing from SFr. 50 to 100 a year) and ensure that you have adequate home contents insurance (see page 273). Most apartment blocks in Switzerland are fitted with a security system, allowing residents to speak to callers before giving them access to the building. In addition, most apartment entrance doors have a spy-hole so that you can check a visitor's identity before opening the door.

There are pickpockets in major cities and tourist centres, so don't walk around with your wallet or purse on display and men should never keep their wallet in their back trouser pocket. Some theft insurance doesn't cover pickpocket thefts, only robbery with violence (so tell your insurance company that you were robbed at gun point!). Mugging and crimes of violence are fortunately still rare in Switzerland and you can safely walk almost anywhere, day or night. Remember to lock your car and put any valuables in the boot or out of sight, particularly when parking overnight in a public place, and look after your expensive skis and other belongings in ski resorts.

The Swiss compensate for the lack of serious crime by making many trivial offences unlawful, such as hanging bedding from your windows at the wrong time or washing your car on a Sunday. All fines (sometimes referred to as administrative measures – the Swiss have many euphemisms for unpleasant things like taxes and fines) around SFr. 50 are entered in a canton register. Single fines over SFr. 200 are entered in a central criminal register (*Strafregister*, *casier judiciaire*) and too many entries in the **BIG BLACK BOOK** may prejudice your residence permit. If you're fined for an offence, you may have the option of doing community service at weekends, rather than pay a fine.

What you may be unaware of as a foreigner (and hopefully will remain so) is the infamous Swiss imprisonment on remand (*Untersuchungshaft, la détention provisaire*), whereby anyone can be imprisoned on suspicion of committing a crime and kept there for months without charge or trial. Despite the exemplary behaviour of the Swiss and most foreign residents in Switzerland, it was discovered in 1990 that the federal police had compiled over 900,000 secret files on its Swiss and foreign residents, who were apparently perceived as a threat to national security (Swiss xenophobia knows no bounds).

ECONOMY & TRADE

Despite its limited size and severe shortage of raw materials, Switzerland is one of the most productive, competitive and prosperous countries in the world. Swiss products are renowned for their quality, reliability and after sales service, and a strong emphasis is given to the refinement and finishing of products, and high quality specialisation. Switzerland's success is due to a combination of technical know-how; enterprising spirit; hard work (particularly by the foreign labour force); virtually no strikes; high investment in plant and equipment; and an overriding pro-business mentality. Like Japan, it's largely dependent on imports, particularly raw materials, semi-finished and finished products, energy sources and food. The majority of Swiss companies are leaders in their fields.

One of Switzerland's most important industries is precision mechanical and electrical engineering, which produces highly specialised equipment and tools, particularly machine tools, and textile and printing machinery. Other important industries include chemicals and pharmaceuticals, tourism, the textile and clothing industries and watch making. The Swiss food industry is also prosperous and Swiss chocolate (much of which is now manufactured abroad – is it still Swiss?) and cheese, among other foods, are exported all over the world. Nestlé is the largest food company in the world. Despite the fact that only a quarter of Switzerland's surface area is productive, Swiss farmers produce around 70 per cent of the country's food.

It's the service sector, however, which contributes most towards balancing the budget, in particular the major Swiss banks and insurance companies. The tourist industry is also important and is one of the country's largest employers, providing work directly or indirectly for some 240,000 people. Tourism is Switzerland's third-largest export source (after the machine and chemical industries) with foreign tourists spending close to SFr. 14bn in 2005 (some 5 per cent of GDP). The Swiss workforce consists of some 4m people or around 55 per cent of the population (55 per cent men and 45 per cent women), some 20 per cent of whom are foreigners. Around 70 per cent are employed in the services sector; 25 per cent in industry, trades and construction; and 5 per cent in agriculture and forestry.

It was feared that Switzerland's rejection of the EEA (and the European Union) could prove an obstacle to future growth and prosperity, as few western countries are so dependent on the outside world for their economic survival. However, Switzerland has negotiated a series of trade treaties with the EU, and in 2014 EU citizens will be able to live and work freely in Switzerland (Swiss citizens will have the same rights in EU countries). The Swiss will therefore be able to enjoy the benefits of EU membership without the bureaucracy and expense (the Swiss really are smart!). Switzerland cannot afford any kind of isolation, either with regard to energy or raw materials, or in relation to capital and labour markets. For this reason, Switzerland's foreign exchange system has always been based on a free market, opposition to all forms of protectionism, and a policy of low customs duties with almost no restrictions on imports.

Agricultural products are virtually the only exception. Most food imports are subject to high duties in order to protect the livelihood of Swiss farmers and ensure sufficient food production in times of need (due to their high production costs, Swiss farmers cannot compete with imports). Swiss farmers receive a large part of their income from federal subsidies, but there are regular battles over milk prices and production quotas. Despite the duties on imported food,

Switzerland imports more agricultural products per capita than any other European country. Other important benefits of the Swiss farming policy are safeguarding the traditional Swiss way of life, particularly in mountainous regions, and the protection of the environment. Agriculture is also considered a vital prerequisite for the tourist industry. Nevertheless, every resident of Switzerland pays some SFr. 500 a year to subsidise Swiss farmers.

The Swiss economy remains strong and competitive, despite the strength of the Swiss franc (which has wiped millions of francs off the profits of Switzerland's multinationals in the last decade), high labour costs and ever-increasing competition. However, Swiss companies are feeling the pinch and are increasingly being forced to move production and other facilities abroad, reduce prices and shave their profit margins. The Swiss are constantly striving to improve their products to meet world demand and are quick to incorporate the most advanced technical innovations (who but a Swiss would invent a prayer mat for Muslims with a built-in compass, calibrated to point towards Mecca from anywhere in the world!).

Switzerland spends more per capita on research and development than any other country, is second only to the US in the number of computers per head, and is sixth in the world in the value of advanced technology exports. It's significant that (per capita) the Swiss have produced more Nobel prize winners (around 25) and registered more patents than any other country. A 'Made in Switzerland' label remains a significant attraction to many buyers, who gladly pay a premium for Swiss quality and durability. However, ominous signs for the future of Swiss industry include the sharp drop in foreign investment and the increasing number of Swiss companies transferring investment and manufacturing abroad. In recent years, Swiss companies have redoubled their efforts to build ties with companies located within the European Union.

GEOGRAPHY

Switzerland is situated in the central Alpine region of Europe and has borders with five countries: Italy (734km/456mi) to the south, Austria (164km/102mi) and the Principality of Liechtenstein (41km/25mi) to the east, Germany (334km/207mi) to the north and France (573km/356mi) to the west. (Due to its 'isolationist' policies, Switzerland has been described as the only island in the world surrounded entirely by land!) It's a small country; the maximum distance from east to west is just 348km/216mi and from north to south only 220km/137mi. The total area is 41,290km^2 (around 15,940mi^2). The Alps, mainly in the central part of the country, reach altitudes of more than 4,000m (13,123ft). Geographically Switzerland can be divided into three main regions:

● The alpine massif, which includes the whole of southern Switzerland, covering some 60 per cent of the country and containing around 20 per cent of the population. Approximately one-fifth of the total alpine range lies within Switzerland.

- The central plateau (Mittelland) north of the alpine massif consists of some 30 per cent of the land area and is home to around two-thirds of the population.

- The Jura mountains in the north-west make up the remaining 10 per cent of Switzerland, with some 15 per cent of the population.

The highest point in Switzerland is the Dufour Peak of the Monte Rosa (4,634m/15,203ft) and the lowest Lake Maggiore (195m/639ft above sea level). The Swiss Alps contain the crossroads formed by the St. Gotthard, Grimsel, Furka and Oberalp passes, and are the source of both the Rhine and Rhône rivers. Due to its central position, Switzerland has long been an important link in communications and transport between northern and southern Europe, a fact that has been decisive in determining the course of Swiss history.

GOVERNMENT

Switzerland is the most politically stable country in the world. The Swiss constitution (reviewed and updated in 2001) provides both the confederation and cantons with the system of a democratic republic, in the form of direct or representative democracy. Switzerland's foreign policy is neutral. A number of important recent referendums (e.g. EEA membership and Swiss UN troops, both of which were rejected) have shown only too clearly that the Swiss government is increasingly out of step (at least in terms of foreign policy) with its people. However, Switzerland's foreign policy isn't entirely isolationist and in 1992 it became a member of the IMF and the World Bank (it's also a member of the Council of Europe, GATT and the OECD). In 2002, the Swiss voted to become a member of the United Nations.

In Switzerland, power is 'devolved' **upwards** from some 3,000 communities (*Gemeinde, commune*), each of which has a local council or municipal authority. A Swiss citizen is first and foremost a citizen of a community (written in his passport), which remains ultimately responsible for his welfare throughout his life. In a community, the executive is the administrative council headed by the mayor, with legislative matters being handled by the municipal council. The community levies local taxes and has self-rule in all matters that aren't the responsibility of either the federal government or the canton. These include the administration of public property such as forests; water, gas and electricity supply; bridges, roads and administrative buildings; schools (primary education); and the civil defence, fire, health and local police departments. Several communities make up a borough or county (*Bezirk, district*).

Next in line are the 26 cantons (*Kanton/Stande, canton*), six of which rank as 'half-cantons' (half a canton is better than none). Each canton has its own written constitution and is in effect a sovereign state subject to federal law. The canton government consists of an executive state council of five to nine members (each head of a department) and a legislative grand council of varying size, depending on the canton. Each canton is responsible for its own civil service; citizenship; church matters; education; finances and income tax; fire service; labour department; land usage; law and order; libraries; public health; public transport; roads; stock exchange supervision; and water and electricity supply.

The federal government is directly responsible for the armed forces; civil, criminal and industrial law; currency; customs and federal taxes; fishing, forestry and hunting; foreign policy; hydroelectric power; monetary controls; pensions; post and communications services; and railways. Legislative power is exercised by the federal assembly (*Bundesversammlung, Assemblée Fédérale*), consisting of two chambers of equal status:

● **The Council of States** (*Ständerat, Conseil des Etats*) comprises 46 representatives of the cantons. The 20 'full' cantons have two representatives each and the six half-cantons one each.

● **The National Council** (*Nationalrat, Conseil National*), is elected for a four-year term and consists of 200 direct representatives of the people. The number of members allocated to each canton depends on their size and population. This results in five cantons with one member only and therefore no proportional representation.

Both chambers hold four regular sessions a year, each of three weeks duration, and bills must be debated and passed by both chambers. Members of both chambers aren't professional politicians and hold other jobs, although most are self-employed or high-ranking corporate executives with the time and money to be part-time politicians. Politicians are paid around SFr. 70,000 a year. As you'd expect in Switzerland, few federal politicians are women (possibly because they've had the right to vote only since 1971), although this is changing. The men of half canton Appenzell Innerrhoden steadfastly refused to give women the right to vote in community and canton elections until being overruled by the federal government in 1990.

The federal assembly elects the seven federal councillors (comprising the federal executive), who serve for four years and head the departments of foreign affairs; the interior; justice and police; defence and sport; finance; economics and environment; and transport and energy (including communications). Re-election of federal councillors is permitted. Each year the assembly elects a councillor as president of the confederation (who remains anonymous to everyone but his/her spouse). The highest judicial authority is the Federal Supreme Court, which sits in Lausanne and consists of 30 members elected by the federal assembly.

The Swiss system of democracy, although not perfect, is among the best ever devised. Almost everyone is represented through proportional representation (with the notable exception of the 1.6m foreigners who comprise around 20 per cent of the population). Local communities and cantons have real powers that cannot be usurped or vetoed by the federal government and all important decisions must be decided by the people through referendums (see page 379). The system functions well because politicians of all parties work together for the greater benefit of the majority, rather than indulging in petty squabbling and party politics. However, Swiss politics are also terminally boring, although the EEA/EU issue has injected a modicum of interest and the Swiss are beginning to debate issues with some passion. If you're an insomniac, you can find out more about Swiss politics via the internet (🖥 www.socio.ch/poli).

LEGAL ADVICE

Many towns and all major cities offer free or inexpensive legal advice for foreigners in English and other languages. Advice encompasses both criminal and civil law, e.g. the interpretation of house rental or purchase contracts. Ask your community or local information office for the address of your nearest legal office (*Notariat, Étude de notaire*). With regard to divorce, Swiss private international law applies only when either spouse is a Swiss citizen or has been residing in Switzerland for more than two years.

If you have reason to complain about faulty goods or bad services and your initial attempts at redress fall on deaf ears, try writing a letter in English to the manager or managing director. This often has surprisingly positive results (see also **Consumer Associations** on page 361). Even when dealing with government bureaucrats or officials, you can be successful if you protest loudly and long enough. The Swiss usually submit meekly to all rules and regulations, and therefore bureaucrats are often flabbergasted when faced with an assertive foreigner. Legal advice and services may be provided by your embassy or consulate in Switzerland, including, for example, an official witness of signatures (Commissioner for Oaths).

MILITARY SERVICE

If you work in Switzerland, you may notice that your Swiss male colleagues have a habit of disappearing for a few weeks every few years. They aren't entitled to more holidays than foreigners, but are simply doing their military service (*Militärdienst, service militaire*). Switzerland has a 'citizen' army of part-time soldiers and can muster up to 220,000 men at arms in 48 hours to defend the homeland (only brigade commanders and above and instructors are full-time professionals, a total of around 3,000). However, don't be concerned as foreign residents aren't liable for military service. If you become a Swiss citizen, military service depends on your age and whether you've already served in a foreign army (if you have, you won't be trusted and will be exempt). You will probably be unaware of it as a foreigner, but success and promotion in the army often opens the door to position and power in Swiss industry, government and finance. The Swiss army was cut by around a third in the last decade from 600,000 to 400,000 and then again to 220,000.

All Swiss males must serve at least 260 days from the age of 19, when they undergo a basic 21-week training course, after which they become 'active' troops. Most ranks (soldiers and non-commissioned officers/NCOs) must complete a number (around six) of 19-days-refresher courses, usually once a year, and remain on 'reserve' until age 35, when military service ends (the exception being senior officers, who serve until they're 50). Senior NCOs and officers undergo additional periods of training. The total length of military training is around one year and includes annual target practice when not on active duty. Military service isn't compulsory for women, although they can volunteer to serve in the women's military service.

To speed up mobilisation in the event of a war, Swiss soldiers keep their uniforms, gas masks, arms and ammunition at home – a sure-fire recipe for civil war in less disciplined countries. An unusual feature of the Swiss armed forces is that in peace time they have no general, one being appointed only in the event of a threat of war. Anyone who's unfit for military service must serve in the auxiliary services, e.g. the civil defence or ambulance service. In 1991, Switzerland finally recognised the status of conscientious objectors, prior to which anyone who refused to serve in the army was imprisoned. An alternative civil service (390 days) has now been established for those who object to military service on religious or moral grounds. Swiss citizens living abroad aren't liable for military service, but are required to pay a military exemption tax (*Militärpflichtersatz, taxe d'exemption du service militaire*) of a percentage of their salary, even if they never intend to return to Switzerland. The tax also applies to anyone excused service on medical, moral or religious grounds. Swiss employers usually pay employees their full salary while they are doing their military service, except in extreme circumstances when they're unable to do so.

Although the majority of Swiss proclaim that they loathe military service, whenever the question of abolishing conscription or the army is raised in a referendum, they vote to retain it. However, in 1989, 35.6 per cent voted to abolish the army, which shocked the complacent military and political establishment to the core, although in a second referendum in December 2001, only 23.2 per cent voted to abolish the army. However, fears in military circles that a future referendum could prove terminal have led to a reduction in the length of military service and the number of personnel.

In 1994, the Swiss voted against allowing their troops to volunteer for UN peacekeeping missions. The army has been reformed twice over the last decade, with one of the goals being the reduction of costs. Switzerland's annual defence budget is over SFr. 4bn – a lot of money for a country without an enemy in the world and which hasn't fought a foreign campaign since 1515! There are, however, plans to slash the military budget in the coming years by reducing manpower, putting equipment and vehicles into storage, and closing military camps.

PETS

If you intend to bring a pet (*Haustier*, *animal domestique*) with you to Switzerland, check the latest regulations in advance. Make sure that you have the correct documents, not only for Switzerland but for all the countries that you must pass through to reach Switzerland. If you need to return prematurely, even after a few hours or days, to a country with strict quarantine regulations, your pet will be put into quarantine.

Swiss Regulations

There's generally no quarantine period for animals in Switzerland. For entry into Switzerland, all dogs and cats over five months old must have an international health certificate stating that they've been vaccinated against rabies (*Tollwut*, *rage*). You must have an official letter stating that your pet was in good health before the vaccination, which must have been given at least 30 days and not more than one year before entering the country. Certificates are accepted in English, French, German and Italian. Dogs and cats under five months of age may be imported from many countries (includin those in Europe except Turkey, Australia, New Zealand and the US) without a vaccination, but require a veterinary attestation of their age and good health. Dogs and cats from countries that don't require rabies vaccinations (Australia and New Zealand) can be imported without a vaccination certificate. People who are resident in Switzerland aren't allowed to import dogs whose ears or tails have been cut, although those coming to live in Switzerland can import such dogs when they enter the country.

British Regulations

The Pet Travel Scheme (PETS – now under the auspices of the EU pet passport scheme), replaces quarantine for qualifying cats and dogs. Under the scheme, pets must be micro-chipped (they have a microchip inserted in their neck), vaccinated against rabies, undergo a blood test and be issued with a health certificate (passport). **Note that the PETS certificate/ EU pet passport sometimes isn't issued until six months AFTER the above have been carried out!** In the UK, EU pet passports are issued by Local Veterinary Inspectors (LVI) only. In other EU countries, passports are issued by all registered vets.

The scheme is restricted to animals imported from rabies-free countries and countries where rabies is under control – 22 European countries plus Bahrain, Canada and the US. To qualify, pets must travel by sea via any major British ferry port, by train via the Channel Tunnel or via Bristol, Doncaster, London Gatwick, London Healthrow or Manchester airports. Only certain carriers are licensed to carry animals and these are listed on the Department for Environment, Food and Rural Affairs (DEFRA) website (🖳 www.defra.gov.uk/animalh/quarantine/index/htm). Additional information is available from DEFRA (☎ 0870-241 1710, ✉ helpline@defra.gsi.gov.uk).

British pet owners must complete an Application for a Ministry Export Certificate for dogs, cats and rabies susceptible animals (form EXA1), available from DEFRA at the above address. DEFRA contacts the vet you've named on the form and he performs a health inspection. You then receive an export health certificate, which must be issued no more than 30 days before your entry into Switzerland with your pet.

General Information

In Switzerland, dogs must have a rabies vaccination every two years from the age of six months. A vaccination for distemper (*Staupe, morve/maladie carré*) is recommended every two years, but isn't mandatory. If you plan to take your dog abroad, it must have had a rabies vaccination at least six weeks before travelling. Cats aren't required to have regular rabies vaccinations, although if you let your cat roam free outside your home it's advisable to have it vaccinated annually. Areas usually become active rabies areas in three to four-year cycles. If your area is active, there are strict rules for pet owners, for example dogs must be kept on a lead. Don't let your children play with wild or strange animals, or approach a pet or wild animal that's acting strangely, as it could have rabies. Report the incident to the police as soon as possible. If your child is bitten by an animal that could have rabies, he requires a series of anti-rabies injections. The authorities set anti-rabies vaccine in bait (chicken heads) for foxes twice annually; don't touch them or let your dog get at them.

A dog needs a licence when it's six months old, available from your local community office on production of its international health certificate. In some cantons owners may require private liability insurance (see page 274) before a dog licence is issued. A card is issued by the insurance company, which must be produced when applying for a licence. When you obtain your dog licence, you're given a small aluminium tag inscribed with the year, licence number and canton. It must be attached to your dog's collar and be worn at all times in public places. If a dog's found without a licence tag, it's usually taken to an animal shelter (*Tierheim, refuge pour animaux*), where they try to find the owner. Licences must be renewed annually by 31st May, when an announcement is made in local newspapers by your community. They cost between SFr. 60 and 150 a year depending on your community. If you have two or more dogs, the cost of licences can be astronomical in some areas. Owners of unlicensed dogs are fined. If you move home within Switzerland, you must re-register your dog in your new community.

Since tags can get lost, you may want to have an electronic microchip implanted in your pet. The Animal Identity Service (ANIS – Morgenstrasse 123, CH-3018 Bern, ☎ 031 371 35 30, 🖳 www.anis.ch) keeps track of owner information and makes it available to animal shelters and veterinarians throughout Switzerland.

If you plan to leave a pet at a kennel or cattery (*Tierpension*, *pension pour animaux*), book well in advance, particularly for school holiday periods. Dogs left at kennels must be inoculated against kennel cough (*Zwingerhusten*, *toux cannine*). All vaccinations must be registered with your veterinary surgeon (*Tierarzt*, *vétérinaire*) and listed on your pet's international health certificate. Dogs must be kept on a lead (*an der Leine*, *être tenu en laisse*) in all public places. There are special areas and parks where dogs are allowed to roam free. Owners of dogs that foul public footpaths may be fined, so take a shovel and plastic bag with you when walking your dog (no joke!). Plastic bags and containers are provided in some towns and some also provide special toilet areas. Brackets or hooks are provided outside many shops and shopping centres, where you can secure your dog while shopping. Dogs require half-price tickets on public transport and are allowed into most restaurants.

Birds (except canaries) need a special import license, obtainable from the Bundesamt für Veterinärwesen, and are quarantined until it's established that there's no danger of parrot fever (psittacosis). Rabbits also need special permission and must undergo a quarantine period of around 15 days. Guinea-pigs, golden hamsters, rats, mice, aquarium fish and canaries may be imported without a health certificate. An import licence and a veterinary examination is required for some domestic animals, e.g. horses. Dangerous animals, for example poisonous snakes, man-eating tigers, teddy-bears, etc., require a special import licence. Note also the following:

● Some apartments have regulations forbidding the keeping of dogs, cats and/or other animals.

● Most major cities and towns have veterinary hospitals (*Tierspital*, *hôpital pour animaux*) and a veterinary surgeon is on 24-hour call for emergencies. Ask the telephone operator (☎ 111) for the number.

● A brochure regarding the keeping of dogs is published by some cantons.

● In some cantons you need special permission to be allowed to have a dog of a potentially dangerous breed, e.g. Bullterrier, American Staffordshire Terrier, Pitbull Terrier, Staffordshire Bullterrier, Rottweiler, Dobermann, Dogo Argentino, Filo Brasileiro and crosses of these breeds.

● The death of a dog or horse must be reported to your community and your vet. Your community or vet arrange to collect and cremate the body of your pet for a small charge, as you aren't permitted to bury a large dead pet in Switzerland, burying cats and other small pets is generally acceptable. You can also have a pet cremated privately and keep the ashes.

● If you take your dog to some countries, e.g. Italy, it must wear a muzzle.

● If you want to take your pets from Switzerland to a country without rabies, e.g. Australia, Ireland, New Zealand or the UK, it may need to go into quarantine for a period. **Check with the authorities of the country concerned.**

● Rats and mice aren't allowed into Switzerland and officially don't exist (except as pets). If you happen to catch or kill a rat or mouse that has eluded the border patrols, your community may pay you a reward (e.g. SFr. 1).

For the latest regulations regarding the importation or keeping of pets in Switzerland, contact the Federal Veterinary Office (*Bundesamt für Vetrinärwesen, Office Vétérinaire Fédéral*), Schwarzenburgerstr. 155, CH-3003 Berne (☎ 031 323 30 33, 🖥 www.bvet.admin.ch).

POLICE

Switzerland has no uniformed federal police force (*Polizei, police*), as law and order is the responsibility of the cantons and police uniforms vary from canton to canton. Besides canton police, Switzerland also has city and town police, and a non-uniformed federal police force. All police are armed, efficient and courteous, particularly when giving you a speeding ticket. However, all isn't sweetness and light. In recent years, Amnesty International has accused the Swiss police of 'unjustifiable and liberal use of violence', particularly against foreigners and Swiss citizens of non-European descent. Law enforcement is generally strict, particularly for any number of trivial offences. There are a significant number of foreigners living and working illegally in Switzerland, and you can be stopped by special plain clothes police and asked for your passport or identity card at any time, particularly if you drive a car with foreign registration plates.

You rarely find a policeman on the streets in towns or cities unless he's directing traffic (another indication of the low crime rate) and if you need one you usually need to phone or visit the local police station. The large number of foreigners in Switzerland take their cue from the Swiss and are generally law-abiding – which is just as well, as their meal-ticket (residence permit) can easily be cancelled.

POPULATION

The estimated population of Switzerland in 2006 was 7,507,300, including 1,553,600 (20.7 per cent) foreigners, living in an area of 41,290km² (some

15,950mi^2). The population density of 182 inhabitants per km^2 is one of the highest in the western world. When the uninhabited areas are excluded, the average population density rises to around 250 people per km^2. This figure reaches 400 inhabitants per km^2 in the central plateau, which incorporates the main centres of population. In 2006, the canton of Basle had about 5,000 inhabitants per km^2, Geneva 1,600 and Zurich 800. The city of Geneva has over 11,500 inhabitants per km^2, making it one of the most densely populated cities in the western world.

Over 50 per cent of the Swiss population live in urban areas, although less than 25 per cent live in cities with 30,000 inhabitants or more. The largest Swiss cities are Zurich (population 370,000), Basle (165,500), Geneva (185,000), Berne (128,200) and Lausanne (128,300). In sharp contrast to the cities, the population density is only 26 inhabitants per km^2 in canton Graubunden and 54 in canton Valais. Geneva has the highest proportion of foreign residents at around 38 per cent.

REFERENDUMS

Direct democracy, as practised in Switzerland, results in numerous national referendums, meaning that the people have a direct say in all important (and many insignificant) decisions. Referendums are also held at the canton level, although their use varies from canton to canton. The voting age is 18 for federal elections and variable for canton elections. The following kinds of national referendums are held in Switzerland:

- **Obligatory referendum** – a change or addition to the constitution proposed by the federal government.

- **Optional referendum** – a change in the law demanded by a minimum of 50,000 voters nation-wide or by eight cantons.

- **Popular liitiative** – a new article or change in the constitution registered by a petition signed by 100,000 voters.

A change in the legislation requires a majority vote by the electorate, while a change in the constitution must be approved by a majority of the votes cast by the people **and** a majority of the Council of States (canton representatives). The decision of the voters is final at all levels (communal, canton and federal), although provided the requirements are met, an issue can be put before the voters repeatedly, perhaps couched in different terms. Many people believe that Switzerland has too many referendums and that it's too easy to call one. Voting isn't compulsory and the turnout is often low, e.g. between 30 and 50 per cent, unless a particularly important or controversial issue is at stake (political apathy is rife in Switzerland). Of the 70 per cent of the population eligible to vote, only some 40 per cent actually vote (around 30 per cent of the population). Votes are usually decided by something over half of the votes cast, i.e. 15 per cent of the population or 25 per cent of eligible voters.

A foreigner will usually be unaware that a referendum is taking place, unless the issue is of national interest and widely publicised. Recent referendums have involved joining the UN, abolishing the army and limiting the foreign population, all of which are unique, these questions having been put to the people of no other country. Foreigners seldom have voting rights in Switzerland, irrespective of how long they've been residents (particularly when the Swiss are voting on whether to throw them out!). However, many foreigners in the French-speaking part of Switzerland enjoy the right to vote at the local and sometimes cantonal level, but this is rarely the case in German-speaking Switzerland.

RELIGION

Around 42 per cent of the Swiss population are Roman Catholics, some 35 per cent Protestants, 8 per cent other religions (e.g. old Catholic, Jewish, Islamic and Hindu) and 15 per cent have no religion. Besides local Protestant and Catholic church services conducted in local languages, there are English churches and English-language services in all major cities, e.g. Catholic, Anglican, Church of England and International Protestant. There are also bible study groups in many areas and Jewish, Islamic, Greek Orthodox and other religious centres in the major cities. In major cities, services are often held in languages other than the local Swiss language. In addition to the established mainstream religions, Switzerland is also home to some 600 religious movements, cults and pseudo-religious organisations.

The curriculum of Swiss state schools includes compulsory religious education, which may be segregated by denomination when the class entails more than simple bible study. Parents can, however, request that their children are excused from religious education classes. Although the Swiss constitution includes freedom of conscience and belief, certain radical sects are banned. Contact your community, tourist, or information office for information regarding local places of worship and service times.

SMOKING

Smoking isn't permitted in cinemas, theatres, on public transport, in many public buildings (e.g. post offices), or in doctor's and dentist's waiting rooms. In 2004, Ticino was the first canton to forbid smoking in all restaurants and bars, and a similar ban is under review in other cantons, but restaurants aren't generally required to have a non-smoking section (non-smoking restaurants are listed on ⌨ www.eatsmokefree.ch). In 2006, all of Switzerland's public transport became smoke-free, including enclosed areas at train stations. Many Swiss are extremely anti-smoking and health conscious, but nearly a third of the population smokes. In 2007, the federal health commission decided to propose a law to protect the healthy majority from secondhand smoke, but it's likely to be at least 2008 before a law is passed.

SOCIAL CUSTOMS

All countries have their own particular social customs and Switzerland is no exception. As a foreigner you will probably be excused if you accidentally insult your host, but you may not be invited again. The following are a few Swiss social customs:

● When introduced to someone, you should use the formal form of address (*Sie, vous*). Don't use the familiar form (*du, tu*) or call someone by their Christian name until invited to do so. Generally the older or more important person, e.g. your boss, will invite the other person to use the familiar form of address and first names (usually after around 50 years' acquaintance in Switzerland). Younger people are much less formal.

● After you've been introduced to a Swiss, address him or her as Mrs. (*Frau, Madame*) or Mr. (*Herr, Monsieur*) followed by his or her family name and shake hands **without** gloves (unless it's 20 degs. below freezing). When saying goodbye, it's a formal custom to shake hands again.

● It's customary to say good day on entering a small shop and goodbye on leaving. Even the checkout cashier in a supermarket often does this (usually apathetically).

● If you're invited to dinner, take along a small present of flowers, a plant or chocolates. If you take flowers, there must be an odd number and you should unwrap them before presenting them to your hostess. Flowers can be tricky, as to some people, carnations mean bad luck, chrysanthemums are for cemeteries and roses signify love. Maybe you should stick to plastic, silk or dried flowers – or perhaps a nice bunch of weeds.

● Don't arrive late for an invitation and don't overstay your welcome (your host will probably fall asleep around 9pm or earlier, which is your cue to leave).

● The Swiss say good appetite (*en Guete, bon appétit*) before starting a meal. If you're offered a glass of wine, wait until your host has made a toast (*Prost/zum Wohl, santé*) before taking a drink. If you aren't offered a (another) drink, it's time to go home.

● It's customary to telephone in advance before dropping in on a Swiss family, unless they're relatives or close friends. Privacy is respected in Switzerland.

- You should always introduce yourself before asking to speak to someone on the telephone and don't telephone at meal times (whenever they are?) or after 9pm.

- If you're planning a party, it's polite to notify your neighbours (so they don't call the police **too** early).

- If you do a Swiss a favour, he usually feels obliged to repay you with a gift. The habit of doing favours for nothing is generally un-Swiss and a Swiss may expect you to reciprocate if he does you a favour.

- Although the Swiss are usually formal in their relationships, their dress habits, even in the office, are often extremely casual. There are generally no office dress rules and many employees wear jeans or shorts (in summer) with sandals or clogs. You aren't usually expected to dress formally for dinner.

- Sunday is a day of peace when the Swiss won't tolerate noise, e.g. electric drills, hammering or loud music (somebody ought to inform the church bell-ringers and shooting ranges). The general Sunday working law (see **Sunday Working** on page 52) even prohibits the glorious Sunday pastimes of car washing and gardening. If you're fortunate enough to have a garden, you may sit, but not work, in it on a Sunday. Washing your clothes on a Sunday is also forbidden, at least in a communal washing machine, as is hanging out clothes to dry.

TIME DIFFERENCE

Like most of the continent of Europe, Switzerland is on Central European Time (CET), which is Greenwich Mean Time (GMT) plus one hour. The Swiss change to summer time in spring (usually the end of March) when they put their clocks forward one hour; in autumn (fall), usually the last weekend in October, clocks are put back one hour for winter time (spring forward, fall back). Time changes are announced in local newspapers and on radio and TV. The international time difference in winter between Switzerland and some major cities is shown below:

SWITZERLAND	LONDON	JO'BURG	SYDNEY	AUCKLAND	NEW YORK
12 noon	11am	1pm	10pm	12 midnight	6am

The time can be obtained by calling the 'speaking clock' on ☎ 161 (SFr. 0.50 per call) or via teletext.

TIPPING

In Swiss hotels and restaurants, a service charge of 15 per cent is included in all bills and tipping (*Trinkgeld, pourboire*) is not necessary. However, it's customary to leave a little extra change after a meal, or to round up when paying for something small, like a coffee. In most major cities and towns, including Basle, Berne, Geneva and Zurich, a 15 per cent service charge is included in taxi hire costs. A service charge is always included in the price of hairdressing. No tipping is generally the rule, although there are a few exceptions, notably railway and hotel porters, wash and cloakroom attendants, and garage petrol pump attendants, e.g. when they clean your windscreen or check your oil. People do, of course, reward good service and if you intend to become a regular customer it often pays to sweeten the staff. Large tips are, however, considered ostentatious and in bad taste (except by the recipient!).

TOILETS

Last, but not least, when you need to go to the little girls' or boys' room, you will find Switzerland has the cleanest and most modern public toilets in the world. Some even have revolving, self-disinfecting seats, automatic bidets, automatic soap dispensers, taps and hand dryers, and even on occasion individual, fresh, cotton towels (free of charge). Public toilets are found everywhere and are generally free, although those located at some railway stations and motorway stops may cost from SFr. 0.20 to 2. Toilet humour is frowned upon, so don't write on the walls!

19.

THE SWISS

Who are the Swiss? What are they like? Let us take a candid and totally prejudiced look at the Swiss people, tongue firmly in cheek, and hope they forgive my flippancy or that they don't read this bit (which is why it's hidden away at the back of the book).

The typical Swiss is scrupulously honest, narrow-minded, industrious, pessimistic, boring, hygienic, taciturn, healthy, insular, tidy, frugal, sober, selfish, spotless, educated, insecure, introverted, hard working, perfect, religious, rigid, arrogant, affluent, conservative, isolated, private, strait-laced, neutral, authoritarian, formal, responsible, self-critical, unfriendly, stoical, materialistic, impatient, ambitious, intolerant, unromantic, reliable, conscientious, obstinate, efficient, square, enterprising, humourless, unloved (too rich), obedient, liberal, thrifty, stolid, orderly, staid, placid, insensitive, patriotic, xenophobic, courteous, meticulous, inventive, prejudiced, conventional, intelligent, virtuous, smug, loyal, punctual, egotistical, serious, bourgeois, cautious, dependable, polite, reserved or shy, law-abiding and a good skier.

You may have noticed that the above list contains 'a few' contradictions, which is hardly surprising as there's no such thing as a typical Swiss. Apart from the many differences in character between the French, German, Italian and Romansch-speakers of Switzerland, the population encompasses a potpourri of foreigners from all corners of the globe. Inevitably when you're sure you have the Swiss neatly labelled and pigeonholed, along comes another friendly, humorous and fun-loving Swiss who ruins all your preconceptions. Nevertheless I refuse to allow a few misfits to spoil my arguments . . .

With 'all' the above characteristics, it comes as no surprise to discover that the Swiss aren't always the best companions with whom to share a deserted island. On the other hand, the characteristics that often make the Swiss so solemn and serious are the foundation of Switzerland's political and financial stability. A revolution or two might make life more exciting, but would do little for the economy or the strength of the Swiss franc. However, there are a few contradictions to the virtuous Swiss image, for example they're often reluctant to admit they're wrong about anything (their way of admitting a mistake is to say that **you** weren't wrong). They rarely compliment anyone on anything, but are generally quick to complain, particularly about trivia.

The Swiss are rather uncommunicative and tend to meet everything foreign with reserve, the general consequence of which is an innate distrust of foreigners (unless you're a tourist). It's difficult to become close friends with the Swiss (even for other Swiss) and they rarely start a conversation with strangers; not just with foreigners but even with other Swiss. In fact, the Swiss have taken the art of non-conversation to new heights. Rumour has it that the French and Italian-speaking Swiss are more open, less stressed and more friendly than their German-speaking countrymen. Most foreigners, however, notice little difference. In fact, social contact of any kind between the Swiss and most foreigners is rare, and the vast majority of foreigners in Switzerland count few Swiss among their friends. This is particularly true in cantons such as Geneva, where a third of the population are foreigners, another third Swiss from other parts of Switzerland

and only a third are born locally. Surprisingly, some foreigners **actually marry Swiss citizens**, although they usually meet abroad.

The Swiss love their guest worker (*Gastarbeiter, travailleur étranger*) as only those who **know** they're superior can (we all need someone to look down upon). It's so convenient to have someone to blame for your troubles (and to do all the dirty manual jobs), whether it's unemployment, crime, pollution, housing shortages or social problems – the guest worker makes a useful scapegoat. Even Swiss with foreign names find themselves the victims of xenophobia. (Foreigners in Switzerland will be pleased to hear that the Swiss government is concerned about their nationals living in other European countries becoming second-class citizens after their rejection of membership of the EEA/EU.)

You may be unaware that you have Swiss neighbours, except when they complain. They won't welcome you when you move into a new house or apartment and if you can speak the local language, it's up to you to invite them round for coffee and introduce yourself. Don't expect your neighbours to drop round for a cup of sugar; the Swiss are much too reserved to do such a thing, and in any case, they never run out of anything. Only close friends or relatives call on each other without making appointments.

In business, the Swiss are even more formal. After many years, colleagues may still address each other as Herr Zürcher or Madame Guisan, using the formal *Sie* or *vous* form of address. Young Swiss are, however, less formal than their parents. The Swiss aren't so strict with foreigners and if you speak to them in English, you may find yourself on first name terms after a relatively short period. You can get away with a lot by being an eccentric foreigner (at least I hope so), as we're all a little strange to the Swiss.

To many foreigners, the Swiss don't appear to be the merriest of people. This is often difficult to understand considering the beautiful country they inhabit (inhibit?) and the high standard of living and quality of life they enjoy. Switzerland has been unkindly referred to by some foreigners as a robotic paradise (or 'land of the living dead'), where many people lack spontaneity and soul, are devoid of a sense of fun and zest for life, and are afraid to open their hearts for fear of looking foolish. This may in part be due to the fact that only some 15 per cent of Swiss consume alcohol daily – it's enough to make anyone dull!

There's no truth in the rumour that laughter is forbidden, although you may sometimes wonder if there's a tax on humour. The Swiss don't even laugh when you tell them they have no sense of humour! It may come as a big surprise that the Swiss have their **very own** book of jokes in English called, *Tell me a Swiss Joke* – **and** the pages aren't blank. Of course, all the jokes could be borrowed (joke!)? Maybe their lack of humour is all the fault of a local wind called the *Foehn*, which gives people headaches and makes them grumpy. Of course not all Swiss lack a sense of humour, although the minority that don't are usually foreigners masquerading as Swiss (or Swiss who have worked abroad). Life is taken seriously in Switzerland and if foreigners followed their example perhaps they too would be rich. Many Swiss, particularly among the ultra-conservative German-speakers, believe it's sinful to be lazy, to retire early or to enjoy yourself.

The Swiss are **very**, **very** careful with their money. There's some SFr. 10,000bn deposited in Swiss banks (although not all Swiss owned) and the Swiss are second only to the Japanese in savings per capita. Maybe they've worked out a way of taking it with them or have ATMs in heaven (all Swiss go to heaven). Alternatively, Hoffman La Roche may have discovered the secret of eternal life. It's no coincidence that the Swiss are pioneers in cellular therapy, rejuvenation and revitalisation. Their meanness is the one characteristic that they deny most vehemently, but then nobody likes to be thought of as a penny-pincher. Be wary if a Swiss invites you to dinner as he may split the bill with you (or leave you to pick up the tab). To be fair (who's trying to be fair!), although the Swiss don't believe in wasting money, it's rumoured that they're gracious and generous hosts in their own homes – if only you could get an invitation!

The Swiss don't approve of flaunting their wealth or their poverty, which officially doesn't exist. Incredibly, over 500,000 inhabitants of Switzerland are considered to live below the official poverty level (probably all foreigners), although most of Switzerland's 'poor' would be considered wealthy in many third world countries. The little old man sitting next to you on the tram could easily be one of the 250,000 or so millionaires in Switzerland. 'If you've got it, flaunt it' isn't the Swiss way of doing things. In fact, modesty is taken to extremes; for example if a Swiss tells you that he's a fair skier, it usually means he's not quite as good as the Olympic champion.

The Swiss are very law-abiding (except regarding speed limits). Any Swiss loitering in town at 3am is more likely to be waiting for the green light to cross the road than preparing to rob a bank. In fact anyone out at 3am is probably a foreigner preparing to rob a bank, as all Swiss will have been in bed since early evening. The Swiss slavishly follow all rules and regulations and delight in pointing out your transgressions: they're world leaders in robotics – there are over 5m in Switzerland (Ouch!). In Switzerland, rules (however trivial) certainly **aren't** made to be broken, and if you use the 'in' door to exit, or park an inch or two outside a parking space, it will be quickly brought to your attention by an upstanding Swiss citizen. Solzhenitsyn left Switzerland, where he arrived after deportation from Russia, complaining that Swiss bureaucracy was worse than Russia's (even the usually placid Swiss were taken aback by this pronouncement). In Switzerland, everything that isn't illegal is forbidden; everything else is compulsory. Switzerland is often described as a benevolent police state and heaven help anyone who steps out of line.

The Swiss like everything to be spotless and are obsessed with cleanliness (it being next to godliness). They employ an army of guest workers to clean up after them and not only vacuum clean their tunnels and footpaths, but scour the streets **between** villages. Swiss streets are so clean you could eat off them and are cleaner than the average kitchen hand in some countries. Swiss banks (colloquially known as laundromats) even wash dirty foreign money so their citizens won't become contaminated.

Switzerland isn't exactly a land of milk and honey for the dedicated career woman, who's considered something of an eccentric. Most Swiss men think that a women's place is in the home, particularly the kitchen (not the bedroom judging by the low birth-rate). What they think of women politicians is unprintable! They don't think much of politics and politicians in general – but then who does? Swiss women didn't obtain the right to vote until 1971 and Swiss marriage laws, which were heavily biased in the husband's favour, were finally revised in January 1988 to give a wife equal rights with her husband (after 81 years). Swiss women are among the least emancipated in Western Europe and the majority appear to like it that way. The Swiss are slow to make changes, both individually and as a nation. However, they're usually quick to embrace new technology, particularly when it will make them rich(er).

The Swiss have enjoyed the good life for so long that they've forgotten what it's like in the real world. However, Switzerland's seemingly permanent prosperity and stability was threatened in the early '90s by the world recession, which shook the Swiss to the core. Among the biggest concerns facing the Swiss are unemployment; drug addiction; asylum seekers and refugees; the environment; provision for the elderly (pensions); relations with the EU; inflation; crime; housing; and taxation (not necessarily in that order). Many Swiss are fearful of what the future may hold. The only certain thing is that (like everyone else) they must adapt to the challenges of the 21st century and can no longer afford to live in cloud cuckoo (clock) land.

Despite their idiosyncrasies, most foreigners could learn a lot from the Swiss, who excel in many things. They're excellent skiers, the world's best hoteliers and have the best public transport services in the world. They're also the world's most prolific flag flyers and best *hornussen* players. In business, they're among the world's best bankers and insurance salesmen, and are renowned for the quality of their products, from precision machinery and watches, to cheese and chocolate. Switzerland is the most ordered and stable (financially and politically) country in the world. If we turned the operation of the world economy over to the Swiss, the rest of us could relax and organise the parties.

The Swiss political system is a (boring) model of democracy, where co-operation and compromise are preferred to obstruction and obstinacy (members of the Swiss Radical Party are actually liberals). Swiss politicians even ask the opinion of the Swiss people when important issues are at stake. It hardly seems credible, but the Swiss could give politicians a **good** name – not only can you believe them most of the time, even government statistics are usually accurate. Finally, despite the famous words of a former British Chancellor of the Exchequer, most inhabitants of Zurich are of average height and bear little resemblance to gnomes. They do, however, have lots of treasure.

The Swiss are a nation of diverse peoples who don't always see eye to eye, although generally Switzerland is an outstanding example of unity in diversity. However, nothing is guaranteed to bring the Swiss closer together than **being made fun of by a bloody foreigner!** (Pssst! Don't **Tell** the Swiss, but **William**, their national hero, didn't exist.)

Long live Switzerland!

20.

MOVING HOUSE OR
LEAVING SWITZERLAND

When moving house or leaving Switzerland, there are numerous things to be considered and a 'million' people to be informed. The checklists contained in this chapter are intended to make the task easier and may even help prevent an ulcer or nervous breakdown – provided of course you don't leave everything to the last minute.

MOVING HOUSE WITHIN SWITZERLAND

When moving house **within** Switzerland the items mentioned below should be considered:

- You must usually give your landlord at least three months notice before vacating rented accommodation (refer to your contract). If you don't give your landlord sufficient notice or aren't resigning on one of the approved moving dates, you need to find someone to take over your apartment (see **Contract Termination** on page 98). **Your resignation letter must be sent by registered post to reach your landlord by the last day of the month at the latest.** This also applies if you have a separate contract for a garage or other rented property, e.g. a holiday home, in Switzerland. Arrange a date with your landlord for the handover.

- Inform the following:

  - your employer;

  - your present community eight days before moving house and your new community within eight days of taking up residence (see **Registration** on page 78);

  - your electricity, gas, telephone and water companies;

  - your insurance companies (for example health, car, house contents and private liability); banks, post office, stockbroker and other financial institutions; credit card and hire purchase (credit) companies; lawyer; accountant; and local businesses where you have accounts;

  - your family doctor, dentist and other health practitioners. Health records should be transferred to your new doctor and dentist, if applicable;

  - your family's schools. If applicable, arrange for schooling in your new community. Try to give a term's notice and obtain a copy of any relevant school reports or records from your children's current schools;

  - all regular correspondents, subscriptions, social and sports clubs, professional and trade journals, and friends and relatives. Give or send them your new address and telephone number. Free address cards are available from post offices. Arrange to have your post redirected by the post office (see **Change of Address** on page 121),

- your canton's motor registration office within 14 days of moving if you have a Swiss driving licence or a Swiss-registered car. If you're moving to a new canton, you will receive a refund of your road tax from your previous canton. You're required to re-register your car in a new canton within 14 days and to return your old registration plates to your former canton's motor registration office;

- your local consulate or embassy if you're registered with them.

● Return any library books or anything borrowed.

● If moving cantons, arrange to settle your income tax liability in your present canton (see page 287).

● If applicable, re-register your dog in your new community (see **Pets** on page 375).

● Arrange shipping for your furniture and belongings (or transportation if you're doing your own move).

● Arrange for a cleaning company and/or decorating company for your apartment, if necessary (see **Contract Termination** on page 98).

● If applicable, ensure the return of your deposit from your landlord.

● Cancel the milk and newspapers.

● Ask yourself (again): 'Is it really worth all this trouble?'.

LEAVING SWITZERLAND

Before leaving Switzerland for an indefinite period, the following items should be considered **in addition** to those listed above.

● Give notice to your employer, if applicable.

● Check that your and your family's passports are valid.

● Check whether there are any special entry requirements for your country of destination, e.g. visas, permits or vaccinations, by contacting the relevant embassy or consulate in Switzerland. An exit permit or visa isn't required to leave, but if you intend to return to Switzerland and want to retain your right to residence, you should obtain an 'assurance of resident permit' or 'authorisation of absence' (see **Leave of Absence** on page 72).

- You may qualify for a rebate on your income tax and federal old age and survivors insurance (see page 261). Your employer and community will assist you with these. Tax rebates are normally paid automatically.

- Your private company pension contributions will be repaid in full (see **Company Pension Fund** on page 263). Before your pension fund repays your funds, you must provide a statement from your community office stating that you've de-registered and are leaving Switzerland.

- Arrange to sell anything you aren't taking with you (e.g. house, car and furniture) and to ship your belongings. Find out the exact procedure for shipping your belongings to your country of destination (see **Removals** on page 102). Check with the local embassy or consulate of the country to which you're moving, as special forms may need to be completed before arrival. If you've been living in Switzerland for less than a year, you're required to re-export all imported personal effects, including furniture and vehicles (if you sell them, you should pay duty).

- If you have a Swiss registered car that you plan to take with you, you can retain your Swiss registration plates for up to one year or until your Swiss insurance expires. When you re-register your car abroad, your Swiss registration plates must be returned to your former canton's motor registration office or can be destroyed, in which case you must provide **official** proof. If you don't return them, the Swiss authorities won't be pleased – and have long memories.

- Pets may require special inoculations or may need to be placed in quarantine for a period (see page 375).

- Contact Swisscom well in advance to recover your telephone deposit, if applicable (see **Moving or Leaving Switzerland** on page 134).

- Arrange health, travel and other insurance (see **Chapter 13**).

- Depending on your destination, you may wish to arrange health and dental check-ups before leaving Switzerland. Obtain a copy of your health and dental records and a statement from your health insurance company stating your present level of cover.

- Terminate any Swiss loan, lease or hire purchase (credit) contracts and pay all outstanding bills (allow plenty of time, as most Swiss companies are slow to respond).

- Check whether you're entitled to a rebate on your road tax, car and other insurance. Obtain a letter from your Swiss motor insurance company stating your no-claims bonus.

- Sell or let your house, apartment or other property.

- Check whether you need an international driving licence or a translation of your Swiss or foreign driving licence for your country of destination (see page 212).

- Give friends and business associates in Switzerland an address and telephone number where you can be contacted.

- If you will be travelling or living abroad for an extended period, you may wish to give someone 'power of attorney' over your financial affairs in Switzerland so that they can act on your behalf in your absence. This can be for a fixed period or open-ended and can be limited to a specific purpose only. **You should, however, take legal advice before doing this.**

- Buy a copy of ***Living and Working in x*** before leaving Switzerland. If we haven't published it yet, drop us a line and we'll get started on it right away!

Gute Reise/Bon voyage !

APPENDICES

APPENDIX A: USEFUL ADDRESSES

Embassies & Consulates

Embassies are located in the capital Berne, consulates and missions in Geneva and Zurich (plus a few other towns). Embassies and consulates are listed in telephone directories under *Konsulate, consulat/ambassade*. A selection of embassies, in Berne, Basle, Geneva and Zurich, is listed below.

Berne

Albania: Pourtalèsstrasse 65, CH-3074 Muri b. Bern (☎ 031 952 60 10).

Algeria: Willadingweg 74, PO Box 5, CH-3000 Berne 15 (☎ 031 350 10 50).

Argentina: Jungfraustr. 1, CH-3005 Berne (☎ 031 356 43 49).

Austria: Kirchenfeldstr. 77-79, PO Box 266, CH-3000 Berne 6 (☎ 031 356 52 52).

Belarus: Quartierweg 6, CH-3074 Muri b. Berne (☎ 031 952 79 14).

Belgium: Jubiläumsstr. 41, PO Box 150, CH-3000 Berne 6 (☎ 031 350 01 50).

Bosnia-Herzegovinia: Jungfraustr. 1, CH-3005 Berne (☎ 031 351 10 77).

Brazil: Monbijoustr. 68, PO Box 1004, CH-3000 Berne 23 (☎ 031 371 85 15).

Bulgaria: Bernastr. 2, CH-3005 Berne (☎ 031 351 14 55).

Cameroon: Brunnadernrain 29, CH-3006 Berne (☎ 031 352 47 37).

Canada: Kirchenfeldstr. 88, PO Box, CH-3005 Berne 6 (☎ 031 357 32 00, ✉ bern@international.gc.ca).

Chile: Eigerpl. 5, CH-3007 Berne (☎ 031 371 07 45).

China: Kalcheggweg 10, CH-3006 Berne (☎ 031 352 73 33).

Colombia: Dufourstr. 47, CH-3005 Berne (☎ 031 351 17 00).

Costa Rica: Schwarztorstr.11, 3007 Berne (☎ 031 372 78 87).

Croatia: Thunstrasse 45, CH-3005 Berne (☎ 031 352 02 75).

Cuba: Gesellschaftstr. 8, PO Box 5275, CH-3000 Berne (☎ 031 302 21 11).

Czech Republic: Muristr. 53, CH-3000 Berne 16 (☎ 031 350 40 70).

Denmark: Thunstr. 95, CH-3000 Berne (☎ 031 350 54 54).

Ecuador: Ensingerstr. 48, CH-3016 Berne (☎ 031 351 17 55).

Egypt: Elfenauweg 61, CH-3000 Berne (☎ 031 352 80 12).

Finland: Weltpoststr. 4, PO Box 11, CH-3000 Berne 15 (☎ 031 351 30 31).

France: Schosshaldenstr. 46, CH-3006 Berne (☎ 031 359 21 11).

Germany: Willadingweg 83, PO Box 250, CH-3000 Berne 16 (☎ 031 359 41 11).

Ghana: Belpstr. 11, PO Box 5272, CH-3001 Berne (☎ 031 381 78 52).

Greece: Laubeggstr. 18, CH-3006 Berne (☎ 031 356 14 14).

Hungary: Muristr. 31, PO Box 149, CH-3000 Berne 16 (☎ 031 352 85 72).

India: Kirchenfeldstr. 28, PO Box 406, CH-3000 Berne (☎ 031 351 11 10).

Indonesia: Elfenauweg 51, PO Box, CH-3006 Berne (☎ 031 352 09 83).

Iran: Thunstr. 68, CH-3006 Berne (☎ 031 351 08 01).

Ireland: Kirchenfeldstr. 68, CH-3005 Berne (☎ 031 352 14 42, ✉ berneembassy@dfa.ie).

Israel: Alpenstr. 32, CH-3006 Berne (☎ 031 356 35 00).

Italy: Elfenstr. 14, CH-3006 Berne (☎ 031 352 41 51).

Ivory Coast: Thormannstr. 51, PO Box 170, CH-3000 Berne (☎ 031 351 10 51).

Japan: Engestr. 53, PO Box 51, CH-3000 Berne 26 (☎ 031 300 22 22).

Jordan: Belpstr. 11, PO Box 5276, CH-3001 Berne (☎ 031 384 04 04).

Kazakhstan: Alleeweg 15, CH-3006 Berne (☎ 031 351 79 69).

North Korea: Pourtalèsstr. 43, CH-3074 Muri b. Berne (☎ 031 951 66 21).

South Korea: Kalcheggweg 38, PO Box 28, CH-3000 Berne 15 (☎ 031 356 24 44).

Lebanon: Thunstr. 10, PO Box 463, CH-3074 Muri b. Berne (☎ 031 950 65 65).

Libya: Tavelweg 2, CH-3006 Berne (☎ 031 350 01 22).

Liechtenstein: Willadingweg 65, CH-3006 Berne (☎ 031 357 64 11).

Luxembourg: Kramgasse 45, PO Box 619, CH-3000 Berne 8 (☎ 031 311 47 32).

Macedonia: Kirchenfeldstr. 30, CH-3005 Berne (☎ 031 352 00 28).

Madagascar: Egelbergstrasse 9, CH-3006 Berne (☎ 031 368 18 63).

Mexico: Bernastr. 57, CH-3005 Berne (☎ 031 357 47 47).

Monaco: Hallwylstr. 34, PO Box, CH-3005 Berne (☎ 031 356 28 58).

Morocco: Helvetiastr. 42, CH-3005 Berne (☎ 031 351 03 62).

Netherlands: Kollerweg 11, PO Box, CH-3000 Berne 6 (☎ 031 350 87 00).

Nigeria: Zieglerstr. 45, PO Box 574, CH-3000 Berne 14 (☎ 031 382 07 26).

Norway: Bubenbergplatz 10, PO Box 5264, CH-3001 Berne (☎ 031 310 55 55).

Pakistan: Bernastr. 47, CH-3005 Berne (☎ 031 352 29 92).

Paraguay: Kramgasse 58, PO Box, CH-3000 Berne 8 (☎ 031 312 32 22).

Peru: Thunstr. 36, CH-3005 Berne (☎ 031 351 85 55).

Philippines: Kirchenfeldstrasse 73, CH-3005 Berne (☎ 031 350 17 17).

Poland: Elfenstr. 20a, CH-3006 Berne (☎ 031 352 04 52).

Portugal: Weltpoststr. 20, CH-3015 Berne (☎ 031 351 17 73).

Romania: Kirchenfeldstr. 78, PO Box 298, CH-3000 Berne 6 (☎ 031 352 35 22).

Russia: Brunnadernrain 37, CH-3006 Berne (☎ 031 352 05 66).

Saudi Arabia: Kramburgstr. 12, CH-3006 Berne (☎ 031 352 15 56).

Slovakia: Thunstr. 99, CH-3006 Berne (☎ 031 356 39 30).

Slovenia: Schwanengasse 9/11, CH-3011 Berne (☎ 031 312 90 09).

South Africa: Alpenstr. 29, PO Box, CH-3000 Berne 6 (☎ 031 350 13 13, 🖳 www.southafrica.ch).

Spain: Kalcheggweg 24, PO Box 202, CH-3000 Berne 16 (☎ 031 350 52 52).

Sweden: Bundesgasse 26, CH-3011 Berne (☎ 031 328 70 00).

Thailand: Kirchstr. 56, CH-3097 Liebefeld (☎ 031 970 30 30).

Trinidad & Tobago: Elfenauweg 24, CH-3006 Berne (☎ 031 352 19 35).

Tunisia: Kirchenfeldstr. 63, PO Box 357, CH-3000 Berne 6 (☎ 031 352 82 26).

Turkey: Lombachweg 33, PO Box, CH-3000 Berne 15 (☎ 031 3529 70 70).

Ukraine: Feldeggweg 5, CH-3005 Berne (☎ 031 352 23 16).

United Kingdom: Thunstr. 50, CH-3005 Berne 15 (☎ 031 359 77 00, 🖳 www.britain-in-switzerland.ch).

Uruguay: Kramgasse 63, CH-3011 Berne (☎ 031 311 27 92).

USA: Jubiläumsstr. 93, PO Box, CH-3001 Berne (☎ 031 357 70 11, 🖳 www.bern.usembassy.gov).

Venezuela: Schlosshaldenstr. 1, PO Box 1005, CH-3000 Berne 23 (☎ 031 350 57 57).

Yugoslavia: Seminarstr. 5, CH-3006 Berne (☎ 031 352 63 53).

Zaire: Sulgenheimweg 21, PO Box 5261, CH-3001 Berne (☎ 031 371 35 38).

Basle

Austria: Lange Gasse 37, PO Box 3740, CH-4002 Basle (☎ 061 271 35 35).

Belgium: Gerbergasse 1, PO Box 525, CH-4001 Basle (☎ 061 261 69 22).

Bolivia: Sevogelplatz 2, CH-4052 Basle (☎ 061 312 44 45).

Brazil: Freie Str. 1, PO Box 1553, CH-4001 Basle (☎ 061 261 76 61).

Cape Verde Republic: Rümelinspl. 14, CH-4001 Basle (☎ 061 269 80 95).

Czech Republic: Unterwartweg 15, CH-4132 Muttenz (☎ 061 462 00 01).

Denmark: Spalenring 163, PO Box 150, CH-4011 Basle (☎ 061 271 88 11).

Ecuador: Wallstrasse 8, CH-4051 Basle (☎ 061 272 03 03).

Finland: Lichtstr. 35, CH-4056 Basle (☎ 061 696 48 14).

France: Aeschengraben 26, CH-4002 Basle (☎ 061 276 56 77).

Germany: Shwarzwaldallee 200, CH-4058 Basle (☎ 061 693 33 03).

Hungary: Hirzbodenweg 103, PO Box, CH-4020 Basle (☎ 061 319 51 48).

Italy: Schaffhauserheinweg 5, PO Box 334, CH-4005 Basle (☎ 061 689 96 26).

Luxembourg: Steinengraben 28, PO Box 3418, CH-4002 Basle (☎ 061 401 36 52).

Malaysia: Centralbahnstr. 17, PO Box 3353, CH-4002 Basle (☎ 061 271 27 12).

Mali: St. Jakobsstr. 30, PO Box, CH-4002 Basle (☎ 061 295 38 88).

Monaco: Wartenbergstr. 40, PO Box, CH-4020 Basle (☎ 061 319 51 19).

Netherlands: Aeschengraben 9, CH-4002 Basle (☎ 061 206 34 00).

Norway: Peter Merian-Str. 45, PO Box, CH-4002 Basle (☎ 061 205 33 33).

Philippines: Innere Margarethenstr. 2, PO Box 3849, CH-4002 Basle (☎ 061 278 99 88).

San Marino: Sternengasse 18, PO Box 3423, CH-4002 Basle (☎ 061 331 82 97).

Sweden: Neubadstr. 7, PO Box 217, CH-4015 Basle (☎ 061 281 00 42).

Thailand: Aeschenvorstadt 71, PO Box, CH-4010 Basle (☎ 061 206 45 65).

Tuvalu: Elisabethenstr. 42, PO Box 314, CH-4010 Basle (☎ 061 273 49 20).

Uruguay: Lange Gasse 15, PO Box 4152, CH-4002 Basle (☎ 061 277 52 42).

Geneva

Afghanistan: Rue de Lausanne 63, CH-1202 Geneva (☎ 022 731 14 49).

Algeria: Rte de Lausanne 308, PO Box 14, CH-1293 Bellevue (☎ 022 774 19 19).

Angola: Rue de Lausanne 45-47, CH-1201 Geneva (☎ 022 732 30 60).

Australia: Ch. des Fins 2, PO Box 172, CH-1211 Geneva 19 (☎ 022 799 91 00, 🖳 www.geneva.mission.gov.au).

Austria: Rue Jean-Sénebier 20, PO Box, CH-1211 Geneva 12 (☎ 022 312 06 00).

Bahrain: Ch. William-Barbey 51, PO Box 39, CH-1292 Chambésy (☎ 022 758 21 02).

Bangladesh: Rue de Lausanne 65, CH-1202 Geneva (☎ 022 732 59 40).

Belgium: Rue de Moillebeau 58, PO Box, CH-1211 Geneva 19 (☎ 022 730 40 00).

Belize: Rue du Mont-Blanc 7, CH-1201 Geneva (☎ 022 906 84 28).

Burkina Faso: Av. Eugène-Pittard 16, PO Box 21, CH-1211 Geneva (☎ 022 704 18 18).

Cameroon: Rue de Nant 6-8, PO Box 6493, CH-1211 Geneva 6 (☎ 022 787 50 40).

Cape Verde Republic: Av. Blanc 47, CH-1202 Geneva (☎ 022 731 35 40).

China: Chemin de Surville 11, CH-1213 Petit-Lancy (☎ 022 792 25 37)

Congo: Rue des Pâquis 11, CH-1201 Geneva (☎ 022 731 88 21).

Cyprus: Rue Pédro-Meylan 1, CH-1208 Geneva (☎ 022 736 34 16).

Czech Republic: Ch. de la Gabiule 110, PO Box, CH-1245 Collonge-Bellerive (☎ 022 855 95 70).

Denmark: Rue de la Gabelle 9, PO Box 1368, CH-1227 Carouge (☎ 022 827 05 00).

Dominican Republic: Rue Grenus 16, PO Box 2205, CH-1211 Geneva 2 (☎ 022 738 00 18).

Egypt: Rte de Florissant 47, CH-1206 Geneva (☎ 022 347 63 79).

El Salvador: Rue de Lausanne 65, CH-1202 Geneva (☎ 022 732 70 36).

Ethiopia: Rue de Moillebeau 56, PO Box 338, CH-1211 Geneva 19 (☎ 022 919 70 10).

Finland: Grand-Rue 25, PO Box, CH-1211 Geneva 11 (☎ 022 311 83 75).

France: Cours des Bastions 2, CH-1205 Geneva (☎ 022 319 00 00).

Georgia: Rue Richard-Wagner 1, CH-1202 Geneva (☎ 022 919 10 10).

Germany: Ch. du Petit-Saconnex 28C, PO Box, CH-1211 Geneva 19 (☎ 022 730 11 11).

Ghana: Rue de Moillebeau 56, CH-1209 Geneva (☎ 022 919 04 50).

Greece: Rue Pédro-Meylan 1, CH-1208 Geneva (☎ 022 735 37 47).

Grenadines: Av. de Frontenex 8, CH-1207 Geneva (☎ 022 707 63 00).

Guatemala: Rue de Vieux-Collège 10, CH-1204 Geneva (☎ 022 311 99 45).

Honduras: Ch. Taverney 13, CH-1218 Le Grand-Saconnex (☎ 022 710 07 60).

Iceland: Rue du Mont-de-Sion 8, CH-1206 Geneva (☎ 022 703 56 56).

India: Rue du Valais 9-11, CH-1202 Geneva (☎ 022 731 51 29).

Iran: Ch. de Fossard 2, CH-1231 Conches (☎ 022 919 05 20).

Iraq: Ch. du Petit-Saconnex 28a, CH-1209 Geneva (☎ 022 918 09 80).

Italy: Rue Ch. Galland 14, CH-1206 Geneva (☎ 022 839 67 44).

Ivory Coast: Av. du Cardinal-Mermillod 6, CH-1227 Carouge GE (☎ 022 343 90 09).

Jamaica: Rue de Lausanne 36, CH-1201 Geneva (☎ 022 731 57 80).

Japan: Ch. des Fins 3, CH-1218 Le Grand-Saconnex (☎ 022 717 31 11).

Kuwait: Av. de l'Ariana 2, CH-1202 Geneva (☎ 022 918 01 30).

Lithuania: Av. du Bouchet 18, CH-1209 Geneva (☎ 022 734 51 01).

Luxembourg: Ch. de la Rochette 13, CH-1202 Geneva (☎ 022 919 19 29).

Malaysia: Rte de Pré-Bois 20, PO Box 1834, CH-1215 Geneva 15 (☎ 022 710 75 00).

Malta: Parc Château-Banquet 26, CH-1202 Geneva (☎ 022 901 05 80).

Mexico: Rue de Candolle 16, CH-1205 Geneva (☎ 022 328 39 20).

Monaco: Cours des Bastions 4, CH-1205 Geneva (☎ 022 708 01 01).

Myanmar Union: Av. Blanc 47, CH-1202 Geneva (☎ 022 731 75 40).

Netherlands: Rue Ferdinand-Hodler 23, 1211 Geneva 3 (☎ 022 787 57 30).

New Zealand: Ch. des Fins 2, PO Box, CH-1209 Geneva 19 (☎ 022 929 03 50).

Nigeria: Rue Richard-Wagner 1, PO Box 2571, CH-1211 Geneva 2 (☎ 022 730 14 14)

Norway: Rue de Jargonnant 2, PO Box 6045, CH-1211 Geneva 6 (☎ 022 736 16 12).

Oman: Chemin de Roilbot 3A, CH-1292 Chambésy (☎ 022 758 96 60).

Panama: Rue de Lausanne 72, CH-1202 Geneva (☎ 022 715 04 50).

Peru: Rue des-Pierres-du-Niton 17, CH-1207 Geneva (☎ 022 707 49 17).

Philippines: Av. Blanc 47, CH-1202 Geneva (☎ 022 731 83 20).

Portugal: Rte de Ferney 220, CH-1218 Le Grand-Saconnex (☎ 022 791 76 36).

Qatar: Rte de Ferney 149B, CH-1218 Le Garand-Saconnex (☎ 022 798 85 00).

Republic of Rwanda: Rue de la Servette 93, CH-1202 Geneva (☎ 022 919 10 00).

Romania: Chemin de la Perrière 6, CH-1223 Cologny (☎ 022 752 10 90).

Russia: Rue Schaub 24, CH-1202 Geneva (☎ 022 734 79 55).

Saudi Arabia: Rue de Lausanne 263, CH-1292 Chambésy (☎ 022 758 22 74).

Senegal: Route de Berne 25, CH-1010 Lausanne (☎ 021 652 18 42).

Sierra Leone: Quai Gustave-Ador 62, CH-1207 Geneva (☎ 022 735 85 78).

South Africa: rue du Rhône 65, CH-1204 Geneva (☎ 022 849 54 54).

Spain: Rue Pestalozzi 7, PO Box 176, CH-1211 Geneva (☎ 022 734 46 06).

Sri Lanka: Rue de Moillebeau 56, PO Box 436, CH-1211 Geneva 19 (☎ 022 734 93 40).

Sudan: Av. Blanc 47, PO Box 335, CH-1211 Geneva 19 (☎ 022 731 26 63).

Sweden: Rue Rodolphe-Toepffer 8, CH-1206 Geneva (☎ 022 700 47 00).

Syria: Rue de Lausanne 72, CH-1202 Geneva (☎ 022 732 56 58).

Thailand: Rue de l'Athénée 6, CH-1205 Geneva (☎ 022 319 87 00).

Togo: Rue Rudolphe-Toepffer 11, CH-1206 Geneva (☎ 022 346 52 60).

Turkey: Rte de Pré-Bois 20, PO Box 1901, CH-1215 Geneva 15 (☎ 022 798 12 32).

United Arab Emirates: Rue Moillebeau 58, CH-1209 Geneva (☎ 022 918 00 00).

United Kingdom: Rue de Vermont 37-39, PO Box 67, CH-1211 Geneva 20 (☎ 022 918 24 00).

USA: Rue Versonnex 7,CH-1207 Geneva (☎ 022 840 51 60).

Vietnam: Ch. Des Corbillettes 30, CH-1216 Cointrin (☎ 022 798 48 90).

Yemen: Ch. de Jonc 19, CH-1218 Le Grand-Saconnex (☎ 022 799 05 10).

Zurich

Austria: Seestr. 161, CH-8002 Zurich (☎ 044 283 27 00).

Bahamas: Bahnhofplatz 9, PO Box 6075, CH-8023 Zurich (☎ 044 226 40 42).

Belgium: Basteiplatz 5, PO Box 5038, CH-8022 Zurich (☎ 044 212 11 55).

Brazil: Bürglistr. 6, CH-8002 Zurich (☎ 044 206 90 20).

Burkina Faso: Sumatrastr. 25, CH-8006 Zurich (☎ 044 350 55 70).

Croatia: Bellerivestr. 5, PO Box, CH-8034 Zurich (☎ 044 422 83 18).

China: Bellariastr. 20, CH-8002 Zurich (☎ 044 201 10 05).

Costa Rica: Stockerstr, 10, CH-8002 Zurich (☎ 044 201 13 52).

Cyprus: Wiesenstr. 7, CH-8008 Zurich (☎ 043 488 61 40).

Czech Republic: Dufourstr. 22, CH-8008 Zurich (☎ 044 262 15 81).

Denmark: Bürglistr. 8, PO Box 56, CH-8027 Zurich (☎ 044 289 30 60).

Djibouti: Othmarstr. 8, CH-8008 Zurich (☎ 043 268 09 18).

Estonia: Bergstr. 52, CH-8712 Stäfa (☎ 044 926 88 37).

Finland: Kronenstr. 42, CH-8006 Zurich (☎ 044 350 25 66).

France: Signaustr. 1, PO Box 1782, CH-8032 Zurich (☎ 044 268 85 85).

Gambia: Rütistr. 13, PO Box 482, CH-8952 Schlieren (☎ 044 755 40 48).

Germany: Freigutstrasse 15, CH-8002 Zurich (☎ 044 201 72 22).

Greece: Bellerivestrasse 67, CH-8034 Zurich (☎ 044 388 55 77).

Grenada: Claridenstrasse 20, CH-8002 Zurich (☎ 044 206 29 34).

Haiti: Forchstr. 182, CH-8032 Zurich (☎ 044 381 69 89).

Hungary: Voltastr. 65, CH-8044 Zurich (☎ 044 262 39 32).

Iceland: Bahnhofstr. 44, PO Box 6040, CH-8023 Zurich (☎ 044 215 12 60).

India: Mühlestrasse 41, CH-8803 Rüschlikon (☎ 044 772 81 51).

Ireland: Claridenstr. 25, PO Box, CH-8027 Zurich (☎ 044 289 25 15).

Italy: Tödistr. 67, PO Box 822, CH-8022 Zurich (☎ 044 286 61 11).

Ivory Coast: Löwenstr. 17, PO Box 7685, CH-8023 Zurich (☎ 044 211 88 44).

Japan: Utoquai 55,CH-8008 Zurich (☎ 044 269 40 46)

Latvia: Gessnerallee 36, CH-8001 Zurich (☎ 044 211 79 75).

Lesotho: Bleicherweg 45, CH-8002 Zurich (☎ 044 201 44 45).

Luxembourg: Seegartenstr. 2, CH-8008 Zurich (☎ 044 383 63 55).

Madagascar: Kappelergasse 14, PO Box 5070, CH-8022 Zurich (☎ 044 212 85 66).

Malaysia: Fraumünsterstr. 29, PO Box, CH-8022 Zurich (☎ 044 210 06 66).

Malta: Limmatquai 3, CH-8001 Zurich (☎ 044 252 70 50).

Marshall Islands: Seehofstr. 4, CH-8045 Zurich (☎ 044 250 87 60).

Mauritania: Bahnhofstr. 52, PO Box 6133, CH-8023 Zurich (☎ 044 214 62 92).

Mexico: Tödistr. 55, CH-8039 Zurich (☎ 044 209 70 10).

Monaco: Chapfstrasse 48, CH-8126 Zumikon (☎ 044 919 04 16).

Morocco: Bahnhofstr. 73, CH-8001 Zurich (☎ 044 211 74 32).

Netherlands: Binzstr. 18, CH-8045 Zurich (☎ 044 455 60 02).

Norway: Utoquai 37, PO Box 581, CH-8024 Zurich (☎ 044 251 69 39).

Panama: Löwenstr. 40, PO Box, CH-8023 Zurich (☎ 044 225 14 88).

Peru: Löwenstr. 69, PO Box, CH-8023 Zurich (☎ 044 211 82 11).

Portugal: Zeltweg 13, CH-8032 Zurich (☎ 044 200 30 40).

Rwanda: Zürichstr. 31, CH-8700 Küsnacht (☎ 044 914 14 91).

Senegal: Schifflände 22, CH-8001 Zurich (☎ 044 251 19 45).

Seychelles: General-Guisan-Quai 22, CH-8002 Zurich (☎ 044 285 79 29).

South Africa: Wiesenstr. 7, CH-8008 Zurich (☎ 043 488 60 01).

Spain: Hotzestrasse 23, PO Box, CH-8042 Zurich (☎ 044 368 61 00).

Swaziland: Lintheschergasse 17, CH-8001 Zurich (☎ 021 211 52 03).

Turkey: Stadelhoferstr. 40, CH-8001 Zurich (☎ 043 343 10 50).

Thailand: Löwenstr.3, PO Box, CH-8001 Zurich (☎ 043 344 70 00).

Turkey: Weinbergstr. 65, PO Box 674, CH-8035 Zurich (☎ 044 368 29 00).

United Kingdom: Hegibachstrasse 47, CH-8032 Zurich (☎ 044 383 65 60).

USA: Zurich America Center, Dufourstr. 101, CH-8008 Zurich (☎ 044 422 25 66).

Vanuatu: Basteipl. 5, PO Box 924, CH-8039 Zurich (☎ 044 212 70 73).

Yugoslavia: Alfred-Escher-Str. 4, CH-8002 Zurich (☎ 044 202 02 73).

Government

Central Compensation Office (OASI/DI): Av. Edmond-Vaucher 18, CH-1203 Geneva 28 (☎ 022 795 91 11, 💻 www.avs-ai-international.ch).

Federal Aliens Office: Quellenweg 6, CH-3003 Berne-Wabern (☎ 031 325 11 11, 💻 www.bfm.admin.ch).

Federal Office for Social Insurance: Effingerstr. 20, CH-3003 Berne (☎ 031 322 90 11, 💻 www.bsv.admin.ch).

Federal Veterinarians Office: Schwarzenburgstr. 155, CH-3003 Berne (☎ 031 323 30 33, 💻 www.bvet.admin.ch).

Head Customs Office: Monbijoustr. 40, CH-3003 Berne (☎ 031 322 65 11, 💻 www.zoll.admin.ch).

Swiss Broadcasting Corporation (SRG): Belpstrasse 48, CH-3000 Berne 14 (☎ 031 350 91 11, 💻 www.srg.ch).

Swiss Bureau for the Prevention of Accidents: Laupenstr. 11, CH-3008 Berne (☎ 031 390 22 22, 💻 www.bfu.ch).

Switzerland Tourism (ST): PO Box 695, CH-8027 Zurich (☎ 0800 100 200 30, 💻 www.myswitzerland.com).

Swiss Radio International: Giacomettistr. 1, CH-3000 Berne 15 (☎ 031 350 92 22, 💻 www.swissinfo.org).

Miscellaneous

Association of Swiss Private Clinics: Sanaweb AG, Höhestr. 28, CH-8702 Zollikon (☎ 044 912 28 18, 💻 www.privatkliniken.ch).

The Automobile Club of Switzerland (ACS): Wasserwerkgasse 39, CH-3000 Berne 13 (☎ 031 328 31 11, 💻 www.acs.ch).

British Swiss Chamber of Commerce: Bellerivestr. 209, CH-8008 Zurich (☎ 044 422 31 31, 💻 www.bscc.ch).

English Teachers Association of Switzerland: ETAS Administration, Rue de l'Hôpital 32, CH-1400 Yverdon (☎ 024 420 32 54, 💻 www.e-tas.ch).

Mobility Carsharing Schweiz: Gütschstrasse 2, PO Box, CH-6000 Lucerne 7 (☎ 0848 824 812, 💻 www.mobility.ch).

Pro Infirmis Schweiz: PO Box, CH-8032 Zurich (☎ 044 388 26 26, 💻 www.proinfirmis.ch).

Pro Senectute Schweiz: Lavaterstr. 60, PO Box, CH-8027 Zurich (☎ 044 283 89 89, 💻 www.pro-senectute.ch).

REGA Administration und Secretariat: Rega Center, PO Box 1414, CH-8058 Zurich Airport (☎ 044 654 33 11 or 1414 in an emergency, 💻 www.rega.ch).

Swiss Accidents and Insurance (SUVA): Fluhmattstr. 1, CH-6002 Lucerne (☎ 0848 830 830, 💻 www.suva.ch).

Swiss-American Chamber of Commerce: Talacker 41, CH-8001 Zurich (☎ 043 443 72 00, 💻 www.amcham.ch).

Swiss Camping Association: Bahnhofstr. 5, CH-3322 Urtenen-Schönbühl (☎ 031 852 06 26, 💻www.swisscamps.ch).

Swiss Hotel Association (SHV): Monbijoustr. 130, PO Box, CH-3007 Berne (☎ 031 370 41 11, 💻 www.swisshotels.ch).

Swiss Red Cross:, Rainmattstr. 10, CH-3001 Berne (☎ 031 387 71 11, 💻 www.redcross.ch).

Swiss Spas: Av. des Bains 22, CH-1400 Yverdon-les-Bains (☎ 024 420 15 21, 💻 www.heilbad.org).

STA Travel: Ankerstr. 112, CH-8026 Zurich (☎ 058 450 40 20, 💻 www. statravel.ch).

Swiss Travel Savings Fund: Neuengasse 15, CH-3001 Berne (☎ 031 329 66 33, 💻 www.reka.ch).

Swiss Youth Hostels: Schaffhauserstr. 14, CH-8042 Zurich (☎ 044 360 14 14, 💻 www.youthhostel.ch).

Touring Club of Switzerland (TCS): Ch. de Blandonnet, PO Box 820, CH-1214 Vernier (☎ 0844 888 111, 💻 www.tcs.ch).

Transport Club of Switzerland (VCS): Lagerstr. 18, PO Box, CH-3360 Herzogenbuchsee (☎ 0848 611 611, 💻 www.verkehrsclub.ch).

Clubs & Organisations

There are many clubs and organisations in Switzerland for foreigners, a selection of which is listed below. Your embassy or consulate in Switzerland may be able to provide you with a list of clubs and organisations. Information about expatriate clubs is also available from Anglo-Phone (☎ 157 5014) and Xpat Xchange (💻 www.xpat xchange.ch).

Allgemeine Lesegesellschaft: Mrs Ruth Marzo, Münsterplatz 8, CH-4001 Basle (☎ 061 261 43 49, ✉ lesegesellschaft@balcab.ch).

American Citizens Abroad (ACA): Mr Karl Jauch, 5 rue Liotard, CH-1202 Geneva (☎ 022 340 02 33, 💻 www.aca.ch).

American Club of Zurich: (☎ 079 243 56 81, 💻 www.acz.ch, ✉ info@acz.ch).

American International Club of Geneva: Hotel Intercontinental, PO Box 371, CH-1211 Geneva 19 (☎ 022 910 25 80, 💻 www.amclub.ch).

American International Women's Club of Geneva: 11, Rte de Chêne, CH-1207 Geneva (☎ 022 736 01 20, ✉ aiwc@bluewin.ch).

American Women of Ticino: c/o Ms Jonsi Andrews, Casa Mimosa, CH-6914 Carona (☎ 091 649 66 13, ✉ jonsi@bluewin.ch, 💻 www.awot.ch).

American Women's Club of Basle: PO Box 2161, CH-4002 Basle (☎ 061 261 40 55, 💻 www.awcbasel.org).

American Women's Club of Berne: PO Box, CH-3000 Berne (✉ information@awcbern.org).

American Women's Club of Lausanne: Av. Eglantine 6, CH-1006 Lausanne (☎ 021 320 26 88, 💻 www.awc-lausanne.org).

American Women's Club of Zurich: Schöntalstr. 8, CH-8004 Zurich (☎ 044 240 44 55, 💻 www.awczurich.org).

Anglo-Swiss Circle, St. Gallen: Ms Eileen Ochsner, Spiserwisstr. 6, CH-9030 Abtwil (☎ 071 311 27 82, ✉ eileen-robert@bluewin.ch).

Anglo-Swiss Club Basle: Mr Marc Leuenberger & Ms Regula Jost, Auweg 8, CH-4450 Sissach (☎ 061 971 30 67, ✉ m.leuenberger@datacomm.ch, 💻 www.fasc.ch).

Anglo-Swiss Club Fribourg: Mr Horst Paul, les Noutes 6, CH-1772 Grolley (☎ 026 475 25 29, ✉ hpaul66@solnet.ch).

Anglo-Swiss Club Geneva: Mrs Rosemarie Schaer, Rue de Contamines 11, CH-1206 Geneva (☎ 022 346 65 53).

Anglo-Swiss Club Locarno: Ms Verena Graf, PO Box 23, CH-6655 Intragna (☎ 091 796 12 59, 💻 www.angloswisslocarno.ch).

Anglo-Swiss Club Lucerne: Mr John Askins, Altegghalde 1, CH-6045 Meggen (☎ 041 377 34 12, ✉ ask.john@bluewin.ch).

Anglo-Swiss Club Solothurn: PO Box 124, CH-4502 Solothurn (☎ 032 622 20 71, 💻 www.angloswissclubsolothurn.org).

Association of the Friends of India: Mr Saleem Ismail, Mettliweg 2, CH-4147 Pfeffingen (✉ sismail@bluewin.ch).

Basel Expats: Mr Nigel MacGeorge (☎ 061 206 88 08, 💻 www.baselexpats.com).

Bharatiya Association Berne: PO Box 71, CH-3000 Berne 15 (💻 www.india-bab.ch).

Big Ben Club: Ms Vivienne Brenner, Via TraversagnaCH-6986 Novaggio, (☎ 091 606 14 76, ✉ brennertheoviv@bluewin.ch).

The Book Nook: Located at: Residenza Pico, Via Pedemonte 2, CH-6962 Viganello (💻 www.booknook.ch). Contact: Robin Bognuda (☎ 091 858 30 85, ✉ bognuda.afk@bluewin.ch).

British-American Club: Av. Avant-Poste 4, CH-1005 Lausanne (☎ 021 323 40 44).

British Circle Basle: Mr. Martin Rudolf, Erlensträsschen 62, CH-4125 Riehen (☎ 061 645 95 55, ✉ martin.rudolf@universal-consulting.ch).

British Residents' Association Basel: Mrs Angela Meier-Jones, Im Wiesengrund 8, 4102 Binningen (☎ 061 461 73 62, ✉ angiemeier@gmx.ch).

British Residents' Association Berne: Mrs Judy Chisholm, Beethovenstrasse 11, CH-3073 Gumligen, (☎ 031 951 93 00, ✉ judy chisholm@bluemail.ch).

British Residents' Association Geneva: Mr Michael R. Rogers, OBE, World Trade Center I, PO Box 896, CH-1215 Geneva 15 (☎ 022 788 05 51, ✉ mrogers@tiscali.ch).

British Residents' Association Neuchâtel: Mrs Anne Droz, Av. du Mail 34, 2000 Neuchâtel (☎ 032 724 03 42, ✉ drozheitz@gmx.ch).

British Residents' Association Tessin: Ms Penny Osti, Via Tamporiva, 19 CH-6976 Castagnola (☎ 091 970 16 54, ✉ alosti@freesurf.ch).

British Residents' Association Zurich: Mrs Joanna Koch, Alte Landstrasse 89, CH-8802 Kilchberg (☎ 044 715 19 46, ✉ joan nakoch@gmx.net).

British Residents' Association of Switzerland: Mr David Pilsworth, Chemin de Sarments 9, CH-1295 Tannay (☎ 021 728 62 55, 💻 www.britishresidents.ch).

British Swiss Chamber of Commerce: Bellerivestr. 209, CH-8008 Zurich (☎ 044 422 31 31, ✉ info@bscc.co.uk, 💻 www.bscc.co.uk).

Centrepoint: Im Lohnhof 8, CH-4051 Basle (☎ 061 261 20 02, 💻 www.centrepoint.ch).

Commonwealth Association of Geneva: Mr Derrick Deane, PO Box 69, CH-1211 Geneva 20 (☎ 022 791 35 03, ✉ deaned@who.int).

Dänischer Verein CUK: Mr Peder H. Nielsen, Zugerstr. 50 K, CH-8820 Wädenswil (☎ 044 780 47 71, ✉ pedernielsen@hth-kuechen.ch).

Danish Club Basle: Mrs Agnethe Christensen, Tiefenmattstrasse 12, 4434, Hölstein (☎ 061 951 29 19, ✉ agnethe.christensen@ bluemail.ch).

Die Dänische Kolonie in der Schweiz: (🖳 www.dansk.ch).

English Club of Berne: Mittelstr. 55, CH-3012 Berne (☎ 031 381 63 34, 🖳 www.englishclub.ch).

English Club Biel/Bienne: PO Box 3462, CH-2500 Biel/Bienne 3 (🖳 www.englishclubbienne.ch).

English Club Zofingen/Langenthal: Mrs Doris Pavel, Hausmattweg 25, CH-4802 Strengelbach (☎ 062 751 94 67, ✉ mike.pavel@ bluewin.ch).

English Club Toggenburg-Wil: PO Box 54, 9604 Lütisburg, Mr Urs Halter, Kirchgasse 4, CH-9532 Rickenbach (☎ 071 912 47 47, 🖳 www. ectw.org).

English-Speaking Club: Mr Horst Schiel, Meilistr. 18, CH-8400 Winterthur (🖳 http://e-s-c-w.ch).

English-Speaking Club Aarau: Mr Walter Hagmann (☎ 062 842 88 42, 🖳 www.escaarau.ch).

English-Speaking Club: Mr K. A. Prevost, Beckenburgstr. 10, CH-8212 Neuhausen.

English-Speaking Club Baden/Brugg: Mrs Penny Maag, Meisenweg 7, CH-5426 Lengnau (☎ 056 241 13 56, ✉ hp.maag@bluewin.ch.)

English-Speaking Club of Zurich: Mr. Jürg Meier, P.O. Box 7321, CH-8023 Zurich (☎ 071 983 04 91, 🖳 www.escz.ch).

English Theatre Group of Zug: Mrs Fiona Schaller, PO Box 2110, CH-6302 Zug (☎ 041 741 28 86, 🖳 www.etgz.ch).

European Women's Management Development: Ms Christine Raemy-Dirks, Raemy Communications Consulting, PO Box 1559, CH-8027 Zurich (✉ switzerland@ewmd.org).

Federation of Anglo-Swiss Clubs, Mr Laurent Belet, Via Massagno 24, CH-6900 Lugano (☎ 091 921 44 30, 💻 www.angloswissclubs.ch).

Friends of Ireland, Bern, Mrs Paddy Quinche, Tägetlistr. 8, CH-3072 Ostermundigen (☎ 031 931 29 78).

Geneva English-Speaking Club: Mr Victor Wolff, Rue du Vélodrome 3, CH-1205 Geneva (☎ 076 396 49 40 or ☎ 078 601 49 41, ✉ victor_wolff@yahoo.com).

Geneva Irish Assoc.: c/o rue Pedro Meylan 6, CH-1208 Geneva (☎ 022 747 64 14, 💻 www.genevairishassociation.com).

Harvard Club of Switzerland: c/o Bellevue Group AG, Mrs. Claudine P. Stäuble, Seestrasse 16, CH-8700 Küsnacht (☎ 044 267 67 77, 💻 www.harvardclub.ch).

Indian Association: Mr Venkatraman Narasimhan, Av. Adrien-Jeandin 12, CH-1226 Thônex.

International Club of Berne: CH-3000 Berne (💻 http://tritt.bizland. com/ic_berne).

International Club of Lausanne: Ms Gabi Cruise, secretary, PO Box 50, CH-1000 Lausanne 21 (✉ icl@urbanet.ch, 💻 http://home.world com.ch/icl).

International English-Speaking Club La Chaux-de-Fonds: Ms Lorna Cruikshank, Prairie 31, CH-2300 La Chaux-de-Fonds (☎ 032 968 22 76).

International Men's Club of Zug: Mr Joop Hubbeling, Flachsacker 18, CH-6330 Cham (☎ 041 780 75 50, 💻 www.imcz.com).

International Men's Club of Zurich (IMC), Mr Robert Grondman, Fohrbachstr. 6, CH-8702 Zollikon (☎ 044 392 18 59, ✉ info@zimc.ch, 💻 www.zimc.ch).

International Women's Club of Lugano: (💻 www.iwcl.org).

International Women's Club of Lucerne: Mrs Björg Jakob, Stegenhalde 30, CH-6048 Horw (☎ 041 340 10 56, 💻 www.iwcl.net).

Learning Tree Cooperative School: Women's Activity Club, Winterthurerstr. 18, CH-8610 Uster (☎ 043 305 92 50, 💻 www. wac.ch).

Library in English: 3, Rue de Monthoux, CH-1201 Geneva (☎ 022 732 80 97, 🖥 www.thelibrary.ch).

Neuchâtel English Speaking Ladies Group: Mrs Carole Clark, Av. de la Gare 49, Neuchâtel (☎ 032 725 46 62, ✉ carole.clark@freesurf.ch).

New Zealand Association of Switzerland: (🖥 www.nzclub.ch).

Nordisk Club Schweiz: Mr Sven-Erik Gunnervall, St. Gallerstrasse 41 A, CH-9034 Eggersriet (☎ 071 877 36 84, 🖥 www.nordiskclub schweiz.ch).

Odd Fellows Haus: Grosspeterstrasse 5, CH-4052 Basle (☎ 061 313 96 96, 🖥 www.oddfellows-basel.ch).

Professional Women's Group Basle: c/o Centrepoint, Im Lohnhof 8, CH-4051, Basle (🖥 www.pwg-basel.ch).

Semi-Circle Theatre Group Basle: Mrs Suzan Wilson, Oberemattstr. 52a, CH-4133 Pratteln (☎ 061 823 04 12).

Six to Eight: Mrs Leona Foldi (☎ 022 346 74 87), Geneva.

Skandinavisk Club Zurich: Ms Carita Benz, PO Box 2828, CH-8022 Zurich (🖥 www.skandinaviskclub.ch).

Society for International Development: Mr Cyril Ritchie, Ch. Rojoux 15, CH-1231 Conches.

Stanford Club of Switzerland: (🖥 www.stanfordalumni.ch).

Swedish Women's Educational Assoc.: (🖥 www.chapters-swea.org/ zurich).

Swedish Women's Educational Assoc.: (🖥 www.chapters-swea.org/ geneva).

Swiss American Society of Lucerne: (🖥 www.sasl-lucerne.ch).

Swiss American Society of Sankt Gallen: c/o Mr Jack Bates, Ruppen, CH-9450 Altstätten.

Swiss English Assoc.: Mr Graham Tritt, Weissensteinstr. 58, CH-3007 Berne (🖥 www.swissenglish.ch).

Swiss Friends of the USA: Mr Martin Frey, Schützenstr. 14, CH-8702 Zollikon (🖥 www.sfusa.ch).

Toastmasters International: groups throughout Switzerland (💻 www. toastmasters.ch).

United Nations Women's Guild: Villa Les Feuillantines, 13 Av. de la Paix, CH-1211 Geneva 10 (☎ 022 917 33 86, (💻 www.unwg.ch).

The Women's Activity Club: The Learning Tree Cooperative School, Winterthurerstrasse 18, CH-8610 Uster (☎ 043 305 92 50, 💻 www. wac.ch).

Zug International Women's Club (ZIWC): (💻 www.ziwc.ch).

Zurich Comedy Club: PO Box 9, CH-8024 Zurich (💻 www.zcc.ch).

Appendix B: **FURTHER READING**

One of the most useful Swiss publications for anyone seeking information about anything in Switzerland is *Publicus, the Swiss Year Book of Public Life* (*Schweizer Jahrbuch des Öffentlichen Lebens, Annuaire Suisse de la vie publique*), also available on CD-ROM. It contains the addresses and telephone numbers of federal and canton government departments, charitable organisations, embassies and much more, and is available from Schwabe & Co. AG, Steintorstr. 13, PO Box, CH-4010 Basel (☎ 061 278 95 65, 🖥 www.publicus.ch).

In the lists on the following pages, the publication title is followed by the author's name and the publisher's name (in brackets). Note that some titles may be out of print, although you may still be able to find a copy in a bookshop or library. Books prefixed with an asterisk (*) are recommended by the author.

Travel & Tourism

All About Geneva, Scott Charles

*Baedekers AA Switzerland (Baedeker/AA)

*Berlitz Discover Switzerland (Berlitz)

Blue Guide Switzerland, Ian Robertson (A & C Black)

*Camping in Switzerland (Swiss Camping Association)

Essential Switzerland, Gerry Cranshaw (AA)

*Fodor's Switzerland, E. Fodor (Hodder & Stoughton)

Frommer's Switzerland & Liechtenstein (Macmillan Publishing)

Guide Gastronomique Schweiz/Passeport Bleu Suisse

*Insight Guides Switzerland (APA Insight Guides)

Karen Brown's Switzerland: Charming Inns & Itineries, Clare & Karen Brown (Karen Brown's Guides)

*Let's Go Austria & Switzerland (Macmillan)

*Michelin Green Guide to Switzerland (Michelin)

*Michelin Red Guide Switzerland (Michelin)

Off The Beaten Track: Switzerland (Moorland Publishing)

*Swiss Hotel Guide (Swiss Hotels Association)

The Swiss Travel Trade Directory (Urs Meierhofer Publications)

Switzerland, A Phaidon Cultural Guide (Phaidon)
*Switzerland: A Travel Survival Kit, Mark Honan (Lonely Planet)

Switzerland at its Best, Robert S. Kane (Passport Books)

Travel Bugs: Switzerland (Sun Tree)

Zurich Dining Out Guide (Andes Publishing)

Economy & Government

An Outline History of Switzerland, Dieter Fehrni (Pro Helvetia)

George Mikes Introduces Switzerland (Andre Deutsch)

How Switzerland is Governed, Prof. Hans Huber

Modern Switzerland, Prof. J. Murray Luck (Sposs Inc.)

The Referendum – Direct Democracy in Switzerland, Kris W. Kobach (Dartmouth)

*The Social Structure of Switzerland, René Levy (Pro Helvetia)

The Swiss Army (La Place de la Concorde Suisse), John Mcphee (Faber & Faber)

The Swiss Constitution, Nicholas Gillet (YES Publications)

Swiss Foreign Policy, Daniel Frei (Pro Helvetia)

*Switzerland (Auge International)

*Switzerland Inside Out, Lydia Lehmann (Bergli Books)

*Switzerland Land, People, Economy, Aubrey Diem (Media International)

Switzerland's Political Institutions, Oswald Sigg (Pro Helvetia)

*Switzerland: People, State, Economy, Culture (Kümmerly + Frey)

*Why Switzerland?, Jonathan Steinberg (Cambridge University Press)

Hiking & Climbing

Adventuring in the Alps, W. E. & M. Reifsnyder (Sierra Club)

The Alpine Pass Route, Jonathan Hurdle

Footloose in the Swiss Alps, William Reifsnyder (Sierra Club)

*Grosse Freizeit und Ferienbuch (Kümmerly + Frey)

*Grosser Wander-Atlas der Schweiz (Kümmerly + Frey)

*Walking in Switzerland, Brian Spencer (Moorland Publishing)

*Walking Switzerland - The Swiss Way, Lieberman (Cordee)

100 Hikes in the Alps, Harvey Edwards (The Mountaineers Seattle)

Miscellaneous

*Berne, Peter Studer, Walter Däpp, Bernhard Giger & Peter Krebs (Bergli Books)

*Christmas in Switzerland (Bergli Books)

Cooking in Switzerland, Mariane Kaltenbach (Wolfgang Hölker)

Culture Shock Switzerland, Shirley Eu-Wong (Kuperard)

Cupid's Wild Arrows, Dianne Dicks (Bergli Books)

Dance and Ballet in Switzerland, Jean-Pierre Pastori (Pro Helvetia)

*Handbook of Swiss Traffic Regulations (Federal Department of Justice and Police)

*Inside Outlandish, Susan Tuttle (Bergli Books)

*Laughing Along with the Swiss, Paul Bilton (Bergli Books)

Malice in Wonderland, Eugine V. Epstein (Benteli)

A Pain in the Alps, Eugine V. Epstein (Benteli)

*The Perpetual Tourist, Paul N Bilton (Bergli Books)

Southwards to Geneva, Mavis Coulson (Alan Sutton Publishing)

*The Surprising Wines of Switzerland, John C. Sloan (Bergli Books)

The Swiss and the British, John Wraight (Michael Russel)

Swiss Cooking, Anne Mason (Andre Deutsch)

The Swiss Financial Year Book (Elvetica Edizioni SA)

Swiss Meals on Wheels, Diana Nial (Littlestone)

Swiss Theatre Scene, Roland Maurer (Pro Helvetia)

*Switzerland by Rail, Anthony Lambert (Bradt Publications)

*Switzerland for Beginners, George Mikes (Andre Deutsch)

Switzerland: An Inside View (Scalo Publishers)

Switzerland: Through the Eyes of Others (Scalo Publishers)

Take Me to Your Chalet, Eugine V. Epstein (Benteli)

*A Taste of Switzerland, Sue Style (Bergli Books)

Tell Me a Swiss Joke, René Hildbrand (Benteli Publishers Bernee)

*Ticking Along With The Swiss, Dianne Dicks (Bergli Books)

*Ticking Along Too, Dianne Dicks (Bergli Books)

Who Put the WIT in SWITzerland, Eugine V. Epstein (Benteli)

Xenophobe's Guide to the Swiss, Paul Bilton (Ravette)

APPENDIX C: USEFUL WEBSITES

Swiss Websites

About Switzerland (🖥 www.about.ch). Detailed information compiled by a Swiss world traveller.

All for Kids (🖥 www.allforkids.ch). Fun learning and creative products in English for families in Switzerland.

Basler Zeitung (🖥 www.baz.ch). The online version of *Basler Zeitung*, covering mainly the northwest of Switzerland. Many articles are translated into English.

Comparis (🖥 www.comparis.ch). Provides interactive comparisons of insurance premiums, telephone charges and bank charges in Switzerland.

Directories (🖥 www.directories.ch). Swiss online telephone book.

Eat Smoke Free (🖥 www.eatsmokefree.ch). A directory of Swiss restaurants that are non-smoking or that offer separate dining rooms for non-smokers.

Educa (🖥 www.educa.ch). Covers all levels of the Swiss education system.

English Forum (🖥 www.englishforum.ch). A forum for English speakers throughout Switzerland.

The English Show (🖥 www.theenglishshow.ch). Magazine-style local radio show broadcast in English.

Federal Office of Immigration (🖥 www.bfm.admin.ch). Provides information on work and residence permits.

Feiertagskalender (🖥 www.feiertagskalender.ch). Lists all public holidays for each canton of Switzerland.

Homegate (🖥 www.homegate.ch). Comprehensive database of apartments and houses for rent or sale.

Inforoute (🖥 www.inforoute.ch). Up-to-date traffic information on Swiss motorways, alpine passes and tunnels.

Matterhorn (💻 www.matterhorn.ch). Search engine with online booking system for holiday homes and package tours all over Switzerland.

Meteo Schweiz (💻 www.meteoschweiz.ch). Actual and historic weather and climate information on Switzerland.

Mothering Matters (💻 www.mmjournal.com). Devoted to parenting in Switzerland.

Museumspass (💻 www.museumspass.ch). A portal which provides access to information on museums in Switzerland.

My Switzerland (💻 www.myswitzerland.com). Swiss tourist office website with comprehensive information and links to accommodation, transport, sports facilities, events etc.

NZZ (💻 www.nzz.ch). Biggest national newspaper in Switzerland, mainly Zurich focused.

SBB (💻 www.sbb.ch). Swiss Railway company website with train schedules and personalized timetables.

Search (💻 www.search.ch). Search engine for Swiss websites. Also shows sports news.

STA Travel (💻 www.statravel.ch). Finds the cheapest flight from Switzerland to any destination of your choice. Also provides last minute travel and hotel bookings.

Swiss Banking (💻 www.swissbanking.ch). Swiss Bankers' association website where the Swiss banking system is explained.

SwissConnex (💻 www.swissconnex.ch). A portal that links to many sites covering health, tourism, sports and business.

Swiss Government (💻 www.admin.ch). The website of the Swiss government with links to all state departments.

Swissinfo (💻 www.swissinfo.org). National and international news provided by Swiss Radio International.

Swissworld (💻 www.swissworld.org). Provides information on Switzerland's history, the political system, the culture and society – and on the history of chocolate production in Switzerland.

The Swiss Portal (💻 www.ch.ch). A wealth of practical information provided by the Swiss government.

XpatXchange (💻 www.xpatxchange.ch). Information and contacts for expatriates in Switzerland.

Youth Hostels (💻 www.youthhostel.ch). List all youth hostels in Switzerland, with online reservation system.

General Websites

British Expatriates (💻 www.britishexpat.com). Designed to keep British expatriates in touch with events in and information about the UK.

Direct Moving (💻 www.directmoving.com). General moving information, tips, and numerous links.

Escape Artist (💻 www.escapeartist.com). One of the most comprehensive expatriate sites, including resources, links and directories covering most expatriate destinations. You can also subscribe to the free monthly online expatriate magazine, *Escape from America*.

Expat Exchange (💻 www.expatexchange.com). Reportedly the largest online 'community' for English-speaking expatriates, including articles on relocation and a question and answer facility.

Expat World (💻 www.expatworld.net). Information for American and British expatriates, including a subscription newsletter.

Expat Expert (💻 www.expatexpert.com). Run by expatriate expert Robin Pascoe, providing advice and support.

Family Life Abroad (💻 www.familylifeabroad.com). A wealth of information and articles on coping with family life abroad.

Just Landed (💻 www.justlanded.com). Useful relocation information for 26 countries.

MASTA (💻 www.masta.org). An advisory service for travel abroad including useful factsheets and personalised health briefs available by telephone (UK ☎ 0906-822 4100).

Save Wealth Travel (💻 www.savewealth.com/travel/warnings). Travel information and warnings.

The Travel Doctor (💻 www.tmvc.com.au). Contains a country by country vaccination guide.

UK Trade Partners (💻 www.uktradeinvest.gov.uk). A UK government-sponsored site whose main aim is to provide trade and investment information on just about every country in the world. Even if you aren't planning to do business abroad, the information is comprehensive and up to date.

World Health Organization (💻 www.who.int). Health information.

Worldwise Directory (💻 www.suzylamplugh.org/worldwise). This website, run by the Suzy Lamplugh charity for personal safety, provides a useful directory of countries with practical information and special emphasis on safety, particularly for women.

The World Press (💻 www.theworldpress.com). Links to media sites in practically every country.

World Travel Guide (💻 www.wtgonline.com). A general website for world travellers and expatriates.

APPENDIX D: WEIGHTS & MEASURES

Switzerland uses the metric system of measurement. Those who are more familiar with the imperial system will find the tables on the following pages useful. Some comparisons shown are only approximate, but are close enough for most everyday uses. In addition to the variety of measurement systems used, clothes sizes often vary considerably with the manufacturer (as we all know only too well). Try all clothes on before buying and don't be afraid to return something if, when you try it on at home, you decide it doesn't fit (most shops will exchange goods or give a refund).

Women's Clothes

Continental	34	36	38	40	42	44	46	48	50	52
UK	8	10	12	14	16	18	20	22	24	26
US	6	8	10	12	14	16	18	20	22	24

Pullovers

	Women's						Men's					
Continental	40	42	44	46	48	50	44	46	48	50	52	54
UK	34	36	38	40	42	44	34	36	38	40	42	44
US	34	36	38	40	42	44	sm	med	lar	xl		

Men's Shirts

Continental	36	37	38	39	40	41	42	43	44	46
UK/US	14	14	15	15	16	16	17	17	18	-

Men's Underwear

Continental	5	6	7	8	9	10
UK	34	36	38	40	42	44
US	sm	med		lar	xl	

Note: sm = small, med = medium, lar = large, xl = extra large

Children's Clothes

Continental	92	104	116	128	140	152
UK	16/18	20/22	24/26	28/30	32/34	36/38
US	2	4	6	8	10	12

Children's Shoes

Continental	18	19	20	21	22	23	24	25	26	27	28	29	30	31	32
UK/US	2	3	4	4	5	6	7	7	8	9	10	11	11	12	13

Continental	33	34	35	36	37	38
UK/US	1	2	2	3	4	5

Shoes (Women's and Men's)

Continental	35	36	37	37	38	39	40	41	42	42	43	44
UK	2	3	3	4	4	5	6	7	7	8	9	9
US	4	5	5	6	6	7	8	9	9	10	10	11

Weight

Imperial	Metric	Metric	Imperial
1oz	28.35g	1g	0.035oz
1lb*	454g	100g	3.5oz
1cwt	50.8kg	250g	9oz
1 ton	1,016kg	500g	18oz
2,205lb	1 tonne	1kg	2.2lb

Length

Imperial	Metric	Metric	Imperial
1in	2.54cm	1cm	0.39in
1ft	30.48cm	1m	3ft 3.25in
1yd	91.44cm	1km	0.62mi
1mi	1.6km	8km	5mi

Capacity

Imperial	Metric	Metric	Imperial
1 UK pint	0.57 litre	1 litre	1.75 UK pints
1 US pint	0.47 litre	1 litre	2.13 US pints
1 UK gallon	4.54 litres	1 litre	0.22 UK gallon
1 US gallon	3.78 litres	1 litre	0.26 US gallon

Note: An American 'cup' = around 250ml or 0.25 litre.

Area

Imperial	Metric	Metric	Imperial
1 sq. in	0.45 sq. cm	1 sq. cm	0.15 sq. in
1 sq. ft	0.09 sq. m	1 sq. m	10.76 sq. ft
1 sq. yd	0.84 sq. m	1 sq. m	1.2 sq. yds
1 acre	0.4 hectares	1 hectare	2.47 acres
1 sq. mile	2.56 sq. km	1 sq. km	0.39 sq. mile

Temperature

Celsius	Fahrenheit	
0	32	(freezing point of water)
5	41	
10	50	
15	59	
20	68	
25	77	
30	86	
35	95	
40	104	
50	122	

Notes: The boiling point of water is 100C / 212F.

Normal body temperature (if you're alive and well) is 37C / 98.4F.

Temperature Conversion

Celsius to Fahrenheit: multiply by 9, divide by 5 and add 32. (For a quick and approximate conversion, double the Celsius temperature and add 30.)

Fahrenheit to Celsius: subtract 32, multiply by 5 and divide by 9. (For a quick and approximate conversion, subtract 30 from the Fahrenheit temperature and divide by 2.)

Oven Temperatures

Gas	Electric	
	F	C
-	225–250	110–120
1	275	140
2	300	150
3	325	160
4	350	180
5	375	190
6	400	200
7	425	220
8	450	230
9	475	240

Air Pressure

PSI	Bar
10	0.5
20	1.4
30	2
40	2.8

APPENDIX E: MAP OF SWITZERLAND

The map opposite shows the 26 Swiss cantons (listed in alphabetical order below). Cantons Appenzell Inner-Rhodes, Appenzell Outer-Rhodes, Basle-Town, Basle-Country, Nidwalden and Obwalden rank as half-cantons and have only one seat in the Council of States (all other cantons have two seats). The letters in brackets are the official canton abbreviations, as shown on vehicle number plates.

Aargau/Aargovia (AG)

Appenzell Inner-Rhodes (AI)

Appenzell Outer-Rhodes (AR)

Berne (BE)

Basle-Town (BL)

Basle-Country (BS)

Fribourg (FR)

Geneva (GE)

Glarus (GL)

Grisons/Graubunden (GR)

Jura (JU)

Lucerne (LU)

Nidwalden (NW)

Obwalden (OW)

Neuchâtel (NE)

St. Gallen (SG)

Schaffhausen (SH)

Solothurn (SO)

Schwyz (SZ)

Ticino (TI)

Thurgovia (TG)

Uri (UR)

Valais (VS)

Vaud (VD)

Zug (ZG)

Zurich (ZH)

INDEX

G

H

I

SURVIVAL BOOKS

Survival Books was established in 1987 and by the mid-'90s was the leading publisher of books for people planning to live, work, buy property or retire abroad.

From the outset, our philosophy has been to provide the most comprehensive and up-to-date information available. Our titles routinely contain up to twice as much information as rival books and are updated frequently. All our books contain colour photographs and some are printed in two colours or full colour throughout. They also contain original cartoons, illustrations and maps.

Survival Books are written by people with first-hand experience of the countries and the people they describe, and therefore provide invaluable insights that cannot be obtained from official publications or websites, and information that is more reliable and objective than that provided by the majority of unofficial sites.

Survival Books are designed to be easy – and interesting – to read. They contain a comprehensive list of contents and index and extensive appendices, including useful addresses, further reading, useful websites and glossaries to help you obtain additional information as well as metric conversion tables and other useful reference material.

Our primary goal is to provide you with the essential information necessary for a trouble-free life or property purchase and to save you time, trouble and money.

We believe our books are the best – they are certainly the best-selling. But don't take our word for it – read what reviewers and readers have said about Survival Books at the front of this book.

To see our current list of titles, visit our website: **www.survivalbooks.net**

CULTURE WISE SERIES

The Essential Guides to Culture, Customs & Business Etiquette

Our ***Culture Wise*** series of guides is essential reading for anyone who want to understand how a country really 'works'. Whether you're planning to stay for a few days or a lifetime, these guides will help you quickly find you feet and settle into your new surroundings.

Culture Wise guides reduce the anxiety factor in adapting to a foreign culture; explain how to behave in everyday situations in order to avoid cultural and social gaffes; help you get along with your neighbours, make friends and establish lasting business relationships; and enhance your understanding of a country and its people.

People often underestimate the extent of the cultural isolation they can face abroad, particularly in a country with a different language. At first glance, many countries seem an 'easy' option, often with millions of visitors from all corners of the globe and well-established expatriate communities. But, sooner or later, newcomers find that most countries are indeed 'foreign' and many come unstuck as a result.

Culture Wise guides will enable you to quickly adapt to the local way of life and feel at home, and – just as importantly – avoid the worst effects of culture shock.

Culture Wise – the wise way to travel

To see our current list of titles, visit our website: **www.survivalbooks.net**

LIVING AND WORKING SERIES

Our *Living and Working* guides are essential reading for anyone planning to spend a period abroad, whether it's an extended holiday or permanent migration, and are packed with priceless information designed to help you avoid costly mistakes and save you both time and money.

Living and Working guides are the most comprehensive and up-to-date source of practical information available about everyday life abroad. They aren't, however, simply a catalogue of dry facts and figures, but are written in a highly readable style - entertaining, practical and occasionally humorous.

Our aim is to provide you with the comprehensive practical information necessary for a trouble free life. You may have visited a country as a tourist, but living and working there is a different matter altogether; adjusting to a different environment and culture and making a home in any foreign country can be a traumatic and stressful experience. You need to adapt to new customs and traditions, discover the local way of doing things (such as finding a home, paying bills and obtaining insurance) and learn all over again how to overcome the everyday obstacles of life.

All these subjects and many, many more are covered in depth in our *Living and Working* guides – don't leave home without them!

To see our current list of titles, visit our website: **www.survivalbooks.net**

BUYING A HOME SERIES

Buying a home abroad is not only a major financial transaction but also a potentially life-changing experience; it's therefore essential to get it right. Our *Buying a Home* guides are required reading for anyone planning to purchase property abroad and are packed with vital information to guide you through the property jungle and help you avoid disasters that can turn a dream home into a nightmare.

The purpose of our *Buying a Home* guides is to enable you to choose the most favourable location and the most appropriate property for your requirements, and to reduce your risk of making an expensive mistake by making informed decisions and calculated judgements rather than uneducated and hopeful guesses. Most importantly, they will help you save money and will repay your investment many times over.

Buying a Home guides are the most comprehensive and up-to-date source of information available about buying property abroad – whether you're seeking a detached house or an apartment, a holiday or a permanent home (or an investment property), these books will prove invaluable.

To see our current list of titles, visit our website: **www.survivalbooks.net**

OTHER SURVIVAL BOOKS

A New Life Abroad: The most comprehensive book available for anyone planning to live, work or retire abroad, containing surveys of over 50 countries.

The Best Places to Buy a Home in France/Spain: Unique guides to where to buy property in France and Spain, containing regional profiles and market reports.

Buying, Selling and Letting Property: The best source of information about buying, selling and letting property in the UK.

Earning Money From Your Home: Essential guides to earning income from property in France and Spain, including short- and long-term letting.

Foreigners in France/Spain: Triumphs & Disasters: Real-life experiences of people who have emigrated to France and Spain, recounted in their own words.

Investing in Property Abroad: Essential reading for anyone planning to buy property abroad, containing surveys of over 30 countries.

Making a Living: Comprehensive guides to self-employment and starting a business in France and Spain.

Renovating & Maintaining Your French Home: The ultimate guide to renovating and maintaining your dream home in France.

Retiring in France/Spain: Everything a prospective retiree needs to know about the two most popular international retirement destinations.

Running Gîtes and B&Bs in France: An essential book for anyone planning to invest in a gîte or bed & breakfast business in France.

Rural Living in France: An invaluable book for anyone seeking the 'good life' in France, containing a wealth of practical information about all aspects of country life.

Shooting Caterpillars in Spain: The hilarious and compelling story of two innocents abroad in the depths of Andalusia in the late '80s.

Wild Thyme in Ibiza: A fragrant account of how a three-month visit to the enchanted island of Ibiza in the mid-'60s turned into a 20-year sojourn.

To see our current list of titles, visit our website: **www.survivalbooks.net**

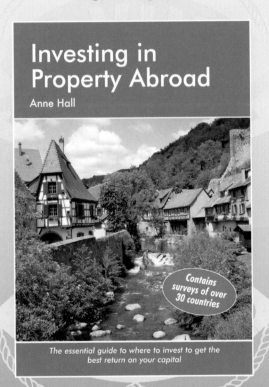